Justice at a Distance

The current global justice literature starts from the premise that world poverty is the result of structural injustice mostly attributable to past and present actions of governments and citizens of rich countries. As a result, that literature recommends vast coercive transfers of wealth from rich to poor societies alongside stronger national and international governance.

Justice at a Distance, in contrast, argues that global injustice is largely homegrown and that these native restrictions to freedom lie at the root of poverty and stagnation. The book is the first philosophical work to emphasize free markets in goods, services, and labor as an ethical imperative that allows people to pursue their projects and as the one institutional arrangement capable of alleviating poverty. Supported by a robust economic literature, *Justice at a Distance* applies the principle of noninterference to the issues of wealth and poverty, immigration, trade, the status of nation-states, war, and aid.

Loren E. Lomasky is Cory Professor of Political Philosophy at the University of Virginia. Lomasky is the author of *Persons, Rights and the Moral Community* (1987), for which he was awarded the 1990 Matchette Foundation Book Prize for best philosophy book published during the preceding two years by an author under the age of forty. He coauthored *Democracy and Decision: The Pure Theory of Electoral Preference* (Cambridge University Press, 1993) with Geoffrey Brennan. His essay, "Is There a Duty to Vote?," also coauthored with Brennan, was awarded the 2003 Gregory Kavka/UC Irvine Prize in Political Philosophy by the American Philosophical Association.

Fernando R. Tesón is the Tobias Simon Eminent Scholar at Florida State University. He is the author of *Humanitarian Intervention: An Inquiry into Law and Morality* (3rd edition) and *Rational Choice and Democratic Deliberation: A Theory of Discourse Failure* (with Guido Pincione). He has written more than fifty articles in journals, including *Ethics & International Affairs*, *Journal of Philosophy*, *American Journal of International Law*, and *Social Philosophy and Policy*.

Justice at a Distance

Extending Freedom Globally

LOREN E. LOMASKY
University of Virginia

FERNANDO R. TESÓN
Florida State University

CAMBRIDGE
UNIVERSITY PRESS

CAMBRIDGE
UNIVERSITY PRESS

32 Avenue of the Americas, New York, NY 10013-2473, USA

Cambridge University Press is part of the University of Cambridge.

It furthers the University's mission by disseminating knowledge in the pursuit of education, learning, and research at the highest international levels of excellence.

www.cambridge.org
Information on this title: www.cambridge.org/9781107536029

© Loren E. Lomasky and Fernando R. Tesón 2015

First published 2015

Printed in the United States of America

A catalog record for this publication is available from the British Library.

Library of Congress Cataloging in Publication Data
Lomasky, Loren E., author.
Justice at a distance : extending freedom globally / Loren E. Lomasky, Fernando R. Tesón.
  pages   cm
Includes bibliographical references and index.
ISBN 978-1-107-11586-6 (hardback) – ISBN 978-1-107-53602-9 (pbk.)
1. Social justice – Developing countries.   2. Equality – Developing countries.   3. Income distribution – Developing countries.   4. Economic development – Developing countries.   I. Tesón, Fernando R., 1950– author.   II. Title.
HN980.L64   2015
303.3′72091724–dc23   2015015719

ISBN 978-1-107-11586-6 Hardback
ISBN 978-1-107-53602-9 Paperback

Contents

Acknowledgments

Both before and after the idea of this joint project germinated, we benefited from the suggestions and criticisms of numerous interlocutors who thereby tested and strengthened the book's arguments. Recalling the names of all who assisted in this regard is beyond our power, and were we to attempt to supply a listing, we would doubtlessly leave out many names that deserve inclusion. To all we are grateful. In particular, though, we wish to acknowledge three workshops on *Justice at a Distance*. The first was sponsored by Georgia State University when the manuscript was still at an early stage of preparation, the second was conducted by the Mercatus Center at George Mason University as we were in the process of tying up loose ends (a task that, we concede, can never be completed), and the third was organized by the University of Arizona Philosophy Department (Freedom Center) after completion of the manuscript. To the organizers and participants of those events we owe a great debt. In particular, we thank Andy Altman, Andrew I. Cohen, Guido Pincione, Peter Boettke, Jason Brennan, Ed Lopez, John Hasnas, Chris Morris, Neera Bhadwar, Dick Miller, Thom Brooks, Claire Finkelstein, Bas van der Vossen, Claire Morgan, David Schmidtz, Carmen Pavel, Allen Buchanan, Tom Christiano, Danny Shapiro, Chad van Schoelandt, and Horacio Spector. Special thanks go to Jonathan Klick, who did the basic economic research and contributed central ideas to Chapter 6. All these criticisms and remarks greatly helped to improve the manuscript.

Fernando R. Tesón thanks the Social Philosophy and Policy Center of Bowling Green University for hosting him as a Fellow in the summer of 2008. This allowed him to write early drafts of what are now Chapters 1 and 6. He also thanks his terrific institution, Florida State University College of Law, and especially Dean Don Weidner for unflinching support of his scholarship. Unfortunately, he cannot thank his colleague and friend Danny Markel, who offered excellent criticisms to the manuscript, because his life was tragically cut short in the summer of 2014. His greatest gratitude goes to his wonderful family: Bettina, Carolina, Fernando, Jr., and Marcelo, who were more than supportive throughout.

Loren E. Lomasky enjoyed a fellowship at the National University of Singapore, during which he enjoyed not only untrammeled research time but also the opportunity to observe a prosperous and free society that a few decades previously had been one of the world's also-rans. The University of Virginia also supported his research efforts. Most of all, he is grateful to his grandchildren, who continually inspire him with hope that the future will be better than the past. And his thanks go to Linda, always Linda.

The State of the World

THE JUSTICE QUESTION

What do we owe other people? An ancient answer is: their due. This is helpful only to the extent that it can be determined what that due may be. The simple answer advanced in this book is that what is primarily owed to others is to *leave them alone*. We say "primarily" because requirements of justice extend in addition to particular performances owed to particular others. For example, to one's children, business partners, clients, students, friends, and lovers, one bears responsibilities that do not extend to people in general.

Exceptional circumstances engender obligations to anonymous others that also go well beyond noninterference. Following an example offered by Peter Singer,[1] suppose that while treating yourself to a recreational walk, you encounter a young child face down in a puddle. You can easily wade in to pull her out; otherwise, she will drown. What should you do? We trust that our readers will not find this an especially challenging dilemma. Not to rescue the child would be wrong; more specifically, it would be to *wrong the child*. You owe her more than merely leaving her alone, even if the cost to you of rescue is wet toes and ruined shoes. Who would demur from saving a life at so minimal a cost? According to Singer, nearly all of us do. Around the world, there are tens of millions of children (and former children) who, in effect, are face down in smothering waters and cannot help themselves. These are the unfortunate others who live on the edge of exigence, where the absence of food or shelter or health care imperils survival. Minimal aid expenditures by those of us who are comparatively wealthy, alleges Singer, could extricate these people from their various puddles. Yet, for the most part, they are left to drown.

This sort of challenge inclines many theorists to think about the demands of justice as requirements to *do something* to ease the plight of the less well-off.

---

[1] "Famine, Affluence, and Morality," *Philosophy and Public Affairs* 1 (1972), 229–43.

Because well-being levels differ profoundly across borders, the urgency of aid provision will seem most acute in the domain of global justice. Succeeding pages examine various global-justice theories that take up this strategy. We begin, though, by announcing that this presumption is precisely to misconstrue the issues at stake. To repeat: justice is primarily about leaving other people alone. This may seem banal when juxtaposed with cases such as the drowning toddler or the suffering millions in poverty. Nonetheless, it is crucial. Our central claim is that most people, but especially the world's poor, are saddled with a host of coercive barriers that impede flourishing. These barriers are quite diverse: political oppression, exploitive institutions, and burdensome regulations, both within and without borders. In particular, we suggest that the plight of the world's poor is caused (mainly) by bad *domestic* institutions and ineffectual, corrupt governance and not by the failures of rich countries to help. To be sure, the wealthy people and polities of the world have much to answer for, but predominantly these transgressions are acts of unwonted interference, not a shortage of aid payments. Such interference falls into three main categories. First, wealthy countries harm the world's poor by maintaining unjustified protectionist and immigration barriers. Second, they project force across borders to the detriment of affected populations. Third, they sometimes cooperate with and thereby abet unjust or incompetent regimes. On these grounds, we add our indictments of the world's haves to those offered by the dominant strand of the global-justice literature. Where we most notably diverge in our assessment of the relevant pathologies is by insisting that wealthy countries are bit players in these sad dramas: most of the damaging interference takes place at the domestic level.

Because injustice is overwhelmingly homegrown, the recommendations of this book are addressed not only to persons in rich countries. Most urgently, they are directed to foreign elites who unjustly interfere with the lives of their subjects. These elites, in other words, must honor the obligation to *leave their people alone*. Of course, persons in rich countries also should leave others alone, both their own compatriots and those who live at a distance. A significant but distinctly secondary task is to exercise prudent pressure for reform in order to persuade local elites to desist from the unjust interference with their subjects' lives. Unfortunately, it is easier for us to issue the recommendations than it is to persuade autocrats and warlords to listen. That is their fault, not ours, but even so, a perceived lack of efficacy is not comfortable for philosophers. This helps to explain, we believe, why most political philosophers emphasize the requirement to *do* rather than to *refrain*.

We conjecture that very few readers of this book have ever encountered even one child inertly lying face down in a puddle. In the unlikely event that one should someday do so, a requirement of rescue would represent a trivial imposition on one's ordinary pursuits. Indeed, most would welcome an opportunity to do so much good at so little cost. This is, however, one of the two junctures at which Singer's analogy breaks down. The world's hungry and sick are not, alas, a rarity. Despite extraordinary gains that have been achieved over the past three or four decades, grinding poverty continues to plague many populations. Were one obliged to address each instance of personal desperation near or at a distance, there would literally be no time to do anything else with one's life. Rather than justice primarily being a matter of leaving people alone, Singer-style justice-as-rescue is maximally intrusive.

The second juncture at which the analogy fails is to treat global distress as on a par with a child's accidental misstep. Poverty, though, is typically no accident. It results, as we shall argue at length, from bad policies, bad people, and bad institutions. Some political elites are merely incompetent; others are vicious. Either way, they generate avoidable human misery. If well-meaning governments or private citizens of wealthy countries transfer resources to those impoverished fiefs, they may relieve some distress, but they equally well may be strengthening the purveyors of that distress and thereby create further distress. To put it another way, subsidizing debilitating poverty is likely to produce more of it.[2]

Those readers of this book who are professional philosophers know that ours is a discipline that glories in outlandish thought experiments: children face down in puddles are joined by runaway trolleys that will kill one or five persons, someone who wakes to find her circulatory system hooked up to that of a great violinist, a nuclear terrorist who will reveal where he has secreted a ticking time bomb only if he is put to torture (or even better, only if his innocent little daughter is threatened with torture), an experience machine that will provide the illusion of any satisfaction but which, once entered, can never then be abandoned, and so on. These are puzzles that are charming in their own right but also philosophically useful as tests of our views insofar as they put them under more pressure than they normally would have to bear. (The greatest philosopher who ever lived, Plato, engineered the single most profound thought experiment ever devised: an invisibility-conferring device. On it he constructs the dialogue *Republic*.) Therefore, readers who pursue some other line of work should not regard philosophers' fancies as altogether idle. Neither, though, should the conclusions elicited from these scenarios be regarded as definitive. No less important than ingenious theoretical jujitsu is attentiveness to empirical results derived at the mainstream rather than at the margins. Although we are not immune to the lure of clever constructions, it is within that mainstream that we will mostly orient ourselves in this book, using the most convincing results of contemporary social science to test and confirm our theory of justice as leaving people alone.

So that potential readers can better determine whether to invest time and effort in the remaining pages of this book, here is a brief indication of how we position ourselves orthogonally in relation to most of the global-justice

---

[2] For an effective dissection of Singer's analogy, see David Schmidtz, "Separateness, Suffering and Moral Theory" in *Person, Polis, Planet* (New York: Oxford University Press, 2008), 145–64.

industry. The dominant approach to global justice is essentially *regulatory*. On this view, justice's most urgent demand is redistribution of global wealth. Accordingly, the main ills of the world, oppression and poverty, should be addressed by appropriate national and international regulation. The dominant approach is to recommend enlarging state institutions and international agencies so as to enforce justice, coercively redistribute wealth, and correct the supposed injustices and inefficiencies of markets. Most of the debate concerns how to do this effectively – whether by robust state-initiated foreign-aid schemes or by reinforcing international redistributive institutions. Strong labor and environmental regulations complete this picture. The world's poor, it is thought, will be best served by substituting good coercion for bad, ineffectual coercion and, above all, by enforcing the duties of global justice that citizens in rich countries are supposed to have toward the world's less fortunate. This strategy is typically dual: on the one hand, states must be *enlarged* so that they can carry out internal duties of justice. On the other hand, international agencies should be empowered to coerce people in rich countries to transfer resources to the poor.

We dissent. The argument advanced here is that what the poor need is *less* regulation, *less* coercion, and *less* state presence in their lives. They need, in other words, more political and economic space where they can engage in the positive-sum games that trade, mobility, and commerce offer. We agree that they need good institutions, but those institutions should be liberty friendly and, especially, market friendly. This classic liberal vision is often characterized as callous because it does not recommend forced aid or redistribution. On the contrary, we contend that this liberal view is truly *humanitarian*. We firmly believe that the evidence shows that freedom will help the poor and vulnerable more than will the alternative regulatory vision. We are convinced that the majority of writers on global justice have simply misdiagnosed the problem and for that reason have recommended ineffectual or counterproductive solutions. As shall be seen, we agree with the preponderance of writers that justice is cosmopolitan, not merely local. But what cosmopolitan justice requires is not that we coercively transfer resources or fatten international bureaucracies but that we everywhere afford people the freedom to pursue their personal projects. This duty of noninterference is global in scope, and transgressions of it are also global. As observed previously, governments and citizens of rich countries sometimes unjustly interfere with the lives of distant persons (and, of course, with the lives of their own citizens).[3] The main culprits, though, the

---

[3] As the economist Angus Deaton put it: "What we need to do is to make sure that we are not standing in the way of the now-poor countries doing what we have already done. We need to let poor people help themselves and get out of the way – or, more positively, stop doing things that are obstructing them." Angus Deaton, *The Great Escape: Health, Wealth, and the Origins of Inequality* (Princeton, NJ: Princeton University Press, 2013), 312.

unjust interferers *par excellence*, are the local elites who have captured their societies' resources for their own benefit.

We proceed as follows: in the remainder of this introduction we summarize the state of the world as it bears on questions to be taken up. We present facts that are relevant to global justice, and we survey various interpretations of those facts. Because we are not social scientists, we rely on what we think is state-of-the-art social-science research. In Chapter 2 we present the philosophical basis of our argument. Our strategy is to counter arguments for the alleged strong moral duties of aid and redistribution of wealth via two responses. First, if we really treated aid as a hard duty of justice (as opposed to an action recommended by virtue), we would engage in counterproductive behavior. Instead of fewer figurative children floating face down in puddles, there would be more. An enforced duty of aid also would disastrously undermine production in the wealthy parts of the world, thus further exacerbating poverty. Our second response is to reject the impersonal view of good and bad that the aid moralist proclaims. Value, we argue, is tied to an individual's own aspirations and well-being. In the philosophical vernacular, it is *agent relative*. Because this is so, it is false that one must be perpetually on call to relinquish one's own cherished personal projects for the sake of facilitating the goods of others.

Chapter 3 develops two themes that are anticipated later in this chapter. First, wealth and poverty are highly determined by the quality of a society's institutions, and second, the most effective poverty-reduction measure of all is liberalizing markets to allow poor people to get richer. Chapter 4 discusses the justice of personal migration. Here again, we argue that entry barriers are *wrong* in principle and *harmful* to persons, especially the poor. We discuss and emphatically reject various attempts to justify such barriers. Chapter 5 examines at length one such purported justification: that open borders cause a brain drain from poor countries. We show why this argument is implausible on empirical and moral grounds. Together these chapters identify injustices of coercively impeding in-migration and out-migration. Chapter 6 examines in depth the justice of international trade. We explicate the law of comparative advantages and its relevance to justice, and we reject various attempts to justify trade barriers. Once again, the case for free trade is overdetermined: protectionism unjustly hurts many, unjustly benefits a few, and reduces national and global wealth.

Chapter 7 addresses the moral standing of states. It reviews the relevant literature, including the work of John Rawls and Michael Walzer, and concludes that the notion of state legitimacy is of little help. People have rights, and violations of those rights are impermissible. There are no fully legitimate regimes because even the best ones violate rights. There are only comparatively good and comparatively bad institutions: good institutions are those that (mostly) leave people alone; bad institutions are those that (mostly) do not.

Chapter 8 examines war. It defends and elaborates the view that war is justified only in defense of persons and their rights. National self-defense and

humanitarian intervention, when justified, are two species of the same genre –
defense of persons. War is justified (when it is) as an effort to make sure that
others leave people alone. We examine just-war theory and the difficult problem of collateral deaths. Finally, Chapter 9 concludes with a discussion of foreign aid, going beyond strict requirements of justice – that is, what people *must*
do – to consider what charitable individuals are *well advised* to undertake. It
defends the view that justifiable aid is mostly that which is extended voluntarily by private parties, not by governmental or quasi-governmental agencies.
There is a limited role for states, however, and we try to work out what that is.
A brief conclusion follows.

THE RELEVANT FACTS: FREEDOM AND WEALTH

A theory of global justice must identify its subject. Philosophers have many
proposals about this: some think that justice is about the basic structure of
society; others that justice permeates all aspects of social life; finally, for others,
justice is all the preceding plus personal virtue. These disagreements about the
matter of justice compound the disagreements about the *scope* of justice. Some
people believe that justice makes sense only within a state; others claim that
justice must be global in scope. Before we take sides on these matters, in this
chapter we identify the *kinds* of facts that a theory of justice should care about.
Whatever else philosophers disagree about, they roughly agree (at least those
of liberal persuasion) about the resources that people need to lead fulfilling
and productive lives: freedom[4] and wealth. Although writers agree that people
need these resources to pursue meaningful life projects, they disagree (again!)
about the *status* of these goods within the theory. Most believe that wealth is
an instrumental good. Some think that freedom is also instrumental (classical
natural-law thinkers, perhaps), whereas philosophers in the Kantian tradition
tend to claim that freedom is an intrinsic good. We will say more about this
later, but in this chapter we sidestep these foundational issues. Here we assume,
as indicated, that people need political freedom[5] and sufficient material wealth
to pursue their life projects and flourish. Global justice is about the fair global
distribution of those goods and about the institutions that are most likely to
secure that distribution. A theory of global justice, then, is centrally concerned
with the *oppressed* – those who have been deprived of their freedom – and
the *poor* – those who lack sufficient material resources. To be sure, people
have more specific needs: they love, they appreciate art, they worship. But they

---

[4] By "freedom," we mean *political* freedom, not transcendental freedom or human agency.
[5] We mean here what is usually styled *negative* political freedom as a necessary condition of justice. At the very least, global justice requires the absence of political oppression. Of course, persons must be able to pursue their life plans – they must enjoy *positive* freedom as well. We do not
enter the rich debate on this topic because we assume that our emphasis on prosperity, material
resources, and alleviation of poverty addresses positive freedom sufficiently at the global level.

cannot confidently pursue these life projects without an adequate amount of freedom and wealth. And there is little that global justice can (and perhaps should) do, directly, about these other aspects of the human condition.

In this chapter we survey the state of the world circa 2014 as prolegomena to thinking about justice. Theories of justice do not have to start with the facts, but unless they connect with the circumstances actually confronted by choice makers, they will lack normative punch. Here we put some of these facts front and center by way of situating our account of global justice. These facts are comprised of empirical data and theories that can be gauged from reliable scientific research. Establishing what the facts are and why they are as they are is extremely difficult. How do we measure poverty? What causes it? Has inequality increased with globalization? Is the planet headed toward environmental collapse? What are the causes of war and tyranny? What counts as oppression? Does political freedom lead to prosperity or the other way around? How do majoritarian institutions enhance freedom and prosperity? What variables should we use to measure these things? Many of these are *not* normative questions; philosophers cannot answer them by just *thinking* hard. These incorporate genuine empirical questions, and the conclusions a theory of justice advances will depend inevitably on the answers to these questions. The authors are philosophers and, as such, are not equipped to conduct the empirical research required to establish these facts about the world. For this reason, we rely on what we take to be state-of-the-art social-science literature, especially economics.

A theory of global justice has additional concerns. On the one hand, tyranny and poverty are not the only facts a theory of justice should worry about. We worry about environmental degradation, disease, conflict, and other ills. However, these problems are important because they threaten freedom and well-being. On the other hand, a theory of justice cares about individual choices. In recent years, philosophers have introduced the idea that the distribution of burdens and benefits in society should be sensitive to individual choices rather than to fortuitous individual circumstances – it should be "ambition sensitive" rather than "endowment sensitive."[6] It seems unjust that some persons suffer a big starting disadvantage in life through no fault of their own. This is a particularly pressing problem for a theory of global justice because persons who share this planet are born to vastly different political environments, causing their life prospects to diverge dramatically. A rich person and a poor person born in Germany have different initial endowments, but at least they are both born in a wealthy *and* politically free society. But a poor person born in Germany is *significantly* better off than a poor person born in Myanmar. The latter is much poorer than the former *and* lacks the political freedom that the German poor person enjoys. (Interestingly, the German poor are *worse* off than the Myanmaran *rich* for a variety of reasons, including the

---

[6] For a useful discussion of "luck" egalitarianism, see Will Kymlicka, *Contemporary Political Philosophy*, 2nd ed. (Oxford University Press, 2002), 72–87.

fact that the rich in unjust societies often obtain their rents from the oppressive nature of the regime.)

In this chapter we describe the current distribution of goods that are especially important for a theory of international justice and introduce some causal explanations of various problems offered by specialists. These explanations are amplified in subsequent chapters. Without prejudging issues of priority, these goods fall, as we indicated, into two broad categories: freedom and wealth. It is possible, of course, to reduce these to a single good, for example, human welfare,[7] but that would prejudge thorny metaethical issues. For now, we prefer to retain neutrality in our classification.

OPPRESSION

As of 2014, there were 195 independent countries in the world.[8] Using three categories, "free," "partly free," and "not free," the well-respected Freedom House reports that, as of December 2013, there were 88 free countries (those scoring 1 to 2.5 on a 1–6 scale), representing 45 percent of the world's states; 59 partly free countries (scoring 2.5 to 4), representing 30 percent of states; and 48 countries that are not free, representing 25 percent of states. So the good news is that free countries make up the largest group of the three. The bad news is that the countries with significant freedom deficits, that is, the group of "partly free" and "not free" taken together, outnumber free countries 107 to 88. To be sure, freedom has made important inroads since 1990. There are more free countries today than was the case ten years ago, and there were more ten years ago than in the 1970s.[9] This classification is not without problems – for one thing, it glosses over threats to freedoms in free countries. But it will do as an approximation because part of what we mean when we say that a country is free is that its institutions can address threats to freedom that will inevitably arise. However, according to Freedom House, respect for civil rights and political rights have declined overall for the last five consecutive years.

Another flaw with counting nations is that they are not persons. It is misleading to count nations as units in any estimate about the extent of freedom in the world because what we want to know is how many *persons* live under unfree institutions. A rough calculation yields the following numbers: the

---

[7] See, in this sense, Eric Posner, "Human Welfare, Not Human Rights," Chicago Law and Economics Working Paper No 394; available at: http://www.law.uchicago.edu/files/files/394.pdf.

[8] See Freedom House, "Freedom in the World 2014: An Eighth Year of Decline in Political Rights and Civil Liberties," Washington, DC; available at: http://www.freedomhouse.org/report/freedom-world/freedom-world-2014#. We choose this source because it is highly respected and because it rates countries. However, we think that other sources largely agree with Freedom House on the issue of individual freedom.

[9] According to the data provided by Freedom House, in 1973 there were 44 free countries out of 151, that is, around 29 percent. In 2014 there are 88 free countries out of 193, about 45 percent. See http://www.freedomhouse.org/images/File/CountryStatus_and_RatingsOverview1973-2010.pdf.

world population is approximately 7 billion.[10] According to Freedom House, the number of people living under free governments is roughly 2.8 million, or 40 percent of the world population.[11] This means that roughly 4.2 billion people, about 60 percent of the world population, live in countries that are partly free or not free (we label these "unfree.") We suspect that the situation is worse because Freedom House is quite generous with the label "free." That category includes "kleptocracies," that is, countries that systematically steal from their citizens but formally respect civil rights. Because, as we will argue, those political systems seriously impair individual freedom, they get an undeserved pass from human rights reports, like Freedom House's, that are indifferent to the relationship between economic stagnation and freedom.

A few remarks about these numbers are appropriate. It is commonly assumed that the fall of communism had a great impact on the advancement of freedom. Although this is not mistaken, the wonder of the fall of the Berlin Wall should not be allowed to obscure the fact that by far the greatest progress has come from political changes in Asia. India, Indonesia, South Korea, and Taiwan count today as free nations. Japan has been a free society for a long time. Considering numbers alone, the greatest coup for the cause of freedom would be an accession of China to the community of free nations, since more than half the people who currently live under unfree institutions are in China. (As of this writing, political liberalization in China is highly uncertain but not impossible, given the dramatic economic liberalization and growth in that country.) Elsewhere, the democracies of the Americas, Europe, and Australia share the badge of honor. Russia is a sad case of regression. Many hoped that after the collapse of the Soviet Union, Russia would join the family of liberal states. Events in 2014 have dashed those hopes, at least for the time being.

The assault on human freedom has many faces. Governments often interfere directly with individual freedom. In Zimbabwe, the government persecutes and tortures dissenters while refusing to step down after electoral defeat.[12] The government of Iran also tortures and, among other things, raids private homes in search of "immorality."[13] Saudi Arabia monitors women with forcibly implanted electronic devices.[14] In Cambodia, authorities forcibly evict poor landowners and give the land to developers.[15] In Guinea, the

[10] U.S. Census Bureau, at http://www.census.gov/main/www/popclock.html.

[11] See Freedom House report, n. 8.

[12] See Human Rights Watch, "Zimbabwe: Runoff Vote Not Credible among Violence and Torture," New York; available at: http://hrw.org/english/docs/2008/05/02/zimbab18734.htm.

[13] See Human Rights Watch report on Iran; available at: http://hrw.org/doc/?t=mideast&c=iran.

[14] See CNN, "Saudi Arabia's Unsolicited Monitoring of Women's Travels Draws Activists' Outrage," November 26, 2012; available at: http://www.cnn.com/2012/11/25/world/meets/saudi-arabia-women/index.html.

[15] See "World Bank Suspends New Lending to Cambodia over Eviction of Landowners," *The Guardian*, August 10, 2011; available at: http://www.guardian.co.uk/global-development/2011/aug/10/world-bank-suspends-cambodia-lending.

government opened fire in a stadium packed with dissenters, killing hundreds.[16] Sometimes governments are guilty of criminal omission. The government of Myanmar has blocked international aid to more than 100,000 victims of a deadly cyclone.[17] And in Darfur, Arab militia have killed and "cleansed" large numbers of people (the twenty-year civil war has claimed about 2 million lives there), apparently with the complicity of the Sudanese government. The area was under genocide alert until Southern Sudan declared its independence.[18] The much-heralded Arab Spring has yet to produce significant freedom gains: as we write, only *two* Muslim countries are free.[19] In Libya, the abject Qaddafi regime is gone, but Libya has descended again into chaos.[20] Similar worries burden Egypt, Tunisia, and other neighbors. In Bahrain, street demonstrations have met with brutal repression.[21] And in Syria, an uprising against the dictatorial regime of Assad is met with violent repression while the world watches in impotence.[22] Oppression is not confined to developing nations. In the United States, the incarceration of millions of persons for morally innocent behavior and recent well-publicized incidents of police brutality are indications that liberal democracies, while on the whole freer, are far from blameless on this score.

Governments are not the only suppressors of freedom. As we write these lines, the so-called Islamic State, a fighting army in Syria and Iraq, is terrorizing civilians to an unprecedented extent.[23] For forty-eight years in Colombia, a powerful guerrilla group succeeded, with some external backing, in terrorizing the general population.[24] In South Africa, violent mobs descended on migrant

[16] See Human Rights Watch, "Guinea: Stadium Massacre Victims Await Justice," New York, September 29, 2012; available at: http://www.hrw.org/news/2012/09/29/guinea-stadium-massacre-victims-await-justice.

[17] See Operation USA, "Cyclone Nargis: Disaster Response in Myanmar," Los Angeles, CA; available at: www.opusa.org/cyclone-nargis-disaster-response/.

[18] See United Human Rights Council, "Genocide in Darfur," Glendale, CA; available at: http://www.unitedhumanrights.org/genocide/genocide-in-sudan.htm.

[19] See Freedom House report n. 8.

[20] See "How Libya Descended into Faction-fighting and Chaos," *The Telegraph*, November 8, 2014; available at: http://www.telegraph.co.uk/news/worldnews/africaandindianocean/libya/11218039/How-Libya-descended-into-faction-fighting-and-chaos.html.

[21] See Courtney C. Radsch and Jennifer Gulbrandson, "Killing the Messenger: Bahrain's Brutal Crackdown," Freedom House, Washington, DC; available at: http://www.freedomhouse.org/template.cfm?page=704.

[22] See Voice of America, "UN Chief 'Firmly Condemns' Syria Violence Escalation," Washington, DC, December 17, 2012; available at: http://www.voanews.com/content/un-chief-firmly-condemns-syria-violence-escalation/1566271.html. For a timeline of events, still unfolding at the time of this writing, see BBC News, "Syria Profile," London, December 12, 2012; available at: http://www.bbc.co.uk/news/world-middle-east-14703995.

[23] See CNN, "ISIS Fast Facts," October 9, 2014; available at: http://www.cnn.com/2014/08/08/world/isis-fast-facts/.

[24] See NPR, "After 48 Years of War, Colombians Plan Peace Talks," Washington, DC; available at: http://www.npr.org/2012/09/26/161432683/after-48-years-of-war-colombians-plan-peace-talks.

workers,[25] and in Nigeria, a warlord by the name of Boko Haram kidnaps girls to sell them as "wives."[26] Crimes of international terrorism are well known, as are the excesses of governmental response.[27] And some states are criminal enterprises from beginning to end.[28] Sometimes the perpetrators deny political rights, such as the right to vote; other times they deny civil rights, such as the right to free speech or freedom of religion. Sometimes, as we noted, governments torture and kill. But other times the problem is not so much government abuse but the *lack* of government, that is, anarchy, the breakdown of minimal social order that leads to failed states. Another species of failure is when organized crime becomes the enemy of freedom, as in Mexico.[29] The Fund for Peace runs an index of failed states, which as of 2012 was headed by Somalia, Congo, Sudan, the new South Sudan, Chad, Zimbabwe, and Afghanistan. This index puts fourteen states in the "red" zone, that is, on the verge of disintegration and civil war.[30] The problem of failed states is important because any theory of global justice must address the moral status of sovereignty. Government is perhaps necessary, but it is also a grave threat to persons.

In this book we take seriously *all* unjust interferences with personal freedom. Human rights advocates understandably focus on the most truculent violations. Our approach to global justice, in addition, is concerned with less obvious but still problematic interferences with personal projects. Examples include various instances of less egregious interferences with *civil liberties*, such as restrictions on speech and worship, and instances of *economic* depredation, such as the erection of trade barriers or the outright expropriation of wealth to pursue ends that are far removed from anything resembling the public good. We thus avoid a formalistic approach to the matter: states do not get a passing grade just because they are formally democratic, and conversely, an undemocratic state, while morally deficient for that reason, may be less obtrusive to freedom than a democratic state.[31] While political democracy is morally preferable, other things being equal, global justice is concerned with unjust interferences with freedom, whether they are perpetrated by undemocratic or

---

[25] See BBC News, "UN Condemns South Africa Attacks on Zimbabwe Workers," London; available at: http://news.bbc.co.uk/2/hi/africa/8370720.stm.

[26] See "Boko Haram Rebels Parade 'Liberated' Nigerian Girls in Propaganda Video," *The Guardian*, May 13, 2014; available at: http://www.theguardian.com/world/2014/may/12/kidnapped-nigerian-girls-paraded-in-boko-haram-video.

[27] For a critical view of targeted killings, see Fernando R. Tesón, "Targeted Killings in War and Peace: A Philosophical Analysis," in *Targeted Killings: Law and Morality in an Asymmetrical World*, C. Finkelstein, J. Ohlin and A. Altman, eds. (Oxford University Press, 2012), 403–33.

[28] There are many historical examples; for a current one, see Human Rights Watch, "North Korea," New York; available at: http://www.hrw.org/nkorea.

[29] The 2014 Freedom House report (n. 8) downgraded Mexico from free to partly free for this reason.

[30] See The Fund for Peace, "Failed States Index 2012," Washington, DC; available at: http://www.fundforpeace.org/global/?q=fsi.

[31] See the discussion of state legitimacy in Chapter 7.

democratic regimes. In the latter case, it should be noted that good institutions may allow redress for intrusions. Alas, majoritarian institutions may *aggravate* denial of freedom. Tyrannical practices are not improved by the fact that a majority decrees them.[32] Our nonformalistic approach distinguishes instead between (relatively) good and bad institutions. Good institutions are those that allow persons to pursue their personal projects; bad institutions are those that fail to do so.

Global justice should strive for all nations on the globe to establish good institutions, but those institutions will not be perfect. It would be a triumph if most of the nations of the world became freedom loving (or if any world state that were eventually established, assuming that it is desirable, were freedom loving), but even that happy outcome would not eliminate *all* human rights violations. The most a theory of justice can do is to devise principles for evaluating institutions and to make recommendations for institutional design.

POVERTY

A theory of global justice must address world poverty. Here we provide facts about poverty and briefly sketch various causal hypotheses found in the extensive literature; we take up the empirical question again in Chapter 3. Experts define poverty as "pronounced deprivation in well-being" and classify poverty into three types: extreme poverty, moderate poverty, and relative poverty. The *extreme* poor live with less than \$1 a day.[33] These people all too often cannot afford the basic material goods they need simply to survive. Persons earning between \$1 and \$2 a day live in *moderate* poverty. These households can barely meet basic needs but lack many of the things (e.g., health care, education) that people in rich countries take for granted. Those in moderate poverty risk survival at every turn because they lack the resources to overcome even minor misfortunes. And finally, those with an income below the national average or below a particular poverty line defined in their own countries are in *relative* poverty. In the United States, a family of four is legally poor if they make less than \$23,850 a year.[34] Of course, the cost of living in rich countries is much higher. Just to compare: in a relatively rich developing country such as Argentina, the line of poverty (called *canasta básica total*) is approximately \$6,000 a year for a family of four. About 30 percent of the Argentine

---

[32] An example: the democratically elected legislature of Ecuador has passed a law to tightly control media critical of the government; see www.reuters.com/article/2013/06/14/us-ecuador-media-idUSBRE95D0YJ20130614.

[33] These facts summarize the massive work on poverty done under the sponsorship of the World Bank. An important source is Jonathan Haughton and Shahidur R. Khandker, *Handbook on Poverty and Inequality* (World Bank, Washington, DC, 2009); available at: http://mail.beaconhill.org/~j_haughton/HandbookPovIneq.pdf.

[34] See U.S. Department for Health and Human Services, "2014 Poverty Guidelines," Washington, DC; available at: http://aspe.hhs.gov/poverty/14poverty.cfm.

population is below this national poverty line.[35] And as an example of a relatively poor developing nation, consider Nigeria. Despite Nigeria's plentiful resources, including oil, poverty is widespread. The country is now considered one of the twenty poorest countries in the world. Over 70 percent of the population is classified as poor, with 35 percent living in absolute poverty.[36] (It is hard to determine what the national poverty line would be.) Relative poverty is morally significant for writers who reject cosmopolitanism and argue for a strong duty to compatriots. On this view (which we discuss later), an American citizen has distributive obligations to the American poor rather than to the world's poor.

According to the World Bank, of 7 billion people on the globe, 2.8 billion live on less than $2 a day, and of those, 1.2 billion live on less than $1 a day. It is estimated that 8 million people per year die from extreme poverty. People in extreme poverty are distributed as follows: 43.5 percent in South Asia, 24.3 percent in sub-Saharan Africa, 23.2 percent in East Asia and the Pacific Rim, 6.5 percent in Latin America and the Caribbean, 2% in Europe and Central Asia, and 0.5 percent in the Middle East and North Africa.[37] The poorest region in the world is sub-Saharan Africa: the thirty-three sub-Saharan African countries in this region have a combined population of 617 million, with a population-weighted average annual income of $271 per person, or 74 cents a day.[38]

Explanations of poverty abound. One disagreement is whether poverty and hunger are due to a *production* failure, that is, to a suppression of markets, or to a *distribution* failure.[39] A related disagreement is who is to blame. Some blame rich countries for world poverty. There are two versions of this view. One blames poverty on deliberate plundering or similar wrongful behavior by rich countries. This view was once fashionable but has since been discredited.[40]

---

[35] See the pertinent data at Index Mundi, "Argentina Population below Poverty Line"; available at: http://www.indexmundi.com/argentina/population_below_poverty_line.html (the official Argentine index is unreliable because of the government's repeated tampering with the numbers). The cost of living is lower than in the United States, but still the Argentine poor are considerably worse off in terms of purchasing power than the American poor.

[36] See World Bank, "Nigeria," Washington, DC; available at: http://www.worldbank.org/en/country/nigeria.

[37] These numbers can be found in a well-known study by the World Bank. "World Development Report, Attacking Poverty (Overview)," Washington, DC, 2000–1, p. 4; available at: http://siteresources.worldbank.org/INTPOVERTY/Resources/WDR/overview.pdf. For an update, see World Bank, "World Development Report 2014: Risk and Opportunity – Managing Risk for Development (Overview), Washington, DC, 2015, p. 5; available at: https://openknowledge .worldbank.org/handle/10986/16092.

[38] See Jeffrey D. Sachs, John W. McArthur, Guido Schmidt-Traub, Margaret Kruk, Chandrika Bahadur, Michael Faye, and Gordon McCord, "Ending Africa's Poverty Trap," *Brookings Papers on Economic Activity* 2004(1), (2004), 118.

[39] We borrow this dichotomy from Partha Dasgupta, "The Economics of Poverty in Poor Countries," *Scandinavian Journal of Economics* 100(1), (1998), 43.

[40] For an example of the new literature rejecting this explanation, see George B. N. Ayittey, *Africa Betrayed* (New York: St. Martin's Press, 1993).

The other, defended by Thomas Pogge and others, is that whatever the cause of poverty, rich countries should be blamed for not ending it, given that they could do so at low cost.[41] Both these views are consistent with either of the two explanations mentioned earlier: poverty as production failure or as distribution failure.

The prevailing explanation, however, is that poverty is mainly the result of bad governance, that is, bad *domestic* institutions and practices. Deficient institutions lie at the heart of economic stagnation and poverty.[42] Poverty abounds when institutions and rulers fail.[43] They unduly suppress markets, or they do not redistribute properly, or (more likely) both. There is a robust consensus that countries can derive substantial economic benefits from better governance (this is sometimes called the *development* dividend.)[44] The extensive literature on the subject identifies several components of the definition of good governance. Without prejudging issues in political theory, good governance may be roughly defined as the traditions and institutions by which authority in a country is exercised to the benefit of its citizens.[45] Different institutions have different impacts on growth and prosperity because they create different incentives. Politics, then, lies at the foundation of wealth and poverty. Scholars who disagree about the influence of other factors (e.g., about the importance of trade openness) nonetheless agree that institutional quality is crucial for economic growth and, consequently, an escape from poverty.

But what *are* good institutions for this purpose, that is, those that will enable nations to escape poverty? Here are some of the institutional deficiencies listed in the literature: (1) lack of protection of traditional human rights, including fairness of elections, (2) high corruption levels, (3) disrespect for

[41] See Thomas Pogge, *World Poverty and Human Rights* (Cambridge, UK: Polity, 2002). We examine Pogge's arguments below and in Chapter 3.

[42] The literature is extensive. Leading works include Daron Acemoglu and James A. Robinson, *Why Nations Fail: The Origins of Power, Prosperity and Poverty* (New York: Crown, 2012); Deaton, *The Great Escape*; Douglass C. North, *Institutions, Institutional Change, and Economic Performance* (Cambridge University Press, 1990); Hernando de Soto, *The Other Path: The Invisible Revolution in the Third World* (New York: Harper & Row, 1989); David S. Landes, *The Wealth and Poverty of Nations* (New York: Norton, 1998); Dani Rodrik, Arvind Subramanian, and Francesco Trebbi, "Institutions Rule: The Primacy of Institutions Over Geography and Integration in Economic Development," *Journal of Economic Growth* 9 (2004), 131; Daron Acemoglu, Simon Johnson, and James Robinson, "The Colonial Origins of Comparative Development: An Empirical Investigation, *American Economic Review* 91 (2001), 1369–1401. Also important is the work of Daniel Kaufmann, available at the World Bank's website: http://siteresources.worldbank.org. As we will see, these scholars differ on the emphasis they assign to different institutions.

[43] None other than John Rawls concurs in this diagnosis: "The great social evils in poorer societies are likely to be oppressive government and corrupt elites." John Rawls, *The Law of Peoples* (Cambridge, MA: Harvard University Press, 1999), 77.

[44] See Daniel Kaufman, "10 Myths about Governance and Corruption," *Finance & Development* 42 (2005), 41.

[45] We adapt the definition from Kaufman.

the rule of law, (4) government ineffectiveness, including rent-seeking and private capture of government agencies, (5) protectionist trade policies, (6) insufficient or unstable protection of property rights and contracts, and (7) excessive regulatory burdens – the presence of market-unfriendly policies and practices.[46] The *relative* impact of these institutional factors on economic performance is hard to gauge, even with the sophisticated empirical methods that characterize economic research these days. In addition, the boundaries among these factors are blurred: corruption *is* a failure of the rule of law, excessive regulation creates more opportunities for bribes and political abuse, and trade barriers often result from rent-seeking and other forms of predatory behavior. In many cases (but not all), the lack of political freedom impairs growth. To complicate things, fair and transparent democratic processes often yield bad laws because of epistemic failures in the electorate and the truth-insensitive incentives that politicians have.[47] While these dangers are even more acute in nondemocratic regimes, the sad truth is that fair, transparent democratic procedures will *not* guarantee the institutions or practices conducive to growth and prosperity and, consequently, will not guarantee poverty alleviation.

Economists who agree on the importance of institutions disagree on the relative weight of the factors just listed. We can classify institutionalists into two camps. Some (*political* institutionalists) emphasize the importance of the rule of law, the absence of corruption, the independence of courts, a healthy regulatory regime aimed at preventing fraud and other abuses by the private sector, and the *stability* of property rights as the main ingredients of the kind of political system that causes economic prosperity and, consequently, is apt to alleviate poverty.[48] Others (*full* institutionalists) agree with this list but point out that a society needs, in addition, *market-friendly* institutions to prosper. Thus *robust* (and not just stable) property rights, absence of excessive regulation, and openness to trade importantly determine economic growth, which,

---

[46] Kaufman, "10 Myths about Governance and Corruption."

[47] For an analysis of this phenomenon, called *discourse failure*, see Guido Pincione and Fernando R. Tesón, *Rational Choice and Democratic Deliberation: A Theory of Discourse Failure* (New York: Cambridge University Press, 2006).

[48] See Rodrik et al., "Institutions Rule." Mathias Risse uses this thesis effectively in his reply to Thomas Pogge's claim that the global order is mainly responsible for world poverty. His enunciation of the thesis bears reproduction:

Growth and prosperity depend on the quality of institutions, such as stable property rights, rule of law, bureaucratic capacity, appropriate regulatory structures to curtail at least the worst forms of fraud, anti-competitive behavior; and graft, quality and independence of courts, but also cohesiveness of society, existence of trust and social cooperation, and thus overall quality of civil society.

Mathias Risse, "How Does the Global Order Harm the Poor?" *Philosophy and Public Affairs* 33 (2005), 349–76. While we are largely sympathetic to Risse's position (especially his refutation of Pogge's central causal claim), we think that this definition understates the importance of free markets.

in turn, is a necessary condition for poverty alleviation.[49] In other words, an economically successful society must be capitalist, come what may. As Adam Smith told us, economic freedom is a central factor in the wealth of nations.

We believe that theory and history support full institutionalism.[50] A society must have healthy political *and* economic institutions to escape poverty. Individuals must be able to interact in an environment that is politically and economically free in order to engage in the positive-sum exchanges that cement economic growth. Yet the empirical question is extremely tough, and some cautionary notes are in order. Political institutionalists are right that free-market policies (which normally create growth) can fail if other institutions are deficient. As Dani Rodrik and his associates put it, "[T]he quality of institutions trumps everything else."[51] Political institutionalists, then, have made a credible case that liberalizing markets *alone* often will not do the trick and especially will not alleviate poverty.

The problem with political institutionalism, however, is that it fails to account for the phenomenon of *democratic kleptocracies*. A kleptocracy is a state that steals from its citizens. Kleptocracies concentrate power in the hands of powerful elites and block the mutual benefits that generate economic growth. In a kleptocracy, the government and its friends run roughshod over property rights and freedom of contract. These regimes prey on those who produce and end up harming everyone except themselves and those who help them stay in power.[52]

Interestingly, kleptocracies can be democratic and observe traditional civil rights. This is so because as long as they can win elections, they do not need to put people in jail to enact confiscatory laws. Moreover, their ability to confiscate wealth is the reason they win elections. It is called *populism*, and majority rule is the tool of choice for effecting economic depredation. This is a challenge for writers such as Leif Wenar who endorse democratic transfers of resources to the state. The global-justice literature, with its exclusive insistence on global redistribution and (less vigorously) on traditional civil rights (to the exclusion of property rights) as the only marks of legitimacy, has overlooked

---

[49] See Hernando de Soto, *The Other Path*; and Daron Acemoglu and Simon Johnson, "Unbundling Institutions," *Journal of Political Economy* 113 (2005), 949–95.

[50] We develop our argument in Chapters 3 and 6.

[51] Rodrik et al., "Institutions Rule," 135.

[52] See Sebastian Edwards, *Left Behind: Latin America and the False Promise of Populism* (University of Chicago Press, 2010). For the case of Argentina, See Roger Cohen, "Cry for Me, Argentina," *New York Times*, February 27, 2014; available at: http://www.nytimes.com/2014/02/28/opinion/28iht-edcohen28.html?_r=0; and "The Tragedy of Argentina: A Century of Decline," *The Economist*, February 15, 2014; available at: http://www.economist.com/news/briefing/21596582-one-hundred-years-ago-argentina-was-future-what-went-wrong-century-decline. For Venezuela, see Moisés Naun, "An Economic Crisis of Historic Proportions," *New York Times*, January 8, 2013; available at: http://www.nytimes.com/roomfordebate/2013/01/03/venezuela-post-chavez/chavez-will-leave-behind-an-economic-crisis.

this serious problem. If a country respects human rights and the rule of law and observes transparent democratic processes, but then the legislature uses those same processes to enact bad laws such as massive plans for government intervention in the economy, expropriations, and the like, one can safely predict economic failure. Societies afflicted with this problem will only prosper by establishing the rule of law *plus* robust private property rights enforced by an independent judiciary and not just protect traditional civil rights and majority rule.

We should comment here on some of the leading scholarship in this area. Among economists, the view that development is a function of good domestic governance, export-led growth, and openness to foreign investment was pioneered by Peter Bauer and Basil Yamey. In contrast to the then-prevailing view that assigned government a central role in pulling societies from stagnation, these authors stated as early as 1957 that development should be judged by how much institutions widen "the range of alternatives open to people as consumers and as producers."[53]

Douglass North, the founder of institutional economics, has provided a theoretical foundation for the view that good institutions are essential for economic development. A central theme in his work is that deficient institutions increase transaction costs, especially informational costs, and for this reason, they seriously interfere with the smooth functioning of markets. North argues that institutions create a path dependency that makes both good *and* bad institutions persist. In his words:

[I]nstitutions matter and shape the long-run path of economies, but as long as the consequent markets are competitive or even roughly approximate the zero-transaction-cost model, the long-run path is an efficient one.... But if the markets are incomplete, the information feedback is fragmentary at best, and transaction costs are significant, then the subjective models of actors modified both by very imperfect feedback and by ideology will shape the path. Then, not only can both divergent paths and persistently poor performance prevail, the historically derived perceptions of the actors shape the choices that they make.[54]

Daron Acemoglu, Simon Johnson, and James A. Robinson have shown that present differences in income among former European colonies can be traced back to the different institutions established by settlers.[55] In the successful cases (i.e., Australia, Canada, and the United States), settlers tried to replicate European institutions, which emphasized private-property rights and checks

[53] Peter T. Bauer and Basil S. Yamey, *The Economics of Under-Developed Countries* (University of Chicago Press, 1957), 151–55, on the centrality of individual decision making for development. See also Peter S. Bauer, *Equality, the Third World, and Economic Delusion* (Cambridge, MA: Harvard University Press, 1984), 8–25.

[54] North, *Institutions, Institutional Change, and Economic Performance*, 95–6

[55] Acemoglu et al., "The Colonial Origins of Comparative Development: An Empirical Investigation," 1369–1401.

against government powers. In the unsuccessful cases (i.e., Latin America and Africa), Europeans powers created "extractive" institutions, that is, systems aimed at plundering as many resources as possible from the colonies. These colonial practices failed to protect private property and to establish checks against governmental expropriation and other abuses.

In their most recent work, Acemoglu and Robinson display in full their version of the institutionalist thesis. They argue that poverty and wealth can be traced to the presence of extractive or inclusive institutions, respectively. Extractive political institutions "concentrate power in the hands of a narrow elite and places few constraints on the exercise of this power."[56] Inclusive political institutions, vesting power broadly, tend to uproot economic institutions that expropriate the resources of the many, erect entry barriers, and suppress the functioning of markets for the benefit of a few. The authors go on to give numerous examples of both: the contrast is marked not only between societies that emerged from English and Spanish colonization, respectively, but also the even more glaring contrast between North Korea and South Korea, two societies with virtually identical resources, geography, and ethnicity. Importantly, Acemoglu and Robinson leave open the question of which, if any, political mechanisms are inclusive – more precisely, whether laissez-faire or (moderate) interventionist policies would pave the way to economic success. One thing is clear, however: inclusive institutions require relatively unhampered markets. In unsuccessful states, elites intervene coercively in the market to secure gains for themselves. Therefore, a constitutional arrangement to prevent elites from perpetuating themselves in power is a necessary (but not sufficient) condition for success. This account supports the proposition that economic and political liberties go hand in hand because they allow the diffusion of power that uproots plundering institutions.

Similarly, the groundbreaking work of Hernando de Soto provides, we believe, convincing proof of the central role that a host of market-unfriendly institutions and practices has played in the stagnation of Latin America. De Soto's extensive research shows that the informal economy that characterizes Latin American societies could not possibly be or become efficient because it is characterized by the absence of clearly defined property rights.[57] These findings comport with the predictions of economic theory.[58] De Soto's main concern was to debunk a political and academic consensus about Latin America and the developing world generally during the 1960s and 1970s: that the problem on that continent is unequal distribution of income fueled by the dependent status of those countries. This consensus (*dependencia* theory) was formed after the

---

[56] Acemoglu and Robinson, *Why Nations Fail*, 81ff.

[57] Soto, *The Other Path*, esp. chap. 5, 158–72.

[58] See, e.g., the seminal paper by Harold Demsetz, "Toward a Theory of Property Rights," *American Economic Review* 57 (1967), 347–59.

war and, unfortunately, was supported by influential academic elites in Europe and the United States. The faulty diagnosis led to the mushrooming of socialist, nationalist, and populist regimes in Latin America and Africa, with disastrous results.[59] De Soto showed that neither disparity of income nor imperialism was the problem. Rather, Latin American nations lacked the institutions and practices that secure growth and prosperity.[60] Sadly, a vicious path dependence still haunts many Latin American societies today. Populist regimes win elections by pursuing electorally effective but economically harmful policies. Scholars have made similar findings for Africa.[61]

Some challenge or qualify the institutionalist thesis. Some scholars claim that countries are *trapped* in poverty. They are too poor to grow, so institutional reform will not help them. Referring to Africa, Jeffrey Sachs and his coauthors write:

[E]xtreme poverty leads to low national saving rates, which in turn lead to low or negative economic growth rates. Low domestic saving is not offset by large inflows of private foreign capital, for example foreign direct investment, because Africa's poor infrastructure and weak human capital discourage such inflows. With very low domestic saving and low rates of market-based foreign capital inflows, there is little in Africa's current dynamics that promotes an escape from poverty.[62]

This explanation rings circular: countries are poor because they cannot save enough, and they cannot save enough because they are poor. But perhaps the point the authors make is simply that once a country has reached levels of extreme poverty *for whatever reason*, including institutional deficiencies, its predicament prevents the creation of the conditions to overcome it. On this view, whatever its origins, poverty persists because there is just not enough wealth even to get the economy started. Still, even if the authors are right about the poverty trap, they misconceive good governance for this purpose. They use the Freedom House report to show that some countries that score high on the report are nonetheless trapped in poverty. But that report does not measure *economic* freedoms, only political freedoms. All their observation shows is that some African countries that are politically free (and perhaps less corrupt) remain poor despite this. The same is true in Latin America, where massive unproductive public spending and corruption prevent economic growth in politically free societies. Sachs and his associates overlook the well-established

---

[59] To be accurate, populism in Latin America is not the result only of a cognitive mistake: populist politicians know well that their policies ruin their countries. But a phenomenon called *discourse failure* (the public's economic mistakes due mainly to high informational costs) prevents the public from reversing this vicious circle.

[60] Along the same lines, see, for the Argentine case, Sergio Berensztein and Horacio Spector, "Business, Government, and Law" in *A New Economic History of Argentina*, Gerardo della Paolera and Alan M. Taylor, eds. (Cambridge University Press, 2004).

[61] See Ayittey, *Africa Betrayed*.

[62] Sachs et al., "Poverty Trap," 122. The authors propose a big influx of public spending financed by rich-country donors.

fact that good governance includes, as we saw, the protection of property rights and effective operation of other market-friendly institutions.[63]

Another critic of the institutionalist thesis is Thomas Pogge, who claims that the global order is responsible for poverty.[64] According to Pogge, the global order, established and dominated by rich countries, confines millions of persons to avoidable poverty. This happens through a variety of mechanisms, of which three are salient. First, rich countries refuse to liberalize agriculture. They protect their own rich farmers, thus harming farmers in the developing world. Second, rich countries have succeeded in enforcing intellectual property rights on pharmaceuticals, which exacerbates health problems in the developing world. And finally, the global order controlled by rich countries is too deferential to sovereignty. This allows corrupt and tyrannical elites in the developing world, in complicity with the West, to exploit their subjects.

Pogge deserves credit for having reawakened new audiences to the awful reality of world poverty, for having called attention to the objectionable protectionist policies of rich countries, and for having challenged the prevailing notion of sovereignty on which the international order relies. On the latter issue, the sanctity of borders and its political incarnations, nationalism and national interest, have harmed many persons in history and done much to undermine justice in the world at all levels. Indeed, Pogge's analysis here converges with Acemoglu and Robinson's identification, already noted, of plundering institutions as the main cause of economic failure. The global order relies too much on sovereignty and established governments, and this reliance is causally linked to the economic stagnation of weak countries. Economic relations, no less than political relations, often proceed without sufficient scrutiny of the moral credentials of governments. Global institutions such as the World Bank and the International Monetary Fund are subject to criticism on this score because they assist developing countries without pausing to consider whether they are thereby consolidating bad governance and, eventually, perpetuating poverty as well. We can say that the international order does not do enough to prevent plundering of people by their own governments. In this sense, then, Pogge is correct.

The problem with Pogge's theory is that his *causal* claim is wrong. If by "global order" we mean not just the objectionable part of international law that protects incumbent regimes but also the mechanisms that have allowed the liberalization of the global economy (globalization), including dismantling of tariffs and other trade barriers, then the global order, far from being the cause of poverty, is responsible for a vast amelioration of poverty over the past

---

[63] The "2012 Index of Economic Freedoms" lists the following nations as the freest, in descending order: Hong Kong, Singapore, Australia, Switzerland, New Zealand, Canada, and Chile, Mauritius, Ireland, and the United States. See Heritage Foundation, "2014 Index of Economic Freedoms," Washington, DC; available at: http://www.heritage.org/index/.

[64] Pogge, *World Poverty*, 13–15.

100 years or so. As Mathias Risse explains, according to Pogge's own benchmarks, the global order "has caused amazing improvements over the state of misery that has characterized human life throughout the ages."[65] Once one controls for domestic institutions, Pogge's attempt to blame rich countries loses much of its superficial appeal. Rich countries got rich for quite diverse reasons, usually anchored in Europe's embracing of capitalism and technological innovation. As we saw, the literature points to two such reasons: the emergence of good, stable institutions and the establishment of efficient markets. Even when those institutions are morally objectionable to modern sensibilities, they nonetheless were hospitable to growth and innovation. As David Landes put it:

> The economic expansion of medieval Europe was … promoted by a succession of organizational innovations and adaptations, most of them initiated from below and diffused by example. The rulers, even local seigneurs, scrambled to keep pace, to show themselves hospitable, to make labor available, to attract enterprise and the revenues it generated.[66]

Pogge's attempt to dismiss the massive evidence in favor of the full institutionalist thesis is, we think, unsuccessful.[67] Some of his more specific empirical claims are dubious as well. For example, Pogge cites the rich countries' protectionist agricultural policies as evidence that the global order (which allows these practices) causes poverty. While those unjust practices exacerbate the problem, for two reasons they are far from being the main cause of world poverty. First, the explanation understates the importance of domestic institutions.[68] It suggests that stagnation in the developing world derives mainly or only from what *others* do and thereby fails to confront local ruling elites' contribution to stagnation.[69] Second, whether the West's protectionist policies harm farmers of a given developing country depends on the size of the market for that country's exports. Argentina, for example, sells its beef and grain to

[65] Mathias Risse, "Do We Owe the Global Poor Assistance or Rectification?" *Ethics & International Affairs* 19 (2005), 9–10.

[66] Landes, *The Wealth and Poverty of Nations*, 44.

[67] Pogge is aware that his views are contradicted by mainstream economic research. This is why he dismisses economists *in totum*. He writes: "While economists like to present themselves as disinterested scientists, they function today more typically as ideologists for our political and economic 'elites' – much like most theologians did at an earlier age." Thomas Pogge, "Real World Justice," *Journal of Ethics* 9 (2005), 30.

[68] See Kym Anderson, "Agriculture, Trade Reform, and Poverty Reduction: Implications for Sub-Saharan Africa"; available at: http://www.unctad.org/en/docs/itcdtab24_en.pdf. The author shows that while trade liberalization in the agriculture sector can bring important gains, developing countries need to change their "anti-agriculture, anti-export and anti-poor bias of current policies." The complex empirical issues are set forth in M. Ataman Aksoy and John C. Beghin, eds., *Global Agricultural Trade and Developing Countries* (Washington, DC: World Bank, 2004).

[69] At several points Pogge suggests that this emphasis on domestic factors, which he calls "explanatory nationalism," may be self-serving. See *World Poverty*, 4, 6, 15.

Russia, China, India, and Egypt. Given that the rising demand for agricultural products (at the time of this writing) comes from these non-Western countries, farmers in developing countries might be in a particularly advantageous situation because they no longer depend on exporting their products to Western markets. They are certainly less likely to be harmed by the West's trade policies. This is an empirical issue and will vary for particular countries and products, but the truth is that protectionist policies harm first and foremost the country's *own* consumers. Of course, we join Pogge in calling for the dismantling of the West's protectionist policies. This is part of the general call to liberalize trade not only for efficiency reasons but also for *moral* reasons.[70] But saying that liberalizing agricultural trade will help is not the same as saying that the current protectionist policies of Western powers are the main *cause* of poverty.

A final major disagreement concerns what to do about poverty. Is the solution to liberalize markets further? Or is it to establish a global system of aid? Or a mix of both? What is the role of immigration barriers? Is national sovereignty the problem so that a world state or a loose world federation would score better on all these fronts? The standard approach to poverty alleviation has been monetary aid, but this method is under fierce attack from many quarters.[71] Proposals to liberalize markets all around as a way to fight poverty also have their critics, although the evidence in favor of their beneficial effects is stronger. And finally, as a corollary of the consensus about governance, many recommend institutional reforms in poor countries – whether or not combined with other remedies such as trade liberalization and aid.

What are we to make of the empirical question? This brief survey of the literature shows that *whatever else people in rich countries can or should do to alleviate poverty*, there are two goals that, if achieved, would reduce poverty. First, nations must practice good governance in the sense discussed earlier (securing political and economic freedoms). Second, the poor must enjoy access to markets. Justice requires opening national and international markets so that the poor can participate as consumers and producers. This includes dismantling burdensome domestic regulations and all trade barriers and liberalizing immigration. The importance of these factors is recognized as well by scholars who advance the "poverty trap" hypothesis. They just do not think that these conditions would be sufficient and urge that something more must be done (in their case, an intelligently targeted high amount of foreign aid that would allow those countries to break the poverty trap). Similarly, all countries will benefit from economic and political freedoms *regardless* of other factors that

---

[70] We expand on these concepts in Chapter 6.

[71] William Easterly, *The White Man's Burden: Why the West's Efforts Have Done so Much Ill and so Little Good* (Oxford University Press, 2007); Chris Coyne, *Doing Bad by Doing Good* (Redwood City, CA: Stanford University Press, 2013); and Paul Polak, *Out of Poverty: What Works when Traditional Approaches Fail* (San Francisco: Berret-Koheler Publishers, 2008). These authors argue that it is impossible to donate people out of poverty. They recommend, essentially, fostering imaginative local entrepreneurship.

arguably may help or hamper their development. Jared Diamond, for example, has argued that geographic factors play an important role in economic success, but even he recognizes that institutions provide at least 50 percent of the answer.[72]

What is the causal relationship between *political* freedom and prosperity? Some hold that political freedom leads to prosperity. Alas, this view is questionable. The experience in Latin America shows that political freedoms and relatively transparent democratic processes cannot alone lift countries from stagnation.[73] In particular, popular democratic processes work, at best, indifferently with regard to economically healthy institutions. As we saw, political freedom will likely *help* development by diffusing political power and reducing the chances for plundering – but only *if* accompanied by economic freedoms. Others believe that the reverse is true: economic freedom leads to political freedom. Those who oppose the U.S. embargo on Cuba and favor increasing trade and economic relations with China and other morally suspect regimes make this argument. The idea is that once people achieve a degree of material wealth, they will naturally want political freedom. The problem with this argument is that, even if true, it is open to serious moral reservations. It would allow, indeed mandate, cooperation with and support of tyranny on the hope that in the long run the country will be prosperous *and* free. One of the principles defended in this book is that (save for a few extreme hypotheses) liberal nations should not cooperate with tyranny, even for the sake of the future liberation of the country. For one thing, we should be reluctant to weigh equally present harms, which are certain, and future benefits, which are uncertain. But more important, people should not be required to suffer political oppression for the benefit of future generations. Perhaps justice requires *economic* sacrifices for the sake of greater prosperity for future generations, but in our view, current generations should not be required to endure tyranny as the putative price of reforms to come.

Devising principles for the alleviation of poverty is a central task of a theory of justice. In succeeding chapters we work to determine more precisely who owes what to whom and which policies are more likely to implement what justice requires. Certainly the fact that extreme poverty deserves the world's urgent attention does not mean that a theory of justice has nothing to say about moderate poverty, relative poverty, and global inequality. Another issue to be addressed is the status of nation-states in any theory about global equality.

---

[72] The two important books by Diamond are *Guns, Germs, and Steel: The Fates of Human Societies: The Fates of Human Societies* (New York: Norton, 2005), and *Collapse: How Societies Choose to Fail or Succeed* (New York: Penguin, 2011). See also his review of How Nations Fail in the New York Review of Books; available at: http://www.nybooks.com/articles/archives/2012/jun/07/what-makes-countries-rich-or-poor/, with a reply by Acemoglu and Robinson.

[73] On populism in Latin America, see Edwards, *Left Behind: Latin America and the False Promise of Populism*.

Must a theory of justice talk about rich and poor *nations* or about rich and poor *persons*? This will depend on the normative pull of methodologic individualism, on the one hand, and the moral status of nation-states, on the other.[74]

CONFLICT

It is a truism that war gravely undermines freedom and human welfare. One of the important achievements of international law since 1945 has been the prohibition of war. But the *jus ad bello*, the normative status of war, is more complex than this consensus about its evils suggests. Sometimes wars liberate; sometimes they stop evil aggressors, which is why pacifism is problematic. We want to say that most wars are morally prohibited but that defensive wars and liberating wars (humanitarian intervention) can sometimes be justified. These are exceptions to the rule, however.[75] Here we want only to provide a snapshot of recent conflicts. We assume that those conflicts harm persons and cause havoc and destruction in many important ways. At the theoretical level, a theory of justice must address the age-old problem of the control of violence. Immanuel Kant understood this well, and various modern scholars have attempted to tackle the problem. The central question is: which institutions can guarantee a just peace (as opposed to the peace "of the cemeteries")? Is the only solution world government, with its monopoly of violence, or can peace be attained by preserving separate nation-states? And assuming that, properly tailored, self-defense and humanitarian intervention are appropriate exceptions to the prohibition, which institutions are likely to keep aggressors and tyrants in check? We will address these and other questions in Chapter 8. Our aim here is purely descriptive: to take a snapshot of conflicts that afflict the world in the second decade of this century.

Enough has been said about the horrific wars of the twentieth century and other events during that period, such as the atrocities perpetrated by Hitler, Stalin, Mao, Pol Pot, and others. Here is a partial list of wars that have erupted in the twenty-first century:

1. *International wars:* Afghanistan war (2001–present), various Israel-Palestinian wars (2001–present), Iraq war (2003–2012?), Al-Qaeda war or "war on terror" (2001–present), Georgia-Russia war (2008), Eritrea-Ethiopia war (2000–2001)
2. *Civil wars:* Libya (2011), Syria-ISIS (2011–present), Chechnya (1999–present), Chad (2005–present), Sudan (2003–present), Ivory Coast (2002–present), Algeria (2000–2001)

We have listed only armed conflicts of magnitude. There are many additional conflict spots in the world where rebels attack sporadically or skirmishes occur

---

[74] We return to the empirical issue of poverty and wealth in Chapter 3.
[75] We discuss war fully in Chapter 8.

at the border. Some of these wars are acts of aggression. Others may be justified: perhaps they are legitimate defensive wars; perhaps they are wars to escape grievous injustice. Tackling the causes of conflict is an extremely difficult issue. As is well known, war theorists agree to condemn wars of aggression and accept genuinely defensive wars. But there the agreement ends. We analyze the phenomenon of war and the problem of justification in Chapter 8.

THE DEMOCRATIC PEACE

We close this chapter by examining a controversial hypothesis about the causes of war – or, more exactly, about the causes of peace: the theory of *democratic peace*. It holds that there is a robust causal link between *domestic liberal institutions* and international peace. It was advanced first by Kant and was revived after the cold war by Michael Doyle and others.[76] Kant's original idea was that democracies (*republics*, in Kant's parlance) are less inclined to war because in a democracy the people know they will bear its burdens. That is to say, citizens internalize the costs of war. In a dictatorship, the despot sends *others* to fight while his perks and riches remain largely intact.[77] He externalizes the costs of war. But history has shown that Kant's thesis is too strong because democracies frequently go to war. Accordingly, democratic-peace scholars have reformulated the Kantian thesis thus: democracies do not go to war *with each other*. However, they often go to war against *illiberal* states. And, of course, illiberal states fight one another frequently. This reformulation has been dubbed the *separate* liberal peace, and it better fits the empirical evidence.[78] Democratic-peace theory has provided support for the American (and perhaps European) policy of promoting liberal institutions overseas. The thesis has attracted vigorous criticism, but it is far from being refuted.[79]

---

[76] Kant's argument is set forth in Immanuel Kant, "To Perpetual Peace: A Philosophical Sketch," in Immanuel Kant, *Perpetual Peace and Other Essays*, trans. Ted Humphrey (Indianapolis, IN: Hackett Publishers, 1983). Leading modern proponents include Michael Doyle, "Kant, Liberal Legacies, and Foreign Affairs," Part 1, *Philosophy and Public Affairs* 12 (1983), 205–35; Part 2, *Philosophy and Public Affairs* 12 (1983), 323–53; John M. Owen, "How Liberalism Produces Democratic Peace," *International Security* 19 (1994), 87–125, and Bruce Russet, *Grasping the Democratic Peace: Principles for a Post-Cold War World*, (Princeton, NJ: Princeton University Press, 1993). For a rather optimistic endorsement of the theory, see Fernando R. Tesón, *A Philosophy of International Law* (Boulder, CO: Westview, 1998), chap. 1.

[77] Writes Kant: "Under a nonrepublican constitution, where subjects are not citizens, the easiest thing in the world to do is to declare war. Here the ruler is not a fellow citizen, but the nation's owner, and war does not affect his table, his hunt, his places of pleasure, his festivals, and so on." *Perpetual Peace*, 113.

[78] See Russet, *Grasping the Democratic Peace*, 30.

[79] Among the critics, see Christopher Layne, "Kant or Cant: The Myth of Democratic Peace," *International Security* 19 (1994), 5–49; David Spiro, "The Insignificance of the Liberal Peace," *International Security* 19 (1994), 50–86; and Sebastian Rosato, "The Flawed Logic of Democratic Peace Theory," *American Political Science Review* 97 (2003), 585–602.

There is little doubt that the empirical correlation holds; this is admitted even by the critics of the theory.[80] By far the largest challenge faced by the theory is to explain *why* democracies do not go to war with one another. What is the causal connection between free institutions[81] and peace? The theory has two main versions that are not mutually exclusive.

One claims that liberal peace is mainly caused by liberal *culture*. The idea is that liberals and their leaders believe in compromise and peaceful settlement of disputes and follow these norms in their external relations as well.[82] To these scholars, "democracy," for purposes of the theory, is a society that not only honors the panoply of liberal constitutional rights and procedures but also where the leaders, the public, and the opinion makers share a liberal worldview. Liberal practices and values make it virtually impossible for a liberal government to fight another liberal government.[83] Liberal *ideas* are thus crucial: the liberal public tends to believe that liberal governments generally pursue the welfare of their people, whereas despotic regimes are seen with distrust because they often have other aims, such as conquest and plundering. And, of course, public opinion in democratic nations, mistaken as it often is on a number of issues, tends to be largely sympathetic and tolerant of political processes that occur within other democratic nations.[84]

The second version of the theory regards the *institutional constraints* that operate in liberal democracies as the main cause of liberal peace.[85] This research, following Kant's suggestion, identifies the domestic *costs* that democratic leaders face: losing wars likely will cause their political demise. Also, the constraints of checks and balances, public debate, and division of powers will slow decisions to wage war. Because other democracies know these constraints, they will not fear a surprise attack.[86] Broader institutional features are also relevant. If a foreign

---

[80] See, e.g., Rosato, "Flawed Logic," 585.

[81] In the rest of the discussion, as elsewhere, we use the terms "democracy," "free institutions," and the like as necessarily consisting of *three* elements: protection of basic human rights, political competition and accountability, and a significant role for markets. In particular, "democracy" does not mean only majoritarian rule or elections.

[82] See Russet, *Grasping the Democratic Peace*, 34.

[83] In this sense, see Owen, "How Liberalism Produces Democratic Peace," 87, and Russett, *Grasping the Democratic Peace*, 30–8.

[84] See Owen's fuller statement of the idea in Owen in "How Liberalism Produces Democratic Peace," 102–4.

[85] In this sense, see Bruce Bueno de Mesquita and David Lalman, *War and Reason* (New Haven, CT: Yale University Press, 1992); Bruce Bueno de Mesquita, Christopher F. Gelpi, and Michael Griesdorf, "Winners or Losers? Democracies in International Crises, 1918–1994," *American Political Science Review* 95 (2001), 633–47.

[86] See Russett, *Grasping the Democratic Peace*, 40. However, perhaps democracies will garner resources *faster* than their rivals, and for this reason, they are unattractive targets. This explains why democracies win a disproportionate number of wars. For this and other advantages that democracies have, see Bruce Bueno de Mesquita, James D. Morrow, Randolph M. Siverson, and Alastair Smith, "An Institutional Explanation of the Democratic Peace," *American Political Science Review* 93 (1999), 791–807.

country is democratic, citizens can more comfortably trust that country's government because its intentions and actions are usually more transparent. If distrust breeds belligerence, then democracies are more peaceful. And a free press and a robust opposition often keep governmental abuse under check, at least in the nation's relations with other countries possessing similar institutions. The secretiveness of the Saddam Hussein regime was arguably a reason why the American public initially had less reason for opposing that war. It would have been unthinkable for any democratic government to err or deceive the public about dangers, real or imaginary, posed by a democratic nation. Some writers emphasize the fact that in a democracy the public controls governmental decisions to go to war. To them, if a country has domestic liberal institutions but the public lacks control over foreign policy decisions, then it will not be a "democracy" for this purpose. Thus, for example, Germany was quite liberal internally in 1914, but the executive's discretion over foreign policy decisions was unfettered. (It is unclear what one would say about a regime that is domestically oppressive but allows popular control over foreign policy. This is probably nonexistent.)

Illiberal states do not possess these peace-producing characteristics. Illiberal leaders use and expect violence from their adversaries as the natural way to resolve conflicts. As Michael Doyle has observed, "[b]ecause non-liberal governments are in a state of aggression with their own people, their foreign relations become for liberal government deeply suspect."[87] In addition, as Kant pointed out, undemocratic leaders are unconstrained in their decisions to go to war and are less likely to pay the price for their blunders because they rule by violence and terror. Importantly, these very features of illiberal states make them unattractive to the liberal public, which is why wars between liberal and illiberal states are more frequent. Liberals view illiberal states as unreasonable, unpredictable, and dangerous.[88]

The two versions of the theory converge. Liberal culture leads to liberal institutions, and (arguably) liberal institutions promote liberal ideals and values. But there are cases where liberal institutions alone will not cause people to behave in a liberal way – thus the need, for some, of spontaneous liberal social norms and values and not just coercive institutions. Good institutions need men and women to defend them. Good values, good institutions, and liberal dispositions are the three ingredients of a stable liberal polity, and perhaps it is the possession of the three that makes a society eligible for the democratic alliance that, according to the view we are discussing, will alone preserve peace.

The democratic-peace theory is controversial, however. It has been challenged from the Realist tradition, which emphasizes national interest and states' global competition for resources in the semianarchical international arena as the main causes of state behavior and of war in particular. Here we mention two criticisms.

---

[87] Michael Doyle, "Liberalism and World Politics," *American Political Science Review* 80 (1986), 1161.

[88] Owen, "How Liberalism Produces Democratic Peace," 96.

As we noted, few deny the empirical correlation; rather, critics question the causal story behind the correlation. Sebastian Rosato has argued that the causal logic offered by democratic-peace scholars is implausible and, in fact, refuted by history.[89] On his view, it is not true that democratic elites tend to treat other democracies with respect. Nor is it true that democratic institutions will curb the occasional war-prone leader: legislatures and others are often more bellicose than the executive they are supposed to contain. Henry Farber and Joanne Gowa, in an empirical study of wars since 1816, claim that the democratic-peace theory is robust only for the cold war years, which suggests that common interests, not common values, are the engine of the democratic peace.[90]

Another criticism challenges the view (held by many, including two recent American presidents) that spreading democracy will decrease conflict.[91] This optimistic belief, critics argue, has to be qualified. The probability of war increases among *mixed dyads*, that is, among any random pair of liberal-illiberal countries. This means that when more countries become democratic, at first the chances of war will *increase* because the number of mixed dyads will increase. This will occur until the democracies become a majority. Then chances of war will decrease as the number of mixed dyads decreases (because there will be more liberal-liberal dyads than before). This view confirms the democratic-peace thesis at the dyadic level but warns that there will be a period in the process of global liberalization during which the world will be particularly dangerous as illiberal regimes feel more isolated and cornered by the rise of democracy.

Democratic-peace scholars have replied forcefully to criticisms. In particular, a study by Gelpi and Grisedorf refutes some of the alternative explanations for the democratic peace. To test the robustness of the theory, these authors extend the democratic-peace theory to include a *new* dependent variable – international crises.[92] They tested the theory's core claim (that there is something special about democracies in international behavior) by investigating whether the common elements that democracies share make a difference in areas cognate to but *other* than war. Their survey of international crises shows that democratic strictures influence behavior in these crises by identifying which causes are worth fighting for. Essentially, the authors find that democratic states face substantial *domestic* costs in using force,

[89] Rosato, "Flawed Logic," 594–6.

[90] Henry S. Farber and Joanne Gowa, "Interests or Common Polities? Reinterpreting the Democratic Peace," *Journal of Politics* 59 (1997), 393.

[91] This criticism (or qualification) is leveled by Nils Gledistch and Havard Hegre, "Peace and Democracy: Three Levels of Analysis," *Journal of Conflict Resolution* 41 (1997), 283–310. See also, in support of this approach, Kelly M. Kadera, Mark J. C. Crescenzi, and Megan L. Shannon, "Democratic Survival, Peace, and War in the International System," *American Journal of Political Science* 47 (2003), 234.

[92] See Gelpi and Griesdorf, "Winners or Losers? Democracies in International Crises, 1918–1994," 633–47.

and as a result, those states tend to select conflicts in which they are likely to prevail. This research undermines the criticism that the democratic peace can be attributed to common *strategic* interests as well as the criticism that democracies seldom go to war because they are powerful states who wish to preserve the status quo. This latter view is undermined by the fact that the "perceived weakness of democracies leads states to challenge them despite their military power."[93] This finding seems supported by the challenges faced at present by the United States and Europe from their much-weaker adversaries. For these authors, then, the "audience costs," that is, the vulnerability that state leaders have vis-à-vis their own constituencies, is the major cause of the democratic peace.

What should we make of the democratic-peace theory? Despite the criticisms, the correlation between peace and liberal institutions is so robust that it calls for *some* explanation, even provisional. Skeptics cannot explain this correlation away: if they are not satisfied with the explanations given by the theory's supporters, they have to come up with an alternative hypothesis. Some have suggested, for example, that the real explanation is the greater military prowess of democratic states[94] and, more specifically, American preponderance after World War II[95] and not the democratic nature of the regimes. But this conjecture is even less sufficiently specified than the democratic-peace thesis and also fails to account for some facts, such as the lack of conflicts among democratic *developing* nations. Some of the factors proposed by defenders of the thesis seem to us plausible, and the critics, while successful in casting doubt on some of the causal mechanisms proposed, have not dispelled the strength of the correlation nor many of the claims suggested by it, even if those claims are conjectural. The counterexamples that critics advance tend to use an insufficiently robust notion of "democracy." For one thing, there are illiberal democracies. The units that count for the theory are only liberal democracies. In addition, as John Owen has argued, *perceptions* are important. Sometimes, as we saw, the liberal public wrongly *sees* an adversary as illiberal and supports action against it. This also may happen because of the adversary's political alliance with a powerful illiberal enemy. Rosato uses the example of Allende's Chile to refute the claim that liberal states behave in accordance with liberal norms toward other democracies.[96] At the time, though, there were persistent rumors that Chilean President Salvador Allende had secretly agreed to grant military bases to the Soviet Union. Whether these rumors were true is irrelevant. The American perception of the Chilean government's forging of a close alliance with the Soviet Union destroyed any element of pandemocratic solidarity that

[93] Ibid., 645.
[94] In this sense, David Lake, "Powerful Pacifists: Democratic States and War," *American Political Science Review* 86 (1992), 24.
[95] Thus Rosato, "Flawed Logic," 599–600.
[96] Ibid., 590–1.

might have existed between the two states. In such a situation, the democratic dyad is nullified, and the Realist logic takes over. And the same can be said of other alleged counterexamples.

The democratic-peace theory is relevant for the argument in this book. We will endorse a sort of modified version of the theory. We conjecture that *good states*, by which we mean states with good institutions in the sense described earlier (and further explained in Chapter 3), are less likely to go to war with each other than any dyad that contains a *bad state*. That is, we argue that the larger the sphere of freedom a society allows to its citizens, the lower are the chances of war against similarly free societies. The pursuit of personal projects through free, voluntary transactions is, we think, a salutary antidote to conflict. And we agree with Kant that economic freedoms facilitate peaceful relations among societies.[97] However, our conception of a good state does not exactly overlap with that of the democratic-peace theorists. Peace-leaning tendencies are not generated only by democratic institutions and respect for basic rights: as the classics clearly saw it, trade and prosperity incline peoples to peace, too.

CONCLUSION

As this brief survey has shown, the state of the world is far from satisfactory. Freedom is not prevalent in most of the world, and global poverty is a great scourge, made even more awful by the fact that we live in a time of great technological and scientific advancement. Political philosophy has something to say about this. But while these facts (widespread oppression and poverty) are objects of moral concern, the question of causation, human agency, and responsibility will become central to any answers and policy proposals. To what extent are we responsible for oppression and poverty in distant lands? What do rich people in the world owe the world's poor? How do we evaluate current global practices and institutions? What institutions can rescue persons threatened with genocide and war and secure individual freedom effectively? And what institutions provide better chances of preventing future conflict? These are some of the questions that this book will try to answer. But we can say this much: *domestic* political and economic liberal institutions are morally overdetermined. If the empirical findings in this chapter are right, then the argument for liberal institutions is unassailable. Liberal institutions are, first, preferred by political morality. They are, second, recommended by the full institutionalist thesis we have endorsed. And finally, they are indicated if our goal is to reduce international violence. In the next two chapters we substantiate this position, first, by exploring and rejecting the impersonal conception of value on which our alleged global redistributive duties rest and, second, by enlarging our discussion on the causes of and remedies for world poverty.

97 Kant, *Perpetual Peace*, 118.

2

What Do We Owe Distant Others?

Before sitting down to write this chapter, one of the authors fortified himself with a freshly brewed tall latte. The cost was a reasonable $3.75 plus tax – reasonable, that is, relative to prices on the American specialty coffee market. From other perspectives, however, the purchase is an extravagance. Over half the world's population subsists on a daily income of less than the cost of that one coffee.[1] That is not how much they spend on food and drink; it is the amount available to spend on *everything*. Those who have $3.75 per day are fortunate compared with the world's truly poor. The World Bank has established the global poverty line at the equivalent of $US1.25 per day.[2] The number who are accounted poor by this standard is not trivial; more than 1 billion people live at or under this level. It might be more accurate to say instead that they *die* under this level. All measures of mortality and morbidity are much worse for the global poor than they are for Western latte drinkers. Life expectancy at birth is dramatically lower. In large measure, this is so because the children of the poor die at distressing rates; almost 10 million children under the age of five perish each year. The vast majority of these deaths are unnecessary; the diseases that produce the carnage are almost entirely treatable in societies that possess modern health-care systems. Hunger, dispossession, infirmity, and death: this is the lot of the world's poor.

Only someone slow or callous could fail to reflect in the light of these data that it would be a wonderful boon to the global underclass if only some small fraction of the plenty enjoyed by the world's upper stratum could be used to relieve their misery. The simplest strategy that might seem to bring about this change is a direct *transfer* from the well-off to the poor. This could be done by governments taxing their citizens, the proceeds going abroad. Alternatively,

---

[1] See http://www.globalissues.org/article/26/poverty-facts-and-stats (accessed July 26, 2013).
[2] See http://data.worldbank.org/topic/poverty (accessed November 30, 2014).

generous individuals could of their own free will give to those in need. One way or the other, transfer might present itself as a moral imperative. How many cups of Starbucks' coffee is a young life worth? The question may seem to be obscene. No one would ask it about her own child or that of an acquaintance. Yet the opportunity cost of the cup that I drank is approximately three days of poverty-level income forgone. Of course, there is nothing special about coffee in these considerations.[3] There are any number of indulgences most of us routinely enjoy without giving them a second thought. The hundreds or thousands of dollars spent on these each year would be enough, if otherwise employed, to save the lives of at least one and probably several of the world's children. Is it not morally insupportable that we give preference to our trivial comforts over the lives and well-being of our billion worse-off global neighbors?

This is the position that has been advanced with commendable consistency for many years by Peter Singer. In a recent book, he formulates the argument this way:

First premise: Suffering and death from lack of food, shelter, and medical care are bad.

Second premise: If it is in your power to prevent something bad from happening, without sacrificing anything nearly as important, it is wrong not to do so.

Third premise: By donating to aid agencies, you can prevent suffering and death from lack of food, shelter, and medical care, without sacrificing anything nearly as important.

Conclusion: Therefore, if you do not donate to aid agencies, you are doing something wrong.[4]

Is Singer right? Unfortunately, an adequate answer to this question will require a response much less simple and straightforward than Singer's compact argument. This is so because the Singer premises conceal some vague and ambiguous notions that stand in need of clarification. In particular, the following questions need to be addressed:

1. Singer says that suffering and so on are bad. Does he mean that they are bad for the sufferer? This claim is uncontroversial. Does he also mean that suffering is bad for everyone, including those who do not themselves suffer but share a world with those who do? Or is the badness an impersonal badness, not bad for Bennet, not bad for Dashwood, not even bad for the sufferer in any distinctive way, but simply *bad in itself*? Is this a notion that even makes sense?

---

[3] Well, perhaps there is. Some readers may concur with the authors in taking coffee to be a *necessity* rather than a luxury. But even those of us who luxuriate in our caffeine dependence will admit that specialty coffee is not strictly necessary for living decently. Maxwell House also can supply a morning jolt.

[4] Peter Singer, *The Life You Can Save* (New York: Random House, 2009), 15–16. The argument is essentially identical to the one offered in his classic essay, "Famine, Affluence, and Morality," *Philosophy & Public Affairs* 1 (1972), 229–43.

2. You should prevent bad things from happening when you will not need thereby to sacrifice anything nearly as important. But again we ask, important for whom? Presumably, not to the one who will otherwise be the victim of the bad thing. However, it is not her latte that will be forgone. Important, then, from the perspective of the one who is bidden to sacrifice. Suppose, though, that Bennet *really wants* the latte. If that wanting is strongly maintained and occupies a central position in Bennet's conception of what adds delight to his life, does that count toward importance? This may sounds selfish, but perhaps it is just routinely self-interested. Bennet does not deny that it matters a great deal to the anonymous stranger that she get the medicine that would cure her dysentery, and he wishes her well. That, though, is properly her concern, not Bennet's. Or so he maintains. Singer may respond that this is to beg the question, that it is precisely Bennet's propensity to view choiceworthiness primarily from Bennet's own perspective that is being called into question. But where is the argument that Bennet (and everyone) should choose based on impersonal importance? Is there really any such thing as a perspective that is of no one in particular? And even if there is, why should it be of interest to beings all of whom are persons whose perspective is uniquely their own?

3. When Singer claims that it is wrong not to make the requisite sacrifice, how are we to cash out the word "wrong"? Does Singer mean that failing to make the sacrifice falls short of being the very best action open to Bennet to perform? If so, perhaps he is right. Many of us might think that someone such as a Mother Teresa who gives up all her worldly creature comforts to minister to the poor and dying[5] is closer to saintliness or moral heroism than is the contented latte sipper. However, to label as wrong any conduct that falls short of the very best is to invoke a high standard indeed. It bespeaks a kind of moral fanaticism. Conversely, Singer may hold that failing to sacrifice constitutes an act of *injustice* to the world's poor, that Bennet is thereby violating their rights. That this is so is far from obvious. The $3.75 is Bennet's; the choice of how to spend it is his to make. Even if we believe that he is acting shortsightedly or with less than laudable consideration, it does seem that he is nonetheless acting within his rights. We may wish that he were more altruistic, may wish indeed that he was another Mother Teresa, but wishes are not moral imperatives. It is not unfair to others not to be a saint.

There are further questions to be asked about what is indeed within our power to do by way of helping and what we ought to do via the political collectivity

[5] Admiration for Mother Teresa is considerable but not unanimous. See Christopher Hitchens, *The Missionary Position: Mother Teresa in Theory and Practice* (London: Verso, 1995), and Neera Badwhar, "International Aid: When Giving Becomes a Vice," *Social Philosophy & Policy* 23 (2006), 69–101.

of which we are part as opposed to what we do in our individual capacity. These will be taken up in subsequent chapters. Here, though, the aim is to make progress on getting clearer about good and bad, importance and triviality, right and wrong, justice and charity.

PERSONAL AND IMPERSONAL VALUE

We know people who call themselves *value nihilists*, who claim that the only properties in the universe are physical properties and that value is an illusion. We do not see how anyone who has ever had a severe toothache can hold to this position. It is patently evident that toothaches are *dreadful*. The world would be a far better place with the toothache gone. More precisely, the toothache is bad for the sufferer. She can have no doubt that something very bad is going on and that it is very bad for her. Conversely, the taste of an expertly brewed latte is good, not in some cosmic sense but in that drinking the coffee makes the drinker's life go better than it otherwise would.

Perhaps the so-called nihilist would acknowledge the reality of value in this sense. (She may herself have experienced toothache or coffee.) There is no doubt that people take various circumstances to be good and bad, but their thinking that it is does not make it so. On this version of nihilism, value exists subjectively, but there is no such thing as objective value.

This is a confusion. It is not believing that a severe toothache is bad that makes it bad (for oneself). Rather, the reason one takes a toothache to be bad is that it genuinely is bad for the one who experiences it. Indeed, there are circumstances that are objectively good or bad for agents about which they have neither awareness nor belief. If a small cancerous tumor is growing in Bennet's skull; that is very bad for Bennet. He may not know that the tumor is there and may never find out about it. (Perhaps he lapses into coma before being diagnosed.) Its presence, though, is an objective disvalue for Bennet. More controversially, a condition may be bad (or good) for the agent despite the fact that he believes the contrary. Woodhouse is a crystal meth aficionado and believes that getting high is good, the best thing in his life. Woodhouse, however, is mistaken. Despite his subjective preference for the drug, he has misestimated whether it is good for him. (It might be objected that if the high from crystal meth is glorious and sustained long enough, it may more than compensate Woodhouse for his blackened gums, inability to function effectively between hits, and his shortened expected lifespan. That, though, is to contend, against common conceptions, that the life of the drug addict is *really*, that is, objectively a good one.)

To say that φ is good for Bennet is not merely to indicate in some not very specific way the location of the good in Bennet's body or consciousness. Rather, it is to indicate that Bennet has a distinctive reason to bring about or preserve φ. If, for example, φ is the cessation of Bennet's toothache, then Bennet has reason to wish it gone and to act so as to produce that state of affairs. This is not to maintain that only Bennet has reason to bring about the cessation of Bennet's toothache. Dashwood, let's say, is a friend of Bennet or perhaps just an ordinarily sympathetic human being. In this case, there is reason for Dashwood to do something to ease Bennet's toothache. One should not, however, conclude that Dashwood's reason is identical to Bennet's. Rather, whatever reason Dashwood has is logically posterior to Bennet's. If Bennet is one of those rare individuals for whom toothache concentrates the mind so wonderfully that it generates a magnificent zest for living, then Bennet would no longer have good reason to wish the toothache gone. Therefore, neither would Dashwood. The reverse is not the case. If Dashwood believes that the toothache is divine recompense for the wickedness of Bennet's life, then Dashwood no longer has reason to act to relieve the ache. However, this in no way lessens Bennet's reason for wishing the toothache gone. There is, then, an asymmetry between the individual for whom φ is a primary (dis)value and others to whom that (dis)value is somehow transmitted.

Value that originates in the weal or woe, flourishing or failing of some particular individual, we call *personal value*. It is *primary* personal value for that individual in whom it originated. It is *secondary* personal value for those to whom it is transmitted. The test of whether it is primary or secondary is the counterfactual test: if φ somehow is no longer valuable for Bennet, does it follow as a consequence that φ is no longer valuable for Dashwood? Value for Dashwood that is parasitic on value for Bennet is secondary.[6]

Transmission of personal value often brings the aims of diverse individuals into harmony. It is also the case sometimes that what is personally valuable for one person thereby becomes disvaluable for another. Suppose, for example, that Bennet and Woodhouse are meeting tomorrow morning on the field of honor to duel with pistols at twenty paces. Bennet's hands are prone to nasty tremors. It is good for Bennet to secure a potion that relieves the tremors, but it is bad for Woodhouse that Bennet be able to do so. Some personal values are inherently competitive. This should not come as a surprise to anyone who has not spent her whole life living in a Disney theme park. It was not a surprise for Hobbes, who in *Leviathan* sketches out a picture of the natural human condition ("state of nature") in which one person's gains come at the expense of all others. This is a dark conception, but sometimes darkness does indeed prevail.

Some may suppose that personal value is not real value; that it is not up there with Plato's Form of the Good or the other resplendent values that moralists invoke. We hold, to the contrary, that personal value is the most basic and epistemically well-certified value there is. Much more dubious is whether, in addition, there exists *impersonal value*. By "impersonal value" is meant something

---

[6] This will not quite do as stated. φ may remain valuable for Dashwood because Bennet, as it were, hands over the value to Woodhouse, and Dashwood stands in the same sort of relationship to Woodhouse as she had to Bennet. In nearly all well-specified cases, it will be easy to determine whether personal value is primary or secondary.

that is good or bad in itself irrespective of being good or bad for any particular individual. If there are impersonal values, all agents stand to them in the same way and same degree, having reason to advance or retard them as the case may be in proportion to their magnitude.[7] Philosopher Eric Mack has argued strongly against the existence of impersonal value.[8] Even if Mack is mistaken, impersonal value plays no role in individuals' decisions concerning how to act in the world until those values are cognized and internalized. Thus a morality that aims to be practical, bringing value considerations to bear on choice, has to orient itself to reasons that attach to the persons who are to act on them.[9]

We have maintained that what is of personal value to Bennet need not be so as a function of any choice or commitment Bennet has made: toothache is a useful example. Sometimes, however, commitment makes all the difference. Friendship is a paradigmatic instance. There are no doubt billions of people in the world in whom it would be appropriate to take some sort of modest interest. (If they step out in front of your truck, you would do better to drive around them than over them.) However, for the small number of these people who are your friends, vastly greater consideration is indicated.[10] Aristotle seemed to have held a kind of impersonal value conception of friendship. The basis for befriending someone is the person's elevated virtue, at least for those who are themselves virtuous. This is not one of Aristotle's happier ideas. Whatever may have been the case in the ancient world, modern friendship is not a virtue contest in which the one who scores highest becomes your friend. Rather, the indicated attitude is *appreciation*, not judging. Your friend is the one to whom, for whatever reason, you have become committed. She is loved not because she is impersonally best; rather, because you love her, she is best for you.

Commitments are extended not only to particular others but also to religious and political creeds, crafts and professions, nations and ethnicities, vocations and avocations, causes hard won and lost, social classes, aesthetic ideals, and much else. These vary sharply from person to person and form in large measure the contours of an individual life. The commitments that are fundamental determine in large measure what will be a candidate to enter into the active life of an individual and what will leave her unmoved. We call these fundamental

---

[7] An "all else equal" clause is needed because individuals will have greater or lesser causal capability with regard to realizing various goods.

[8] See "Against Agent-Neutral Value," *Reason Papers* 14 (Spring 1989), 76–85; "Moral Individualism, Agent-Relativity and Deontic Restraints," *Social Philosophy & Policy* 7 (1989), 81–111.

[9] In the contemporary philosophy lexicon, the terms "agent-relative value" and "agent-neutral value" have largely supplanted "personal/impersonal value." Because this terminology is likely to court confusion with the ethical theory *moral relativism*, we prefer the latter usage.

[10] In a Facebook world, the concept of a *friend* has been devalued, perhaps to the edge of extinction. Speaking of extinction, though, now that communism has died, perhaps the term "comrade" can be recycled to substitute for what "friend" used to do.

commitments *projects* because (warning: verb coming) they *project* through the episodes of a person's life.[11] The projects that inform a life determine more than anything else what counts as practical reason for that individual.

If something is a distinctive end for Bennet, then Bennet has a stake in that end not shared by Dashwood, Woodhouse, or anonymous others. Its importance is not vested simply in the nonrelational properties of that end but that it is cherished specifically by Bennet. It may be something profound and elevated such as writing the great American novel or something as humble as staying in good shape. Regardless, the reasons generated by the project are personal reasons, reason for Bennet but not necessarily transmissible to others. Dashwood may be entirely unmoved by Bennet's commitments. A more sympathetic Dashwood will be modestly moved by Bennet's desires, wish Bennet well, but assign considerably higher value to the success of her own projects than to those of Bennet. This does not represent some failure of moral identification. Rather, it is embedded in the logic of individuated practical reason. To be committed to a project is to stand toward its being carried out with a degree of engagement radically greater than that of unconcerned others. What would be distinctly odd is if this were not so, if Bennet had no more reason to work on behalf of Bennet's own ends than those of some random person. Valuation and reason are inherently perspectival. This is not because people tend to be more selfish than they ought to be but because, as a matter of logic, to stand toward an end as primary personal valuer is to have a unique stake in its pursuit.

Attention to the salience of personal value indicates why Singer's argument is defective. Recall the second premise: "If it is in your power to prevent something bad from happening, without sacrificing anything nearly as important, it is wrong not to do so." This premise begs the questions *bad for whom?* and *important for whom?* Consider two individuals, Sufferer and Benefactor. Some circumstance constitutes personal disvalue to Sufferer. It may, like a toothache, be disvaluable for reasons quite apart from any specific commitments. Alternatively, the badness may be a function of those particular projects to which Sufferer is wedded. Suppose, for example, that Sufferer deeply desires to make the Hajj pilgrimage to Mecca, that doing so constitutes a fundamental building block of his religious identity. Being precluded from doing so by the bankruptcy of the travel operator constitutes for Sufferer a disaster, one for which he would willingly trade a severe toothache provided only that it occur in Mecca. It will cost Sufferer $100 either to have his tooth filled by a competent dentist or to reserve a spot on the next passage to Mecca. Unfortunately, Sufferer has no money beyond that required to procure his next meal. Benefactor is a middle-class American of ample but not overwhelming means, perhaps a professor of philosophy. She has been told of Sufferer's situation and

---

[11] The nature and importance of projects are investigated at some length in Loren Lomasky, *Persons, Rights, and the Moral Community* (New York: Oxford University Press, 1987).

could wire him $100. That, though, is the money she was planning to spend on the rent-a-clown for her daughter's sixth birthday party. What should she do?

Take the question to be a straightforward moral inquiry. Some theorists, Singer among them, take morality to be reasoning that is conducted from a scrupulously impartial perspective. What makes choice moral is its lending equal weight to the interests of all affected parties and then adhering to the vector of concerns thereby generated. If Benefactor is not merely a dedicated pursuer of her own ends but is instead morally motivated, then she will impartially weigh the importance of spending the $100 on what appeals to her[12] versus that which matters to Sufferer.

This, we maintain, is incoherent. If staging the perfect birthday party is a significant component of her child-raising project, then to leave out of consideration the fact that this is not just someone's much-loved daughter but *her daughter* is to misunderstand in a fundamental way what it is to be an engaged parent. Santa Claus or a professional utilitarian may be neutral among all the children in the world, but this is not an attitude that ordinary mothers and fathers are obliged to take up. Quite the reverse: they have reason firmly to reject it. That reason is inescapably personal, based on their own affective situatedness in a world of circumstances they will appraise differently than anyone else not in their situation. "This is *my* daughter!" constitutes for Benefactor a compelling reason. If on certain conceptions it is not sufficiently detached to count as a moral reason, then so much the worse for those conceptions of morality. Or to put it another way, some people may commit themselves to the project of viewing the world's weal and woe impersonally and then, to the best of their ability, acting accordingly. This is not in itself an unreasonable thing to do, any more than is tending to the upbringing of a six-year-old. However, if generalized as an imperative binding on all agents, a preference allegedly necessary to being a morally good human being, then it bespeaks fanaticism or invalid reasoning or both.

Back to Benefactor: what should she do? Our answer, unsurprisingly, is this: it depends on her personal valuations. This does not mean that the only feasible choice is to rent the clown. Benefactor may value her daughter's happiness more than that of any other person in the world, more even than her own, but she realizes that there are indeed other people in the world, and she wants to live well among them. She also wants her daughter to grow up learning to live well among them. So maybe this year, unlike the preceding five, she will forgo the clown and wire the money to Sufferer. The lesson actually may be to the daughter's ultimate good, but even if not, it probably is not to her ultimate

---

[12] It is important in this context to observe that Benefactor's own concern does not mean her own *selfish* or even *self-interested* concern. Rather, the concern here has the daughter's happiness as its object. If you believe that this must then redound to Benefactor's own benefit – to someone who has been nagged by a disappointed six-year-old, this supposition will come easily – then you are free to modify the example as seems fitting.

harm. At any rate, the decision should not be oversimplified to one between the daughter's happiness and Sufferer's happiness but rather in the full context of all the things that Benefactor cares about (including what she would like her daughter to grow up to care about). It is, as the economists say, a determination made *at the margin*, meaning that it takes as given all those other episodes of acting on her personal values that have constituted her life up to now. Perhaps in the fullness of consideration, Benefactor is most true to her conception of how best to live by spending the money on the clown – or perhaps by wiring it to Sufferer. That Sufferer strongly prefers the latter is some reason for Benefactor, but it is not sufficient reason. Nor is there an algorithm for making choices like this.[13] People take responsibility for their own moral lives by the tradeoffs they accept and those they reject. Others may protest that the agent has decided wrongly, and the agent herself may later come to believe that the choice she made was an error. But even then, that judgment will be issued from her own personal value perspective.

Suppose that Benefactor decides to send the money. (This is why we named her.) Would it be unreasonable of her to purchase dental care for Sufferer rather than the ticket to Mecca, even though Sufferer intensely prefers the latter? Not at all. This is so because in providing the benefaction, she is operating in accord with *her own* standard of what is valuable, not Sufferer's. A decent person will no doubt pay heed to the expressed preferences of those with whom she deals, but those preferences are not determinative. Benefactor is an agent, not the instrument, of the wishes of another person – not those of Sufferer, not even those of her six-year-old daughter. She may for her own respectable reasons assign high value to a world free of dental distress and be willing to take some small part in advancing that ideal. However, and equally respectably, she may assign little or no value to the world being such that millions of people complete the Hajj. This can be the case in a couple of different ways. First, Benefactor may believe that those who go to great trouble to get themselves to Mecca are making a mistake concerning what is truly in their own interest. You may be like that with regard to panhandling winos for whom you offer to buy a cup of coffee and scrambled eggs but not to contribute to their next bottle of Thunderbird. This is a kind of paternalism. More interestingly, Benefactor may believe that Sufferer has excellent reason from his own point of view to finance the trip, even at the price of toothache, but she has her own reasons not to be a partner in this kind of tradeoff. This is not paternalism. Rather, it is acknowledgment of the fact that over a wide range of determinations, independent moral agents are entitled to give effect to their own conceptions of what is better and what is worse.[14]

---

[13] The most distinctive and enduring feature of the utilitarian tradition from which Singer emerges is its insistence on reducing moral choice to an algorithmic procedure.

[14] A classic discussion is Tim Scanlon, "Preference and Urgency," *Journal of Philosophy* 72 (1975), 655–69.

This is not to maintain that individuals' preferences concerning how to live are beyond rational criticism.[15] Those preferences can be deformed by ignorance, unreason, or vice. To profess neutrality between the projects of Albert Schweitzer and Julius Streicher would be absurd, evil. This is so because they are other-regarding in diametrically opposed ways. We discuss later the constraints to project pursuit set by the rights of others. However, self-regarding modes of life are not immune from negative assessment. The individual possessed of a modest trust-fund income who devotes his days to sitting on the couch watching soap operas (or, if you prefer, *Fox News*), drinking beer, eating ice cream, and scratching himself can be judged to be a lamentable failure. If you were the parent, sibling, or childhood friend of this person, you would not be neutral concerning whether this is a life well-lived. It does not, of course, follow that you possess standing to stage an intervention, let alone forcibly to set the person's life on a different trajectory. This is so because the entitlement to live one's life pretty much as one sees fit is, in large measure, an entitlement to make a botch of living that life.

Personal value does not afford unlimited hegemony to subjectivism. Even if one succeeded in becoming "nonjudgmental" concerning the life choices of others (but why?), this is not a stance one can reasonably take toward oneself. In asking the question, "How ought I to live?" the answer is not sought by paying close attention to one's actual current preferences. Rather, it is an inquiry into what I *ought to prefer*, which commitments are *best* for me to undertake. This involves assessment of the good-for-me. It is barely possible that someone may hold that this is entirely a matter of one's own free creation, that whatever you can bring yourself to prefer is as good-for-you as any other set of preferences you might come to obtain. This is one way in which the ideal of *autonomy* can be expressed. We are skeptical of autonomy so understood – and, indeed, the apotheosis of autonomy that characterizes so much of contemporary moral philosophy. That, however, is a battle for another occasion. Here it is enough to observe that for the vast majority of individuals, their lives are enhanced by objects of regard that never presented themselves as items they are at liberty either to accept or reject. No one chooses her patrimony or country of origin. Some children are adopted, but others just come into one's life and thereby profoundly transform it. In advanced secular societies of the twenty-first century, religion is more and more a matter deliberately to take on or lay off like a suit of clothes, but over much of the world's history and geography, this sort of stance was inconceivable. Similarly for other objects of affection. To personalize the contrast, one of the authors of this book was born to the attractions of English prose;

---

[15] This surely is the case for criticism understood as forming in one's mind the judgment that the person has erred. One learns, however, that the overt criticism of one's friends' choice of romantic partners is almost never a good idea until after the divorce papers have been filed – and even then may backfire.

the other later in life chose to immerse himself. Neither stance is inherently superior to the other.

VALUE AND RIGHTS

Singer's great utilitarian predecessor, John Stuart Mill, argued:

> No reason can be given why the general happiness is desirable, except that each person, so long as he believe it to be obtainable, desires his own happiness. This, however, being a fact, we have not only all the proof that the case admits of, but all which it is possible to require, that happiness is a good: that each person's happiness is a good to that person, and the general happiness a good to the aggregate of all persons.[16]

This is one of the most commonly scorned arguments in the history of philosophy. It is often presented as a simple logical howler, of the same form as inferring from the fact that each person has a mother that therefore there is some mother of all people.[17] If read in context, however, Mill's object appears laudable even if this manner of approaching it is suspect. Mill is quite aware that in pursuing their own personal happiness individuals can come into violent conflict with one another. The result then will be that they achieve much less than they might have done. There is an antidote to this poison of social dissonance: the aggregate of all persons recognizing the general happiness as their highest object of concern. Presumably Mill means for it to supplant in each moral agent the primacy of his own personal happiness when the general and particular conflict, although that would seem to cut the ground out from under the premise on which the argument rests. In principle, though, the standard of greatest overall utility offers a centralized, monolithic, universal decision procedure for resolving competition among right-minded persons.

An alternative strategy for addressing conflict radically decentralizes questions of value. Because persons differ in their projects, they will quite reasonably differ in their valuations. There is no such thing as a common measure of value to which they can all subscribe. It is not a question of being morally motivated; it is that they are individuated. Therefore, they will have different and potentially opposed ideas concerning what is to be done.

---

[16] John Stuart Mill, "Of What Sort of Proof the Principle of Utility Is Susceptible," chap. 4 in *Utilitarianism*, Oskar Piest, ed. (New York: Library of Liberal Arts, 1957), 44–5.

[17] The fact that this is preceded by a passage in which Mill takes "desirable" as of the same semantical form as "visible" (= what people actually see) and "audible" (= what people actually here) rather than meaning what *ought to be desired* makes Mill's apparent transgression against basic logic all the more obvious. Among the critics, Mill's younger contemporary, F. H. Bradley, is second-to-none in his derisory commentary. See F. H. Bradley, *Ethical Studies* (Oxford University Press, 1988), especially essay 3, "Pleasure for Pleasure's Sake." More recently, philosophers have proffered vindications in whole or in part of Mill's "proof." See Geoffrey Sayre-McCord, "Mill's 'Proof' of the Principle of Utility: A More than Half-Hearted Defense," *Social Philosophy & Policy* 18 (2001), 330–60.

Bennet quite properly takes Bennet's projects to define the center of the valuational universe – for Bennet. But, unless Bennet is literally insane, he will not suppose that all other project pursuers acquiesce to Bennet's perspective. Rather, Bennet will readily agree that Dashwood has reason to act in accord with Dashwood's own lights, Woodhouse with Woodhouse's, and so on. The parties also understand that in the complete absence of some constraint on their behavior, they will bump into each other far too often and far too hard. They will, therefore, have reason to accept a system of constraints – or, to put it from the reverse angle, a system of prerogatives – that is binding on each. It is important to observe that they do so not because this best serves the general happiness – they may well believe that there is no such thing – but because each is thereby well served in terms of her own favored mode of life. They rationally maintain

1. Each agent has reason to act with partiality on behalf of the ends that deeply matter to her; and
2. Each agent realizes that all other agents also have reason to act with partiality on behalf of the ends that matter to them; and therefore
3. All agents have reason to adhere to rules that impartially constrain themselves and others from disrupting agents' efforts to show partiality on behalf of what matters to them.

This is a rough sketch of an argument that needs to say quite a lot more about how all interacting parties are vulnerable to hostile moves by others, that all or nearly all parties find themselves better off from their own perspectives if they forgo intruding on others provided that they themselves are thereby rendered immune from intrusion, and that an order of constrained project pursuit can under favorable conditions prove to be stable. We have previously thought about these issues and will refrain from repeating ourselves at length.[18] Forgoing all opportunities to build suspense, we announce that the indicated solution to the problem of interpersonally agreeable constraints in a world of divergent personal valuations is an order of *rights*. More specifically, these constraints are *liberal rights*, for which life, liberty, and property/pursuit of happiness are the usual triumvirate. The controlling idea is that I refrain from interfering with your enjoyment of the triumvirate and you with mine. The result is a substantial improvement on what is traditionally referred to as the "state of nature": a condition in which interference is rife and life thereby endemically hazardous.

This is only a shell of a theory. It cannot be made operational until content is given to *interference*, but to understand what constitutes interference with some individual, it first has to be determined to which actions or items the individual has a right. (When you decline to hand over all the cash in your pocket to a mugger, you are not thereby interfering in the relevant sense with his

---

[18] A fuller discussion is provided in Lomasky, *Persons, Rights, and the Moral Community*.

pursuit of a livelihood.) This is a pretty narrow circle. The first attempt within the liberal tradition to square this circle was to find bases grounded in nature concerning what the purview of each person is. The outer perimeter of human bodies is a good starting point, but after that, demarcations become murkier. John Locke, one of the patron saints of the movement, claimed that to mix one's labor with things out in the world made it one's own property, on which others for that reason are no longer at liberty to encroach.[19] Others argue that it is the chancing on a previously unclaimed thing that makes it one's own irrespective of whether labor has been invested in it or not. Again, we take the high road and demur from advocating any particular theory of rights. Perhaps basic rights are "natural" in the traditional sense, or perhaps they are conventional, or perhaps they are some combination of nature and convention. For the purposes of this discussion, it is less important to track the source of rights down to their foundations and then up again than it is to observe that liberal rights understood as predominantly claims against interference are the indicated solution to the problem of multiplicity of personal valuations. Readers who (correctly) find the sketch of an argument provided here less than compelling are invited to see whether the fuller versions provided in our other works satisfy better. *Justice at a Distance* does not aim to demonstrate the truth of classical liberalism/libertarianism but rather to spell out its implications for important questions of global justice. We hope that even readers ideologically opposed to our foundational theory will find its implications for these matters of some use. Indeed, the extent that the account of global justice worked out in these chapters seems reasonable may influence individuals' assessments of the libertarianism from which it springs.

Although there are numerous theories of how rights are, in the first instance, to be understood, the relation that undergirds all these variations is *reciprocity*. What each party concedes to all others is noninterference, and what each receives in exchange is noninterference. This is the indicated solution to the problem of cooperation among parties who differ along almost every evaluative dimension.[20] Bennet may have every sympathy with Woodhouse's projects, may willingly enroll himself on behalf of Woodhouse's ventures. In this case, Bennet's moral relationship to Woodhouse will extend far beyond noninterference. However, not all meetings are meetings of minds. Bennet may find Dashwood's pursuits antithetical to how he believes life to be well lived. Much less is being demanded of Bennet if only forbearance toward Dashwood is required then if, in addition, positive assistance must be tendered. Even if Bennet regrets the fact that he is not at liberty to quash Dashwood's ventures, it is of no little consolation to reflect that Dashwood is barred from interposing

---

[19] John Locke, "Of Property," § 27, chap. 5, in *Second Treatise of Government*, in *Locke: Two Treatises of Government*, Peter Laslett, ed. (Cambridge University Press, 1988), 287–8.

[20] If, however, they differ concerning whether peaceful coexistence is preferable to war, then it is war they shall have.

her benighted views on him. This is live and let live, almost literally. (It is also "liberty and let liberty," but that is ungrammatical.) In a world in which no consonance of value can be presumed but rather diversity of ends predominates, this is far from an unsatisfactory conclusion. No one is obligated actively to assist distasteful projects of distasteful others, but each must minimally forbear. In this way, people are enabled to pursue their idiosyncratic ends without having to subscribe to and serve some one sovereign conception of a general good.

Liberty understood as noninterference is a distinctive good. Although the immediately preceding discussion has emphasized the heterogeneity of personal value, liberty seems to be an exception to that rule. Critics will charge that this is special pleading. Why should only liberty be allowed the status of a universal value as opposed to, say, toothache prevention? If everyone is supposed to prize noninterference, is it no less the case that everyone prefers to be free of toothache? Why should one of these universal goods be taken as a foundation for civil society and not the other? This special pleading gives the appearance of a libertarian coup d'etat, a rather clumsy one at that.

The criticism incorporates a confusion. The claim is not that liberty as such is universally valued. Rather, it is that Bennet has reason to value *Bennet's liberty*, Dashwood to value *Dashwood's liberty*, Woodhouse to value *Woodhouse's liberty*, and so on. And, of course, the projects for which they desire the corresponding liberty may be entirely diverse: Bennet a liberty to prove theorems, Dashwood a liberty to pray to her God, Woodhouse a liberty to construct an industrial behemoth. No one of them need prize universal liberty as such. Indeed, each might be happier if he or she were free of interference from others but entitled forcefully to intrude his or her nose into their business. This, though, is an unlikely equilibrium. It could not be attained through uncoerced acquiescence. Stalin enjoyed a position something on this order, but he had his guns and gulags to enforce that status. If mutual acceptability is required, then this kind of asymmetry is ruled out. Bennet gets noninterference from Dashwood and Woodhouse if and only if like is returned for like.

Whatever one's projects are, one needs noninterference to pursue them successfully. Even, in the limiting case, if someone merely wants above all to sit in his easy chair until he perishes from starvation, he needs that his door not be broken down and that he *not* be hauled away to hospital for undesired resuscitation. The undertakings of most individuals are more active than allowing nature to take its course, and for these there are numerous nodes at which unwanted intrusion can prove destructive. To follow John Rawls's usage, liberty is a *primary good* – instrumental in one's pursuits – regardless of the particular nature of one's conception of the good.[21] Moreover, the requisite noninterference is to be supplied by everyone. It is not good enough if 99 percent of the people around you refrain from imprisoning you or shooting bullets into you. Of course, there are many people with regard to whom interference

[21] *A Theory of Justice* (Cambridge, MA: Harvard University Press, 1971), 62.

never becomes a significant question: for example, those on the other side of the globe who plan to remain there. In such a case, the question of whether they will intervene in your life's affairs becomes moot. Nonetheless, in principle, the noninterference requirement extends to everyone and is reciprocated by everyone.

It is important to understand that the emphasis on liberty as the basic right does not *depend* on an assertion that somehow liberty is transcendentally finer than other goods people may want. "Give me liberty or give me death!" satisfies rhetorically in a way that "Give me dental treatment or give me death!" does not, but we do not deny that it might be entirely reasonable for people to be willing to give up a bit of their liberties for a bit of pain relief. Imposed servitude is awful, but so too is an excruciating toothache. Liberty's special significance is more formal than substantive. First, the demand is ubiquitous. The authors happily announce that as we write this, we stand in need of no toothache relief. (This has not, alas, always been the case.) We do, however, require noninterference with our typing just as you, the reader, need people not to pull these pages out of your grasp if you are to be able to see what is on them. Freedom permeates everything.

Second, for virtually every other invaluable good, provision is sufficiently attended to by a small number of people. The person with the toothache does not need the commiserations of everyone; he needs a dentist. And what if he lacks the means to pay for dental services? Then he needs a benefactor. By saying that the numbers required to address this particular need are small, we do not mean to impugn its urgency. Rather, it is to distinguish between those ends that require something close to universal subscription if they are to be feasible and those that depend on cooperation with a few willing others. Viewed from another perspective, though, even treatment of an abscessed tooth depends on wide cooperation. It is cooperation via noninterference with the relationship between patient and dentist. This species of cooperation is a refraining rather than a doing. It is what renders liberty unique among the Rawlsian primary goods. Over an extremely wide range of conceptions of the good, one needs income and wealth to serve them. However, one regular paycheck from one employer can meet this nicely. Those who are called on not to pilfer it are everyone.

Third, noninterference is a uniquely other-directed good. Many of the things we need to make our lives go tolerably well are things we can provide for ourselves. Instead of heading out to a restaurant for dinner, you can cook the meal for yourself. The ingredients you toss into the pot were probably provided by diverse other parties, but your possession of means of exchange allows you actively to procure them as you see fit. This is not a hermit's autarky, but it is possession of a capacity through one's own goal-directed choices to get what one needs. The exception, again, is liberty. It is a logical truth that only others can tender noninterference with you. This is not to say that persons are altogether passive with regard to whether that noninterference is forthcoming.

Locking one's doors when one goes out raises the likelihood that one's property will not be snatched; avoiding leisurely strolls at midnight through Central Park conduces to one's person being unmolested. Liberty is not the only other-directed central good. People need friends to live a decent human life, probably a job, and yes, a dentist. But only the claim to noninterference always looks outward and over an arc of 360 degrees.

This explains why the innovators of early modern political philosophy introduce the concept of *human rights*. These are, in a nutshell, what is needed by all from all. John Locke summarizes the content of these rights as *life, liberty, and property*. The triad is rhetorically effective but generates a fount of subsequent misunderstandings. By "property," Locke does not mean only things external to the self such as chattel or land but that over which one enjoys a legitimate proprietorship. He explicitly states that this proprietorship includes one's own life and liberty. Therefore, the triad is better expressed as *life, liberty, and estate*, the three of them taken together constituting one's property.[22] Locke's claim that the founding purpose of civil society is protection of individuals' property should not be construed then as a naked materialism in which "stuff" counts for more than people do.[23] A second respect in which the formulation misleads is in the impression that liberty is one right (or family of rights) juxtaposed with a right to life and property rights. It is clear, though, that all three are rights primarily to noninterference. A right to life is not, for example, a right to be given whatever might be sufficient to sustain a person's existence but rather is a right not to be (unjustly) killed. A right to property is not a claim to be given goods in a certain amount but rather is a protection against trespass on whatever property one may have (rightfully) come to acquire. Just as the triad can be summarized as the right to property, so can it be expressed as the right to liberty (as noninterference).[24]

It would be unduly distracting in a work mostly directed at other targets to go into much greater detail concerning the contours of the basic right to noninterference. We freely acknowledge that questions both of interpretation and justification are numerous and deeply controverted. We have taken positions on these elsewhere and offer in this book a sprinkling of references to our prior

---

[22] See Locke, *Second Treatise*, § 87.

[23] The favored term for this mischaracterized position comes from the title of C. B. Macpherson, *Political Theory of Possessive Individualism: Hobbes to Locke* (Oxford University Press, 1962).

[24] This is its primary signification. A more complete exposition of Locke's account will bring in that Locke recognizes entitlements in extremis to charitable provision from the surplus of others. The key text is *First Treatise of Government* § 42: "We know God hath not left one Man so to the Mercy of another that he may starve him if he please.... As Justice gives every Man a Title to the product of his honest Industry, and the fair Acquisitions of his Ancestors descended to him; so Charity gives every man a title to so much of another's Plenty, as will keep him from extream [*sic*] want, where he has no means to subsist otherwise." The most important feature of this declaration is not that it recognizes some title to positive provision but how hedged that recognition is with qualifications and contingencies.

writings sufficient to assist those who are interested without unduly detaining those who wish to move straightaway into global policy issues. This brief review has been by way of identifying a theoretical position that will undergird the various arguments that follow. We would be pleased if we could simply provide for it the rubric *liberal rights theory* and move on. Unfortunately, here, too, confusions abide. Over the century between the careers of J. S. Mill (1806–73) and (John Rawls 1921–2002), the term "liberal" underwent a sea change, especially in the United States. From a theory that emphasized the primacy of liberty, the protection of which is the primary function of the political order, it transmuted into a call for positive provision of an extensive range of welfare goods, more often than not at the cost of some significant limitation on the liberty of those who are called on to provide them. (The term "liberty" also has bred extensions and transmutations such as a cloudy distinction between *negative liberty* and *positive liberty*.) We therefore alert readers that when we speak without qualification of *liberalism*, we mean the range of theoretical stances explored and developed with extraordinary philosophical acumen in the period from the closing years of the seventeenth century into the second half of the nineteenth century, when they are largely overtaken by a "new liberalism." In part, we do so because no neologisms are adequate in replacement. "Libertarianism" is the name of a twentieth-century ideology into which, among others, neither Locke, Kant, nor Adam Smith fits. "Classical liberalism" suggests something antiquated, not a view fit for robust contemporary deployment. So "liberal" it will have to be.[25]

JUSTICE AND OTHER VIRTUES

Critics will contend that it is a harsh and constricted picture of human moral dealings that confines them to reciprocated demands to be left alone. The critics will be right. If the extent of Bennet's concern for those around him is to observe their rights, then Bennet is not an admirable person. He is, though, minimally tolerable. This is so because Bennet thereby shows himself to possess the virtue of *justice*. The defining character of justice is that it is a settled disposition to give each her due, period. On the one hand, this is not to give a lot. On the other hand, it is to give to many. These balance out. Rights proclaim demands that are universal, incumbent on all who interact with the rights holder. They establish a minimum that is due to all individuals, including those whose projects and person one finds distasteful. Not only misanthropes will find that this class includes a substantial number of one's

[25] The preference is not entirely or even for the most part semantic. Rather, it is our view that recognition of the primacy of noninterference is key to addressing satisfactorily the problems we take up in these chapters concerning ramifications of justice at a distance. Those theorists who have accepted a more expansive understanding of the range of claims individuals have on distant others thereby commit themselves to conclusions neither plausible nor practical.

neighbors and countrymen. People who have well-defined conceptions of the good will thereby also have pronounced views concerning what lacks goodness. There may be an awful lot of the latter going around.

Simple forbearance with regard to designs found unattractive and idiotic is already no small thing to ask of an agent. ("You want me not to interfere with him counting grass all day?!) What can make this acceptable is recognition that this is the price to be paid for the corresponding forbearance of those who might find one's own projects of dubious worth. Such reciprocal payment is the coin in which liberal toleration is priced. Much more demanding is to be required to lend positive assistance to others' unattractive pursuits. ("I will *not* count blades of grass with him!") This is why demands of justice are overwhelmingly phrased in the negative and only rarely, if at all, take the form of mandatory positive assistance to anonymous others.[26]

Justice, the proverb tells us, is no respecter of persons. If this is all there is to say on this score, then we might conclude: so much the worse for justice! Because people are arrayed everywhere along the spectrum from noble to base, it would be absurd to fail to reflect in conduct toward them their estimability or lack of same. With regard to possession of basic rights, however, saints and scoundrels stand on the same level of moral considerability. It is not adequate to defend snatching the property of someone by saying that he would just proceed to use it for unworthy ends – unworthy, at least, when compared to one's own shining purposes. This is to misunderstand the scope of justice. It is the aspect of morality that is most general and thus responsive to the lowest common denominator. Only when that floor is breached, by deliberately (crime) or inadvertently (tort) infringing the rights of others, is it then permissible to deprive the perpetrator of what would otherwise rightfully be his.

A moral mistake even worse than trying to stretch justice to account for degrees of worthiness among rights-respecting individuals would be to suppose that dealings with intimate others require nothing more than acting justly toward them. If Bennet always deals justly with his children, neither more nor less, then he is not much of a father. If one's neighbor is struggling to extricate herself from a predicament, then the virtue of neighborliness is not well served by concluding that she has no right against you for assistance and then putting her out of your mind. Although moral life is necessarily founded on scrupulous concern to do justice to all, it extends well beyond that basic proviso. Justice tells us what we *must do*; virtues such as generosity, compassion, good humor, and inventiveness suggest to us what we *may to some credit do*. Charitable giving, for example, is not a dictate of justice; if one is strictly required to give,

---

[26] "Good Samaritan laws" that require individuals to lend assistance to those confronting grave peril when no corresponding danger would threaten the rescuer herself are instances of positive assistance construed as a demand of justice. We will not here examine the case for Good Samaritan legislation except to note that the carefully qualified and exceptional circumstances in which it would apply underscore the predominantly negative character of duties of justice.

then complying with the requirement does not count as charity. (It was not charity to the barista when she was given $3.75 for the latte.)

It is a good thing for individuality that the demands of justice are minimal and that nonmandatory permissions and suggestions are many. This enables individuals to form for themselves lives that give expression to their own distinctive personal valuations. There is no option whether to respect the rights of others, but once one has satisfied the justice side of morality, options are everywhere. Not all these are objects of deliberated choice. Whom to befriend rather than hold at arm's length is more often a matter of serendipity than decision. However, one is accountable for these relationships both in their initial formation and in terms of the actions responsive to the relationship. "Accountable" used in this context is not the bottom-line accountancy of justice in which one pays one's due but rather is an accounting for the shape of a life, for whether it is going well or ill from the perspective of the agent in question. Everyone has a stake in whether Bennet acts justly, but whether Bennet is noticeably generous, studious, gregarious, or pious – these are matters concerning which the primary stake is Bennet's. Others will have secondary stakes correlating with their closeness to Bennet. If Dashwood is Bennet's longtime comrade, whereas Woodhouse knows Bennet barely well enough to nod in passing, then Dashwood has greater reason than Woodhouse to respond to Bennet's being preoccupied, behaving atypically. None of this, however, has anything to do with justice.[27]

RIGHTS, WRONGS, AND WRONGINGS

It is an inconvenient linguistic fact that the word "right" is used with two related but importantly distinct meanings: right as possession ("right to life") and as commended conduct ("It was right to help her out of that jam"). This makes it sound slightly paradoxical to say that persons have a "right to do what is wrong." But rather than paradox, this is a necessary component of any moral conception that affords to individuals wide latitude with regard to the scope of their choices. Young children are often afforded inconsequential choices: what flavor of ice cream to order, which shirt to wear to school, which nonviolent cartoons to watch on Saturday morning. Because nothing hangs on whether it is to be strawberry or vanilla, there is no such thing as making the "right" or "wrong" choice in these contexts other than what satisfies the child's transient preferences. To allow the child to decide whether to proceed on to

[27] Immanuel Kant is more responsible than any other philosopher for confusions in this area. Kant affirms that nothing can have ultimate moral worth other than doing one's duty because it is one's duty. Moreover, that duty is pronounced via an *imperative*, one that is categorical. This is the language of justice. Kant explicitly recognizes other moral virtues, but the initial adoption of the justice template deforms what follows thereon. Kant has been enormously influential in purveying the idea that what moral life is about is identifying one's moral duties and then fulfilling them. This has been a stumbling block for subsequent moral philosophy.

the fourth grade or instead to go off to sea would, however, be making far too much of the desirability of choice. Kids are not prepared adequately to consider and bear the consequences of such choices; this is why we treat them as kids. Adults, however, are not to be infantilized. Over a wide range they enjoy a liberty to undertake momentous commitments. Because these will count for much toward the flourishing or failing of their lives (most of all as seen from their own perspectives), it is ludicrous to maintain that there is no distinction between making the right choice and the wrong one. Dashwood has the right to marry or to remain single, but one of these might be disastrously inappropriate for her. This is the sort of case in which friends often see with much sharper vision than does the party in question. Because they are friends, they decide to take on themselves the onus of trying to talk Dashwood out of what will surely leave her worse off, even at the cost of creating some rough edges to the friendship. "This isn't right for you," they may say – properly. What they certainly should not say, however, is, "You have no right to do this."

The word "wrong" does not carry the same ambiguity but is susceptible to a related one. As an adjective, "wrong" attaches to actions, decisions, choices that are somehow defective. As a transitive verb, however, "to wrong" is to treat someone injuriously or discreditably. Unless used metaphorically ("She wrongs Truth itself!"), it takes as its object a person.[28] The verb is irreflexive; Bennet can wrong Dashwood, but as a matter of logic, Bennet cannot wrong Bennet.[29] Bennet certainly can, however, make disastrously wrong choices that result in Bennet's life going poorly. This is an unfortunate but inescapable upshot of the right to do what is wrong.

People are wronged when their rights are violated. If Bennet murders Dashwood, then Bennet wrongs Dashwood by violating her right to life. If, however, Bennet turns the gun on himself, then he may be acting in a way that is not right, but he is not violating his own right to life.[30] Violating someone's rights is to act unjustly toward that person; one cannot act unjustly toward oneself. Other vices, however, can well come into play. Bennet's choice can be rash, intemperate, craven, foolish, and altogether imprudent, in which case it is true that Bennet *harms* himself. Generally, it is wrong for people to bring harm onto themselves, but they do not thereby wrong themselves.

---

[28] Some will contend, for example, that we can through our actions wrong the ecosphere. This is implicitly to assign to the ecosphere a moral status similar to that enjoyed by individual human beings.

[29] A qualification: if Bennet at different stages of life is seen as significantly discontinuous between earlier and later, then there is sense to speaking of Bennet-at-thirty wronging Bennet-at-seventy by squandering the resources that would have allowed for a comfortable old age. This is to take young Bennet and old Bennet as being (almost) separate persons. A wonderfully provocative discussion of how the usual importance of personal identity can break down is Derek Parfit, *Reason and Persons* (Oxford University Press, 1984).

[30] Locke believed that suicide constitutes a rights violation, but the right in question is that of God, who possesses ultimate ownership of all human beings. Locke, *Second Treatise*, § 6.

Can Bennet wrong Dashwood despite not violating any rights of Dashwood? The answer is not clear-cut. There are many ways in which Bennet might disappoint or anger Dashwood that do not constitute wrongs done to Dashwood. Even some harms that Bennet brings about will not constitute wrongs to Dashwood. For example, if Bennet opens up a store that drives Dashwood's shop to the wall, Bennet has caused a harm to Dashwood but has not wronged her. It is plausible to maintain that the only way in which someone can actually wrong an anonymous other is to violate that person's rights. However, the case is different with regard to those with whom one has an ongoing relationship. Suppose that Bennet routinely gives Dashwood a ride to work but then one day – perhaps Bennet is in a hurry or perhaps Bennet simply is tired of Dashwood's incessantly humming the tune of "You Are the Wind Beneath My Wings" – Bennet does not stop for Dashwood. Has Dashwood been wronged? An affirmative answer can take two different forms. First, it can be argued that Bennet's prior conduct has constituted a tacit promise to Dashwood of transportation and that in violating the promise Bennet has breached Dashwood's right to specific performance. Second, one can maintain that Dashwood has no right against Bennet, strictly speaking, but that Dashwood has an expectation that Bennet has fostered (and that Bennet ought to know that he has fostered) and that to dash the expectation constitutes a wrong. Our view is that some wrongs done to individuals are violations neither of a general nor specific right. It is a mistake to compress all of morality into the box of right and duties. Those with whom we engage on a personal basis will not fit. They have justified expectations of special solicitude and concern. Anonymous others do not. What we strictly owe them is respect for their rights, nothing more.

Recall Singer's second premise: "If it is in your power to prevent something bad from happening, without sacrificing anything nearly as important, it is wrong not to do so." Previously, we argued that it is defective in leaving open the question: important to whom (and the corresponding question of bad for whom)? To this charge a second is now added: Singer fails to specify what he takes the *wrongness* of nonprevention to be. One possibility is that he holds that not preventing harm wrongs those who are harmed. Although this sometimes is the case, especially in the context of a well-established special relationship, usually it is not. Without in any way wishing to diminish the status of anonymous others – each of *us* is an anonymous other from the perspective of billions of other people – they do not possess a claim for rescue against each other person. Indeed, it is hard to see how we could conceive the nature of such a dispersed entitlement. The person who is without rice in his bowl does not need rice from everyone. One provider will do (including the one such that the act will constitute self-provision). Let's suppose that there are 2 billion people who possess abundant means to donate the cash equivalent of a bowl of rice. Is each one of them guilty of 0.0000000005 of a wrong to the hungry individual (and to each of the other equally hungry people out there)? In the absence of a universal moral database matching each person in need with some unique benefactor, the idea of generalized wronging is far-fetched. Note that no such conundrum of dispersed duties attaches to the liberty right against interference. *Everyone* is obligated not to interfere with Dashwood, and there is no conceptual problem in imagining this obligation to be simultaneously met by everyone.

It is better to take Singer as maintaining that the failure to lend assistance is wrong but not a wronging, barring special antecedent ties, to the person not aided. Its wrongness is constituted by a deficit of beneficence. The basis for this judgment is, however, less than clear. Suppose that Dashwood is passionately devoted to opera. She attends Met performances when she can and otherwise contributes to the sustenance of that artform. Her beneficence is directed toward assisting aspiring singers in pursuing their training. Opera, in a word, *matters* to her. The anonymous hungry individual halfway around the world does not similarly matter to her. (How could he matter to someone who does not know anything about him, including perhaps even that he exists? Is this not a conspicuously bloodless employment of the notion of mattering?) Dashwood does not deny that this person's well-being is as important to himself and to his intimates as her well-being is to her. She will acknowledge that if they were to fail to aid their friend/family member, then they would be doing something wrong as entailed by their own standards of personal value. But she is not them. While wishing all people everywhere well, she has her own life to live. This involves two components: (1) refraining from violating the rights of others and (2) advancing her own projects. From Dashwood's point of view, devoting her resources to opera rather than to Oxfam makes sense. So how is it wrong for her to do otherwise?

Singer might respond that flesh-and-blood human beings are more important than operatic performances. And in one sense he is certainly correct: they are more important to themselves and to those who know and care about them. But without again begging the "important to whom?" question, Singer does not seem to have any compelling response to the question of why someone she has never met and about whom she knows nothing must be important to Dashwood. Alternatively, he might argue that the project of supporting opera is one of lower value than a project of saving lives everywhere on the globe and that the wrong that Dashwood does is to commit herself to the lower-value project instead of a higher-value one. This, though, is to misunderstand the nature of personal value. One's projects are not whatever is judged to score highest on some impersonal standard of value, the same standard for all. If this were all there was to it, then there would exist only one project, the universal project of acting for the sake of the one mandatory good. Utilitarians basically do believe this, although they will qualify it by saying that, of course, one's individual circumstances, endowments, predilections, assets, and so on will dictate for each person different strategies to the same overriding end. Singer is a utilitarian, so he is not inclined to acknowledge the legitimacy of the pull of individual commitments. (We are antiutilitarians – more specifically, antiaggregationists – so we are not inclined to acknowledge the legitimacy or, indeed, existence of the monolithic standard of impersonal value.) This, though, is not to provide an argument against the person who says, "Look, I really do love opera."

This response should not be misinterpreted as a critique of Singer's own personal commitments. He has made both a career and a life in the service of cosmopolitan humanitarianism. For this, Singer deserves respect. But so too does Dashwood for her consistent devotion to opera.

RATIONAL BASES FOR CHARITY TO DISTANT OTHERS

There is a great deal to be said on behalf of sacrificing some of one's own goods – yes, even that much-prized steaming cup of latte – for the sake of bringing relief to others. It ought, however, be said from the multiple perspectives of individuals and their personal commitments.

First, following a line from Aristotle, we observe that human beings are social animals, some much more so and some less. Exceedingly rare is the complete hermit or misanthrope. It is difficult to live an adequate human life without entertaining and being entertained, tending to and being tended by, loving and basking in the love of others. The relationships through which this tendency is best expressed are idiosyncratic and highly personal. Someone who values, say, mothers in general and not his own mother would be distinctly odd. Our sociality is brought to fruition in very particular communions that are both small and intimate.[31] There is, however, a degree of similarity between helping out a cherished friend and helping out a slight acquaintance or even an anonymous other. The similarity is that one is extending oneself for the sake of another person. Almost without exception, a life well lived will incorporate episodes of generosity. It seems likely that those who are open to helping those with whom no special ties are shared also may be more open to the needs of their intimates. The two brands of forthcomingness are complements, not substitutes. If so, then generosity to the distant can be commended even to those whose particular commitments are only to people near and dear.

Second, for the people who matter most to me, I will want to set an example of living well among others that might do them some good. I do not want them to think me narrow-minded, vain, closed off. (Bigots do want sharply to distinguish those for whom they have some care from those whom they disregard or despise, but they are unlikely to lead good lives. Or so we perhaps too optimistically hope.) If, for example, I want to bring my children up to value openness

---

[31] Aristotle believed that the size can extend up to the scope of an entire *polis*, the characteristic Greek city-state numbered in no more than tens of thousands of citizens, and he worked hard to make the case for a kind of "civic friendship" that can embrace others on so massive a scale. That it could extend across borders to humankind everywhere is nowhere within his compass of thought.

of hand toward those less fortunate, I had better exemplify that attitude in my own conduct. Of course, this thought does not generate any globe-spanning leaps of charity. The point can be made most effectively in one's own community. It is difficult to think what to do about the homeless in Chad other than to write a check, but the local homeless can be tended in the soup kitchen, by tutoring, by gifts of old clothes in their size, by faith-based evangelizing if that is one's taste, and so on. Nonetheless, some degree of attentiveness to the distant needy expresses as little else can an understanding that the boundary between those who matter significantly to me (and who, I hope, will matter to my children) and those who matter less is not hermetically sealed, all or nothing.

Third, attentiveness to the world beyond one's nose is epistemically more satisfactory than is insularity. All else equal, we do not prefer to associate with stupid individuals – and we do not wish to be the stupid individual with whom they associate. Attentiveness and responsiveness are virtues. Knowing about phenomena distant from our own everyday experience is to be valued.[32] To familiarize oneself with people distant in geography but also distant with regard to material circumstances, religion, language, history, and so on is almost invariably to come to identify more closely with them and thus to wish them well. (If acquaintance convinces one that they are enemies of all we hold dear, then affections take a different turn.) To value φ is to have reason to act on behalf of φ when the occasion arises. The strength of this reason is proportionate to how much one values φ relative to other objects of one's concern. Insofar, then, as people come to extend the bounds of their knowledge, they will tend to have greater reason to act at a distance. This consideration also works in reverse. Insofar as one extends one's activity into what had previously been mostly unknown realms, one comes to want to know them better.[33] Knowledge and efficacy are complements.

Fourth, the slippery slope can show itself to good advantage. It is impermissible to violate the rights of anyone, whether near or distant. One is more likely to violate the rights of those toward whom one has little knowledge or concern. By developing some measure of compassion toward people in Chad, and by acting in a manner prompted by that compassion, one becomes less likely to overstep the rights of those people. Moreover, to the extent that one develops compassion toward *some* distant others, one becomes more likely to take care for the rights of *all* distant others. A variation on this consideration: one may wrongly believe that distant impoverished people have a right to redistributive

---

[32] It is barely conceivable that someone might have a project of keeping at a distance the events and governing principles of the world. A monk might do so in order not to be distracted from communion with his God, but this would be a determination to sacrifice an extended finite horizon for one that is infinite. Of course, the monk might thereby be getting things wrong.

[33] This should not be taken as exclusively a reflection about aid to distant others. Extending one's horizons to the Cretaceous period may rationally lead one to devote more time to reading up on dinosaurs and volunteering for archaeological digs and less, say, on working for Oxfam.

transfers from those who have much.[34] For one who holds this belief, giving is not an optional exercise of beneficence but expresses attentiveness to rights. A variation on the preceding: people whose rights have been violated are entitled to claim compensation from the violators. For those who deem themselves to have been rights violators in their own person or complicit in violations perpetrated by some collective to which they belong, it may be appropriate to make voluntary transfers by way of paying their pro rata shares of indicated compensation. Note that in this case the reason being given for aid is not that it would be *wrong* to withhold the sum but that it would be *wronging* the potential recipient. This becomes a claim of justice, not charity.

The tentative upshot of these four points is that it will often be the case that individuals' own personal projects afford them reason to act on behalf of distant others. This is a cheering result, if only because it suggests that distant others will have reason to be fonder of those far from them than might otherwise be the case. In a world in which interactions are frequent, extended, and complex, good will is more valuable than ever. Most of all, however, it is a good thing for those of us who are well-wishers although not necessarily well-actors. That Dashwood chooses to devote her efforts mostly to support of opera and not at all toward relieving hunger in Africa does not mean that Dashwood is indifferent toward African hunger. She wishes it gone, but to wish that φ and to take on responsibility for φ are two different things. Dashwood is delighted that Peter Singer and those of like mind are enrolled in the project of cosmopolitan humanitarianism. Dashwood would be more delighted still if Singer et al. rejoiced in Dashwood's resolute support of opera, but perhaps that is too much to hope for. The point, though, is that it is not unfortunate that we do not all subscribe to the same standard of value. Those who would be ashamed of themselves if through their own inattentiveness they let the local opera company fail but who do not attend even a little to the circumstances of Chad are not thereby rendered moral inferiors.

JUSTICE AND DISTANCE

As is often the case, Adam Smith said it best:

Let us suppose that the great empire of China, with all its myriads of inhabitants, was suddenly swallowed up by an earthquake, and let us consider how a man of humanity in Europe, who had no sort of connection with that part of the world, would be affected upon receiving intelligence of this dreadful calamity. He would, I imagine, first of all, express very strongly his sorrow for the misfortune of that unhappy people, he would make many melancholy reflections upon the precariousness of human life, and the vanity of all the labours of man, which could thus be annihilated in a moment. He would too, perhaps, if he was a man of speculation, enter into many reasonings concerning the effects which this disaster might produce upon the commerce of Europe, and the

[34] That this belief is mistaken is argued in the next section and returned to in Chapter 3.

trade and business of the world in general. And when all this fine philosophy was over, when all these humane sentiments had been once fairly expressed, he would pursue his business or his pleasure, take his repose or his diversion, with the same ease and tranquillity, as if no such accident had happened. The most frivolous disaster which could befall himself would occasion a more real disturbance. If he was to lose his little finger to-morrow, he would not sleep to-night; but, provided he never saw them, he will snore with the most profound security over the ruin of a hundred millions of his brethren, and the destruction of that immense multitude seems plainly an object less interesting to him, than this paltry misfortune of his own.[35]

What a person cares about is not a function of a metric of impersonal value. Rather, it depends on her own particular attachments – including the attachment to her own little finger. Whether or not this partiality is desirable can be debated. If subjectivity were not the constant rudder to our valuations, then we might more easily take a position of disinterested universal benevolence. It is not clear what sort of creatures we would then be. Smith's report on the general human tendency to attend to one's own prospects with greater urgency and interest than those of others is not an endorsement of selfishness. He follows the thought experiment with a declaration that the world has never known such villainy as one who would sacrifice those hundred million lives for a finger's sake. Not being privy to the history of the twentieth century, Smith is demonstrably too optimistic in this assessment. Nonetheless, there are moral demands on us to concern ourselves with others. These extend to distant others.

University ethics courses are typically taught as a set piece with the Egoist – "I should act to maximize only my own happiness" – in one corner and the Utilitarian – "I should act to maximize universal happiness" – in the other. Pretty quickly the decision is awarded to the latter (except in the rare case when the instructor is a disciple of Ayn Rand), but then it is off to tussle with Immanuel Kant waiting in the wings. This manner of opposing an ethic of one against an ethic of all goes back at least to the nineteenth century's most masterful treatise on moral theory, Henry Sidgwick's *Methods of Ethics*. The implication that ethical options are so diametrically opposed is unfortunate. As David Hume observed, neither egoism nor impartial benevolence characterizes most agents: "I am of opinion, that tho' it be rare to meet with one, who loves any single person better than himself; yet 'tis as rare to meet with one, in whom all the kind affections, taken together, do not over-balance all the selfish."[36] Affections tend to vary as a function of closeness to the agent, with self being closest of all, near kin and special friends next, casual acquaintances further down on the roster, and countrymen eliciting greater concern than foreigners.

---

[35] Adam Smith, *The Theory of Moral Sentiments*, Kund Haakonsen, ed. (Cambridge University Press, 2002), 157.

[36] David Hume, *A Treatise of Human Nature*, book III, part 2, 2nd ed., L. A. Selby-Bigge, ed. (Oxford University Press, 1978), 487.

If this does indeed represent individuals' concerns, then they will have reason to direct themselves accordingly. What would be a trivial sacrifice to make on behalf of one's child or best friend would be preposterously extravagant for an anonymous other.

The moral sentimentalism of Hume and Smith connects well to the rights theory of Lockean liberalism.[37] Because a demand of noninterference is the most minimal that can be imposed on agents,[38] and because it is the least we can reasonably accept from those with whom we deal, it is the linchpin of a universal morality. It is owed to the most distant of people. To those nearer at hand either emotionally or geographically – the two usually but not always go together – requirements typically will be more extensive, but respect for liberty constitutes a moral minimum. It is, at least under favorable conditions, the basis for a stable equilibrium. First, it is often easily met. At this very moment, there are literally billions of people you are not assaulting! Abiding by their rights is easier even than refraining; it is just a not doing. Second, you are at this very moment the beneficiary of those many billions not interfering with you! Third, simply to recognize others as moral beings with lives of their own to lead is to have some incentive to afford them the space within which they can go about their affairs. The alternative is what the tradition calls a "state of war." If peaceable accommodation is to be had, its minimal condition is generalized noninterference. Nietzscheans may sneer at this pusillanimous acquiescence to a passivist ethic, but it ought to be noted for the record that Nietzsche could not have written his books had he been compelled constantly to defend his own hearth. The upshot is that we act wrongly toward others, both distant and near, if we wrong them and that the most general form of wronging is to infringe rights.

Insofar as the latte drinker is not violating rights of distant others, he is not acting in a morally subpar manner. Or rather, he *need not* be doing so. It depends on the content of his own personal projects. If he is a professed utilitarian universalist, then he is acting in bad faith. (The authors have, though, from time to time observed utilitarians drinking fancy coffees.) If he professes a commitment to charity but never performs it, he is a hypocrite. If, however, he wishes well to all but directs his own energies toward those persons and causes that infuse his own life with meaning and direction, then he is as morally creditable as we are entitled to demand of another person. Or of ourselves.

---

[37] That despite their underlying philosophical methodologies sharply differing. Hume in his essay, "Of the Original Contract," argued that government did not and could not arise from multiple parties contracting with each other. David Hume, *Political Essays*, Knud Haakosen, ed. (Cambridge University Press, 1994), 186. Hume and Smith also are suspicious of the category of *natural* rights, taking the foundational precepts of justice to be conventions that have endured because experience shows them to be useful to human pursuits.

[38] This is not to say that refraining from interference will always come easily. Temptations to interpose one's own enlightened convictions about the good on benighted others is surely one of the most appealing to which human beings are heir. It is the foundation both of ancient evangelizing and modern state paternalism.

RIGHTS AND WRONGS

We have argued that no wrong is done to distant others except insofar as one violates their rights. It has been tacitly assumed in the foregoing that the person sitting in an easy chair in Starbucks enjoying a caffeine infusion is not thereby violating the rights of someone on the other side of the world. There are various grounds on which this assumption can be challenged.

1. Suppose that the beans from which the coffee was brewed had been stolen or extorted from their legitimate owner. Then, in drinking the coffee, one is the unwitting beneficiary of a felony. Or perhaps not so unwitting if one's lack of knowledge of the crime is willful.

2. Perhaps the beans were purchased from their grower in a licit transaction, but the system of trade through which the commerce was conducted is distorted by advantages coercively imposed. Although the consumer has not been an active party to the exploitation, he may nonetheless be implicated in a manner that calls for rectification.

3. As citizens of democracies, "we the people" are the ultimate authors of our country's national policies. To the extent that these incorporate rights violations, we bear responsibility for the harms done to those, distant and near, who have been victimized. If so, our liability may not be personal but rather as a citizen/taxpayer called on to bear a pro rata share of the country's debt to those it has harmed.

4. Locke, Hume, and Smith may have believed that the basic demands of justice are satisfied by respecting the person and property of others. Contemporary liberals such as John Rawls recognize a *distributive* aspect to the requirements of justice. Assuming that all people have a right to a share that is roughly equal – or at least not too grossly inferior – then we might conclude that the individual who earns less in three days than the latte drinker expends for one mug of his favorite brew is being wronged.

These are not trivial accusations. Nor are they altogether implausible. The question to be addressed is: do contemporary practices constitute rights violations against distant others? We shall answer in the affirmative. There are some things that we do as individuals but yet more things done either on our behalf or in our names by governments that are indefensible. They are indefensible not because we enjoy our simple pleasures too much when others are suffering but also because their suffering is a direct consequence of their rights being violated. It is important to observe that neither all nor the most important rights violations against distant others are attributable to the latte drinker and his compatriots. Enough are, however, for citizens of the United States to be made uneasy. We turn now to an examination of wrongings done to distant others and the means through which these might be effectively addressed.

3

Choosing Wealth, Choosing Poverty

Hundreds of millions of people live in desperate conditions of bare subsistence or worse. Hundreds of millions of others enjoy enormous wealth, enormous at least compared to the lot of their unfortunate brethren. That so many are poor is a terrible misfortune. Does it, however, signify an injustice?

An affirmative answer can take either of two forms. First, the inordinate incidence of poverty in Africa, Asia, and the world's other misery spots can be held to be the result of unjust actions that *cause* the poverty under which so many labor.[1] Second, though, the disparity between rich and poor can be said to *constitute* an injustice. That is, the fact of wealthy people retaining possession of nearly all their holdings while refusing to transfer more than a pittance to the less-well-off is itself a failure of justice, specifically a failure of *distributive justice*.

There are many ways to commit acts of injustice, and several of these will be addressed shortly. However, in the burgeoning literature of global justice, it has become common to focus nearly all attention on distributive justice and its absence. One reason for this emphasis is that in canvassing world populations, the most obvious disparity between countries such as the United States and Sweden, on the one hand, and Burkina Faso and Bangladesh, on the other, is that citizens of the former enjoy so many of the goods that make life go well, whereas those in the latter do without. What is good for us and bad for Burkina Faso is, then, how wealth is distributed. Another rationale for the focus on distributive justice is that when wealthy citizens of Organisation for Economic Co-operation and Development (OECD) countries are called on to take note of the plight of the world's wretched, the one means by which they are told they can make a difference is to redistribute either privately or through political

---

[1] And it could, in turn, enable further injustices. We are grateful to Loy Hui Chieh for this observation.

means to the less-well-off. For the fraternity of moral philosophers, however, the single most compelling reason to focus on issues of distributive justice is the towering example of John Rawls. In *A Theory of Justice*,[2] Rawls argues that justice requires society's basic structure to be organized so as maximally to benefit the least-well-off stratum. This does not mandate a strict equality in holdings among all citizens, but it does mean that only those inequalities that improve the position of the least-well-off are justifiable. This is the upshot of his celebrated *difference principle*.[3]

Distributive shares, then, are a criterion of social justice within the Rawlsian framework. They are not, however, the only criterion or even the one that ostensibly is primary. The essence of the theory is expressed in two principles of justice, and the difference principle appears only as the second half of the second principle. Pride of place is taken by the first principle:

First: each person is to have an equal right to the most extensive basic liberty compatible with a similar liberty for others.[4]

This enjoys *lexical priority* over the difference principle, meaning that should there be any conflict between the equal right to basic liberty demand and the distributive shares demand, the former is in every case to be preferred. Officially, then, what matters most within the Rawlsian theory of justice is liberty, not economic egalitarianism. We say "officially," because throughout the enormous literature spawned by *A Theory of Justice*, reflection on the first principle is barely a trickle, whereas the number of treatments of the difference principle is a philosophical torrent. Indeed, Rawls himself plays down the significance of the first principle, progressively qualifying and watering it down in subsequent restatements in *A Theory of Justice* and later writings.[5] This is why from the moment of publication of the book it has served as a stimulus for objections to patterns of wealth or income in which some have very much and others little.

In two respects, however, Rawls' original discussion was less accommodating to their ideological aspirations than egalitarians might wish. First, it applied only to the basic structure of society, not to interpersonal relationships. Therefore, for example, if Bennet is rolling in his millions while Dashwood barely owns two sticks to rub together, it is not a violation of Rawlsian justice for Bennet to choose to retain every last penny and donate nothing to Dashwood. To some readers, this limitation has seemed arbitrary.[6] Second, Rawls explicitly limits the scope of the two principles to a self-contained

[2] John Rawls, *A Theory of Justice* (Cambridge, MA: Harvard University Press, 1971).

[3] Ibid., 75–83.

[4] Ibid., 60.

[5] This history is spelled out in Loren E. Lomasky, "Libertarianism at Twin Harvard," *Social Philosophy & Policy* 22 (2005), 178–99.

[6] Most notably to G. A. Cohen, *Rescuing Justice and Equality* (Cambridge, MA: Harvard University Press, 2008), esp. 27–86.

political society into which individuals enter at birth and exit only at death. The theory, then, has no implications in its pure form concerning wealth transfers across borders. (Nor does it speak to issues of immigration, foreign trade, humanitarian intervention, and others that extend beyond the society's internal structure.) Rawls does not deny that pressing concerns of justice can arise in interstate contexts; he simply begs off addressing them in the already long and complex treatment that is *A Theory of Justice*. Other Rawlsians were, however, more ambitious. To them, it did not seem a very difficult task to devise a strategy for extending Rawls' theory to include all peoples of Earth. Instead of envisioning the hypothetical contract setting as restricted to the citizens of one nation meeting behind a veil of ignorance in an original position in which each person is stripped of specifically individuating information that might allow unfair self-favoritism, they urge that it be reconceived as a global original position with the veil of ignorance extended to encompass knowledge about the social and economic conditions of one's own country. Piggybacking on Rawls' original reasoning, cosmopolitan Rawlsians concluded that the outcome of the global contract would include some variation on a difference principle not just for the basic structure of one nation but rather across all borders. Justice, then, would be globally redistributive.

The shift to global justice enjoyed much popularity among Rawls' disciples.[7] Only one prominent Rawlsian demurred, but that exception counted for much because the dissident was Rawls himself. When he finally turned to writing up a full-scale treatment of international justice in *The Law of Peoples*,[8] Rawls rejected the suitability of the difference principle as a standard for distributive justice among all the world's peoples.[9] Indeed, in the framework he set out for global justice, there is no general requirement of transfers from the world's haves to the world's have-nots. Only for those peoples who are undergoing acute distress, called by Rawls "burdened societies" (essentially the equivalent of what are more commonly referred to as "failed states"), is assistance mandated as a precept of justice. Even then the demand terminates at the "point at which a people's basic needs (estimated in primary goods) are fulfilled and a people can stand on its own."[10] Unlike the discussion of *A Theory of Justice* in which the liberty principle recedes more and more into the woodwork while distributive concerns take center stage, the later book reverses direction. Concern for the autonomy and self-directedness of each individual society renders peoples nearly immune from requirements to set aside their own conceptions of the good and busy themselves instead with relieving the deficits

---

[7] See, e.g., Charles Beitz, *Political Theory and International Relations* (Princeton, NJ: Princeton University Press, 1979); Thomas Pogge, *Realizing Rawls* (Ithaca, NY: Cornell University Press, 1990).

[8] John Rawls, *The Law of Peoples* (Cambridge, MA: Harvard University Press, 1999).

[9] For reasons that need not detain us here, Rawls prefers to speak of the benefits and requirements of international justice as primarily attaching to *peoples* rather than to *countries* or *states*.

[10] Rawls, *Law of Peoples*, 119.

of less-fortunate others. The one ongoing and fundamental demand that each people can properly make of all others is noninterference. It is at the international level that the theory of justice's equal liberty principle truly assumes the sweeping lexical priority that it only nominally enjoys in *A Theory of Justice*.

Cosmopolitan egalitarians object to Rawls' internationalist extensions of his own theory. Thomas Pogge writes:

Rawls strongly rejects the difference principle as a requirement of global justice on the ground that it is unacceptable for one people to bear certain costs of decisions made by another – decisions affecting industrialization or the birth rate, for example. But he fails to explain why this ground should not analogously disqualify the difference principle for national societies as well. Why is it not likewise unacceptable for one province, township or family to bear such costs of decisions made by another?[11]

This is an excellent question. There is strong reason to believe that if the concern to be left at liberty to go one's own way blocks extensive redistributional policies with regard to national entities, it does so as well for subgroups within a particular state. The strand can be extended one step further: redistribution will be blocked between distinct individuals within the subgroups. Indeed, the inference in this limiting case is more compelling than in the others because persons are project pursuers and towns, provinces, and nationalities are not. Only in a loose sense can the latter be said to possess a conception of the good. No such looseness attends offering such a characterization of Bennet or Dashwood or you. Therefore, if the guiding theory of one book or the other must be sharply scaled back, our vote is for modifying *A Theory of Justice*. This, though, is an argument that has been pursued elsewhere.[12] Here we content ourselves with advancing a less contentious claim. A demand for sacrifice, for bearing the burdens of others' choices and making their weal and woe largely one's own, is persuasive in proportion to the closeness of those others to oneself. For family and friends, it defines the nature of the relationship; for casual acquaintances, its salience is muted. To distant others, peoples whose system of laws, cultural traditions, and histories are distinct from our own, the tie is more attenuated still. This is not to maintain that it is altogether absent. To them, we owe our good will for their success on their own terms; our pledge of noninterference with their lives, liberty, and property; and in extreme cases and depending on many factors, our willingness to rescue them from the most abject forms of tyranny.[13] Arguably, this is all. If there is a case for more extensive principles of global redistribution, it must be *made*. An argument based on the assertion that a suitably defined original position of all the world's people (or peoples) would opt for a universal difference principle begs the question of why we should take that model to be morally dispositive. In *A Theory of*

---

[11] Thomas Pogge, *World Poverty and Human Rights* (Cambridge, UK: Polity, 2002), 105.
[12] It is central to Lomasky, "Libertarianism at Twin Harvard."
[13] See Chapter 8.

Justice, Rawls explains, "In justice as fairness men agree to share one another's fate."[14] This seems right. Whatever may be the case within a liberal national political entity, it simply is not credible to maintain that any agreement so profound and far-reaching in its implications does or could obtain globally. If the claim that the disparity between poor and rich peoples betokens injustice stands or falls on a general theory of distributive justice, then it falls.

Readers may protest that this is to give too short shrift to apprehension that the prevalence of misery in so many corners of the world betokens significant injustice. We agree. It is not simply a misfortune that hundreds of millions of distant others are mired in poverty and hopelessness; it is overwhelmingly strong evidence that they have been and continue to be wronged. The questions that demand answers are: what are the wrongs that have been done to them? Who are the primary agents of the harms they suffer? Who are the secondary but nonetheless culpable contributors to the misfortunes they unjustly suffer? And most important, what is to be done, and by whom? Credible answers to these questions will not be secured by recycling Rawls' or anyone's theories of distributive justice. This is so because the significant wrongs endured by the global poor are not essentially distributive in character but rather are impositions on their basic rights. The remainder of this chapter and those that succeed it are addressed to identifying the wrongs and the wrongdoers.

THE GREAT TRANSFORMATION

Poverty is the natural human condition.[15] We enter the world with nothing except the breath that fuels our angry first cries, and we leave with less. In between, we live through the fruits of our labor. Throughout the great preponderance of human civilization, those fruits have been meager, barely adequate to secure subsistence, if that. When Jesus said, "The poor will always be with you," he knew whereof he spoke. In every society for which there is record, wealth was the exception. Most of the population was divided among the desperately poor, moderately poor, and near poor. When weather or the expansionary designs of neighboring tribes were favorable, most people would enjoy enough to eat, although some would not. When one or the other condition turned less favorable, then even the relatively well-off might well find themselves thrust below subsistence level. There were, of course, variations within and among civilizations, but almost without exception wealth, understood as possession of a surplus well beyond that which is needed for subsistence, was a privilege of the very few.

Only gradually did this seemingly fixed point of the human condition begin to give way. Between the seventeenth and nineteenth centuries, along narrow

---

[14] Rawls, *Theory of Justice*, 102.
[15] This section builds on the discussion of Loren Lomasky and Kyle Swan, "Wealth and Poverty in the Liberal Tradition," *Independent Review* 13 (Spring 2009), 493–510.

strips on both sides of the Atlantic, wealth became if not the norm, then an increasingly more common exception. A margin of comfort beyond bare subsistence could be not only the expectation of a growing middle class but also even a realistic aspiration of workers. In part, this was due to the technological eruptions of forge and factory brought about by the industrial revolution. Of similar explanatory importance, however, was the era's new financial technology. Preceding and thereby enabling the wealth explosion was eclipse of the feudalism of an idle landowning class and overworked peasants by the commercial society theorized and celebrated in Adam Smith's *Wealth of Nations*. Capital formation of an unprecedented magnitude was made possible by the development of limited-liability corporations that pooled the funds of numerous independent investors who may have been quite unknown to each other but who concurred in forgoing current for future consumption. Families in the money-lending business evolved into investment and commercial banks that could underwrite the issues of these new corporations and provide them with the liquidity they needed to nurture operations. Stock exchanges and bond markets emerged. Perhaps most important was the steady development of *rule of law* adequate to the increasing complexity of commercial relations. Parties secure in the knowledge that property rights would remain inviolate and that contracts would be honored, if need be via judicial intercession, became willing to trust their accumulated wealth to ventures that would not pay off for many years. The result was persistent and steady growth, which, through the grace of compounding, utterly transformed the economic status of millions of ordinary men and women of Western Europe and North America who were lifted not only out of poverty but into middle-class affluence. Of course, the progress was not frictionless. Blake's "dark Satanic Mills" were harrowing for those who labored therein, and Engels' *The Condition of the Working Class in England in 1844* was powerful contemporary testimony that the progress of industry was in fact the regress of workers. In retrospect, however, it is clear that these observations were premature. The mills were more purgatorial than infernal, and the working class had taken their first step onto an escalator that would improve their own lives[16] and yet more drastically those of their children, grandchildren, and great-grandchildren. Revolutions, we have come to learn, often are more productive of misery than of melioration, but the commercial/industrial revolution constituted a decisive improvement for the lot of those swept up in it. Among its chief gainers were those huddled in society's lowest tiers.[17]

---

[16] The economic historian Jeffrey Williamson declares in *Did British Capitalism Breed Inequality?* (Boston: Allen and Unwin, 1985), 18: "[U]nless new errors are discovered, the debate over real wages in the early nineteenth century is over: the average worker was much better off in any decade from the 1830s on than any decade before 1820."

[17] For a sweeping telling of the story, see Deirdre McCloskey, *The Bourgeois Virtues: Ethics for an Age of Commerce* (University of Chicago Press, 2006).

And then the other shoe dropped. Sometime around the middle of the twentieth century, the geographic bottleneck that had confined the privilege of widespread wealth to the West gave way. Suppositions that economic dynamism were dependent on one particular cultural strand or geographic situation were falsified by postwar experience. (So too were Marxian predictions that capitalism was on its last staggering legs and that socialism would usher in a regime of plenty for all, but that is a story for another occasion.) In places where people since time immemorial had lived mostly in shackles of indigence, production and accumulation quickly launched populations into heretofore inexperienced realms of plenty. Most striking was the extraordinary rapidity of the process compared with the original Western takeoff. Because capital and expertise could be transferred in a matter of weeks – and, with the advent of computer internetworking, microseconds – from where they were plentiful to where they could be put to useful work, developing societies did not have to undergo the slow and painful process of accumulation that the first generations of wealth creators had to endure.

There was something wonderfully democratic to this second wealth explosion, although few of the participants were democracies in the standard sense of the word. The escalator to wealth proved to be accessible to societies spanning entire continents and those no larger than the environs of a single city, East no less than West, countries rich in natural resources and those possessing little more than the industriousness of their own populations, those that had been politically independent for centuries as well as the recently decolonized, and so on. Unfortunately, numerous other societies of all shapes and sizes remained mired in endemic poverty despite the earnest well-wishing and cash infusions of aid bureaucrats. Any serious discussion of the parameters of global justice and global well-being has to attend to the question: what accounts for the divergent paths of the newly wealthy as opposed to the persistently poor?

Here is the quick answer: the average person's prospects of living a long, healthy, and comfortable life are excellent where robust protection of private property rights under the rule of law obtains – that is, under conditions of economic liberalism. We are not unaware that this compression into a one sentence the pronouncement of a mountainous literature in development economics debates will be regarded by some as procrustean. We believe that we can get away with this shortcut because we do not advance this proposition as an *ultimate* causal factor in understanding poverty. Why some societies have achieved the appurtenances of liberal justice and others have failed to do so may well depend on deeper underlying cultural and physical parameters that we have not stipulated. Nor can we do so, except to the very limited extent of identifying in the paragraphs that follow certain behaviors that demonstrably propel or impede wealth creation. Our argument rests on a premise that the presence or absence of certain liberal institutions tends to be crucial to the task of social wealth formation. We confess ourselves unable to provide a blueprint for the genesis of these institutions. Providing a rich theory of why and how those behaviors emerge is a task worthy of a Nobel Prize in Economics.[18]

If one were to pick a poster child for economic development, it would be hard to choose better than Singapore. When granted self-rule by the United Kingdom in 1959, the island-nation sported every appearance of impending failure. It was a miniature-sized political entity surrounded by much larger powers – seven Singapores could fit comfortably into the small American state of Delaware – and possessed of no homegrown defense capabilities in a region in which military adventures were not uncommon. Aside from a minuscule agricultural sector, Singapore enjoyed no natural resources other than its location at the tip of the Malay Peninsula. The majority population was Chinese but with substantial and potentially restive Malay and Indian minorities. Because the Chinese segment spoke a number of dialects, no first language was common even to half the residents. The experience of brutal occupation by Japan between 1942 and 1945 had been seared into Singaporean consciousness, and indignities of colonialism fed the resentments of many. As independence neared, socialists of the People's Action Party (PAP) under the leadership of Lee Kuan Yew contended for political supremacy with communists inside and outside the structure of the PAP. Merger into the Federation of Malaysia in 1963 seemed to solve Singapore's size problem, but less than two years later, after race riots pitted Malays against ethnic Chinese, Singapore was spit out by Tunku Abdul Rahman's federal Malaysian government as indigestible. When in 1967 the British announced plans to close their military bases by the end of 1971, that appeared to some to be the final nail in Singapore's coffin. British troop presence had accounted for up to 20 percent of gross domestic product (GDP) and most of the diminutive nation's deterrent capacity.[19] How would Singapore fare steering solo in dangerous waters?

Over an unbroken forty-year stretch the answer Singapore provided was, "Quite well indeed, thank you." From 1965 to 2005, GDP grew at an average annual rate of 8 percent, almost 6 percent per capita. In an age of extraordinary growth in Asia and beyond, no other country in the world had done as well. It had achieved European standards of affluence, life expectancy, and

---

[18] The wise men of Sweden concur. Douglass North, 1993 Nobel laureate, establishes the foundations of a theory of how institutions are decisive factors in the generation of prosperity. See Douglass North, *Institutions, Institutional Change, and Economic Performance* (Cambridge University Press, 1990). A compelling narrative of the history of wealth creation is David Landes, *The Wealth and Poverty of Nations: Why Some Are So Rich and Some So Poor* (New York: Norton, 1998). A useful overview of the economics debate is provided in Mathias Risse, "What We Owe to the Global Poor," *Journal of Ethics* 9 (2005), 81–117. See also Daren Acemoglu and James Robinson, *Why Nations Fail*, discussed in Chapter 1.

[19] Henri Ghesquiere, *Singapore's Success: Engineering Economic Growth* (Singapore: Thomson Asia, 2007), 139. This book is a wonderfully lucid and informative account not only of post-independence Singapore's political economy but also of the imperatives for development in a competitive world economy.

environmental enhancements while virtually eliminating absolute poverty.[20] Singapore enjoyed some good luck over this period – as does every society that manages to avoid devastating war, disease, or natural disaster – but mostly its success can be attributed to wise policy choices.[21] These include but are not limited to the following:

1. Maximal openness to global markets has been a keystone of Singapore's success. The country parlayed its deep-water port into one of the world's busiest container shipping sites by eliminating almost all tariff and non-tariff barriers. Goods shipped into and out of the country amount to more than three times GDP.[22] Participation of multinational corporations is encouraged by the absence of restrictions on capital transfers and profit repatriation. Singapore is the major regional banking center. Both Singapore Airlines and Changi Airport are at or near the top of world rankings, crucially assisting Singapore's efforts to be a major travel and commerce hub.

2. Liberal immigration policies afford entry both to low-skilled workers and professionals. Although mobility of persons into the country is regulated (see Chapter 4), those who have secured employment offers are not held back at the borders to satisfy the political demands of domestic labor interests.

3. Taxation is moderate. Overall tax revenue amounts to approximately 16 percent of GDP, less than half of which is secured through taxation of income, profits, or capital gains. The maximum marginal tax rate on individuals is 20 percent. Both corporations and individuals thereby get to keep the vast bulk of what they earn.

4. The government provides a social safety net, but only for those who are genuinely in distress. There is no social security program; individuals and families are expected to be the primary providers for their own health-care needs, retirement pensions, and temporary bouts of employment adversity. In Singapore, individual responsibility works: health-care services and outcomes are comparable to those of the United States at less than a third of U.S. costs, unemployment is usually under 3 percent, and the aged live comfortably, often in homes that they themselves own. The government conceives of its primary role as enabler of conditions favorable to the creation of wealth rather than as redistributor of wealth that has already been generated. For most of its existence, Singapore's means were too modest to allow the alternative emphasis. This policy has stuck despite ascendance into the ranks of the world's most prosperous.

---

[20] Ghesquiere, *Singapore's Success*, 12–20.
[21] Unless otherwise indicated, the information provided in the following twelve points is primarily or entirely extracted from Ghesquiere, *Singapore's Success*.
[22] Key Singapore statistics are accessible at http://www.singstat.gov.sg/.

5. Although Singapore spends a relatively high 5 percent of GDP on defense and demands two years of military service from all male citizens at age eighteen, it has avoided both destructive adventures abroad and military meddling in domestic politics. It is one of the relatively rare developing states whose defense spending has actually gone almost entirely for defense.

6. The independence of Singapore's judiciary has been called into question by critics of the ruling PAP who find themselves in the dock for public criticisms of the government. But with regard to enforcing contracts and protecting private property, those courts are world class.

7. Bureaucrats and government officials are paid salaries enormous by comparative world standards,[23] but in return, Singapore has an enviable record of low corruption. According to Transparency International's 2012 survey, it ranked fifth in the world. By comparison, Germany was thirteenth and the United States nineteenth.[24]

8. Although the Singapore government has a finger in numerous economic pies, it refrains from subsidizing local champions. Rather, it maintains a level playing field on which domestic firms either compete effectively against the world's best or die. This has led over the course of Singapore's half century of independence to several cycles of no-longer-competitive industries being allowed to expire as others more responsive to prevailing demand factors take their place. The result is an economy that has remained flexible and dynamic.

9. Organized labor in Singapore has bought into the conception of the economy as positive sum and expects salary increases to reflect productivity gains rather than coziness with politicians. Labor market rules are flexible, retraining is frequent even for older workers, and openness to foreign best practice has allowed Singapore workers to sharpen their skills. Few resources are wasted in industrial actions or rent-seeking.

10. Singapore turned its problem of no one common language into a virtue by capitalizing on its British colonial antecedents and making English the official language of government and education. This afforded it an easier entry into world communications than otherwise would have been the case.

11. Although the government is prime mover in most housing construction, it avoids establishing the sorts of public housing projects or council flats that blight the United States, France, and England. Instead, it provides assistance so that even families of modest income can buy their own residences. One of the most important of these strategies is to allow individuals to use the enforced savings that have gone into

---

[23] At least thirty governmental ministers receive an annual salary in excess of US$1 million. See http://www.yeocheowtong.com/Salaries.html.

[24] http://www.transparency.org/cpi2012/results.

their pension funds for a down payment on a home mortgage. The result is that Singapore is truly an "ownership society," with a residential home ownership rate of 93 percent. People whose most important financial asset is the home in which they live have a strong incentive to preserve its value and to work to prevent their neighborhood turning into a slum. And because Singapore's high rises are demographically integrated, home owners – that is, the vast majority of citizens – have compelling reason to seek solutions rather than conflict across racial lines.

12. In a way summing up the preceding points, surveys of global competitiveness and economic freedom regularly list Singapore at or near the very top of the world's nations. The Heritage Foundation's "Index of Economic Freedom" for 2013 puts Singapore as second to Hong Kong. By comparison, the United States is ranked tenth, Germany nineteenth, and Argentina one-hundred and sixtieth. The World Economic Forum's "Global Competitiveness Report 2012–13" lists Singapore second behind Switzerland and ahead of Germany (sixth), the United States (seventh), China (twenty-ninth), Argentina (ninety-fourth), and Venezuela (one-hundred and twenty-sixth).[25] To make it a clean sweep, the Fraser Institute's "Economic Freedom of the World: 2012 Report' puts only Hong Kong ahead of Singapore. (Somewhat ominously it observes, "The United States, long considered the standard bearer for economic freedom among large industrial nations, has experienced a substantial decline in economic freedom during the past decade. From 1980 to 2000, the United States was generally rated the third freest economy in the world, ranking behind only Hong Kong and Singapore. After increasing steadily during the period from 1980 to 2000, the chainlinked EFW rating of the United States fell from 8.65 in 2000 to 8.21 in 2005 and 7.70 in 2010. The overall ranking of the United States has fallen precipitously from second in 2000 to eighth in 2005 and 19th in 2010.")[26]

This is not to maintain that in every respect Singapore is a paragon. On independence, the country embraced a policy of import substitution which, to its good fortune, was quickly abandoned. In the 1960s, the government's heavy-handed propaganda to encourage people to limit their family size to two children was as risible as its turnaround some two decades later to beseech people into marriage and larger families. With regard to civil liberties and democratic freedoms, Singapore fares distinctly less well than on the economic front. Freedom House in its 2103 report judges Singapore to be only "partly free," criticizing in particular government domination of election procedures and the

[25] For Heritage Foundation, see http://www.heritage.org/index/ranking; for World Economic Forum, see http://www3.weforum.org/docs/WEF_GlobalCompetitivenessReport_2012-13.pdf: http://www.freetheworld.com/release.html.

[26] http://www.freetheworld.com/2012/EFW2012-complete.pdf.

media.[27] Depending on how one thinks about capital punishments' appropriateness as a response to murder, one may believe that Singapore's criminal justice system is unduly draconian, and even supporters of the ultimate penalty may draw the line at its practice of executing traffickers in recreational drugs. Americans in particular will find Singapore's banning of chewing gum intolerable.[28] Nonetheless, and with full acknowledgment that no society this side of paradise is without flaws, we affirm that Singapore's trajectory over the course of the past half century is truly remarkable.[29]

The rationale for the preceding excursus is to announce the good news that a hardscrabble society that plays all its cards right can ascend the wealth ladder with remarkable rapidity. This, though, is only by way of a preface to yet better news: countries that possess even middling good institutions also make the ascent to wealth, albeit with less rapidity than Singapore. To put it another way, achieving excellence matters less than simply not being awful. The leading exemplar of this phenomenon is, of course, China. Under the rule of Mao, it had lurched from ordinary tyranny to mass starvation to bizarre autos-da-fé Asian-style. Its subsequent transformation under the guidance of Deng Xiaoping and his so-called market socialist colleagues is the great economic story of the past quarter century. It is important, however, to keep in mind that the transformation was far from a complete makeover. China continues to labor under the existence of a reduced but still substantial state-owned industrial sector that employs millions of workers (and that therefore is politically hot to handle), consumes capital and other productive resources, and yet in many instances is a value subtracter. The country's banking system operates under constraints other than profitability and lacks skills routine in Western best practice. (Admittedly, post-2008 it is debatable whether this is a curse or a blessing.) Development decisions have grossly failed to account for negative externalities with regard to environmental quality. Courts are not independent, and Chinese citizens have little recourse when the state engages in property takings with little or no compensation to those who are thereby shunted aside. And lest anyone forget the images of Tiananmen Square 1989, this is still very much a despotism that shows its teeth when it feels the need to do so. One would not do well to display in public support for the grievances of Falun Gong or the political rights of Tibetans. Moreover, China is a reliable supporter

[27] http://www.freetheworld.com/2012/EFW2012-complete.pdf.

[28] The authors are quite at ease with the crusade against sticky, dirty, unsightly chewing gum, but we freely admit that we find Singapore's high excise tax on wine and spirits all but intolerable.

[29] Josh Lerner's "Jamaica vs. Singapore," *The American*, November 19, 2009 (online magazine of the American Enterprise Institute), is an illumination comparison of two island nations of essentially the same area, population, and linguistic inheritance that, in 1965, enjoyed roughly the same GDP per person but which in 2006 had climbed, respectively, to $4,800 versus $31,400. In explaining the different experiences, Lerner emphasizes the countries' opposed levels of hospitality to entrepreneurship. See http://www.american.com/archive/2009/november/jamaica-vs-singapore.

of numerous other of the world's most appalling despotisms, including Sudan and North Korea. In other words, China still has a lot of catching up to do.

But catching up is precisely what China's citizens have enjoyed. Over the decades of the 1980s and 1990s, at least 200 million individuals have been boosted out of the roles of the very poor, and many millions are firmly on a trajectory toward affluence.[30] It is hard to think of any historical transformation that compares to this with regard to overall alleviation of misery. For those who believe that global poverty ought to be the key concern for justice theorists, the case of China ought to be paradigmatic. It is a proposition that we strongly endorse. By opening itself to world markets, protecting the property rights of investment capital (although not, unfortunately, the property rights of ordinary citizens), and allowing markets to take over territory that had previously been the prerogative of central planners, Chinese wealth creation took off. To some extent, this is an artifact of the wretched starting point that Maoist frenzies had brought about; simply eliminating a few of the most conspicuously enervating hindrances to wealth creation would lead to a high rate of growth, albeit from a small base. However, those eye-catching growth rates continue in a China that is as we write the world's second largest economy and may, by the time you read this, have become the biggest.[31]

It might be objected that China is an exceptional case, that the overwhelming size of its potential workforce gives it a heft in circles of money, power, and influence that no other developing economy enjoys. The point is well taken. China has been able to overcome institutional defects that do greater harm to less formidable countries. However, lesser actors also have managed to move from poverty to wealth despite considerable policy imperfections. Indonesia is an instructive example. Among the dynamic Asian Dragons, it had been more of a tree sloth. Its recent history, even when not horrific, has displayed self-stultification. Formerly a Dutch colony, Indonesia achieved independence after World War II under a charismatic Sukarno presidency supported by the Indonesian Communist Party. That regime came to an end in a sea of blood when an army faction under General Suharto revenged the assassinations of six fellow generals. A purge of communists and other supporters of the old regime resulted in at least half a million persons perishing. The toll was roughly equivalent to that of the American Civil War but compressed into a much shorter period. As generals are wont to do, Suharto assumed the Indonesian presidency in 1967, a position he held for more than thirty years. Although statistics in this area are hard to come by, Suharto and family distinguished themselves by corruption on a world-class scale, sharing ownership of assets and foreign bank accounts with compliant military supporters. The Asian financial crisis

---

[30] Vigorous debate over the quality of governmental statistics does not call into question the fact that China's transformation has been epochal. See Albert Park and Sangui Wang, "China's Poverty Statistics," *China Economic Review* 12(4) (2001), 384–98.

[31] On a per capita basis, China remains far down on world league tables but is ascending there, too.

of 1997–9 blew the kleptocracy away, but it left an Indonesia with doubtful
political leadership, ethnic rioting, Islamic terrorist attacks such as the October
2002 Bali nightclub bombing, and fissiparous provinces. Oh yes: in 2004, a
devastating tsunami wreaked havoc across Indonesia's many islands.

A narrative of economic disaster? Surprisingly, no. Although Indonesia
has not scaled the heights that Singapore (or Taiwan, Hong Kong, and South
Korea) has achieved, it is far from being one of the world's basket cases. In
1960, Indonesia's per capita GDP adjusted for purchasing-power parity was
a low 5.2 percent of that in the United States. In 1970, after the murderous
period of regime change, it had fallen to 4.6 percent. However, despite the
generous gratuities pocketed by Suharto, it had advanced in 1980 to 9.4 percent. Despite the financial crisis of the 1990s, it was 11.2 percent in 2000
and 12 percent in 2007. That is, Indonesia not only had achieved genuine
growth, but over this period it also had done so at more than twice the rate of
the United States.[32] Moreover, it had successfully effected a transition to functional democracy, largely removed the overpowering influence of the military
in politics (despite the president serving until late 2014 being a former general),
addressed religious and racial animosities, cracked down on corruption, and
with the exception of East Timor, held the country together.[33] Indonesia is by

---

[32] Statistics accessed July 8, 2013, from Alan Heston, Robert Summers, and Bettina Aten, *Penn
World Table Version 6.3*, Center for International Comparisons of Production, Income and
Prices (CIC), University of Pennsylvania, August 2009; available at: http://pwt.econ.upenn.edu/
php_site/pwt63/pwt63_form.php. GDP is, of course, only one measure of economic well-being,
and it is insensitive to distributional inequalities relevant to overall assessments of how burdens
are distributed within the borders of a country. We are keenly aware that the brief vignettes we
offer in this chapter speak only superficially to the quality of the lives that are experienced under
these different political orders. Our goal, however, is not so much to offer current assessments of
well-being across different income and wealth strata as it is to speak to what promotes within
countries' borders a march to greater affluence and what retards that progress. Of all readily
attainable and generally reliable measures, GDP growth is perhaps the single most revealing
indicator of achievement. Those wishing to take into account a broader range of factors bearing
on the freedom and livability of a country may wish to consult the Legatum Institute's Prosperity
Index at www.prosperity.com. The site self-describes: "The Legatum Prosperity Index is the
world's only global assessment of wealth and wellbeing; unlike other studies that rank countries
by actual levels of wealth, life satisfaction or development, the Prosperity Index produces rankings based upon the very foundations of prosperity – those factors that help drive economic
growth and produce happy citizens over the long term." Its 2012 rankings, for example, list
Singapore third in terms of economic fundamentals but only nineteenth overall because of various noneconomic shortfalls. (By way of comparison, Norway ranks first overall and the United
States twelfth.) Of course, this measure, too, is subject to interpretive disputes. Another attempt
to derive a more inclusive measure of well-being has been prepared by a committee appointed
by French President Nicolas Sarkozy under the chairmanship of Joseph Stiglitz. See "Report by
the Commission on the Measurement of Economic Performance and Social Progress"; available
at: http://www.stiglitz-sen-fitoussi.fr/en/index.htm.

[33] *The Economist*, September 12, 2009, includes a fourteen-page special report on Indonesia that
gives a good sense of the country's checkered past and current prospects. The report incorporates political and environmental discussions along with economic appraisal.

no means flawless. It suffers from serious infrastructure deficits, inflexible labor laws, and lingering suspicions of foreign investment. Its direction, though, continues to be clearly positive. This is so because even during the most grasping period of the Suharto years, producers enjoyed enough confidence in the stability of their property holdings to inject capital into the economy rather than sequester it in distant secret bank accounts. Tax rates are moderate, and government budgets are under control. Thus, despite a series of ups and downs worthy of an afternoon soap opera, Indonesians consistently find themselves becoming wealthier.

These are, of course, breathtakingly quick recaps of the economic history of not even a handful of countries. Much more analysis would be necessary to identify the relevant parameters for economic development, interpret the data, and give reasons to believe that these are truly representative cases. Fortunately, an extensive literature exists in which these questions are pursued by experts.[34] We leave interpretation of subtle details to others. The moral we draw is broad and unqualified: *if countries are not massively corrupt or incompetent (or both) with regard to the task of domestic economic development, they will become wealthier.* How quickly and with what effect on the incidence of poverty will differ based on policy soundness and the vagaries of local conditions. It is to say, however, that the problem of eradicating high levels of poverty has been solved – in theory. Practice is, of course, another matter. The practice in question is not, except to a very limited extent, that of potential foreign benefactors.[35] Although the governments of the world's well-off countries were distributing bushels of aid elsewhere, Singapore went matter-of-factly about its business and achieved wealth. China and Indonesia are riding the same train a few cars back. Far too many other societies, however, are still at the station – or rolling in reverse. This is so because they are set back by domestic failures.

HOW TO REMAIN POOR

Discussions of global justice sometimes soft pedal or entirely skirt the centrality of domestic inadequacies for explanations of poverty out of a misplaced concern not to "blame the victim." However, the real victims of, say, North Korean malnutrition, disease, and oppression are not the Kim Jong-un coterie that has continued a six-decade tradition of family despotism. The despair that is the lot of ordinary citizens owes very little to policies issuing from Washington, London, Brussels, or other wealthy capitals.[36] Rather, it is conceived, manufactured, and

---

[34] Of the hundreds of contributions to this literature, two that we have found especially compelling are Paul Collier, *The Bottom Billion: Why the Poorest Countries Are Failing and What Can Be Done about It* (Oxford University Press, 2008), and Daron Acemoglu and James A. Robinson, *Why Nations Fail: The Origins of Power, Prosperity and Poverty* (New York: Crown, 2012).

[35] We discuss foreign aid, both governmental and private, in Chapter 9.

[36] We exclude China from this list because if there is any foreign power properly held accountable for North Korean miseries, it is the one that has most conspicuously held out support to the current regime.

delivered from Pyongyang. Similarly, it is not the unlucky citizens of Myanmar who are to be blamed for the desperation of the lives they have been forced to endure. For half a century they were victims of tyrannical masters who are in a neck-and-neck competition with those of North Korea for the title of world's most odious rulers. Both countries have been islands of misery in an expanding sea of prosperity, but as we write, the noose around the necks of Myanmar's citizens has been loosened, if not yet entirely removed, by its military masters. Its post-2011 performance will provide more evidentiary grist for the mill of explaining wealth and poverty. So, too, does the example of South Korea. It has become something of an exemplar of how to do things right, and its prosperity stands in glaring contrast with the poverty and oppression of the sibling from which it was separated at birth. However, when the two Korean halves went to war in 1950, both were similarly impoverished outposts in a cold war where each was a supporting actor.[37]

The contrast between Myanmar and its neighbors is less pronounced but also worth noting. Equally worth noting is that the rulers of both global laggards have been in the grip of *ideologies* that motivate their undertakings to a considerably greater extent than does concern for the well-being of the citizenry. North Korea is, of course, one of the world's shrinking number of self-professedly communist regimes. Since 1962, Myanmar was ruled by cabals of generals professing a "Burmese way to socialism" vaguely based on Soviet models. These cases suggest a generally reliable indicator for developmental failure: countries that profess themselves "socialist," especially of a communist variety, will persistently underachieve. Cuba amply confirms this prediction, as do a fistful of African nations that, on gaining independence from colonial masters, looked eastward for doctrinal inspiration. China, too, fit this model until 1979. It is now a communist economic dynamo, but the communism of its economic planning owes a great deal more to Adam Smith than to Karl Marx. The single greatest contribution that outsiders could provide to these regimes would be to hold forth an eloquence so persuasive as to shock them out of the ideological sclerosis that now chains them down. Alas, no tongues that silver are in existence.

Socialisms less vicious than those that subscribe to the practices of Lenin and Stalin also can do considerable damage to wealth prospects. The classic example is postwar India, which, under Nehru's Congress Party, embraced a regime of central planning, suspicion of big business, and suffocating regulation enforced by armies of civil servants.[38] The consequence for more than

---

[37] It is difficult to secure reliable figures concerning North Korea's economic product and the proportion of it that trickles down to ordinary citizens. That the representative southerner's life prospects are massively more favorable than those of the representative northerner can hardly be in doubt.

[38] See Raghuram G. Rajan, "India: The Past and Its Future," *Asian Development Review* 23(2) (2006), 36–52.

four decades was the proverbial "Hindu rate of growth" that perpetuated the country's endless expanse of poverty. Only in recent years has the Fabian socialism that was India's patrimony begun to give way to freer markets. The result, as anyone who has phoned a help desk and received instructions in Bangalore-accented English realizes, is a country that is rapidly extending its presence in world markets and building a trajectory of growth that will make it the second megacountry to achieve a 100 million-plus reduction in the number of people who live under the $1.25 per day poverty level. Other countries of modest means that shortly after their birth emulated first-world practice by funding an elaborate welfare-state apparatus also have seen growth rates dragged down or sent into reverse. They would do better to look to Singapore, contemporary China, or Indonesia rather than to the European Union.

Socialism is not the only ideological construct that reliably saps the economic energies of its population. Any system that puts the productive resources of a society in thrall to governors with grand visions of remaking the social order by throttling markets is a likely candidate to put the brakes on wealth creation. One of the authors experienced this phenomenon in the name of Peronism, the political movement that has bedeviled Argentina off and on since 1945. (The current president of Argentina, Cristina Fernandez, self-identifies as a member of the Peronist Party, as did her late predecessor and husband Nestor Kirchner.) The legacy has been political instability, periodic economic crisis, and long-term stagnation. At the turn of the twentieth century, Argentina was one of the world's wealthier countries, roughly on a par with Canada. By the turn of the twenty-first century, it was well down on world tables and boasted not much more than a third of Canadian per capita GDP. Argentina is a country of abundant resources with an educated population, rich cultural tradition, and entrepreneurial energy. But, if current trends continue, it will become a South American laggard.[39] Not to the extent, however, we predict, of Venezuela. In good Popperian fashion we put our theory to the test of a falsifiable prediction. Venezuela labored under the autocratic rule of Hugo Chavez from 1999 until his death in 2013. His less charismatic but similarly illiberal successor, Nicolás Maduro, vows to continue Chavez's "Bolivarian Revolution." We confess that we have been unable to comprehend the fine points of this revolutionary program, but its practical effect is clear: increasing domination of the means of production by rulers who take as their inspiration Fidel Castro. The prediction is that Bolivarian Venezuela will spiral downward into economic and political distress. Readers are invited to remind us of this prediction five or ten years

---

[39] For a somewhat dated but lucid explanation of the Argentine decay, see Carlos S. Waisman, *Reversal of Development in Argentina: Postwar Counterrevolutionary Policies and Their Structural Consequences* (Princeton, NJ: Princeton University Press, 1987). The story is updated in an *Economist* survey essay, "The Tragedy of Argentina: A Century of Decline," *The Economist*, February 15, 2014; available at: http://www.economist.com/news/briefing/21596582-one-hundred-years-ago-argentina-was-future-what-went-wrong-century-decline.

from now, whether to our pleasure or pain. Of course, on another level, what would genuinely please us would be if, via one means or another, Venezuela would enjoy the good fortune to inter Chavez's ideas with his body.[40]

The other great destroyer of growth prospects is *corruption*. Surprisingly, perhaps, it is a lesser menace than ideology. This is so because national ideologies aspire to being all-encompassing, whereas corruption admits of degree. There is no country in the world in which officials are 100 percent spotless. In the United States, governors have a long history of outstretched hands – and not just for shaking those of constituents. Illinois has an especially keen tradition of gubernatorial graft, but others are not far behind. Spiro T. Agnew, Richard Nixon's first vice president, resigned from that office when offenses to which he had been party while governor of Maryland came to light. Nor is corruption confined to state capitals; the District of Columbia receives its full share. When lobbyist Jack Abramoff came under investigation in 2005, congressmen who formerly were his golf buddies scurried off like cockroaches when the lights are turned on. This sampling should not lead one to suppose that corruption is a peculiarly American phenomenon.[41] We are unaware of any wealthy country in the world that has not suffered from some amount of high-level corruption, and that is to leave out ordinary day-by-day practices of police, immigration officials, building inspectors, and so on who do not mind accepting under-the-table gratuities. These are not good either for the economy or regime legitimacy, but the harm they do is contained. So long as entrepreneurial risk-takers are assured that their gains will not be confiscated, they will be willing to generate wealth that is clipped in some small measure by their political silent partners. And, as the example of Indonesia suggests, even high levels of corruption can be endured when the profits left over are adequate to motivate productive investment.

Corruption can be thought of as like the loss of blood. When a healthy individual donates a pint (or loses that amount because of a mishap), the effect on activities is minor and temporary. When, however, the flow is large and unstanched, a tipping point will be reached on which health and life itself are imperiled. Countries, too, can lose their lifeblood. Within living memory (independence came in 1980), Zimbabwe (nee Southern Rhodesia) was perhaps the greatest hope for economic and political takeoff among recently decolonized African nations. It was in possession of a productive agricultural base, functional legal institutions, and a comparatively well-educated citizenry. Today, it is a shambles. Internecine violence has wrecked the country for the

---

[40] Some readers will complain that we have miscategorized Argentina and Venezuela under *ideology* rather than *corruption*. It is a close call, and the two tend to go together. Outcomes that are the misbegotten product of toxic ideologies are apt to stimulate rulers to steal in order to maintain the dream, and corrupt autocrats are liable to manufacture fantastical ideological propaganda to explain away the squalor they leave in their wake.

[41] For example, prior to Labour being cast out of office in the 2010 election, the United Kingdom underwent its greatest parliamentary financial sleaze scandal of recent times.

past decade, industrious wealth creators who were not expropriated have fled, the government cannot pay its debts despite – or because of – inflating its currency by more than 11 million percent, and poverty grew apace. The life expectancy of citizens fell by more than twenty years. One of the few measures that has shown a strong gain is the incidence of HIV infection.[42] This disaster is directly attributable to the predatory appropriations carried out by the government of Prime Minister Robert Mugabe and his ZANU Party, who have ruled the country since independence. In order to pay off supporters and ensure the loyalty of security forces, Mugabe engineered land "reforms" that progressively despoiled the country. Although Mugabe's personal wealth is undoubtedly very great, his holdings do not seem to have come close to those of Suharto (or former fellow African kleptocrat Mobuto Sese Seko). His thefts were more for the sake of buying enduring power than fat foreign bank accounts, and in that he succeeded brilliantly. Even when he lost the election of 2008, Mugabe refused to leave office. Opposition was met with increasing levels of brutality by his hired thugs and official misfeasance. Zimbabwe's descent was breathtaking and heartbreaking. Those who suffered most were, of course, the poor and powerless.

Nigeria's distress is comparable, but with a twist. Although possessed of abundant oil resources that could have provided the basis for a quick leap into prosperity, Nigeria's oil became more a curse than a blessing.[43] Resources so abundant were worth fighting over, and Nigeria has rarely enjoyed internal peace since achieving independence in 1960. Civil war between 1967 and 1970 with breakaway province Biafra cost the lives of a million civilians and combatants before unitary rule was restored. Mostly, Nigeria has been governed by generals, and mostly, they have been corrupt and vicious. By general consensus, the worst of this bad lot was Sani Abacha, who seized power in a 1993 coup and terrorized and bribed his way to an immense fortune before dying some five years later under circumstances that are said to be connected with an imprudent quantity of Viagra consumption. But even under restored civilian rule, property rights are insecure, graft considerable, violence against persons endemic, and, according to the CIA's *World Factbook*, some 70 percent

---

[42] Taken from the *World Factbook* (Washington, DC: Central Intelligence Agency, 2013), accessed July 8, 2013; available at: https://www.cia.gov/library/publications/the-world-factbook/rankorder/2155rank.html?countryname=Zimbabwe&countrycode=zi&regionCode=afr&rank=5#zi.

[43] In this, it is hardly unique. One problem with very large holdings of oil or some similarly valuable resource is that it affords governments an opportunity to live off of royalties rather than attempt to cultivate a widely distributed base of support among the citizenry at large. Large inflows of cash can readily be turned into armaments, soldiers' pay, bought-and-paid-for officials, bribes to voters whenever some semblance of an election is conducted, and the like. Moreover, it artificially enhances the value of the local currency, thereby rendering all other nonextractive industries uncompetitive. This phenomenon became known as the "Dutch disease" when manufacturing declined sharply in the Netherlands after a large natural gas field was discovered. For the coining of that term, see *The Economist*, November 26, 1977, 82–3.

of the population subsisting below the poverty line.[44] Not only with regard to oil but also rich farmland, minerals, and harbors, Nigeria is well endowed with resources. It is potentially among the world's wealthy societies, yet it is an underperforming state that fails to suppress domestic terrorist groups such as Islamist Boko Haram and regularly impoverishes and murders its citizens. As with Zimbabwe, Nigeria's misery is homegrown.

There are some two hundred nominally independent countries in the world, and it would strain patience to try to run through them one by one to test our theory of global poverty. The instances featured earlier are high-profile cases that have enjoyed considerable prominence in headlines as well as prompting numerous efforts in global statesmanship during recent years. A somewhat more obscure example may be illuminating precisely because classification is less clear-cut than for Singapore, on the one hand, or Zimbabwe, on the other. While thumbing through the pages of the June 20, 2009 issue of *The Economist*, we came across the obituary of Omar Bongo, late ruler of Gabon. We confess that this item tested both our geographic and political knowledge, but some side digging informed us that Gabon is a smallish country tucked in along the middle of the west coast of Africa and that it achieved independence from France in 1960. The obituary explains

Mr. Bongo made no distinction between Gabon and his private property. He had ruled there so long, 42 years, that they had become one. It was therefore perfectly natural that an oil company, granted a large concession for coastal drilling, should slip him regular suitcases stuffed with cash. It was natural that $2.6m in aid money should be used to decorate his private jet, that government funds should pay for the Italian marble cladding his palace, and that his wife Edith's sea-blue Maybach, in which she was driven round Paris, should be paid for with a cheque drawn on the Gabonese treasury. Of the $130m in his personal accounts at Citibank in New York, it was probable – though Citibank never asked, and nobody ever managed to pin a charge on him – that much of it was derived from the GDP of his country.[45]

By every reasonable standard, Bongo stands as an epitome of corruption. Nor is there any doubt that his country suffered therefrom. However, by local standards, Gabon was well favored in its governance. Bongo was harsh with opponents when necessary, but he was not a homicidal tyrant like other strongmen in the vicinity. Gabon did not undergo genocidal bloodletting or wholesale persecutions. Even Bongo's expropriations were moderate compared to those that took place in Zimbabwe and Nigeria, and during his long reign, the country enjoyed steadily increasing prosperity. According to the *CIA World Factbook*, its rate of growth was four times that of most of sub-Saharan Africa. "Mr. Bongo brought decades of tranquility, a rare enough commodity in Central Africa: order, and prosperity for a close and favoured few," *The Economist*

---

[44] https://www.cia.gov/library/publications/the-world-factbook/geos/ni.html.
[45] *The Economist*, June 20, 2009, 90.

sums up. Should Gabon be classified among the globe's failures or its qualified successes? It's a close call.

EFFECTIVE THERAPY REQUIRES ACCURATE DIAGNOSIS

We join the champions of global redistribution in affirming that where extremes of poverty are observed in the world, it is almost certain that injustice is being perpetrated. Where we take issue with them is in the conclusion that responsibility for the injustice is reflexively to be lodged against the wealthy nations of the world. To be sure, those nations have been and remain far from faultless in their policies toward the world's least-well-off. Commencing in Chapter 4, we have much to say about the specific wrongs that are done by the global rich to the global poor. It is important to keep in mind, however, that this is something of a sideshow. (Not all sideshows are epiphenomenal.) Primary responsibility for the poverty of the poor lies in the manifold indignities visited on them by their own masters. As Rawls himself observed, "[T]he problem [of poor countries] is commonly the nature of the public political culture and the religious and philosophical traditions that underlie its institutions. The great social evils in poorer societies are likely to be oppressive government and corrupt elites."[46] That these depredations are conceived and carried out domestically does not, of course, reduce their sting. Unless etiology is clarified, however, prospects for therapeutic measures are dim. Without wishing in any way to call into question the commitment and sincerity of the redistributionists, we must judge their program to be profoundly misguided. By looking westward ever westward, they obscure rather than clarify the nature of endemic global poverty.

Another respect in which we diverge from the global redistribution enthusiasts is in our assessment of whether the glass should be understood as being half full or half empty. Should one be heartened by inroads on global poverty that have been made during the preceding half century, or should one rather be disheartened by the magnitude of its persistence?[47] The answer, unsurprisingly, is some of each. However, stepping back just a bit from today's events to gain a bit of perspective, the case for optimism is overwhelming. Society-wide establishment of wealth has penetrated corners of the world in which it was heretofore unknown. The result is that hundreds of millions more people go to bed at night with full bellies in adequate shelters that house them and their children who have survived diseases of infancy and who will awaken in the morning to pursue occupations and educational opportunities that promise yet more to them and their families. Even self-contained philosophical types should be excited by what must justly be reckoned a world-epochal moment. In a way, though, it makes the poverty that persists yet more bitter in that it

---

[46] Rawls, *Law of Peoples*, 77.
[47] Paul Collier asks this question in *The Bottom Billion: Why the Poorest Countries Are Failing and What Can Be Done about It* (Oxford University Press, 2008).

has been shown to be *avoidable*. We salute the impatience of our redistributive colleagues who share this conclusion, although we reject their judgment that the preferred means of eliminating poverty is large-scale transfer from haves to have-nots. Considerations of justice aside – why should societies be penalized for their productivity? – such a strategy has been tried and found wanting. The general ineffectiveness of foreign aid is examined in Chapter 9. But failure of the aid paradigm need not be a cause for gloom. A different strategy has repeatedly shown itself to be an effective eradicator of poverty: free markets, robust property rights, rule of law. It has succeeded in Europe and North America, Japan, much of Southeast Asia, even to a limited but indicative extent in sub-Saharan Africa, the world's most recalcitrant region for wealth creation.[48] We cannot prove that this strategy is able to succeed elsewhere, but the burden of proof surely lies on those who contend that it cannot.

Thomas Pogge does not share our optimism. The glass, for him, is half empty or worse. He acknowledges that life expectancy and infant mortality figures have improved markedly in many countries, "[b]ut the number of people in poverty has not declined since 1987 – despite the fact that this period has seen exceptional technological and economic progress as well as a dramatic decline in defense expenditures.... These trends are all the more disturbing as the ranks of the poor and undernourished are continuously thinned by some 50,000 premature deaths daily from poverty-related causes."[49] In a footnote tied to this passage, Pogge explains, "The number of people below the doubled international poverty line has increased by 9.9 percent – or 20.7 percent if the special case of China is excluded."[50] Global population growth during the same period (1997–8) was about 18 percent. Do the data Pogge cites support the morose interpretation?

To the contrary, they tend to substantiate that this has been a period of marked progress in overcoming poverty. The figures reveal that the absolute number of the world's poor people grew during this period at a rate only half that of global population. Or, to give it a positive spin, even though birth rates in the world's wealthiest countries are low compared to the rest of the world and in some falling below zero population growth, the rate of increase in the world's nonpoor population is twice that of overall population growth. No credence should be given to exclusion of the "special case" of China. It is true that if all the gainers in some field of endeavor are left out of the accounting, what is left are only the laggards. This is not one of the more illuminating tautologies

---

[48] In any other region of the world, their success would be judged modest at best, but Botswana and Mauritius stand out as African exemplars. Two passionate yet hard-headed analyses of Africa's many failures but potential to break free from this cycle are Dambisa Moyo, *Dead Aid: Why Aid is Not Working and How There is a Better Way for Africa* (New York: Farrar, Straus and Giroux, 2009), and Robert Calderisi, *The Trouble with Africa* (New York: Palgrave Macmillan, 2006).

[49] Pogge, *World Poverty and Human Rights*, 99.

[50] World Bank, *Report 2000–2001*, 23.

that we have encountered. Rather than setting China to one side, it should be embraced as the single most revealing example of transformative possibilities. Were there special circumstances that account for the spectacular progress of China since 1979? Of course there were. For any country that enjoys accelerating growth, there are causal factors why it is so, factors that will not obtain in countries not experiencing growth. China is indeed a special case, but so too are Singapore, South Korea, and Botswana, as, for that matter, are Zimbabwe, Myanmar, and North Korea. There are no general covering laws in development theory (or perhaps anywhere in social science), so the best we can do is observe factors that usually are conducive of growth and those that are not. This is what the institutionalist accounts of Douglass North and David Landes cited earlier in footnote 18 do, as do Acemoglu and Robinson in *Why Nations Fail*. It is freely granted that what constitutes best practice in China may not work very well in India, and vice versa, Then again, it might. Lifting millions of people out of penury is to be celebrated and, if possible, learned from wherever it occurs. China is both cheering and instructive.

Focusing on absolute numbers of those in poverty rather than percentage is dubious because it is arbitrary. Shall we bemoan the increased numbers of the poor or instead take satisfaction from the (greater) increased numbers of the nonpoor? This is to circle back to the glass half-full/half-empty conundrum. There are other reasons, though, why looking primarily at absolute numbers is misleading. World population grew substantially over the period Pogge takes as his reference point. This occurred for two reasons: (1) babies being born and (2) people not dying.[51] These can, of course, go together in that decreases in infant mortality rates count as people who did not die. We take it to be all but uncontroversial that fewer people dying in any given period is a good thing. Note, though, that it is apt to appear as a negative in an accounting of total numbers of poor people.[52] Suppose that the infant mortality rate among the most destitute of the Earth is 100 out of every 1,000. Suppose further that their condition is improved as a result of a modest increase in nutritional and health-care access so that now only 50 infants die out of each 1,000. By any reasonable accountancy, this should be taken as an improvement worth acclaiming. Yet, if one simply counts noses of poor people, we will find that their number has increased by 50. Actually, the number will be much more than 50 because fewer poor mothers are dying in childbirth, fewer older siblings are dying, and so on.[53] Basic improvements in the condition of the least-well-off

[51] This is the sort of tautology more to our liking.

[52] It also can give a misleading appearance to figures of proportionate poverty. If poor people die off at an increasing rate compared to the rich, they will, all else being equal make up a decreasing percentage of the total.

[53] These numbers are used only for illustrative purposes. That there have been momentous gains in the health status of the poor is confirmed by numerous sources. To cite just one example, the World Health Organization's *Progress on Health-Related Millennium Development Goals*, dated May 2009, reports: "The proportion of under-nourished children under five years of

will mean that many more of them survive. Only to the misanthrope or the statistically challenged is this a cause for regret.

One final observation on the statistic Pogge cites: the poverty measure he invokes is the World Bank's *doubled* poverty line. This is $2 per day, which, confusingly, is defined as purchasing power equal to what $2.15 had in the United States in 1993. This is a Spartan level of existence, but it is far superior to the basic poverty line of $1 per day. Individuals who manage to ascend from below the basic line to somewhere below the doubled poverty line have thereby substantially improved their life prospects and those of their children. Yet that improvement will not be reflected in consideration only of the number of those who are categorized as poor on the basis of the more generous number.

In a way, this dispute between ourselves and Pogge does not matter. The point is not to debate how best to describe the status of the glass but to *fill it*! Far too great a number of the world's people are poor. That the poverty blighting their lives ought to be a central concern for ethics and, more specifically, justice is not a proposition concerning which we are in disagreement with Pogge. Nonetheless, it is not idle to attend seriously to the question of whether and how the plight of the world's poor has improved. If, like Pogge, you believe that the poverty problem has grown worse over recent decades, then you will not look to strategies that have been employed during that period as the primary engines for melioration. If, however, you believe as we do that enormous strides have been made all across the world in conquering endemic poverty and that establishment of market orders in which property rights are legally validated is a key to economic ascent, then you will believe that the basic problem is one of implementation, not discovery. The search for new global justice nostrums is apt to be not only unnecessary but positively pernicious insofar as it distracts theorists and practitioners from what has actually shown itself to be efficacious. Moreover, if you believe that the injustices that render people poor are mostly domestic – corrupt and despotic rulers, suffocating bureaucracies, suborned judges, redistributive schemes that sap incentives to produce – then you will not suppose that primary actors in global poverty alleviation will be the world's wealthy nations. Rather, their role is that of supporting actors: creditable but not puffed up with an inflated conception of their own centrality. In particular, one will give up the idea that solutions must take the form of greater willingness on the part of the well-off to transfer cash to foreign destinations. One should, therefore, be wary of declarations such as the following:

[S]evere and extensive poverty persists while there is great and rising affluence elsewhere. The average income of the citizens of the affluent countries is about 50 times

age declined from 27% in 1990 to 20% in 2005" and "Some 27% fewer children died before their fifth birthday in 2007 than in 1990." The same document also notes substantial improvements with regard to treatment for HIV/AIDS, a drop in malaria incidence, and enhanced access to safe drinking water. Available at: http://www.who.int/mediacentre/factsheets/fs290/en/index.html (accessed November 25, 2009).

greater in purchasing power and about 200 times greater in terms of market exchange rates than that of the global poor. The latter 2,800 million people together have about 1.2 percent of aggregate global income, while the 903 million people of the "high income economies" together have 79.7 percent. *Shifting merely 1 percent of aggregate global income – $312 billion annually – from the first group to the second would eradicate severe poverty worldwide.*[54]

Shifted where? To Kim Jong-un's North Korea? To Robert Mugabe's Zimbabwe? It could then be used to buy more uranium and build more prisons. Or perhaps to the late Omar Bongo's Gabon, where, to the surprise of absolutely no one, the son of the late president succeeded his father in office? He might be desirous of moving out of his father's old digs into a new presidential palace of his own. If the task of poverty alleviation were as simple as shifting accounting entries, then the world today would be a more humane place. To anticipate the upcoming discussion of foreign aid, it suffices for now to observe that those states that are most in need of external subventions are the ones that have shown themselves most conspicuously inept at managing the resources they already possess. One might as well try to alleviate poverty by handing crisp $100 bills to the derelicts on skid row. The stimulus to the heroin and cheap fortified wine industries would be temporary, after which the intended beneficiaries would, if anything, be worse off.

MORAL RESPONSIBILITY REVISITED

The case for transfers from the wealthy would be stronger if it can be made out that their gains are ill gotten, that they grow wealthier on the backs of the poor. After we spell out in upcoming chapters what we take to be the major injustices committed against the poor (including those committed by wealthy countries), we turn to questions of rectification. We conclude this chapter by examining a related contention – that domestic governance failures are not really domestic at bottom but rather the responsibility of the wealthy. This would seem to be a hard case to argue after even a cursory look at truly evil characters such as Robert Mugabe or even lukewarm despots such as Omar Bongo. Pogge contends, however, that the deep responsibility for their depredations lies with their enablers. It is the wealthy nations of the world that recognize their right to rule, contract with them to extract and purchase the country's resources, and extend loans that become the responsibility of their successors in office and, ultimately, the citizenry to pay off. And, of course, it is countries like the United States that sell them the armaments that delight the generals and oppress the masses.[55]

We acknowledge merit to some of these charges. In particular, supplying military tools to tyrants is itself a violation of basic rights when it is

---

[54] Pogge, *World Poverty and Human Rights*, 2 (emphasis added).
[55] Ibid., 112–17.

predictable by the seller that their primary employment will be as means of oppression. Toward the remainder of the complaint, however, we are less sympathetic. Ultimately, Pogge's dissatisfaction lies with the Westphalian model of state sovereignty that has endured some three and a half centuries. Would the world be better off if it were not divided up into exclusive domains of undivided sovereignty? The question is unanswerable unless one is told what is to replace a world of states. If it is to be one monolithic world government, a United Nations with teeth and without members to which it is beholden, we share Kant's worries that this would likely be inefficient and unrepresentative.[56] Anarchistic capitalism probably deserves more serious consideration than it usually receives, but although its ideal theory is attractive, the stability of patches of anarchy ringed by conventional states is doubtful. Imperial orders are distinctly out of fashion; even if one believes that some of today's faltering states were much better governed when they were colonies of one of the European powers, that train has left the station. At any rate, it is distinctly utopian to conjure up a world in which states have lost their political primacy. Although an honorable part of philosophy is contemplation of what has never been and may never be, the part in which we (and, we presume, Pogge) locate ourselves is less metaphysical and more practical. Tempting as it is to imagine away states, this chapter restricts itself to consideration of which of their actions are permissible, which commendable, and which deplorable.

Receiving loans is, as Pogge observes, often a snare and a folly for countries in need of some picking up by their own bootstraps. Crippling debts can be taken on for projects that feed the megalomania of their presidents-for-life more than they do hungry mouths back in villages. Added to the manifold burdens of poverty are additional burdens of fealty to the barons of global finance, burdens that persist so long as balances remain outstanding. That period can extend through the reigns of several despots as costs come due to the children and grandchildren of those who were the original recipients of the financing. For poor countries, then, the bankers are a curse. There is, though, one thing worse than free access to world capital markets: the absence of such access. The poverty of the poor is not so much a shortage of natural resources or willing labor; it is disproportionately the paucity of its capital stock (including, but not directly relevant in this context, human capital). If only internal resources are relied on for expansion of that pool, the progression toward affluence will necessarily be glacial. This is so because even high rates of saving and investment from a microscopic base yield small returns. If, however, internal sources are multiplied many times over by external investments from those economies that have already achieved abundance, the progress is speeded up. This largely explains why the second great economic explosion that took place after 1945

---

[56] See "Perpetual Peace," esp. 113–14 and 127; "Metaphysics of Morals," 171, both in H. S. Reiss, ed., *Kant: Political Writings* (Cambridge University Press, 1970).

proceeded so much more quickly than the first. The gains that England and America achieved over the course of a century took barely a generation to emulate in Singapore. This is so because Singapore could and did avail itself of mobile capital from abroad. Now that Singapore has achieved affluence, it, in turn, is possessed of vast capital resources that are finding deployment beyond its borders.[57] We are not claiming that acquiring indebtedness is without risk. As the events of 2008 should remind one, such risks are borne both by wealthy and poor countries. The difference is that those who already are wealthy can better afford to play it safe; those subsisting on the edge of exigence cannot. They are not in a position to forgo the perils of globally interdependent relationships for the dubious charms of autarky. Those societies that do wall themselves off from capital markets are among the most unpleasant places on the planet. North Korea is a cautionary example. The problem, then, is not taking on debt; it is taking on foolish, unproductive debt.

Similar comments apply to entering into contracts for the extraction and export of resources. Countries on the bottom of the economic food chain usually will not have sophisticated industrial operations and services to market beyond their borders. If they are to engage in trade at all, that trade is liable to be dominated by primary products and, after a sufficient quantity of investment is made, labor-intensive manufactured products.[58] The process of selling primary products is risky. One of the risks is that naive leaders of poor countries will peddle their nation's patrimony to sly and cunning international capitalists for a pittance. The greater risk, though, is that sly and cunning rulers of these poor countries will drive a market price for the resources but then themselves appropriate a disproportionate share of the proceeds for tanks, palaces, and, of course, numbered bank accounts. Despotism is almost always a bad thing, but fabulously wealthy and powerful despots are a greater plague than those of modest means and ambitions. When multinational corporations do business with some general-turned-president-for-life, do they thereby commit an injustice?

This is a difficult issue, but in general, we believe that the answer is no.[59] The dollars or euros that pour into a poor country can be used for nutrition, education, and health services for the populace while simultaneously putting a great number of people to remunerative work. Alternatively, they can be used to clamp down more firmly on a distressed citizenry. Only rarely will the purchasing corporation be in a position to choose which it is to be. In a sense, such corporations are enablers, but whether it is good or evil that they enable is not up to them. The case is roughly analogous to that of a retail merchant

---

[57] See chap. 3, "Pro-Growth Economic Policies," in Ghesquiere, *Singapore's Success*.

[58] India's sophisticated service industry is something of an exception. It has burgeoned because of a plentiful supply of competent speakers of English and pockets of higher education excellence in an otherwise ghastly swamp of state schooling.

[59] See our discussion of trade in Chapter 5.

selling items such as guns and poisons that are capable of either benign or malign uses. Walmart is not to be blamed or praised for what its customers do with the items they buy. Nor, for that matter, are shoppers to be blamed for what the CEO of Walmart elects to do with his paycheck. It is a principle of law that a chain of responsibility terminates in the free choice of another agent. To be accountable for one's own actions is quite enough of a moral burden, let alone to be held responsible for the actions of those with whom one transacts. Purchasers of oil or diamonds or bauxite are morally obligated to take no more than what the seller agreed to relinquish, to pay the full price as contractually specified, to comply with the tax laws of the jurisdictions under which they operate, to make required disclosures to shareholders, and so on. They are not obliged in addition to plumb the conscience of the party with whom they do business.[60]

On occasion, though, it is precisely the conscience of that party – or lack of same – that fuels the transaction. If one knows or has abundant reason to know that the transaction is meant to supply the means for carrying out an injustice, then a choice to take part in it renders one complicit in those wrongs that predictably result. The paradigm case is the company that happily sells electric cattle prods to the dictator of a country that does not have herds but is well supplied with prisons. A company that does this in full knowledge cannot plead with any plausibility that it was just "doing business." Similarly, it is not usually the responsibility of a Walmart clerk to delve into customers' intentions. However, if asked, "Is this gun powerful enough to put away a lying, cheating, no-good husband?" the indicated course is not to tout the firepower of the weapon so as to complete the sale. Some cases are easy, and others hard. The burden of proof, though, is on the critic to show that a particular transaction crosses the line from ordinary business dealing to the moral equivalent of conspiracy to commit a felony. It will not be enough to know that the rulers of the country with which one transacts are generally a thuggish or kleptocratic sort. Almost never are autocrats exclusively in the business of oppressing citizens. Rather, there will be some kind of balance between exploiting and assisting, between waving carrots and brandishing sticks. It is true that money not paid for the country's goods is money that will not buy tools of oppression. But neither is it money that will pay for teachers or nurses. To turn away a profitable business offer is to take a morally risky position with regard to one's shareholders and employees. To do so when the effect of the proposed venture may well have been net benefit to the citizens of that country magnifies the moral risk. Sometimes executives will be in a position to ascertain where the balance of harm and benefit lies, but this is not likely often to be the case. Their expertise is primarily with regard to costs and benefits that accrue to their own

---

[60] For a vigorous defense of a position contrary to the one we argue here, see Leif Wenar, "Property Rights and the Resource Curse," *Philosophy & Public Affairs* 36 (2008), 2–32. We discuss further Wenar's views in Chapter 6.

company; delicate calculations of burdens and benefits in distant societies is not what they have been trained to carry out.

Indeed, no small measure of arrogance attaches to usurping from the citizens of an independent country responsibility for the actions of their leaders and placing it for better or worse on the heads of foreign corporate executives. This is reminiscent of an old-style imperialism now thoroughly out of fashion: reminiscent but worse. At least the imperial power explicitly assumed responsibility for providing the colony institutions of governance and justice. Notoriously, failures in this regard were many, but it was then clear whose failures they were and who was responsible for making shattered lives whole. Multinational corporations, however, do not enjoy even a pretension of legitimacy in decision making for those distant others. Should they follow the strictures of moral critics who bid them to remove themselves from dealing with unsavory regimes, they do not thereby act to enhance justice. They simply abdicate their corporate role. It hardly needs adding that their unwillingness to transact does not mean that the regime will be unable to market its primary goods or secure financing. Rather, they will simply turn to less scrupulous business partners, those even less inclined to whisper reminders in the dictators' ears about the weal of the masses. The most conspicuous contemporary ask-no-embarrassing-questions business partner is China. There is no regime so murderously sordid that it is off-limits to Chinese purchasers. Were the United States completely to boycott, say, Sudan and Congo, conceding the trade road to China, it is exceedingly unlikely that the result would be an efflorescence of justice and well-being in those states.

Nor does promulgating multilateral boycotts seem very useful. Usually when these gather some steam it is not because the target regime is especially noxious but because of political considerations. Apartheid South Africa labored under vile governance, but so too did many of its neighbors, all of whom remained sanction free. As we write, the United States is working hard to impose sanctions on would-be nuclear power Iran but not nuclear power India or nuclear power Israel. However, all sorts of other states and politically engaged groups do wish to engineer sanctions on Israel, the only remotely democratic and liberal nation in its part of the world. Boycotts tend to be flagrantly violated by those parties that have an interest in doing business with the denounced country. Only rarely, if ever, can we be confident that a boycott is doing more damage to the oppressive government than to the oppressed populace. Iraq between the Gulf wars was a country in which Saddam Hussein continued to ride high while babies died of malnutrition. Perhaps the single most striking effect of that boycott was to increase the United Nations' level of corruption, a feat akin to making the sea saltier.

The conclusions we reach with regard to the value of access to credit markets and vending natural resources will disappoint readers in search of handy rules of thumb that can be applied across the board. Sometimes a citizenry is mired in a deeper and deeper pit by the extravagant borrowings of its masters, but in other environments citizens become the beneficiaries of a growing capital stock that enables them to escape the poverty trap. The record of resource sellers is also mixed. Pogge claims, "It has been well known among economists for quite some time that there is a significant *negative* correlation between a developing country's resource endowment and its rate of economic growth."[61] At best, this describes the tendency of a few decades' standing. One observes that formerly developing countries United States and Australia achieved considerable wealth despite the "handicap" of vast natural resources. Brazil may currently be emulating those earlier successes, and someday even a post-Putin Russia may choose to follow suit. Botswana fares better than almost any other African country: is this despite or because of being a repository of diamonds? Note that even if the presence of resources does on average retard growth, it is a non sequitur to infer that a policy of not marketing these resources will advance the rate of growth. What a casual empiricism reveals is that those countries in which economic liberties are protected do well both if they possess abundant natural resources and if they do not. There are, of course, mixed cases. One is Omar Bongo's Gabon. Bongo was by any account an autocrat, an accumulator, an anachronism. In these various regards, he was worse than some of his peers yet better than many. Gabon did not prosper under his reign as well as it might have done. Neither, though, did it completely stagnate or, worse, regress. Was it a good thing that international corporations chose to do business with Bongo? To a high degree of probability, yes. Was the Bongo regime worthy of accolades? Clearly not. Putting those two kinds of questions together is an invitation to muddle.

Pogge's urging developed countries to avoid resource purchases and long-term loans to *undemocratic countries* seems particularly ill judged.[62] The extent to which countries are democratic is not a very good predictor of whether loans taken out and resources sold will redound to the eventual benefit or misery of the population. It is clear that many of the world's great success stories with regard to marching toward prosperity began that journey as undemocratic satrapies. These include Taiwan, South Korea, Thailand, and, of course, China. All but the latter have become markedly democratic either in spite of their international economic entanglements or, as we think more likely, in large measure because of them. Singapore itself is a highly civilized place to live and work but not distinguished for vibrant democracy. Zimbabwe, however, became progressively more predatory in service of the ruling party's desire to reward electoral majorities with the proceeds of it appropriations. Other countries also have managed to combine democracy with demagoguery to the

---

[61] Pogge, *World Poverty and Human Rights*, 163.

[62] See chap. 6, "Achieving Democracy," in Pogge, *World Poverty and Human Rights*, 146–67. Pogge proposes implementation by "creation of a standing Democracy panel under the auspices of the UN" (156). Given the makeup of the United Nations and its internal political dynamics, this does not strike us as a promising nostrum.

detriment of their citizenry. Argentina's record over the past eighty years is a cautionary example of the limited value of the trappings of democracy. More important than democracy per se is protection for property and a legal order that strives toward impartiality. Where these obtain, democracy well may follow, and its absence will be less inimical to the aspirations of citizens. Where they are absent, prospects for a sweeping diminishment of poverty are meager.

The international legal order is such that, over a wide range, the say over what form of governance is acceptable for any given state belongs primarily to its own citizens. John Quincy Adams in his Independence Day 1821 oration said of America, "Wherever the standard of freedom and Independence has been or shall be unfurled, there will her heart, her benedictions and her prayers be. But she goes not abroad, in search of monsters to destroy. She is the well-wisher to the freedom and independence of all. She is the champion and vindicator only of her own." Both prudentially and morally, this is remarkably good advice. On occasions when the United States has adopted a contrary policy, including in the current century, results have often been other than desired. Moreover, attempts by it and other wealthy and powerful countries to superintend internal arrangements of others have often generated resentment on the part of the intended beneficiaries. This is a good reason to eschew opportunities to climb up on the moral soapbox and deliver instructions to the world's benighted. To be sure, there really are benighted regimes; we are no more devotees of a vapid cultural relativism than is Pogge. We do, though, recognize the desirability of a division of labor among the world's various polities, a division that makes each the champion and vindicator of its own liberty.[63]

This chapter's argument has been that quagmires of distress are avoidable, that where they nonetheless fester it is very likely that the cause is great injustice, but that for the most part the relevant injustices are homegrown. Wealthy countries such as the United States are, with very few exceptions, off the hook as primary perpetrators of endemic poverty. There are, however, other hooks. Wealthy countries can properly stand accused as secondary victimizers, as culpably making worse a distress of which they are not themselves the agents. This is the theme of the next three chapters.

[63] This prudential advice does not preclude the philosophical inquiry about the moral standing of states that we undertake in Chapter 7.

4

Immigration

However else one may choose to evaluate the argument of Chapter 3, it should not be taken as an apologia for rich countries' impositions on the poor. Just the reverse: although it is always and everywhere impermissible to wrong others, all the more so is this the case with inflictions on those already down and out. Duties of special care are owed to those who are most vulnerable, and this surely includes the billion or so people who live under the $1.25 per day poverty line. Saying, "We are not the ones who put them there!" is not an adequate defense. Response to a further question is called for: "Do your policies and actions help to keep them there?" Unfortunately, the answer far too often is yes.

BEYOND RAWLSIAN GLOBAL JUSTICE

Traditionally, the search for a theory of justice across borders began with consideration of *jus ad bellum*, conditions that must be met in order to wage a just war. This is also pretty much where it ended, with a few codicils thrown in concerning reception of diplomatic emissaries, extension of princely courtesies, and fidelity to pacts duly sworn between sovereign entities. Although in *Law of Peoples*, Rawls' concerns extend beyond those of predecessors such as Grotius and Pufendorf, the genre is the same: duties owed by one state (or in Rawls' preferred locution, *people*) to another. That is, the parties involved are political collectivities, not the individual citizens of which they are comprised. However one appraises, then, the success of Rawls' account as far as it goes, it is facially incomplete. Along with an appraisal of state-to-state relations, the fuller account of global justice will include actions across borders that involve (1) states acting on private individuals, (2) private individuals acting on private individuals, and (3) private individuals acting on states. Further complicating the taxonomy is existence of entities such as international organizations (the

United Nations, the World Trade Organization [WTO], etc.) and nongovernmental organizations (NGOs), which are not sovereign states but neither are they purely voluntary assemblages of private parties. Some NGOs operate mostly to serve the philanthropic and other ends of private parties: Oxfam is an example. Some straddle the public/private divide. It is not our intention to offer a comprehensive global-justice account that fills in each of these boxes. Rather, the primary goal in this and the next two chapters is to speak to significant types of state policies that unjustly impose hardships on people – not peoples – of other nationalities. A secondary goal is to identify ways in which private parties knowingly or inadvertently act as accomplices to state-imposed wrongings.

Several important species of global injustice will receive only a passing glance in these pages. At one time it would have seemed reasonable to excuse omission of the third category, private individuals acting unjustly against states. These, one might suppose, at worst count as trifling inconveniences, mere flea bites to the tough hide of leviathan. After September 11, 2001, such a dismissal is no longer so plausible. The phrase "war on terror" is unfortunate, giving the impression that the opposition in question is to certain methods of conducting combat. Nonetheless, either war or something very much like *war against terrorists* is being conducted by the United States and other countries in multiple theaters across the globe. Because counteroperations against terrorists can be carried out with greater or lesser adherence to principles of justice, attentiveness to this aspect of global justice is of undoubted salience. It is, however, either a proper part or a closely related adjunct to theories of just war and justice in war. We discuss war in Chapter 8, with only a passing reference to injustices imposed as a consequence of state counteroffensives against terrorist foes.[1]

In this chapter the focus is migration restrictions that thwart efforts to live, work, or study temporarily in a would-be host country as well as intentions to settle there permanently. Chapter 5 discusses the brain-drain objection to freer borders, whereas Chapter 6 addresses barriers to free trade imposed by states either unilaterally or through multilateral agencies such as the WTO. As was observed in Chapter 3, many millions of people are not only impoverished but also brutalized by their own governments, so Chapters 7 and 8 take up questions concerning the legitimacy of states and our duties not to assist bad regimes, as well as what positive duties, if any, states have to defend themselves and to intervene to put down foreign tyrants. In each case, the argument developed will claim not only that distant others are rendered worse off because of the policies of wealthy countries such as the United States but also that they are *wronged*: their rights not to be interfered with in their lives, liberty, and

---

[1] For an examination of the concept of terrorism and the morality of unconventional war, see Fernando R. Tesón, "Targeted Killings in War and Peace: A Philosophical Analysis," in *Targeted Killings: Law and Morality in an Asymmetrical World*, Claire Finkelstein, Jens Ohlin, and Andrew Altman, eds. (Oxford University Press, 2012), 417–19.

property are violated. To err in this regard is not merely to be less charitable or compassionate than one might have been; it is to perpetrate an injustice. As Chapter 2 argued, we are not generally obligated to extend ourselves to provide positive relief to distant (or even nearby) others, but we must not erect barriers that block their own peaceful pursuits. Distressingly often, however, policies adopted by wealthy countries (and, of course, poor ones) culpably worsen the position of those who are already hard-pressed. These policies typically are not thought of as raising issues of justice; they are simply classified under *border control* or *commerce* or *diplomacy*. So regarded, they unproblematically fall within the ambit of ordinary domestic politics. Is it not a bit melodramatic, one might ask, to treat these as being on a par with theft, unlawful imprisonment, or assault? In fact, they are precisely equivalent. Disguising awareness of the equivalence are the distance of victims and familiarity of the offenses. Innumerable practices – for example, slavery, enforced female subservience, persecution of homosexuals – were at one time taken for granted but now are clearly seen to be unjust. Moral myopia strikes in different ways in different environments and ages. To suppose that our current state of enlightenment has put all species of invidious discrimination behind us is an optimism called into question by that prior experience.

FREEDOM OF ASSOCIATION

Human beings, Aristotle famously informs, are social animals. More distinctively, they are animals that *choose* the company they keep. Not all of it: we are born into families we did not choose and that did not exactly choose us. Also, the communities in which we find ourselves constitute the basis of associations that will give form to our lives. However, within the unchosen parameters of the feasible, our own voluntary undertakings establish for each of us a personal society in which our most important relationships are established. In some measure or other this has always been the case for post–hunter-gatherer humanity, but under conditions of modernity, the ratio of self-determined to antecedently given social ties has greatly expanded. Both fueling and being fueled in turn by that expansion is the philosophy of *liberalism*. Liberalism's stake in freedom of association can be traced along many dimensions.[2] The early liberal campaign for *freedom of religion* was in part a demand to be permitted to dissociate on grounds of conscience from a community of faith incompatible with one's own convictions and instead to participate in another found to be more congenial. Liberal *abolitionism* was predicated on the injustice of coerced bondage of slave to master, and emancipation promised no less and no more than liberty to associate with others on a voluntary basis. *Freedom of assembly* was the right to come together with willing others to

---

[2] This section builds on the discussion of Loren Lomasky, "The Paradox of Association," *Social Philosophy & Policy* 25 (Winter 2008), 182–200.

promote a cause to which all mutually subscribe. It goes hand in hand with *freedom of speech*.

Not least among the early liberal aspirations was breaking shackles that impeded *residential and occupational mobility*. Adam Smith is rarely more eloquent than when he is protesting laws that restricted the job-seeking ventures of would-be workers: "To remove a man who has committed no misdemeanor from the parish where he chooses to reside, is an evident violation of natural liberty and justice.... There is scarce a poor man in England of forty years of age, I will venture to say, who has not in some part of his life felt himself most cruelly oppressed by this ill-contrived law of settlements."[3] Bit by bit, oppressive guilds and monopolies were stripped of their coercive privileges to the betterment of the prospects of ordinary workers who asked simply to be allowed to proffer their services to willing employers. People demanded and won the liberty to leave impoverished rural areas for industrial labor in the cities. The U.S. Constitution recognizes the right of citizens to trade and to travel beyond the borders of their home states on equal terms with those who reside in other states. One is put in touch with a matter of some national shame by reading the passages in John Steinbeck's *The Grapes of Wrath* in which the Joad family is stopped at the California border and denied entry because the quota of Okies had already been filled up, but it is a corresponding matter of national pride that nothing like that could ever again be allowed to happen.

Yet happen it does, not only in California but also along every other port of entry into the United States. A denial of mobility that would be intolerable if enforced between one of the fifty states against another is merely business as usual, unexceptionable to all but a handful of libertarians, when it occurs along the border separating one of those fifty states from foreign territory. The right by a host country to exclude on almost whatever grounds it sees fit to impose[4] is generally taken for granted. However, it is not easy to develop a convincing rationale for that judgment, especially as the onus of proof would seem to rest on the party that wishes to thwart the liberty of would-be peaceful migrants. This is to say, unless there is compelling reason to block entry, whether it is from Oklahoma to California or Mexico to California, then there is compelling reason *not to block* entry. People's life plans, their aspirations for themselves and for their loved ones, rest crucially on a capacity to pick themselves up and resettle in a venue where they are better able to pursue that which matters to them. Moreover, their ability to move to the desired location constitutes a good also for those with whom they will interact once they arrive. Potential employers, landlords, friends, relatives, and lovers all have a stake in the would-be migrant's liberty to choose a place of domicile. For reasons such as these, established systems of apartheid, Jim Crow, and caste exclusions have been disassembled *within* many

---

[3] Smith, *Wealth of Nations* (Indianapolis, IN: Liberty Press, 1981), 157.
[4] A limited exception is refugee status, discussed later.

jurisdictions. However, similar exclusion *across* jurisdictions does not seem to trouble enlightened opinion nearly as much. It is maintained, or perhaps more often tacitly assumed, that national citizenship is not only a relevant factor but one decisive in buttressing a case for differential treatment. On examination, this case is seen to be thin.

Parceling out burdens on the basis of nationality is *morally arbitrary*. Bennet is born two miles north of the Rio Grande, whereas Dashwood at just the same moment is born two miles to its south. From the moment of birth on, Bennet is the recipient of an infrastructure that favorably conditions his life prospects. He can avail himself of health care and educational services that are of world-class standing, and eventually he will be welcome to enter an economic system in which employment and earning prospects are strong. In each of these areas, Dashwood's prospects are inferior. Investment in her human capital is apt to be a small fraction of that enjoyed by Bennet, and her lifetime earning prospects are correspondingly diminished. How unfortunate her choice not to have entered the world farther north!

Of course, there was no choice in the matter, at least not by Bennet or Dashwood, so this difference in life prospects is not something that either can be said to deserve.[5] Rather, the difference is a brute fact to be confronted. People may debate whether it is the proper business of political institutions to meliorate the disparity by transferring additional resources to Dashwood, but what seems to be beyond debate is that no additional impediments to well-being should be imposed on her. This, though, is what exclusionary border controls do. If Bennet is at liberty to pursue excellent life prospects from which Dashwood is barred on dubious grounds of geography, an injustice has been committed.[6] Note that this is not an argument to subsidize Dashwood's travels to the opportunities she seeks. No claim to positive assistance need be advanced here, although we presume that many global egalitarians would be sympathetic to that addition. Rather, it is purely an argument against coercive interference. Blocking Dashwood's mobility in pursuit of a better life is wrong. More precisely, it is a wrong done to her.[7] The armed guards at the border harmfully coerce potential immigrants by preventing them from interacting in valuable ways with others. Coercively

---

[5] The point about lack of desert is modeled on that offered in John Rawls, *A Theory of Justice* (Cambridge, MA: Harvard University Press, 1971), 15, 72–4. We are skeptical, however, of the idea that *inborn talents* can be deserved or undeserved: see our discussion of brain drain in Chapter 6.

[6] It is possible but less likely that Bennet might suffer from the denial of a liberty to take up employment or some other opportunity in Mexico. There exists a theoretical symmetry between the cases, but the size of the gulf between equality in theory and in practice is precisely the measure of how much border exclusions systematically disadvantage the least-well-off.

[7] The argument is developed more extensively in Loren Lomasky, "Toward a Liberal Theory of National Boundaries," *Boundaries and Justice*, David Miller and Sohail Hashmi, eds. (Princeton, NJ: Princeton University Press, 2001), 55–78.

stopping a person from crossing a political border is, then, a violation of that person's right to free association.[8]

Sympathies tend to be a decreasing function of distance. It is not, therefore, surprising that most of us are more attentive to the weal and woe of compatriots than of foreigners. Nor is this necessarily morally discreditable. As argued in Chapter 2, individuals are not required to be scrupulously impartial between the interests of the near-and-dear and distant others. Favoritism with regard to sponsorship of personal travel is no vice. Therefore, for example, Bennet does no wrong when he purchases for his daughter an all-expenses-paid trip to attend a U2 concert when, for the same amount of money, he might have funded Dashwood's urgent job-seeking quest. The limit to permissible partiality is set, however, by the rights of others. Anonymous others as much as valued compatriots must be treated with justice. Thus, although it is psychologically explicable why people tend to be more disturbed by wrongs done to countrymen than to foreigners, those emotional reactions do not constitute a justification for disparate treatment. Note, though, that phrasing the issue in this way misleadingly suggests that the only rights in question are those of foreign nationals. In most instances, this will not be the case. Association is a two-way (or more) relationship. If Dashwood is denied entry, then the liberty of everyone north of the border who may have wished to interact with her is compromised. If Bennet is desirous of hiring Dashwood to tend his garden and clean his swimming pool, then Bennet's liberty every bit as much as Dashwood's is impugned by her exclusion. The difference, of course, is that Bennet very likely will suffer much less from this foreclosing of the relationship than will Dashwood. This is one of the many privileges of affluence. Some will be unmoved by this example, holding that minor inconveniences to the very fortunate amount at most to moral trivialities. We regard this response both as invidious reverse discrimination against the well-off and a manifestation of insufficient appreciation of the importance in people's lives of commercial relationships. But in deference to the sensibilities of critics, we are willing to change the example. Dashwood, let us imagine, is someone's lover, kept apart from him or her by the inflexible regulations of the immigration control people. (She has not filled out the right papers; there are no right papers to fill out; whatever.) It ought to be even clearer in this case that harms are multiple, that they are located on both sides of the domestic/foreign divide, and that they are wrongs done to those who are thereby rendered worse off.

There is, then, a strong presumption against barriers to entry. In a previous version of this argument, the point was put: state boundaries should be very much like the boundaries of states.[9] This seemingly tautologous statement is a play on the word "state," a designation of both national entities such as

---

[8] See Michael Huemer, "Is There a Right to Immigrate?" *Social Theory and Practice* 36 (2010), 429, 435.

[9] Lomasky, "Toward a Liberal Theory of National Boundaries," 73.

Mexico and the United States and also of subnational political divisions such as North Carolina and South Carolina. Although states in the second sense have their own geographically specified areas of jurisdiction, codes of law, and regulatory institutions, they present no barriers to personal mobility. Unlike national entities, their borders are *soft*. The first approximation to a satisfactory theory of justice in personal mobility is that the borders that separate nation-state from nation-state should be similarly softened. The United States will remain a jurisdiction separate from Mexico with its own distinctive laws and institutions and culture, but it will afford unencumbered passage to those who wish to come over and try their luck. To this should be added a proviso acknowledging legitimate considerations of national and personal security. On any theory of what nation-states are for, defense against aggressors foreign and domestic is part of the package. (For the so-called night-watchman state it is the whole package.) Those who have demonstrated through their words or behavior (or, in cases such as being afflicted by a highly contagious disease, their condition) a likelihood of harming those they encounter can justifiably be excluded. The standard of proof to be met need not be nearly as high as that required for a verdict of guilty in a criminal trial. Nor need it involve any showing of culpability, as the disease example illustrates. This is so because the government acts as an agent on behalf of citizens who have a substantial interest in avoiding harms. It is not the agent of noncitizens. To them it owes only the universal duty of not violating their basic rights.

This proposal of qualified open entry will strike many as fanciful: utopian at best, chaotic at worst. Yet it is a close likeness to actual U.S. immigration policy during the hundred years preceding the passage of the *Immigration Act of 1924*.[10] If you could get yourself to a port of entry, and if you were not disqualified by some medical condition or morals charge, you were entitled to enter the country and remain however long you liked, typically for life. Certainly poverty was not an exclusionary factor; rather, it was the typical condition of those who arrived. They yearned to escape oppression, and they yearned to make money. More often than not, the two went together. Emma Lazarus' lines about "your tired, your poor, your huddled masses yearning to breathe free" were well placed and well acclaimed when inscribed on the Statue of Liberty in 1903. They may not strike the contemporary ear quite so favorably. Perhaps this is due to a lessened taste for sentimentality in verse (but then why continuing success of the Hallmark cards company?), but perhaps it is instead the vast gulf that has emerged between Lady Liberty's fine welcoming words and contemporary practice. More often than not, huddled masses are invited to continue huddling in their lands of origin. Some explanation is needed to account for this hardening of hearts and borders.

It does not seem plausible to attribute the change to increased racism or ethnic chauvinism in the United States. To the contrary, every indicator points to

---

[10] The most conspicuous and shameful exception to free access is the Chinese Exclusion Act of 1882.

the citizenry's greater tolerance. Nor is it plausible to attribute greater wariness about migrants to diminished economic opportunity available for outsiders. This might temporarily be the case during periods of recession, but the country's long-term growth trend has remained distinctly positive since 1620. Rather, the one factor most likely to account for immigration wariness in the United States and other typical destinations for would-be entrants is the *rise of the welfare state*. The doughty folks who made their way to and through Ellis Island received the inestimable benefit of not being interfered with by the national government in the pursuit of their dream. That, though, was one of the very few benefits they were afforded.[11] They were not handed food stamps, subsidized public housing, clothing allowances, medical insurance, social security eligibility, unemployment insurance, or minimum-wage-law protection.[12] The result was that many were obliged to live under squalid conditions in cramped, dark, and unhealthy slums. This can be judged a misfortune for them if the comparison invoked is to the perquisites today enjoyed by their grandchildren. Compared, however, to their mode of life in the old country, whichever old country it may have happened to be, they were immeasurably better off than would have been the case had they been excluded. Escaping the potato famine in Ireland or pogroms in the Czar's Russia was literally a matter of life and death. This is why the ships kept coming and coming, with new cohorts of ragged people disembarking and seeking their chance. They did so at only minimal expense to the indigenous population: a dollop of taxation to fund the immigration service itself and the few public conveniences enjoyed by the new Americans. The benefits the migrants supplied in return are inestimable.

It has been consistently argued in these pages that there is a fundamental moral distinction between duties not to interfere and duties to provide aid. Only rarely do the latter come into the picture as demands of justice. Individuals may quite justifiably demur from embracing policies that impose a drain on their own resources. But this is what welfare programs of social democracies do. Insofar as these programs mandate transfers from one group to another, they generate discrete sets of net winners and net losers. They are in this regard decisively unlike the positive-sum transactions that individuals generate through market and other voluntary interactions or that the state affords through public goods provision, including most of all the public good of law and order.[13] The greater the number of people who are eligible to put

---

[11] An important additional one is that their children became eligible for the same free public education that was provided to the native born. Also, immigrants could immediately avail themselves of public goods such as police and fire protection, roads and parks, use of the Carnegie free public library, public hygiene such as it then existed, and the like. The bearing of public goods availability on arguments for exclusion is considered later.

[12] The last properly understood is no benefit to the poor but rather an impediment to their chances of securing desired employment.

[13] This is not to maintain that all welfare-state programs are zero sum (actually, with transaction costs taken into account, negative sum). It can be argued that various public insurance measures provide overall net benefits to citizens in a way that private insurance could not because of

their hands out for a handout, the greater are pro rata tax shares. Therefore, it is rational to oppose measures that will enlarge the class of net beneficiaries – in theory, the least-well-off[14] – and to welcome inclusion of additional parties to bear the transfer burden. Giving full weight to the relative niggardliness of the American welfare state compared to those found in the European Union, it is clear that penniless new immigrants will be net subtracters from the pot. Even if they withdraw little, they will contribute even less. Therefore, it is in the interest of current residents to restrict entry to those banging on the doors. Professionals and well-heeled investors, yes; huddled masses, please call somewhere else.

Desire to accumulate and preserve wealth is honorable whether it is the motivation of impecunious migrants or of long-established natives. In the context of social democracy, the desire expresses itself as a strategy of restricting entry. Our response is: so much the worse for the welfare state! It would please us a great deal if the apparatus of transfers and subsidies throughout the Organisation for Economic Co-operation and Development (OECD) were pared back to the level that obtains in Singapore (see Chapter 3). We do recognize, though, that this is thoroughly utopian (or, if you so incline, dystopian). Egalitarians who defend sweeping transfers from the more-well-off to the less-well-off should, if they are honest, add to the costs of their favored system the drastically limited welcome to aspiring entrants that inevitably follows. This means that the domestic egalitarian agenda has as a corollary disregard of the much greater inequalities that obtain globally. Clear-thinking domestic egalitarians such as Rawls in *Law of Peoples* recognize and accept this corollary. Because the egalitarianism that we find attractive is equality of basic rights, we cannot endorse the program of social democracy. This is the case for a multitude of reasons, not least of which is that an ideology of domestic wealth redistribution leads to hardened borders that deprive persons of a liberty to associate freely with like-minded others.

If the welfare state in some form or other is here to stay, then melioration of border exclusion has to be sought in the realm of second best.[15] One option is to admit all comers but with an explicit blanket denial of access to welfare programs for a period of, say, five years. In many ways this is appealing in that it would essentially confer on today's migrants the same sort of risks and

---

adverse-selection concerns that will degrade any scheme that is not coercively mandated for all. Nonetheless, the general proposition that the preponderance of welfare-state measures is at best zero sum is strongly confirmed.

[14] We say "in theory" because a substantial amount of redistribution proceeds from the less-well-off to the more-well-off. Because of the conditionality and complexity of many policy provisions, it can be difficult to identify the direction of net redistribution. Among the programs that most clearly involve regressive transfers are agricultural price supports, subsidized higher education, and support for the arts.

[15] This discussion builds on ideas put forth earlier in Loren Lomasky, "Liberalism across Borders," *Social Philosophy & Policy* 24 (2007), 206–33.

rewards that were assumed by their forerunners of a century earlier – except, of course, that for the earlier arrivals there was no five-year provision. It is doubtful, however, that any such policy could be sustainable. If because of bad luck or bad economic times even a small fraction of entrants became unable to support themselves, it would be impossible to view with equanimity their hunger, homelessness, and lack of decent health care – nor would many of us wish to live in a society in which equanimity was the standard response to such misfortunes. The problem with people fainting from hunger on the sidewalks is not primarily that one must then carefully step over them.

In an earlier time, humane impulses to assist the unfortunate were largely channeled through religious and secular private charities. The infrastructure that supported such charitable relief was mostly disassembled with the coming of the New Deal in America and even further-reaching governmental assumption of philanthropic activities in advanced European countries. Until and unless a (very unlikely) privatization of most welfare functions is brought about, no denial of access to migrants is feasible or, from the perspective of the indigenous population, desirable. For the migrants themselves, it would be a considerable blessing to be afforded an opportunity to run the risk of disease and destitution in America against the much greater risk of doing so in the country of origin. For better or worse, this is not a wager that they are likely to be allowed to make.

More palatable might be to allow entry to all peaceful candidates who provide surety that they will not become a charge on the public. This could be done, for example, by posting of a bond that would be forfeited should they become applicants for public assistance. The obvious drawback with this suggestion is that the impecunious people who most need access to enhanced economic opportunity are in no position to post that bond. Others could, however, do so on their behalf. Earlier arrivers from the same village might post the bond, with an understanding that when the newcomers are on their feet, they will take over responsibility for their own continued financial position and will, in turn, offer guarantees for new cohorts. A side benefit of this structure would be to enhance ties of community that underpin valuable social capital.[16] Alternatively, prospective employers who value the labor that these new hands will provide might be willing to provide an up-front assurance payment that will be paid back over time by the migrants out of wages. Yet another possibility is that for-profit ventures might post bond for migrants much as bail bondsmen do for individuals who would otherwise remain incarcerated. If the idea of professional bondsmen for migrants seems to verge on being a coercive offer imposed on poor entrants with very few options, it should be kept in

---

[16] For discussion of the concept of social capital and its currently diminished status in the United States, see Robert Putnam, *Bowling Alone: The Collapse and Revival of American Community* (New York: Simon & Schuster, 2001).

mind that rejection of this business model would leave them with yet fewer and worse options.

Many problems remain to be solved before any such policy could be put into practice. What conditions could legitimately be placed on migrants by those who sponsor their entry? Would these policies be a convenient avenue for pimps to import sex workers or drug dealers to bring in fresh talent for street corner distribution? Will workers sponsored by an employer effectively forfeit a liberty to leave their current job for one that is more attractive? And so on. It is not our intention to advance here anything resembling a fleshed-out scheme for softening borders. Inventing schemes is not where philosophers' comparative advantage lies. (Even Plato, philosopher beyond compare, comes off rather questionably with regard to the particular devices manufactured for the superintendence of his *Republic*.) Better to identify general precepts of normative acceptability and leave to others – especially, if possible, to market participants – details of implementation. The relevant general precepts include the following:

1. To deny people access to valued associations merely because those associations entail some crossing of conventional political boundaries is a prima facie violation of rightful liberty.
2. One legitimate defeater of that prima facie liberty is demonstration of actual or likely harms to others that will be caused by the exercise of that liberty.
3. Among alternative measures to prevent harms, those less draconian are to be preferred.
4. Soft borders impose less draconian restrictions on would-be entrants and those desirous of transacting with them than do hard borders.
5. The borders of contemporary welfare states are, with few or no exceptions, harder than they need to be to meet the legitimate security needs of current inhabitants.

We invite those who wish to dispute these suggestions concerning enhanced access not to focus on particular policy details. We concede that some or all of those that we have brainstormed may harbor difficulties of implementation that have not been foreseen. Instead, focus ought to be kept on the five precepts that underlie them.

LIBERAL DEMOCRACY AND ITS ILLIBERAL OPPONENTS

It is of the nature of electoral majorities to shift. Denial of the franchise to some demographic group on the grounds that it might vote against the party currently in power is to repudiate the ground rules of democratic governance. What, however, if the group in question is not opposed to some particular political party or policy but rather is hostile to the fundamental tenets of a liberal democratic order? Does adherence to democratic norms entail their

extension to those who reject the norms? Is participation in democratic practices open to people whose aim is to roll back those practices?[17]

Some will respond that full faith in democracy means confidence to allow
it to fight for itself; if democracy wins by using undemocratic means, then it
loses. (Pacifists offer similar arguments as to why they refuse to meet force
with force.) Perhaps there is something to be said for pushing consistency
to this extreme, but there is also something to be said against it. The value
of democracy is first and foremost its capacity to afford a population more
of the things that make lives worthwhile than are on offer with competing
political systems. Among these goods is a lively prospect of future decisions
being made via democratic means. Better to restrict participation in elections
than to endanger conditions of democratic continuity. Strictly speaking, such
restrictions characterize every democratic system; none embraces a universal
franchise for all affected parties. The United States, for example, allows only
adult U.S. citizens to vote, not American toddlers or mature Chinese citizens,
although both groups are affected by U.S. political decisions. Restricting the
franchise is sensible insofar as it improves the quality of expected outcomes,
however improvement is understood. If it is permissible to withhold the vote
from foreign nationals, including those who wish American institutions well,
then it is no less permissible to withhold it from those either within or outside
borders who would cheer the destruction of those institutions.

If it is possible to identify with reasonable accuracy demographic characteristics of aspiring migrants who are dismissive of democratic structures, then it
is not only permissible but strongly indicated that they not be afforded entry.
This is a corollary of the proposition that defense is a (or *the*) fundamental
function of states. Keeping potentially dangerous people at a distance tends
to render them less threatening than if they are literally next door. It can be
objected that exclusion based on general rather than individual characteristics
is to punish someone before finding her personally guilty. This, though, is to
misunderstand the rationale for exclusion. *Punishment* is indeed only appropriate in response to a wrong previously committed, but *prevention* aims to
preclude commission of a wrong. The distinction is ubiquitous in common
practices. People who have never secured a driver's license are not permitted
to operate a motor vehicle on public roads. The prohibition is not because
they are being punished for culpably avoiding lines at the Division of Motor
Vehicles but because they are judged to pose an unduly high degree of risk
to other drivers and pedestrians. Quarantine is another example of denial of
liberty predicated on risk avoidance. There are many complexities involved in
setting out an adequate theory of when people may be prohibited from engaging in risky activities as opposed to being allowed to perform such activities

---

[17] See Lisa Blaydes and James Lo, "One Man, One Vote, One Time? Modeling the Prospects for
Spontaneous Democratization in the Middle East"; available at: http://www.jhfc.duke.edu/disc/
events/documents/blaydes-lo-DukePaper9-2-2008.pdf (accessed November 19, 2009).

subject to compensating those who may be harmed,[18] but any reasonable theory will strike some balance between the two. Denying access to those who pose significant risks of harm should they be allowed entry into the country does not as a matter of principle violate mobility rights of would-be entrants. (That, in practice, governments are liable to misapply risk judgments is obvious, perhaps most obvious of all to airline passengers who have experienced Transportation Security Administration screening procedures).

Opposition to democracy is, in the contemporary world, opposition to *liberal* democracy. It includes not only suspicion of the results of plebiscites but also hostility toward free speech, freedom of religion (including freedom not to practice religion), insistence on equal rights for women, racial equality, acceptance of homosexual persons, and so on. This is why it may not be enough to countenance migration but deny eventual access to citizenship; those of a thoroughly illiberal cast will, if allowed past borders, pose an ongoing risk of enmity toward the practices of the host country. We say "risk" because it is also quite possible that immersion in the institutions of liberal society will over time corrode prejudices brought along from less tolerant venues. The entire history of immigration into the United States has been laced with dire warnings that the new entrants carry with them strange beliefs and traditions that do not fit in and that they will subvert the republic's traditions. Such were the indictments lodged against the Irish, Italians, Poles, Jews, Greeks, Hispanics, Chinese, and others[19]; without exception, they proved misguided. Over time, in some cases a remarkably short period of time, old ways were largely cast off and new ones donned; the melting pot did not produce homogeneity, but it did produce a population that was unmistakably American. Had any of the anti-immigrant campaigns from the Know Nothings of the 1850s to CNN's Lou Dobbs carried the day, the fabric of the United States would have been rendered poorer for it. This heritage of misplaced nativist ranting provides powerful inductive reason for skepticism concerning the current crop of dire predictions. Induction is not, however, an unfailing key to the future, especially when background conditions are continually undergoing change. (There was good inductive support throughout the history of human beings that none of them would in the coming year set foot on the moon. Those thousands of years of confirmation went by the boards in 1969.) If, for example, a country's increased openness to diversity begins to create a space in which a culture of opposition to liberal democracy finds room to establish itself and to seek further adherents, the rules of the game may thereby have changed sufficiently to mandate a reappraisal of border security concerns.

The discussion of this section has proceeded along lines of general principles. These are the lines with which philosophers are most comfortable. It is

---

[18] A seminal discussion can be found in Robert Nozick, *Anarchy, State, and Utopia* (New York: Basic Books, 1974), chap. 4.

[19] Because the transit of Africans was involuntary, it does not fit into this pattern.

no secret, however, that the primary application of these remarks in the first years of the twenty-first century is Muslim immigration to the United States and, especially, Europe. The openness of U. S. borders, coupled with the feck-lessness of the nation's intelligence-gathering agencies, levied a great cost on September 11, 2001.[20] In March 2004, bombs set by Islamic radicals rocked Madrid, killing almost 200 people and injuring another 2,000. Coordinated suicide bombings by four British Muslim men spectacularly disrupted London in July 2005 and killed more than 50 people. A few months thereafter, rampaging young Algerians in France burned cars and public buildings; Netherlands saw assassinations of leading political and cultural figures; Denmark became the unlikely pretext for riot and murder when its free press published cartoons disliked by certain persons who do not normally peruse Danish journalism, and, most recently, the entire editorial staff of a satirical magazine in Paris was massacred in broad daylight: in each case, the perpetrators were Islamic. Other sanguinary bombings and assassinations were thwarted before they became fully ripe, including, it may be presumed, some that were never announced. Less spectacularly but perhaps ultimately more sinister, those quarters in the West that have welcomed Muslim immigrants find a theology of enmity to liberal institutions increasingly preached to receptive congregations. With all due heed to injunctions not to "demonize the Other," sober assessment[21] has to take seriously the concern that the growing Islamic populations of Western states will prove indigestible.

For not only demographic but also philosophical reasons, problems posed by Islamization are graver in Europe than in the United States. They are not, however, negligible in the latter. On November 5, 2009, at Fort Hood military base in Texas, Major Nidal Malik Hasan opened fire in a crowded medical processing center, proclaiming "Allahu Akbar!" as he shot. Before he himself was felled, thirteen people lay dead or dying and numerous others injured. A full picture of the underlying motivations for the carnage remains to be determined. The scale of the massacre is sufficient, though, to overcome in part inhibitions on publicly acknowledging the ramifications of a growing Islamic presence.[22] The pat response that crazed killers come in all ethnicities and religions (e.g., Timothy McVeigh, the Oklahoma City bomber) are seen to be more and more shopworn as troubling incidents present themselves. Christopher Hitchens framed the issue well when he observed, "I do not say

---

[20] It should not be forgotten that some of this cost was borne by foreigners who wished peacefully to study, work, or merely do a bit of tourism but who were caught up in the ensuing frenzy.

[21] One such is Christopher Caldwell, *Reflections on the Revolution in Europe: Immigration, Islam and the West* (New York: Doubleday, 2009).

[22] For a related outcropping of political correctness that is amusingly Orwellian, see "Government Renames Islamic Terrorism as 'Anti-Islamic Activity' to Woo Muslims," *London Evening Standard*, January 20, 2008; available at: http://www.thisislondon.co.uk/news/article-23433081-government-renames-islamic-terrorism-as-anti-islamic-activity-to-woo-muslims.do (accessed November 20, 2009).

that all Muslims are terrorists, but I have noticed that an alarmingly high proportion of terrorists are Muslims."[23] It is not a manifestation of laudable liberal toleration to ignore risks to persons and institutions consequent on policy
decisions, including immigration policy. That frank deliberations undistorted
by cant and wishful thinking should be carried out in Washington, London,
Paris, Amsterdam, Jerusalem, Canberra, and other capitals is a matter for the
liberal democracies in question. These deliberations will reflect local conditions
concerning which we lack all expertise. There are, however, two points that we
do believe ourselves competent to contribute.

First, we acknowledge that applying a religious test to would-be migrants
is odious on the face of it, in tension with basic liberal principles. There exists
a strong presumption that as far as politics is concerned, religion is a personal
matter that is the business only of the believer himself. This presumption is
nonetheless defeasible. More particularly, to the extent that reliance by the
state on religious (or ethnic) data is found to be essential for avoidance of
serious harms to those whose safety it is charged to defend, then such reliance
should not be peremptorily rejected on theoretical grounds. The defining commitment of liberalism to the overriding importance of liberty does not yield a
priori prescriptions in cases where different persons' liberties come into actual
or potential conflict. And, of course, a liberty to deny others their rights car-
ries no weight at all. An order of mutual respect and noninterference does not
go of itself. Its smooth functioning requires continuous upkeep and lubrica-
tion. Keeping dangerous distant others both distant and other is one important article of programmatic political maintenance. Invariably, this means that
some individuals whose intent is entirely peaceful and unthreatening will be
caught up in the surveillance and exclusion net. This a matter for regret but
not remorse. Governments are at best well-meaning but oafish entities that step
on some as they race to the assistance of others. (And that is at best.) Holding
them to ultrafine standards that cannot realistically be met in a morally and
epistemically conflicted world would be to undercut their reason for being. To
paraphrase Justice Jackson, a nation's immigration policy is not a suicide pact.

But second, in the great majority of cases it will be abundantly clear that
the migrant harbors no ill will toward the country in which she hopes to provide for herself a nest egg and, perhaps, someday put down roots. Nor should
it be suspected absent compelling evidence to the contrary that migrants are
crossing borders with a primary intention of gaming the welfare system. The
demagogic rhetoric that equates *alien*, especially when prefixed by *illegal* or
undocumented, with *terrorist threat* or *sponger* is as unprincipled as it is inac-
curate. The peasant crossing the Rio Grande in search of a paycheck harbors
no malign design to make a second assault on the Alamo. American nativists
and their cousins abroad should be exposed for the frauds that they are. Note,

---

[23] "Hard Evidence: Seven Salient Facts about Maj. Nidal Malik Hasan," *Slate*, November 16,
2009; available at: http://www.slate.com/id/2235760/.

however, that the persistence of the apparatus of social democracy stands in the way of doing so. Unless applicants for entry can demonstrate that they are unlikely to be net claimants on the body politic, they will be resisted by principled objections but also by outrageous ones that are parasitic on the others.[24]

OBJECTIONS

Critics may accept some or all of the preceding arguments for a softening of borders yet deny that they belong in a discussion of global justice. Or if they are relevant to global-justice concerns, it might be contended that they are so in a direction opposite to the one the authors intend. Three objections to softer borders have surfaced in the literature. The first is that allowing freer immigration will result in a major exodus of talented persons from the poor countries that need them the most (the brain-drain objection). The second is that the domestic poor have moral priority over the global poor. The third one is that fellow citizens of a legitimate state have a right to exclude outsiders with which they do not want to associate, as they see fit (the self-determination objection). We discuss brain drain in Chapter 5; here we address the other two.

1. The Priority of the Domestic Poor

It is difficult to formulate a persuasive argument that justice requires that indigenous engineers and radiologists be protected from harmful competition by foreigners. That the already privileged should be advantaged further at the expense of persons both foreign and domestic who are considerably less well-off than they themselves are is manifestly dubious. But when recycled as a *muscle-drain* argument, it fits better with certain strands of egalitarian justice theory. For the foreseeable future, the paradigmatic egalitarianism is that of Rawls' *A Theory of Justice*, which requires that inequalities, to be permissible, must pass the test of advantaging the least-well-off. Rawls does not in that work consider inflows or outflows of individuals across national borders, but a plausible way of extending his theory to a world in which populations are mobile is to insist that the immigration policies of Country A are permissible on grounds of justice only to the extent that they do not diminish the prospects of the least-well-off in Country A. It is not strictly relevant to questions of justice in Country A whether the effect of these policies damages the prospects of the worst-off in Country B, not even if persons in Country B are on average much poorer than those in Country A.[25] Implications concerning

---

[24] For a defense of liberal immigration policy as *required* by the welfare state, see Joseph Carens, *The Ethics of Immigration* (Oxford University Press, 2013), esp. chap. 11.

[25] Something like this position is developed by Thomas Nagel, who writes: "Every state has the boundaries and population it has for all sorts of accidental and historical reasons; but given that it exercises sovereign power over its citizens and in their name, those citizens have a duty of justice toward one another through the legal, social and economic institutions that sovereign

the availability of access may seem to follow straightforwardly: because penniless foreigners with low skill sets will, if allowed admission into a wealthy country, compete with the domestic poor for the limited number of low-end jobs, they should be excluded. It is not enough simply to require that entrants be self-supporting, for the means through which they will support themselves predictably work to the disadvantage of the worst-off of those already present.

There are at least five respects in which this objection is lacking. First, we confess to not being enamored of a Rawlsian egalitarianism confined to the purely domestic context of *A Theory of Justice*. Even if it should become clearer just who Rawls has in mind when he speaks of the least-well-off, it would remain obscure why their well-being should count for more, indeed, infinitely more, than that of all other members of the society. Nor is Rawls' understanding of the scope and value of liberty one that we can endorse. Nonetheless, that egalitarianism is considerably more attractive than one extended to immigration policy. To the credit of the original version, the least-well-off possess the property of being those who are, well, the least-well-off. This is not the case with a Rawlsianism rejiggered so as to harden borders. The United States designates as poor a family of four with an income of less than $23,850.[26] This sum, though, is more than enough to punch the ticket for admission into the world's elite. That those who are relatively well off with regard to nutrition, shelter, health care, and access to educational services should be protected against competition from people markedly worse off along all these dimensions does not plausibly present itself as any kind of egalitarianism worthy of respect. The position denies to the desperate the sort of human equality that has been urged throughout this book: equal liberty to engage in consensual relationships with willing others. Surely the better term for the so-called egalitarian position is *nativism*, a smugly satisfied expression of a nationalistically based "we've got ours" attitude. By criticizing this stance, we do not mean in any way to take back earlier assertions that it is not only permissible but honorable for individuals to insist on the continued validity of their property rights even when there are others who have much less. But to deny those others a liberty to better their conditions in order to favor the competing interests of others who have much more is to get the worst of two worlds: it is to embrace a chimera neither libertarian nor genuinely egalitarian.

Second, this argument will, at most, support restricting access to the hardscrabble poor. Migrants who possess substantial financial or human capital

power makes possible. This duty is *sui generis*, and is not owed to everyone in the world.... Furthermore, though the obligations of justice arise as a result of a special relation, there is no obligation to enter into that relation with those to whom we do not yet have it." Thomas Nagel, "The Problem of Global Justice," *Philosophy & Public Affairs* 33 (2005), 121. Although most of Nagel's nuanced and challenging discussion focuses on cash transfers to the foreign poor, a straightforward reading of the text seems to indicate rejection of the sorts of principles of justice in migration that have been urged in this chapter.

[26] See "2014 Poverty Guidelines"; available at: http://aspe.hhs.gov/poverty/14poverty.cfm.

improve the prospects of the domestic poor both indirectly insofar as they add value to the overall economy and directly because they employ gardeners, cleaners, freelance handymen, and the like. Again, the implication is professionals to the head of the line; huddled masses to the rear.

Third, the claim that entry of poor migrants harms the domestic least-well-off class is contentious.[27] It is often claimed (and often denied) that foreign laborers will gladly take jobs that citizens spurn. If true, this is less a commentary on the lesser industriousness of citizens than a reflection of their greater opportunities for income. To the extent that it is true, though, it means that complementary employment positions will be greater. That is, more busboys means more restaurants, which means more jobs for suppliers to those restaurants, which means more jobs to those who provide goods and services to the suppliers. Moreover, those migrants will themselves purchase products that sustain yet further jobs. Because economic modeling is not an exact science, judging whose macroeconomic projections are correct is too difficult for the authors of these pages – and, we suspect, for anyone else. To call the competition a draw, though, is to obliterate whatever egalitarian case there may be for keeping the outs firmly out.[28]

Fourth, the preceding comments do not get to the heart of the matter. Under virtually any reading of economic tea leaves, it will not be the case that the only or best method to protect the domestic poor is at the expense of the weakest and most vulnerable. If, for example, immigration by poor from abroad is to the disadvantage of the indigenous poor, then the latter could be given either cash transfers or in-kind provisions such as job training by way of compensation. These could be paid for either out of general funds or by a special assessment on employers who have applied for a permit to hire external workers. This is not the place to try to develop in detail an optimal policy for the United States or other wealthy countries, but it is precisely the place to offer a reminder that setting up roadblocks at the border is only one way, and almost certainly not the best, to act on behalf of the domestic least-well-off.

Fifth, it should be observed that this whole debate ought to stand as a considerable embarrassment to domestic egalitarianism. Consider, for example, marginal workers in the United States compared with potential competitors from Mexico who seek entry. The U.S. citizen is probably a native speaker of English (or has from an early age had substantial exposure to English), whereas the Mexican is not. The U.S. citizen has enjoyed the advantage of early education in much more generously funded U.S. schools and has enjoyed greater

[27] See Howard F. Chang, "The Economic Impact of International Labor Migration: Recent Estimates and Policy Implications"; available at: http://papers.ssrn.com/sol3/papers .cfm?abstract_id=946204 (accessed November 28, 2014), and "Migration as International Trade: The Economic Gains from the Liberalized Movement of Labor," *UCLA Journal of International Law and Foreign Affairs* 3 (1998), 371.

[28] It is hardly a draw, however. See the section entitled, "The Benefits of Immigration."

access to health care, nutritional support, and virtually every other aspect of welfare assistance. If she is nonetheless hard pressed to compete with the new entrant, that fact stands as a searing indictment of the prevailing welfare state. And so it should stand; despite expenditures on the less-well-off that are quite enormous by world standards, the U.S. welfare apparatus has managed somehow to become a conspicuous subtracter from human potential. By way of assuaging bruised U.S. sentiments, we hasten to add that in this regard it is only slightly, if at all, a laggard when compared with other wealthy countries. The failure of welfare-state nostrums on their home turf where they possess every advantage ought to have been a great story of the twentieth century; perhaps it finally will be widely told in the twenty-first century. It is difficult to avoid concluding that the proposal to show solidarity with the domestic least-well-off by excluding desperate people from abroad is a desperation move from an ideology at the end of its tether.

2. The Self-Determination Objection

Another objection relies on the special relationship that citizens have with their own institutions. This special relationship, it is argued, entitle citizens to exclude outsiders more or less at will. The objection, in turn, has two versions. Under the first one, *democratic self-determination*, natives are entitled to decide democratically to associate with whomever they want, and this includes the freedom not to associate with immigrants. Under the second one, *cultural self-determination*, natives are entitled to determine the future direction of their country, and this entitles them to limit immigration if they believe that it will take them in the wrong direction – take them in turn.

Democratic Self-Determination

Some critics will contend that our principles pay insufficient attention to democratic determination. Just as individuals by right are at liberty to refuse or admit whomsoever they choose into their homes, so too many democratic electorates through their chosen representatives decide who to admit and who to exclude. Nor is there any onus on them to provide good reasons to justify refusal. Bennet may be an altogether upright and virtuous person, but if for whatever reason Dashwood chooses not to associate with him, she is well within her rights in keeping her doors firmly barred. Similarly, if the United States should choose to admit only 100 or 1,000 or 100,000 or 1 million migrants, that is purely its own decision. It can be faulted on grounds of economic efficiency, perhaps, but not in terms of any injustice done to those denied entry. It is not their country, so whatever entitlements they have are those of guests – or, as the case may be, those from whom guest status is withheld. In this vein, Christopher Wellman claims that "legitimate states are morally entitled to unilaterally design and enforce their own immigration policies, even if these policies exclude potential immigrants who desperately want to enter."[29] The reason is that citizens have in some sense chosen to associate with one another. This association entitles them, it is thought, to exclude outsiders. A state, in Wellman's view, is like a private club: outsiders have to be admitted as new members; they cannot impose themselves on the association already formed.

The analogy to private ownership of a property is faulty. Most land in the United States is not owned by the government but by private parties. Because Yellowstone National Park is the property of the United States, the government is entitled to set conditions of access, including the number of people who will be allowed in. Dashwood's house, however, is owned by Dashwood. She is the one who gets to decide matters of access. If her neighbors vote in the next election that Dashwood be required to have Bennet over for tea at least six times during the upcoming year, that result has no standing. The scope of plebiscitory democracy is constrained by the prior rights of individuals. This includes their property rights. Migration restrictions of the sort maintained by the United States and other OECD countries transgress those rights. They interfere with the free movement of noncitizens as well as with the choices of citizens. Dashwood may have a rental property that she would like to make available to Bennet or a job for which she would be glad to hire Bennet. To the extent that a majority of Dashwood's fellow citizens are allowed to block those choices by refusing entry to Bennet, they unjustly restrict the scope of Dashwood's rights – and, of course, Bennet's. That this is the case is entirely obvious with regard to strictly domestic impairments. Electoral majorities are not permitted to establish policies: "This is a proud, God-fearing Christian neighborhood; no Jews permitted!" or "Marriage between white individuals and persons of color is strictly prohibited." At an earlier period in American history, these and other similarly discreditable restrictions were widely accepted. Their utter disappearance is grounds for congratulations: disappearance, that is, except with regard to foreign nationals. As the law stands, the government can still forbid mutually beneficial hirings and rentals. Even marriage to a foreign national is beset with annoying hurdles to jump or stagger over. And if that affectional relationship is expressed in some form other than marriage, perhaps because the parties are of the same sex or one of them has been unable to achieve extrication from a prior marriage, then the hurdles are yet more numerous and more onerous. We freely grant that many questions of lawfulness and policy are best decided via majoritarian institutions. Those that involve usurpations of individuals' rights to free association are not among them.[30]

[29] Christopher Heath Wellman and Phillip Cole, *Debating the Ethics of Immigration: Is There a Right to Exclude?* (Oxford University Press, 2011), 13.

[30] For a view that the state's title to territory is derived from individual property title, see Fernando R. Tesón, "The Mystery of Territory," *Social Philosophy and Policy* (in press).

Moreover, states are not voluntary associations; they are coercive institutions. This means that the idea of self-determination cannot be cashed out, as Wellman does, in terms of freedom of association.[31] Simply put, citizens have not associated voluntarily with one another, and therefore, the reasons that apply to private clubs are inapplicable to the state. The value of freedom of association resides in the voluntary nature of that association, a freely agreed-on relationship that third parties are not entitled to disturb. Those reasons do not apply to states, where most individuals have been coercively recruited into citizenship.

Ironically, freedom of association supports *our* view, not Wellman's. If a democratic majority enacts immigration restrictions, it violates the freedom of association of *both* the potential immigrant and *those who want to associate with immigrants*. Freedom of association is an individual right; it is not a right of collectivities. When the state coercively prevents me from associating with someone, it is violating that right. The right to exclude, therefore, cannot be based on freedom of association but on some other property ascribed to the coercive apparatus of the state (such as the power to coercively determine the future direction of the society.)[32] And, as we said, we are skeptical that such property can be defended in a manner consistent with respect for individual freedom.[33]

When Wellman considers the libertarian objection similar to the one we make here, it seems to us that he analogizes too quickly from cases where

---

[31] See Bas van der Vossen, "Immigration and Self-Determination," *Politics, Philosophy, and Economics*, July 3, 2014, online version, p. 9; available at: http://ppe.sagepub.com/content/early/2014/07/02/1470594X14533167 (accessed November 30, 2014). Except for what we say here and in "A Note on Territory" in Chapter 7, we do not address the difficult issue of national self-determination, but our inclination is to say that group agency, autonomy, or rights must be derived from voluntary individual decisions and interactions. See Fernando R. Tesón, *A Philosophy of International Law* (Boulder, CO: Westview Press, 1998), chap. 5. See also the essays collected in Fernando R. Tesón (ed.), *The Theory of Self-Determination* (New York: Cambridge University Press, 2015).

[32] Michael Blake likewise criticizes Wellman by pointing out that freedom of association is part of a package of liberties that must be considered as a whole, and that therefore freedom of association cannot be a trump card when other liberty considerations are at stake. Michael Blake, "Immigration, Association, and Antidiscrimination," *Ethics* 122, (2012), 748–62. But Blake concedes too much: we believe that freedom of association is *inapplicable* at the state level.

[33] We reject Ryan Pevnick's views for similar reasons. Pevnick rejects Wellman's freedom-of-association argument (as do we) and says instead that citizens "own" their institutions and "have a prima facie right to make their own decisions about the policies under which they live (including policies regarding membership.)" Ryan Pevnick, *Immigration and the Constraints of Justice: Between Open Borders and Absolute Sovereignty* (New York: Cambridge University Press, 2011), 27, 33. But from the claim that persons own the fruits of their labor one cannot conclude that citizens "own" institutions, over and above their private rights of property. Surely, this must be a different sense of ownership. And if it is different, we are skeptical that the rules that allow owners to exclude others from their property can apply to states, at least when that exclusion infringes important liberties on both sides of the border.

democratic decisions inevitably will trump individual rights of association, such as a referendum to join another state.[34] He thinks that the fact that the losing minority cannot validly resist the merger proves that the state can collectively close borders in violation of the individual right of association. To begin with, it is not obvious at all that a majority that votes to join another state fully respects the rights of the dissenters. To defend this view, we need a full theory of secession and self-determination that somehow vindicates the rights of the collective. It is far from certain that such a theory can be convincingly established.[35] But even accepting the relevance of Wellman's merger case, that merger decision, by its very nature, can only be adopted by majority vote. It does not follow from the fact that *some* democratic decisions that conflict with individual freedom of association must inevitably be made by vote that *any* democratic decision that conflicts with self-determination can *legitimately* be so adopted. In other words, the merger example is disanalogous to the immigration example.[36] Whether the democratic decision to close borders is legitimate must be examined on its merits. As we have repeatedly argued, moral and empirical reasons cast doubt on that legitimacy.

There is, however, another sense in which democracy is in tension with policies allowing freer access. If the electorate of some country is comprised of N voters, then each enfranchised citizen's voting power is $1/N$ of the total. Now add an additional person to the voting rolls; each citizen's voting power has been diminished to $1/N + 1$. The change is small, but it is real, and arguably it amounts to a worsening of one's political condition. People who are permitted entry into the country have taken the first step in a process that eventually will entitle them to cast a ballot. Even if they never join the electoral rolls, their children will. Can citizens argue that they will be politically harmed by the entry of substantial numbers of migrants?

We would like to deny legitimacy to this sort of reasoning, but it must grudgingly be granted some cogency. The degree of that cogency is a function of how extensively political determinations impinge on the persons and property of individuals. If, for example, a country's constitution forbade the taking of property from some to transfer it to others for reasons of so-called social justice, then majorities would be less threatening to potential minorities and less alluring to those with hopes of reaping rewards via deft political

---

[34] Wellman and Cole, *Debating Immigration*, chap. 3.

[35] For such a skeptical view, see Fernando R. Tesón, "The Conundrum of Self-Determination," in Tesón (ed.),*The Theory of Self-Determination*.

[36] Wellman also analogizes freely at the beginning of his chapter: he writes that the fact that foreign nations must respect the judicial system of the state proves that the state has self-determination, and that, in turn, proves that the state can legitimately control borders. Wellman and Cole, *Debating Immigration*, 13–19. But these two situations are not sufficiently analogous. The first one is a jurisdictional question (who should exercise the punitive power of the state?); the second is a human-rights question (can a democratic majority prevent potential immigrants from entering the territory to associate with those who welcome them?).

maneuvering. To the best of our knowledge, no constitution anywhere in the world incorporates such a restriction. Rather, redistribution for the sake of greater equality is altogether common (as is redistribution that in fact fosters greater inequality). There is nothing surprising or ignominious with desiring to protect oneself from predatory incursions by electoral factions. If large numbers of immigrants obtain the right to vote, they can form such a faction, voting either their class or their ethnic interests. For current residents who fear that this is likely to work out to their detriment, there exist reasons grounded in self-defense to keep them out.

As suggested earlier, one solution to this conflict is to limit scope for redistribution by political means. Although a campaign for this sort of rollback may enjoy occasional successes at the margin, it is unrealistic to expect any significant enhancement of individual economic rights against the regulatory and redistributive functions of the state. For better or worse, the Lochner era is well in the past. Nonetheless, there are other ways to respond to the worry of electoral outflanking than by drastically restricting migration. It is imperative not to be trapped by nineteenth-century models while assessing twenty-first-century conditions. Readers' great-great grandparents who emigrated to the United States (or Canada, Argentina, Australia, etc.) did so in the expectation of never again seeing the native country left behind. Resettlement was wrenching, and it was permanent. Now, however, in an era of inexpensive intercontinental jet travel and globalized production, it is entirely common for someone to grow up in one country, attend university in another, take a corporate job that involves postings over a decade in a third, fourth, and fifth country, and then perhaps to return to the country of origin. Or, at the other end of the wealth spectrum, a typical narrative may involve leaving one's home village to spend a couple of years working abroad as a domestic or construction worker and then, with the money saved from the venture, return home and open a beauty shop or purchase a used automobile to operate as a taxicab. For those who are in transit, economic rights are paramount; questions of political rights are moot.

In Chapter 3, Singapore was displayed as the paradigm of a developing country that rose to affluence with hardly a misstep along the way. It has increasingly become a site of aspiration for many people around the world and especially for the Asian poor. Singapore is relatively accommodating to economic migrants despite offering them limited prospects of political assimilation. Recent governmental statistics give the overall population of the country as 4.8 million, of which 3.2 million are citizens. This is a percentage of noncitizen residents some three times that typically found in the United States and the European Union. Of the noncitizens, 478,000 are listed as permanent residents, whereas 1.2 million are nonresidents, meaning that they will be expected to leave once their stipulated period of access has expired. Only a minority of the permanent residents will ever become Singapore citizens, and only a very small percentage of the nonresident population will be afforded status as permanent residents. In one respect, this is disadvantageous to sojourners. They are denied the various educational and housing benefits afforded to long-stay residents, and of course, they are also denied the benefit of being able to set down roots. On balance, however, the limitations probably are a plus in that they render the presence of a large migrant population politically palatable to a citizenry that understands that these individuals are adding value through their labor yet subtracting very little from welfare programs and not diluting the power, such as it is, of citizens' ballots. If the realistic alternatives for access across borders are few entrants but with immediate entitlement to full social benefits and a fast track to citizenship versus many entrants but without access to most transfer payments or eventual citizenship, then it is highly plausible that the second of these represents a better alternative for would-be entrants and, importantly, for the indigenous population.

These are not, however, the only two feasible alternatives. An intermediate one is generous original entry requirements coupled with more demanding criteria for subsequent extended residence and more demanding still for eventual full entitlement to citizens' benefits, including the franchise. We are unable confidently to identify the particular policy that stands best with reference to considerations of equity and economic efficiency, but our confidence is massively greater when we maintain that highly restrictive immigration policy is significantly deficient in both regards. It denies to both foreign and domestic persons valued opportunities without securing compensating benefits to any except the xenophobic and those shy of competing with ambitious and industrious new entrants. Through one mechanism or another, the case for softening borders in the United States and other wealthy countries that are migrant magnets is morally compelling. We are under no illusions, however, that the politics for such a reform will be easy, not when the economy is booming and certainly not in the wake of wrenching economic dislocations. When George W. Bush advanced a reform proposal during his second presidential term that would have regularized the position of millions of illegal Mexican migrants currently in the country and would have established quotas for guest workers who would remain for a limited period and before being required to depart, the proposal was excoriated from both the left and the right. Conservatives fulminated that this would be to reward prior illegal activities and to forfeit control of the nation's own authority to determine the population it will have. Liberals denounced what they took to be exploitation. The *New Republic*, a journal that usually is literate and thoughtful, declared, "Bush's guest-worker program would codify a large group of people in the United States as second-class citizens. Although they would enjoy many of the same legal protections as American-born workers, they would never be viewed by Americans as equals. Instead, they would be seen as transient figures here only to make a buck." The complaints are bizarre. Of course the new entrants would not have been second-class citizens because they would not have been any class of citizen. And it is true that they would have been seen as transient figures because, like foreign university students, tourists, au pairs, and numerous others, guest workers are indeed transient. Why this should be supposed a blot on American democracy is mysterious. Logic is omnipotent in philosophy essays but a rare interloper in Congress. Beset from all sides by criticisms that bordered on the hysterical, the proposed reforms went down in flames. We are pleased not to be members of Congress, so we do rest our case on logic, specifically the logic of liberalism.

We note in passing that our argument turns the usual precedence of bona fide refugees over "mere" economic migrants on its head. Current international law ascribes only to the former a justiciable right to sanctuary (assuming that their fear of persecution is well founded and that other necessary conditions obtain), whereas the latter may rightfully be turned away even if the alternative for them is destitution. It is not because of any ill will harbored toward refugees that we reject the legal status quo. Rather, it is because refugees' claim to positive assistance is grounded in moral sensibilities of *pity* or *compassion*. Because these people are incapable of helping themselves, others must do so for them if they are to get by. Should funds to support them not be forthcoming through private charitable means, the money will secured through taxation of current residents. The claim of economic migrants, however, is grounded in precepts of *justice*. It is a claim of liberty to transact with willing others located on the far side of the border. Should that liberty be denied, both the migrants and their transactors have been wronged.

Because in most matters claims of justice outweigh those of (supererogatory) beneficence, it may be wondered why with regard to migrants the priority is reversed. Here is a supposition: by recognizing the unique status of refugees' rights to sanctuary, the moral status of nonrefugee claimants is implicitly diminished. All the easier to keep them out, no matter how desperate they may be, without any incursions on one's conscience. That this hypothesis is cynical does not prove that it is true, but cynicism is an attitude that fits wonderfully well with the rhetoric and observed behavior of countries that naturally attract refugees. Coast guards of the United States, Australia, and Italy patrol home shores with an aim to interdict and repel desperate boat people hoping to set foot on shore and thus make themselves eligible to apply for refugee status. According such treatment to people who may well satisfy the formal requirements for being refugees should they only reach land is disgraceful. But to refuse a liberty to rescue themselves to migrants who are not refugees is also disgraceful – and it is unjust.

Cultural Self-Determination

The cultural argument holds that people have an interest in controlling their country's culture.[37] Wellman, for example, observes that citizens have the right

---

[37] In this sense, David Miller, "Immigration: The Case for Limits," in *Contemporary Debates in Applied Ethics*, Andrew I. Cohen and Christopher Heath Wellman, eds. (Oxford, UK: Blackwell, 2005), 200.

to determine the future direction of their society. He says that it is natural for citizens to care about how immigration will affect their culture, their economy, and the like.[38] Because freer borders may significantly alter that culture, citizens can reasonably control immigration to avoid undesirable changes. There are, of course, wildly implausible versions of this view (those that border on racism and xenophobia), but here we consider a more plausible version.

The plausible version of the cultural-conservative argument is that culture is a public good. Like any other public good, it is vulnerable to being underproduced. Public goods are defined by nonexcludability and nonrivalry in consumption. Take, for example, the Pacific Heights neighborhood in San Francisco. Locals and tourists alike enjoy the magnificent buildings and the architectural beauty of the Victorian houses and splendid hotels. Neither the owners of those buildings nor the city government can exclude nonpaying consumers of the good. We enjoy it for free just by walking by. Nor does my enjoyment of the good detract from your enjoyment: consumption is nonrivalrous. Now imagine that an owner wants to sell her Victorian house to someone who intends to build a video-game arcade painted pink. This transaction would destroy the public good, which is based on the stunning architectural ensemble. The owner would, it may be hoped, agree that the good has to be preserved, but she is seeking a profit and hopes that *others* will do whatever is needed to preserve the character of the neighborhood. She is a free rider. However, everyone reasons similarly, so the good is underproduced or not produced at all. The government, then, can permissibly prohibit the sale in order to preserve that public good that all want but the market cannot salvage.

Now let us apply this reasoning to immigration. Our culture is a public good just in the same sense as Pacific Heights. The market cannot preserve culture because some people will opportunistically undermine the efforts to preserve it. Suppose that most people in my small border town believe that the English language is an essential feature of our public culture. Suppose further that a business owner wants to hire a number of Spanish-speaking immigrants who, the neighbors fear, would alter that feature. The public-good justification of prohibiting the immigration of these workers is that the business owner is free riding on the efforts of the rest of the town folks to preserve the English language. Therefore, it is thought, the government can permissibly prohibit immigration to preserve this cultural trait, language purity.

We offer three responses to this line of argument. The first is that the public-good justification of state coercion requires that the defector *really* be a free rider. The argument supposes that the person who wants to sell the Victorian house in Pacific Heights really wishes to preserve the architectural beauty of the neighborhood but decides to go ahead with the profitable sale in the hope that others will do their share to preserve the neighborhood. She is acting opportunistically and thus is a genuine free rider. But whether or not

[38] Wellman and Cole, *Debating Immigration*, 9.

she is a free rider cannot be presumed: maybe she *does not care* about the public good at all. Maybe she is what David Schmidtz has called an "honest holdout."[39] Because the public-good argument depends on the actual preferences that people have, whether coercion to stop free riders is justified cannot be established a priori. If the person does not care about the public good, then the question becomes whether or not others can enforce *their* attachment to the good on someone who wishes to exercise her property rights and does not share that attachment. It is one thing to prevent free riding; it is quite another to impose a cultural project on persons who do not share that project and thus are not free riders at all. If we are right, then the business owner who wishes to hire an immigrant and who does not care whether the town's residents will speak English, Spanish, or a mix or both is not a free rider. He cannot, therefore, be prevented from hiring immigrants on the grounds that the community needs to stop those who free ride on the efforts of others to preserve English as a public good.

The second reply goes further: we deny that cultures can be coercively imposed, even on free riders. Our contention here is simple and direct: people do not have a right that their cultural environment remain unchanged.[40] In our view, cultures are valuable to the extent, and only to the extent, that they are the result of voluntary interactions (we allow, of course, for the exception of children who, inevitably, will be socialized into the culture by their parents). Cultures are valuable only if individuals value them and voluntarily try to preserve them. We do not endorse a collectivist notion of culture, one in which some people (even a majority) are entitled to coerce others to participate in the culture's practices. Cultures, however we define them, have dissenters and innovators. As we said, the proper moral claimants are individuals, not groups, communities, or the cultures that these groups supposedly embody. If cultural practices evolve as a result of voluntary exchanges during which no one's rights have been violated, then the result is morally permissible. Those who lament the loss of the old ways cannot use the coercive machinery of the state to impose their preferences that *others* behave in accordance with (what they regard as) the proper cultural code.

Finally, the future direction of the country will be determined by many internal factors besides immigration, such as economic policy, birth rates, and different social equilibria between cooperators and defectors, to name a few. If the

---

[39] David Schmidtz, *The Limits of Government: An Essay on the Public-Goods Argument* (Boulder, CO: Westview, 1990).

[40] Although we think Samuel Scheffler gives too much weight to the worries of cultural preservationists, we agree with him when he writes: "It cannot be the aim of a reasonable immigration policy to insulate either the host country or the new immigrants against cultural change. To think that we must choose between preserving the national culture of the host country and preserving the imported culture of the immigrants is to accept a false dilemma. The truth is that we cannot preserve either of them." Samuel Scheffler, "Immigration and the Significance of Culture," *Philosophy & Public Affairs* 35 (2007), 102.

reason to close the borders is that citizens are entitled democratically to control the future, then they should be equally entitled (democratically) to impede internal movement, control birth rates, impose school curricula, and so forth – measures that, we presume, Wellman does not support. The future direction of the state of Florida, for example, will be determined by how many people move there from other states. Wellman's argument, then, begs the question against immigration solely on the grounds of alienage because we do not suppose that he would allow Florida to prohibit immigration in order to preserve the future direction of Floridian society. The claim that citizens have a right to determine the future direction of their country, then, even if morally defensible (which it is not), proves too much, unless we prejudge the issue in favor of the state.

Our position may seem extreme to those who think national culture and identity are constitutive elements of our moral personality and that therefore countries (at least as long as they are not oppressive or unjust) are entitled to preserve those elements against the challenges that immigration poses. This view, however, is false because it unduly credits *authoritarian* preferences. Let us explain. Preferences can be classified into *personal* preferences, *external* preferences, and *authoritarian* preferences.[41] Personal preferences are preferences about what I myself shall do. My decision to convert to Catholicism, for example, is a personal preference. My action affects (mostly) me. In contrast, external preferences are preferences about what *others* should do. My preference to live surrounded by a Catholic culture is an external preference because it refers to the behavior of others, that others be Catholic. I wished that everyone around me converted to Catholicism because I believe that only in such an environment will I be able to pursue my projects. (Of course, if I express the preference to live in a Catholic culture by *moving* to an existing one, then it would be a personal preference because realizing my preference does not entail any *change* in the conduct of others.) In a sense, there is nothing wrong with an external preference per se *as long as it does not mature into coercive action*. I may have the preference that others be Catholic but reject attempts, by myself or by others, to *coerce* them into Catholicism. I might lament the fact that I am surrounded by nonbelievers, but I am not willing to enlist the coercive power of the state to enforce that preference.

We need, therefore, a third category: my preference will be an *authoritarian* preference when it is a preference that people be *coerced* into doing something they would not do voluntarily. For example, a preference (as Fernando and Isabel, the Catholic Monarchs of Spain, had) that Jews either convert to Catholicism or be expelled is an authoritarian preference. An authoritarian

---

[41] This taxonomy builds on Ronald Dworkin's distinction between personal and external preferences and Brian Barry's distinction between privately oriented and publicly oriented judgments and wants. Ronald Dworkin, *Taking Rights Seriously* (Cambridge, MA: Harvard University Press, 1978): 234–237; Brian Barry, *Political Argument* (London: Routledge, 2011). It is developed at some length in Guido Pincione and Fernando R. Tesón, *Rational Choice and Democratic Deliberation*, chap. 9.

preference is, then, a *reinforced* external preference. Now we hasten to concede that not all authoritarian preferences are impermissible. The community's preference that criminals go to prison is an authoritarian preference in this sense. However, as Dworkin once argued, an authoritarian preference is trumped by individual rights. If you have a right to dress any way you like, I cannot enforce a dress code against you. If you have a right to speak freely, the state may not enforce against you the majority's authoritarian preference that you shut up.

The desire to impose cultural standards is an authoritarian preference that clashes with a nonwaived individual right, the right to move about and interact with whom you please. The cultural conservationist favors using the power of the state to prevent changes in the culture. These changes, which immigration inevitably causes, are the result of spontaneous, voluntary processes: immigrants do not coerce the natives into abandoning their hamburgers and adopting Indian curries. The cultural conservative proposes to interfere with these voluntary processes and thinks that closing borders is a good way of doing it. But, as we have repeatedly stressed, these border-closing actions coercively interfere with people's right to personal mobility. This is true in all cases where immigrants have all sorts of commendable personal preferences, such as improving their lives by engaging in mutually advantageous transactions with natives. Cultural conservatives do not merely prefer to preserve the culture: they are willing to foist the culture on those who, for whatever reason, do not want it.

THE BENEFITS OF IMMIGRATION

The argument of this chapter so far has been largely deontological: immigration barriers violate important rights of the potential immigrants and of those in the host country who want to associate with them. But our case would not be complete without showing that softening borders is not only the morally right thing to do: it portends enormous national and global benefits.

The benefits of freer immigration are intuitively easy to see by straight application of elementary economic principles. Immigration barriers are a form of protectionism. As such, the deadweight losses they cause are easily predicted under the law of comparative advantages.[42] Immigrants increase efficiency by filling needs in the local labor market and thus reducing labor shortages. They move to places where they are more valued. Even without looking at actual numbers, this much is obviously true.

What is less obvious is *how much* the world loses by governments preventing people from crossing national borders. Michael Clemens has shown that the *size* of the losses caused by immigration barriers "should make economists' jaws hit their desks."[43] According to Clemens:

---

[42] See Chapter 6 on trade.

[43] Michael A. Clemens, "Economics and Emigration: Trillion-Dollar Bills on the Sidewalk?" *Journal of Economic Perspectives* 25 (2011), 83. See also Bryan Caplan, "Sitting on an Ocean

The gains from eliminating migration barriers dwarf ... the gains from eliminating other types of barriers. For the elimination of trade policy barriers and capital flow barriers, the estimated gains amount to less than a few percent of world GDP. *For labor mobility barriers, the estimated gains are often in the range of 50–150 percent of world GDP.*[44]

These are staggering numbers: we are talking about trillions in losses. If Clemens is even approximately right, hard national borders are probably the worst human invention in history. These economic benefits of immigration are undeniable and can be measured quite easily. It is true that some experts worry about immigration costs, in particular, the decrease in wages for native workers that immigration may cause, especially in the short term.[45] But even these more guarded specialists concede that "the majority view is that immigration yields a positive aggregate welfare effect in the host country, based on *technological complementarity* between immigrants and *some* domestic factors."[46]

Other benefits of immigration are harder to quantify but quite visible: do we really think that the United States would be better off without Chinese food or that Germany's Turkish *doner kebabs* have sabotaged the native culture? Contrary to the cultural-conservative argument discussed earlier, we think that immigration generally *improves* cultures. The economist Tyler Cowen has perceptively analyzed the effects of cross-cultural exchanges and concluded that they *enhance*, not undermine, aesthetic and other cultural values in the societies in which these exchanges take place.[47] We concur. Freedom, including freedom across borders, encourages human flourishing and creativity, while cultural nationalism encourages stifling government control.[48]

As is the case with liberal trade policy, the case for liberalizing immigration is overdetermined. Freer borders are morally mandatory because they respect individual rights. They are also economically *and* culturally desirable to a high degree. Even someone who insists that states have the constitutional power to

---

of Talent," Econlog, Library of Economics and Liberty; available at: http://econlog.econlib.org/archives/2014/01/sitting_on_an_0.html (accessed January 7, 2014).

[44] Clemens, "Economics and Emigration," 83 (emphasis added).

[45] See Gabriel J. Felbermayr and Wilhelm Kohler, "Immigration and Native Welfare," *International Economic Review* 48 (2007), 731–60, and George J. Borjas, "The Economic Benefits of Immigration," *Journal of Economic Perspectives* 9 (1995), 3–22. The question of the effects of immigration on native wages is controversial in the specialized literature, however. For a less pessimistic view, see Christian Dustmann, Tommaso Frattini, and Ian P. Preston, "The Effect of Immigration along the Distribution of Wages," *Review of Economic Studies* 80 (2013), 145–73.

[46] Felbermayer and Kohler, "Immigration and Native Welfare," 732 (emphasis in original). Similarly, Borjas writes that "natives do benefit from immigration mainly because of production complementarities between immigrant workers and other factors of production, and that these benefits are larger when immigrants are sufficiently 'different' from the stock of native productive inputs." Borjas, "Economic Benefits," 5.

[47] See Tyler Cowen, *Creative Destruction*, (Princeton, NJ: Princeton University Press, 2002). Cowen addresses all cross-cultural exchanges, not just those caused by migrations, but his conclusions apply, of course, to the exchanges between the immigrant and native cultures as well.

[48] Ibid., 145.

close borders (as is the case with the U.S. Constitution) would have to concede, in light of the evidence, that, most likely, closing borders is bad policy.

CONCLUSION

We do not labor under any illusion that the prescriptions set forth in this chapter will be adopted any time soon. One main reason is that the national and international *laws* of immigration place few limitations on the power of states to exclude foreigners. Under international law, that power is one of the attributes of sovereignty.[49] Under U.S. constitutional law, the federal government has an unlimited power to control borders, in turn based, according to the courts, on the international law principle just mentioned.[50] None of this should surprise us: the main feature and purpose of international law is to protect nation-states and their rulers. From a political angle, because poor and powerless noncitizens possess negligible political heft, their rights and interests carry little weight in the calculations of wealthy countries' political elites. This is true at all times but becomes intensified when economic conditions worsen. Then more than ever it is every man for himself and devil take the hindmost. The devil has indeed been busily engaged with the hindmost in the wake of the financial crisis of 2008, and reactive nationalist sentiments have waxed. This is especially the case with regard to openness to migrants, but it also has clouded prospects for international trade. We turn to trade in Chapter 6; Chapter 5 discusses the brain-drain argument for immigration barriers.

[49] Modernly, this power is thought to derive from the sovereign equality of states (UN Charter, art. 1.1) and its corollaries, the exclusivity of jurisdiction over its territory and the power of the state to "perform all activities deemed necessary or beneficial to the population living there." Antonio Cassesse, *International Law*, 2nd ed. (Oxford University Press), 51. This does not mean that states have complete freedom to set the conditions for admitting foreigners. Today, racist criteria (which were acceptable yonder) are prohibited by international law.

[50] In the *Chinese Exclusion Case*, the Supreme Court said: "That the government of the United States ... can exclude aliens from its territory is a proposition which we do not think open to controversy. Jurisdiction over its own territory ... is an incident of every independent nation. It is part of its independence." 130 U.S. 581, 604 (1889). While exclusion of aliens on account of race is not permissible today, this *dictum* is, unfortunately, still good law.

5

Emigration and the Brain-Drain Objection

The brain-drain argument in its purest form maintains that when wealthy countries open their borders, the predictable effect is to induce the brightest and most productive citizens of poor countries to transfer their labor to a location where it will be more personally remunerative. Economies that already enjoy the benefits of ample human capital will be piling up yet more at the expense of those that have precious little. It is not nice to abscond with the widow's mite, but neither is it very neighborly to entice away her daughter, the computer programmer. In the interests of justice, the rich should refrain from acquiring precious personnel from the poor. The brain drain is, on this view, a curse for developing countries because it hurts those left behind. Because human capital is an important determinant of economic growth, the loss of skilled individuals, it is thought, undermines the economic performance of the country.[1] Taking this empirical claim as true, critics deplore the brain drain as unfair and suggest that governments should try to stem it. But are these claims sound?

We argue that they are not.[2] The brain drain is not as harmful as critics believe, and to the extent that it does harm some people, the harm is permissible for two reasons: first, the state does not own its citizens, and second,

---

[1] One researcher summarizes the conventional view: "The brain drain increases the scarcity of highly needed skilled labour in developing countries and consequently reduces long-run economic growth and income." Research Group on the Global Future, Center for Applied Policy Research, "Brain Drain," CAP Report, July 20, 2005, 1; available at: http://www.cap-lmu.de/fgz/statistics/brain-drain.php (accessed March 12, 2010).

[2] The first version of this chapter, Fernando R. Tesón, "Brain Drain," *University of San Diego Law Review* 45 (2008), 899, was, to our knowledge, the first philosophical treatment of the topic. See now Kieran Oberman, "Can Brain Drain Justify Immigration Restrictions?" *Ethics* 123 (2013), 427–55, and Gillian Brock and Michael Blake, *Debating Brain Drain: May Governments Restrict Emigration?* (Oxford University Press, 2015). The literature on global justice, usually favorable to freer migration, has kept silent on this issue. Allen Buchanan, for example, recommends that the international community should support "efforts to liberalize immigration policies to

the right to leave is central to the pursuit of personal projects. Critics of the brain drain make problematic empirical and philosophical claims. The empirical assumption that the brain drain invariably hurts developing countries is controversial. Although a number of authorities endorse the conventional view, a contrarian literature suggests that the brain drain may help those left behind in various ways. We show that the philosophical claims associated with the objection are flawed as well. The claims we reject are as follows: because natural talents are morally arbitrary, those who have them are not entitled to the income those talents generate, and talented persons owe duties of reciprocity or gratitude.

We first examine the facts and summarize various proposals to stem the brain drain. The evidence shows that it is far from clear that the brain drain always, or most of the time, harms those left behind. In general, because the brain drain allocates resources efficiently, it is likely to benefit many people globally, especially the world's poor. Moreover, these benefits often accrue to persons in the emigrant's home state. We then concede for the sake of argument that those left behind are harmed in some relevant sense and ask whether this harm is unjust. We conclude that it is not. The claim that natural talents are undeserved makes no sense. Moreover, the state has no claim over the skilled individual who emigrates because he has prepolitical ownership of his talents.

We then examine claims that the talented citizen has duties of reciprocity or gratitude to her native country and find them wanting. Finally, we discuss the views that skilled emigrants, in most cases, act wrongly when they leave and that host countries act wrongly when they attract them. We doubt that in most cases those claims can be sustained. In cases where the emigrant arguably acts unethically, still the state has no claim over him. And we do not think that host countries act improperly either when they receive talented immigrants. On the contrary, as we saw in Chapter 4, liberal immigration laws help persons to pursue their personal projects.

THE FACTS

International migration of talent has increased substantially since World War II. A 2005 statistical study of selected countries shows that emigration of talent surpasses 50 percent in some countries.[3] The brain drain occurs mostly, but by no

---

increase economic opportunities for the world's worst off." Allen Buchanan, *Justice, Legitimacy, and Self-Determination: Moral Foundations for International Law* (Oxford University Press, 2004), 193. Similarly, Moellendorf criticizes current immigration restrictions in developed countries but does not mention the brain drain. Darrell Moellendorf, *Cosmopolitan Justice* (Boulder, CO: Westview Press, 2002), 54, 61–7.

[3] See CAP Report, n. 1. In some cases, the percentage of skilled population that emigrates is staggering: 82.5 percent of Jamaicans with tertiary education live in Organisation for Economic Co-operation and Development (OECD) countries. Devesh Kapur and John McHale, *Give Us Your Best and Brightest: The Global Hunt for Talent and Its Impact on the Developing World*

means only, from poor to rich countries. This is the brain drain that raises ethical concerns because unlike most rich countries, poor countries urgently need scientists and doctors. A German doctor who leaves for the United States presumably does not hurt Germany much; a doctor from Ghana who makes the decision to emigrate is likely, it is thought, to hurt his home country. The causes of brain drain are not hard to fathom. On the demand side, the explosion of knowledge-based industries in rich countries has increased the need for skilled workers there. This demand creates the wage differentials that attract educated immigrants. On the supply side, people leave because of poor salaries and deficient working and living conditions. The emigrant's expected benefits offset the considerable emigration costs. These benefits are not only financial: brains go where other brains are, where they can face challenges. The brain drain, then, occurs by simple operation of the law of labor supply and demand.

As indicated earlier, the conventional view is that the brain drain hurts the home country. In a classic treatment, noted economist Jagdish Bhagwati took this harm for granted when he proposed taxing the foreign-earned income of the migrant.[4] Others have echoed this sentiment, including the informed press.[5] The idea is that emigration of human capital stymies economic growth. Poor countries that lose their talented citizens are likely to remain trapped in poverty. This occurs in part because, as we saw in Chapters 1 and 3, good institutions are crucial for economic and political success. Because educated citizens are pivotal for institution building, the country cannot take off if they leave.[6] Critics of the brain drain conclude that because the benefits of education are externalities that persons do not take into account when making private decisions, "policies to curb the brain drain may be warranted."[7]

A number of scholars have challenged the conventional view. First, allowing emigration of talented persons raises the returns on education.[8] If people have a nonnegligible probability of migrating to a richer country, they will

(Washington, DC: Center for Global Development, 2005), 19. There are some surprises, though; not all source countries are developing countries. New Zealand and Italy experience high brain drain, whereas the brain drain from Italy and Russia exceeds the brain drain from Mexico and Thailand. For updated numbers, see World Economic Forum, *Global Talent Risk-Seven Responses* (Geneva: World Economic Forum, 2011).

4 Jagdish N. Bhagwati, "The Brain Drain Tax Proposal and the Issues," in *Taxing the Brain Drain*, Jagdish N. Bhagwati and Martin Partington, eds. (Amsterdam: North Holland, 1976), 3. For a more recent reevaluation of this proposal, see the articles collected in *Journal of Development Economics* 95 (2011).

5 See "Go for It," *The Economist*, May 6, 2000, 20.

6 See Kapur and McHale, *Give Us Your Best and Brightest*, 5–6.

7 William J. Carrington and Enrica Detragiache, "How Extensive Is the Brain Drain?" *Finance and Development* (1999), 49.

8 The dissenters include Andrew Mountford, "Can a Brain Drain Be Good for Growth in the Source Economy?" *Journal of Development Economics* 53 (1997), 287–8; Oded Stark, "Rethinking the Brain Drain," *World Development* 32 (2004): 15; Jean-Pierre Vidal, "The Effect of Emigration on Human Capital Formation," *Journal of Population Economics* 11 (1998), 589–90.

predictably invest in their education. The possibility of brain drain, then, creates an incentive for more education, and this benefits the country, assuming that only some of the people will in fact emigrate. Even conceding that the country may experience some loss, this *brain gain* – defined as the increased investment in education in the source country – must be computed to calculate the effect of migration. The brain gain may well exceed the brain drain. Second, many people who study or work abroad return to their home countries. This benefit of temporary emigration, called *brain circulation*, likewise must be computed.[9] And third, those who emigrate are likely to generate knowledge and research that is available universally. Everyone benefits from this, including those in the home country. This phenomenon has been dubbed the *brain bank*.[10] Although some of these findings have been disputed,[11] they are weighty enough to question the view that the harm to source countries is as devastating or univocal as critics had earlier assumed.

So there is no reason to accept the assumption that migration from Country A is, in general, bad for those who remain in Country A. For one thing, the great preponderance of economic migration is less well described as *brain drain* than as *muscle drain*. Landless peasants or unemployed urbanites who flee in the hope of prospects for a better life take with them their malnutrition, not reserves of scarce skills. Insofar as the result is one mouth less to feed out of minimal resources, the sums are apt to be positive for those left behind. This, though, is vastly to understate the typical economic consequences of migration. When Bennet leaves Country A, he does not thereby abandon all ties to it. Bennet's wife, children, parents, and extended family remain behind, and Bennet will be better able to support them with the income he can earn in Country B. Remittances make up a large proportion of the income of many of the world's poor. The amount fluctuates in response to changes in economic conditions around the world. According to the World Bank, it totaled $305 billion in 2008, but in the wake of that year's financial crisis and global slowdown, it was predicted to fall to $290 billion in 2009.[12] This still-substantial sum represents the difference between minimal decency and destitution for tens of millions of the world's poor.

[9] A recent study argues that return migration may mitigate the loss caused by the brain drain. See Christian Dustmann, Itzhak Fadlon, and Yoram Weiss, "Return Migration, Human Capital Accumulation and the Brain Drain," *Journal of Development Economics* 95 (2011), 58–67.

[10] The brain-bank effect is examined in A. Agrawal, D. Kapur, J. McHale, and A. Oettl, "Brain Drain or Brain Bank? The Impact of Skilled Emigration on Poor-Country Innovation," *Journal of Urban Economics* 69 (2011), 43–55.

[11] By Maurice Schiff, "Brain Gain: Claims About its Size and Impact on Welfare and Growth are Greatly Exaggerated," in *International Migration, Remittances, and the Brain Drain*, Caglar Ozden and Maurice Schiff, eds. (New York: Palgrave Macmillan 2006), 201–24.

[12] http://web.worldbank.org/WBSITE/EXTERNAL/NEWS/0,,contentMDK:22115303~pagePK:6 4257043~piPK:437376~theSitePK:460700.html (accessed November 21, 2009).

In Chapter 4 we cautioned against thinking of migration in nineteenth-century terms. It is not only cash transfers that can make the reverse transit back to the country of origin. Those who have gone abroad will, if unimpeded, often choose to return either temporarily or permanently. When they do so, they bring with them both financial capital and human capital acquired abroad. This benefits not just themselves but also those with whom they subsequently interact. In particular, they provide knowledge externalities both insofar as others emulate particular skills that the returnee has acquired and also as he is the incarnate illustration of what is achievable by someone possessing ambition and willingness to take risks. Of course, the countries that play the brain-drain card to denounce as turncoats those who have fled (e.g., as did East Germany with its splendid wall) will thereby diminish incentive to return at all.

Persons who migrate in order to secure greater wealth are not thereby collecting a gratuitous bonanza as a result of being in a more fortunate location. Rather, economic relationships newly opened up to them often allow them to be far more productive than would have been the case had they remained at home. This observation is true of ordinary occupations, such as driving a cab or weeding a garden, but it is especially salient in the context of entrepreneurship. America has from its earliest days to the present been a fount of entrepreneurial activity, and from the time of John Jacob Astor to the present, many of the most innovative and successful entrepreneurs entered as immigrants. In recent years they have jump-started the information revolution. Andrew Grove fled Hungary during the 1956 revolt against Soviet oppression and made his way to America, where eventually he became one of the architects of Intel. Sergey Brin came to the United States as a young child when his parents despaired of prospects in Russia. Twenty years later he had become cofounder of Google. Grove and Brin both became enormously wealthy men. Their adopted country profited handsomely because of their presence. All this is obvious. Easier to overlook, though, is that people all over the world benefited from their migrations. Anyone who has operated a computer with an Intel CPU inside or conducted a Google search is a beneficiary. Had Grove and Brin remained confined to their dreary communist lands of upbringing or had they encountered a *CLOSED!* sign at the American port of entry, those benefits almost certainly would have never come into existence, although none of us would be in a position to know what had been lost. Nor are we in a position to know what has been lost by withholding entry from persons who also might have opened new wealth-creating vistas but were never afforded an opportunity to do so. We repeat because it deserves emphasis: gains accrue not only to the welcoming country but also to people across the world.[13]

---

[13] It is probably not coincidental that both Grove and Brin are of Jewish origin. Their capacity to create wealth is a product both of their intellectual gifts and of the fact that they were able to evade barriers associated with Eastern European anti-Semitism. It is also probably not coincidental that alongside the United States, one of the world's most fertile sites for entrepreneurship is Israel.

Asian immigrants constitute a substantial proportion of those who make Silicon Valley hum.[14] The music may have been louder and sweeter but for visa quotas that interfered with firms' ability to hire additional skilled personnel.[15] That other countries do an even worse job of affording access to bright, creative foreigners does not constitute an encomium to U.S. policy. Perusal of a listing of tenured faculty at Massachusetts Institute of Technology reveals that something on the order of 50 percent were born outside the United States. In no small measure does the country's relative openness to foreign talent compensate for the lackluster performance of its public schools.[16] This is good for those who live within U.S. borders and also good for those who benefit directly or indirectly from research done by scientists and other scholars.[17] Most of all, though, it is a good for those who have been enabled to give fuller effect to their energy and talents. Even if all the other blessings of liberty were in question, this one by itself would be enough to justify claims to unimpeded mobility.

A couple of caveats about the economic literature are in order. First, economic studies assume that wage differential is the only relevant incentive to emigrate. In reality, immigration has many other costs and benefits. In terms of costs, the emigrant leaves her culture and her family, perhaps to go to a place where she will not speak the language or will feel otherwise alienated or isolated. In terms of benefits, as we indicated, she may seek values other than money, such as quality of institutions or intellectual and scientific challenges. Second, economists cast the brain-drain debate in terms of whether it hurts the source country. Yet any normative assessment of the brain drain should take into account its effect on two other groups: the immigrants themselves and their families, of course (after all, their decision to emigrate is central to *their* life projects), and the world population at large and, in particular, the world's poor, who may benefit from what the emigrant produces. These variables are rarely addressed in the brain-drain literature, which focuses, simplistically, only on the harm to the source country. The importance of the decision to emigrate for the emigrant herself and her family is obvious. Although the effect of the brain drain on the global population is difficult to establish, there is no suggestion in the literature to dispute the obvious conjecture that if talents are put to their best and highest uses, they will end up benefiting a larger number of people.

---

[14] AnnaLee Saxenian, "Silicon Valley's New Immigrant Entrepreneurs," Working Paper 15, Center for Comparative Immigration Studies, University of California, San Diego, May 2000; available at: http://www.ccis-ucsd.org/PUBLICATIONS/wrkg15.PDF.

[15] See Matt Richtel, "Tech Recruiting Clashes with Immigration Rules," *New York Times*, December 4, 2012; available at: http://www.nytimes.com/2009/04/12/business/12immig.html (accessed April 11, 2009).

[16] There is a case for suggesting that the Statue of Liberty's message of welcome be revised to "huddled masses/physics classes."

[17] If readers harbor suspicions that this may constitute a pitch for welcoming migrant philosophers, we cannot deny that they have grounds.

This is not hard to accept in the aggregate, although it may or may not be true in a particular case. A scientist who is poorly paid and lacks laboratories and qualified assistants is less likely to contribute beneficial knowledge than a scientist who works under favorable conditions. However, a doctor who practices in poor rural areas in a developing country seems to be helping more deserving persons more than a doctor who treats millionaires at the Mayo Clinic, even though the latter's services are put to their economically best and highest use.[18]

PROPOSALS TO STEM THE BRAIN DRAIN

Critics of the brain drain have proposed several measures to curb it. They can be grouped into three categories: measures adopted by source states, measures adopted by host states, and measures adopted via international agreement.[19] In turn, the source country may use the "stick" and enact measures of control or use the "carrot" and enact measures to increase the incentives to stay. The most obvious control measure is the exit visa, which subjects emigration to the government's permission. The exit visa is the staple of the authoritarian state, a device to prevent all persons from leaving. Slightly less drastic measures forcibly delay emigration, for example, by requiring years of local medical training or practice. The country also may enact fiscal controls. The government can tax the foreign-earned income of the emigrant or establish financial burdens such as an exit tax. These measures do not prohibit emigration but raise its cost, sometimes prohibitively. Alternatively, governments may create incentives to stay by improving salaries and working conditions and, more important, pursuing economic and social policies that bring progress, freedom, and prosperity to their society. Finally, governments may strengthen the relationship with the diaspora of talented nationals, thus softening the (supposedly) adverse impact of the brain drain.

Receiving countries may discontinue immigration policies that lure talented immigrants either by tightening immigration laws or by refraining from direct recruitment of skilled persons in poor countries. Thus, for example, in the United States, the federally funded Fulbright Scholarship Program requires foreign graduates to return to their home countries. Finally, countries may agree, by treaty, for example, that the rich country will compensate the poor country for the brain drain.

THE STATE AND THE EMIGRANT

There are several ways to evaluate the brain drain and the proposals to regulate it. One could take a purely economic approach and say that the brain

---

[18] We say "seems" because even this cannot be said with certainty. What if the Mayo Clinic patient is a great economist or scientist who, if cured, will help to rescue *millions* of persons from poverty?

[19] For a list, see Kapur and McHale, *Give Us Your Best and Brightest*, 177–209.

drain simply allocates human resources efficiently by putting talents to their best and highest use.[20] Because skilled workers migrate where their talents are most wanted and rewarded, total output is maximized. On this view, asking whether the brain drain is fair is like asking whether the fact that Americans buy Japanese DVD players is fair. The brain drain is a free exchange across borders, like free trade: the foreign employer hires the immigrant, and everyone benefits.

But, of course, the question is not so simple. An efficient outcome may be unfair. Perhaps citizens who consider leaving owe their fellow citizens a duty to reconsider. Some may suggest that the government, acting on behalf of the citizenry, has the power to enforce such duties and make emigration difficult or impossible. Just as the government, it is thought, has the power to enforce our political duties by redistributing wealth through taxes, so the government can legitimately induce the wayward sheep to stay in the herd. And it might be argued that rich countries are wrong to actively entice educated immigrants by enacting generous immigration laws and aggressively recruiting foreign talent. It might be thought that in so doing rich countries are preying on an important resource that developing countries need to grow.

Suppose that it is the case that migration is bad for the country from which migrants flow. We would nonetheless utterly reject the contention that those would-be migrants can properly be barred from egress except at a prohibitive cost. People are not possessions of their home country, to be deployed in service of its collective goals. Rather, moral priority runs in the other direction. Individuals are the primary rights holders; to the extent that associations or corporations or states can be said to have rights at all, their entitlements are derivative. Speaking in terms of the interests or well-being of poor countries is liable to obfuscate the secondary status of all such collective ascriptions. Moral clarity is better attained by keeping the focus clearly on the ultimate moral claimants. There is a word for holding one person hostage so that he will be obliged to continue to serve the interests of those who will find themselves worse off if he is allowed to depart, but it is not a word that opponents of the brain drain are likely to wish to employ. Thus, even if Country A is rendered worse off by Bennet's departure to Country B, it has no claim against Country B to block the migration regardless of the comparative wealth and poverty of the two countries. This is a corollary of the earlier observation that global justice is not primarily what Rawls calls a "law of peoples" but is rather at its foundations a theory of how states and nonstate entities may permissibly treat people.

---

[20] For a defense of liberal immigration laws – and not just brain drain – along these lines, see Alan O. Sykes, "The Welfare Economics of Immigration Law: A Theoretical Survey with an Analysis of U.S. Policy," in *Justice in Immigration*, Warren F. Schwartz, ed. (Cambridge University Press, 1995), 158–9.

This is why the language (often used by migration specialists) that describes individuals as "human capital" of the state is objectionable. It suggests that talented persons belong to the state and hence that the state may regulate how many of them leave or stay. This approach personifies the state: the state owns its human capital like an investor owns her financial capital. Such an anthropomorphic view of the state fails to treat persons as autonomous agents. Any liberal theory should give pride of place to individual choices, and while occasionally a decision to leave may be open to moral criticism, this does not mean that the state should have the power to impede emigration. Any political measure to address the brain drain should cohere with the central place of individual freedom in a theory of global justice. Only a police state tells persons that they should work here or there. Scientists, doctors, and teachers in principle should be free to seek employment wherever and whenever they want.

To be sure, few disagree that citizens have a right to leave their country.[21] Indeed, only oppressive regimes have subjected emigration to the government's permission.[22] Although exit visas have sometimes been defended, that position is mercifully discredited today, and governments that prevent people from leaving violate international law.[23] A major purpose of the right of exit is to allow citizens to choose among different cultures, institutions, and legal systems. It is an essential moral right of persons because it is pivotal to their pursuit of personal projects.

Once the right of exit is accepted, it is tempting to say that this settles the issue of brain drain: the emigrant would simply be exercising his right to exit, and the state has no legitimate power to stop him. However, this conclusion, while correct as it goes, would be too quick because although it is true that the state cannot legitimately force the emigrant to stay, the state may perhaps raise the cost of leaving. If the brain drain is bad and something ought to be done about it – even though that something cannot be forcing persons to stay – arguably, state measures short of force that create incentives to stay are not necessarily objectionable. Moreover, even conceding that the emigrants have a right to leave, one could still argue that, as a matter of personal morality, they ought to stay. Political principles, that is, principles about the proper role of the state, may tell us that a liberal state cannot validly prevent someone from

---

[21] Thus John Rawls says that a well-ordered society must recognize the right of emigration as a human right. John Rawls, *The Law of Peoples* (Cambridge University Press, 1999), 74.

[22] See R. Adam Moody, "Reexamining Brain Drain from the Former Soviet Union," *The Nonproliferation Review* 3 (1996), 92; available at: http://cns.miis.edu/pubs/npr/vol03/33/moody33.pdf (accessed September 7, 2008). Interestingly, Soviet bloc regimes gave brain drain as their reason to control all immigration. In Cuba, for example, the regime routinely denies exit visas to health-care professionals. "Denial Exit Visas a Health Care Professionals in Cuba" [*sic*], *Medicina Cubana*, November 17, 2006; available at: http://medicinacubana.blogspot.com/2006/11/denial-exit-visas-health-care.html (accessed January 10, 2010).

[23] As provided, inter alia, in art. 12 (2), International Covenant on Civil and Political Rights (December 16, 1966).

leaving, but they do not address the personal moral issue. That a scientist has a *political* right to leave does not mean that she would be acting ethically if she left, because she may still owe her fellow citizens a moral duty to remain in her native land.

We turn, then, to arguments that may be invoked in support of measures to curb the brain drain.

THE MORAL ARBITRARINESS OF TALENTS

Does a state have a moral claim on its subjects' talents? Many philosophers have answered in the affirmative. They claim that the state can extensively tax people's talent-generated income. The reason is that a central role of justice is to neutralize the effects of morally irrelevant factors. Because natural talents are not deserved –they are morally arbitrary – it is unfair for talented persons to gain advantage from their use, unless in doing so they benefit others, especially the poor. For example, John Rawls thinks that a central aim of justice is to "nullif[y] the accidents of natural endowment" not only because this is necessary to implement equality but also because we do not deserve our talents.[24] For Rawls, "[T]he most obvious injustice of the system of natural liberty [that is, a system where, among other things, people can use their talents as they please] is that it permits distributive shares to be improperly influenced by these factors so arbitrary from a moral point of view."[25] But Rawls goes further: he also criticizes what he calls "the liberal conception," that is, one that improves on natural liberty by securing equality of opportunity. Rawls writes that "even if [the liberal conception] works to perfection in eliminating the influence of social contingencies, it still permits the distribution of wealth and income to be determined by the natural distribution of abilities and talents." Rawls immediately adds that "[t]here is no more reason to permit the distribution of income and wealth to be settled by the distribution of natural assets than by historical and social fortune."[26] In other parts of the book he is even more explicit: "[T]he difference principle," for Rawls, "represents, in effect, an agreement to regard the distribution of natural talents as a common asset and to share in the benefits of this distribution whatever it turns out to be."[27] Natural talents are, indeed, "a collective asset."[28] Many writers have uncritically accepted the premise of this argument.

The consequence of this view for brain drain is that the emigrant does not own his talents because his having them is a mere accident of nature and

---

[24] John Rawls, *A Theory of Justice* (Cambridge, MA: Harvard University Press, 1971), 15. The quotations that follow are from this work.

[25] Ibid., 72 (emphasis added).

[26] Ibid., 73–4.

[27] Ibid., 101 (emphasis added).

[28] Ibid., 179.

therefore an inadequate basis for justifying differential earnings. Hence his natural assets are part of a common pool that services his fellow citizens. This obligation, it is thought, entitles the state to impose some burden on the emigrant, even if that burden cannot be, consistently with the priority of liberty, a prohibition from leaving. The government can freely tax the income generated by the use of his natural assets. Under this view, a person is only entitled to whatever income shares are allotted to him by a theory of justice, and the fact that he does not deserve his natural assets frees the state to redistribute the income generated by those assets in the way justice requires. The only reason why the state allows a person to keep some of his talent-generated income is because doing so maintains that person's incentive to remain productive, and others, especially the poor, are thereby better served. To be sure, there is no morally permissible way for the state to literally appropriate his talents, but he has a duty to compensate others for his greater gains.

The problem with this argument is that its premise is false. Simply put, it makes no sense to say that natural talents are undeserved (or deserved).[29] Talents are neither deserved nor undeserved. The reason is that in order to evaluate whether Meredith deserves the talent T (which she now has), we must evaluate what Meredith did prior to her having T. But before having T, Meredith did not exist. Therefore, there is nothing that Meredith could have done or omitted prior to her coming to have T that may authorize us to say, meaningfully, that T is deserved or undeserved. Of course, if we define "I deserve T" as "I have T as a result of a (meritorious, wise) choice I made in the past," then the statement "T is not deserved" is trivially true because I could not make a choice before birth. This vacuous understanding can hardly form the basis of the state's appropriation of someone's holdings. Talents are not deserved and not *un*deserved; the concept of desert simply does not apply to them.[30]

It is false, then, that the possession of talents is morally arbitrary. But what we can say is that, deserved or not, persons own their natural talents. John Locke famously claimed that "[t]hough the Earth, and all inferior Creatures be common to all Men, yet every Man has a Property in his own Person. This no Body has any Right to but himself. The Labour of his Body, and the Work of his Hands, we may say, are properly his."[31] Here Locke distinguishes between

---

[29] Here we follow Ezequiel Spector, "Do You Deserve to Be Talented," *Utilitas* 23 (2011), 115–25.

[30] Spector shows that the problem is not solved by saying that talents are "morally arbitrary" instead of "undeserved." This simply begs the question: if one asks why talents are morally arbitrary, the answer is "because they are undeserved." And if the claimant protests that the person did nothing to deserve her talents *precisely* because she did not exist, then *all* this sentence says is that the person did not exist before her birth. Ibid., 121–2. It is weird indeed to say that I do not deserve to be the person I am, but this is the claim that Rawls and his followers make. True, sometimes we talk this way, for example, "Why does Pavarotti have such a beautiful voice? He does not deserve it! Why not me?"

[31] John Locke, *Two Treatises of Government* [1690], P. Laslett, ed. (Cambridge University Press, 1967), 287–8.

property in one's own person and property in external things. Because external things, such as land, were initially owned *in common*, first appropriators owed, perhaps, some compensation to latecomers. The idea here is that taking resources from the commons worsens the remaining co-owners. Some think that this original duty of compensation provides a moral foundation for the distributive state because it knocks down the first-appropriation rule as a basis for the right of private property.[32] Locke thought that individuals could appropriate resources by mixing their labor with those resources, as long as they left "enough, and as good ... in common for others" – the Lockean proviso. Many writers have pointed out, however, that the Lockean proviso cannot possibly be satisfied in a world of scarcity. Therefore, first possessors and their descendants in the chain of title have a standing obligation, as it were, to compensate others, and the state can implement this duty through redistributive taxation.

However, this argument, whatever its weight to justify the state redistribution of external resources, cannot possibly apply to natural talents. Individuals did not appropriate their natural assets from the commons: they came attached to them. Consequently, a person's claim over himself – his body, his talents, his mind – is stronger than his claim over external things because with respect to these assets he does not (on this view) have a standing duty to compensate others that the state can enforce through taxation.[33] One may perhaps concede that the government can tax my talent-generated income in order to provide genuine public goods, but the government cannot tax me to realize social justice because others lack any justice-based claim over my natural assets. Because my talents have come attached to me, and they are not goods that I have taken from the commons, the income I generate from them is entirely mine (subject perhaps to the state's power to collect taxes to pay for the provision of public goods). These personal talents are not traceable to any violent or otherwise suspect appropriation in the past. If someone traces the chain of title of the land I own, they may find that at some point in the past someone stole the land from somebody else. But no examination of the chain of title of my natural assets will reveal any blemish. Those assets came with me from the day I was born; I did not take them away from anyone else.

---

[32] Typical in this sense is Will Kymlica, *Contemporary Political Philosophy: An Introduction*, 2nd ed. (Oxford University Press), 116–21. For a contemporary presentation of self-ownership, see Michael Otsuka, *Libertarianism without Inequality* (Oxford University Press, 2003), 11–19, and Peter Vallentyne, "Libertarianism," in *Stanford Encyclopedia of Philosophy*, 2006; available at: http://plato.stanford.edu/entries/libertarianism. For Robert Nozick's take on self-ownership, see *Anarchy, State, and Utopia* (New York: Basic Books, 1974), 171.

[33] Of course, virtually no one claims that the state can *physically* appropriate parts of a person's body or mind. As Warren Quinn put it, "[A]ny arrangement that denied him that say would be a grave indignity." Not everyone agrees, however. *See* Kasper Lippert-Rasmussen, *Against Self-Ownership: There Are No Fact-Insensitive Ownership Rights over One's Body, Philos. Pub. Aff.* 36(86) (2008), 117 (claiming that most of the intuitions that are said to derive from self-ownership are better explained by other principles).

The argument we make here is conditional: *if* one reason for taxing people's wealth is that they do not morally own that wealth because they or their predecessors in the chain of title took that wealth from the commons without compensating others, then there is no reason to tax people's talent-generated income because it is not traceable to any first appropriation. We do not necessarily accept the premise of the argument, that the failure to compensate others in first appropriations of external goods justifies redistributive taxation, nor, conversely, do we necessarily endorse the Lockean view that self-ownership can ground, through labor, the acquisition of external assets. We just do not address it here. Similarly, supporters of redistributive taxation surely have other arguments; for example, they may think that inequality per se is objectionable regardless of the quality of title (or other such considerations.) Our argument here does not address those either.

There are additional reasons to reject the view that the state has a claim on its subjects' natural talents. First, it is not true that income distribution influenced by natural talents is as worrisome as income distribution influenced by social position because, as observed earlier, there is a significant moral gap between a person's body and her mind, on the one hand, and the estate that she inherited, on the other. The claims that others press on a person's material wealth are stronger than the claims that others press on her natural assets. Arguably at least, if someone in the past took material things from the commons, fairness may require that the present holder be willing to give some of that back to others. But no one took her natural assets from the commons, and that makes an important difference in the claims that others have over her person.

Second, as we saw, Rawls and his followers think that the reason why people should not be able to generate differential income from their natural talents is that people do not deserve them. We have suggested that this claim does not make sense. But even assuming that it does, it is fallacious to say that not deserving X is a sufficient reason for not being entitled to X. And it is equally fallacious to suggest "that a person earns Y ... only if he's earned (or otherwise deserves) whatever he used (including natural assets) in the process of earning Y."[34] To be sure, we do say that someone owns something because she deserves it: someone has earned this award by her work, and so forth. Deserving something is, perhaps, a sufficient condition for coming to own it. People should get what they deserve.[35] But the concepts of owning and deserving are not coextensive. Persons can be morally entitled to things they do not deserve. If I give you a gift, you may not deserve it, but my giving it to you surely counts against dispossessing you.[36]

[34] Nozick, *Anarchy, State, and Utopia*, 225.

[35] For a perceptive treatment, see David Schmidtz, "How to Deserve," *Political Theory* 30 (2002), 774–99.

[36] To our knowledge, this fallacy by Rawls was first detected by Robert Nozick, *Anarchy, State, and Utopia*, 225–7. See also Fred D. Miller, Jr., "The Natural Right to Private Property", in *The Libertarian Reader*, Tibor R. Machan ed. (Lanham, Maryland: Rowman and Littlefield, 1982), 278, and Douglas B. Rasmussen, "Liberalism and Natural End Ethics," *American Philosophical Quarterly* 27 (1990), 158–9.

This weakness of the argument is especially glaring when applied to natural assets. My limbs, my keen or deficient eyesight, and my modest or sharp intelligence are mine even if, in a cosmic sense, I do not deserve them. They are mine simply because they are attached to my person in a fundamental and intimate way, and it does not matter that my having them is in some sense morally arbitrary. The fact that my head, with my brain in it, is attached to my body is enough to justify title. Alternative arrangements that authorize others to have the primary say over what is to be done to my body and mind lead, in the vast majority of cases, to grave assaults on human dignity.[37] Institutional arrangements that give others title to my natural assets are akin to slavery. Each person is the morally rightful owner of himself because the contrary view clashes with our intuitions against slavery and domination.[38]

Third, those who deny self-ownership and its Lockean extension to private property assume an unquestioned power of the state to redistribute everything. That is, they apply what we call here the *collectivist default rule*. They conclude that because persons cannot invoke self-ownership, the state can take their assets, natural or worldly, and give them to others who deserve or need them more. However, the conclusion does not follow: an additional argument is needed to show that the *state* has the power to appropriate unowned things. Perhaps a person cannot claim ownership of anything, but it does not follow that others can, and it does not follow that the state should. Moreover, the collectivist default rule overlooks government failure. Even if it might be an ideal practice for the government to take things away from those who hold them in order to further the common good, governmental institutions often fail to further the common good. It is an open question, in such cases, whether empowering the failure-prone government is a better solution than returning to self-ownership and strong Lockean rights. Even accepting that the self-ownership premise does not hold in all possible worlds, establishing institutions which deny self-ownership is morally problematic.

Self-ownership was uncontroversial in the liberal literature before Rawls, and this may be the reason why classical writers did not think they needed

---

[37] Perhaps there is no more fundamental justification to be had for self-ownership. Perhaps self-ownership is derivative of other principles, such as the right to pursue personal projects, but it is no less important for that reason. The central point of self-ownership is simply to establish barriers to bodily invasions by others. Because we are concerned with the morality of actual institutional arrangements, we need not address the fancy counterexamples imagined by Kasper Lippert-Rasmussen. Among the counterfactuals used by Lippert-Rasmussen are a world in which half the population is blind and the other half consists of people with two regular eyes as well as a spare pair lodged in their shoulder, and a world where persons are just Cartesian minds with artificial limbs. See Lippert-Rasmussen, "Liberalism and Natural End Ethics," 96–9, 110–15. For a critique of self-ownership that does not, however, affect our argument here, see David Sobel, "Backing Away from Libertarian Self-Ownership," *Ethics* 123 (2012), 32–60.

[38] See G. A. Cohen, "Self-Ownership, World-Ownership, and Equality," in *Justice and Equality Here and Now*, Frank S. Lucash, ed. (Ithaca, NY: Cornell University Press, 1986), 109.

to argue for it; it was self-evident to them. Rawls's view is a radical departure from the liberal tradition. Robust property in one's person is the better view under a liberal political theory that prizes autonomy and human dignity. The contrary view, that the state owns its subjects' natural assets, does not sit well with a liberal conception of society. To be sure, this view is not necessarily incompatible with claiming that the state must respect many choices that people make regarding their natural talents. Typically, though, proponents of the social ownership of talents claim that people are allowed those choices for *instrumental* reasons, namely, that using their talents productively helps others, especially the worse-off. In contrast, the view defended here is that self-ownership, while not perhaps an entirely foundational principle, has intrinsic value as a necessary condition for the pursuit of personal projects. To respect persons' self-ownership is one sure way to leave them alone to pursue their projects. It follows that the state must show a strong reason to interfere with self-ownership. The state cannot simply say that talented persons must compensate others.

Our position contrasts with the one defended by Liam Murphy and Thomas Nagel in their treatment of the philosophy of taxation.[39] They think that people do not own anything independently of what justice says their fair share of income should be, and they especially dispute the view that government needs a special justification to take people' labor earnings.[40] To them, it is false that what persons have earned is presumptively theirs. Persons are entitled to whatever justice allots them; this may or may not include what they have earned. To be sure, these authors do not support an unlimited state power to confiscate people's incomes. But, again, their reason for this restraint is purely instrumental, as it is for Rawls: society must provide incentives for wealth creation.[41] To these authors, there are no justice-based reasons against dispossession. In contrast, we reject society's ownership of natural assets for moral reasons as well. We rely on intuitions about the centrality of personal projects and about personal identity and autonomy – about what it is to be a person. Whatever else each is obligated to share with others, each has a stringent right to exclude others, and especially the state, from his mind and body.

The consequence of the principle of self-ownership for brain drain is straightforward. If the emigrant owns his talents, the claim by the state to place burdens on his personal project is correspondingly weaker. He owns his natural assets even in the state of nature. The state has no moral power to

---

[39] Liam Murphy and Thomas Nagel, *The Myth of Ownership: Taxes and Justice* (Oxford University Press, 2005).

[40] This is the central argument of the book. See especially ibid., 74–5, where they claim that property rights are entirely conventional.

[41] Thus "the most important function of a market economy in any conception of justice is not as an end in itself, but as a means to the encouragement of production and the generation of wealth." Ibid., 69.

interfere with his decision to take his talents – his decision to take *himself*, really – elsewhere.

There is another consideration that weakens the claim by the state to raise the cost of emigration. Thus far we argued that the state does not own a person's talents and that the moral right to pursue personal projects trumps the state's desire to keep talented persons within its borders. However, for the sake of argument, let us concede that the state has a power to tax the income generated by natural assets in order to realize social justice and not just to pay for the provision of public goods. Even then there is no plausible moral argument for taxing the income that persons earn *abroad* from using their skills. Assuming distributive principles of justice, emigrants simply decide to break ties with their political society and join another political society. They will discharge their (presumed) distributive duties in that new society. Those left behind cannot claim that the emigrants are breaching their duty to share with them their talent-generated income because the emigrants will from now on be taxed elsewhere. They will be sharing their talent-generated income with their new compatriots. The taxing power of the state ends once a person breaks her ties with the homeland.[42]

PERSONAL MORALITY

Someone may object that although talented persons have a right to emigrate and the state, therefore, cannot validly stop them, they *could* choose to stay and benefit their compatriots with their skills. Surely this choice is morally preferable because the decision to leave – if we believe the economic literature – is motivated by their desire to improve their earnings. The doctor who leaves is selfish, whereas the doctor who stays is altruistic because he is willing to incur an opportunity cost. If this is accurate, we can criticize those who leave and deplore the brain drain, just as we deplore alcoholism, teen pregnancy, and other social ills, while accepting that the state cannot coerce people to do the right thing. The brain drain would be the result of objectionable individual decisions, and for that reason, it is vulnerable to criticism and social pressure.

As a preliminary point, even if the decision to leave is blameworthy, it is outside a theory of justice, global or otherwise. It is a matter of personal morality and not one where our *political* duties toward others, distant or proximate, are implicated. This means that even if the talented emigrant acts selfishly, the state does not have the moral power to stop her.[43] Nonetheless, the issue is interesting and deserves examination.

---

[42] Blake describes this entitlement as the right of renunciation: "Individuals have a moral right, once outside the jurisdiction of the state, to renounce particular obligations of justice toward the inhabitants of that state." *Debating Brain Drain*, 192.

[43] Oberman overlooks this point in his defense of a limited right of states to force talented emigrants to stay. He writes: "The general rule here is that coercion should only be used against a person when that person is subject to a moral duty." Oberman, "Can Brain Drain Justify

The claim that the decision to emigrate is morally objectionable fails to make important distinctions. Whether someone acts immorally depends on all the circumstances. First and foremost, as we explained in Chapter 2, a moral assessment of action must take into account the importance of personal projects to those who pursue them. A self-interested act is not automatically worse than an altruistic act. Immoral self-interested acts are typically opportunistic acts that interfere with the personal projects of others. But the typical cases of brain drain are not like that; rather, the talented person who considers emigrating has dreams and aspirations about what she wants for herself and her family, and any moral assessment of her decision to emigrate must take into account the value of that project *to her*.

Two contrasting examples illustrate this point. Imagine a talented scientist in a developing country who receives no support, public or private, for her research. She cannot pursue her scientific interests under those conditions. In addition, the ineffectual policies pursued by her native government have plunged the country into poverty and stagnation. Crime is rampant, and the scientist does not feel that her family is safe anymore. She then accepts an offer to work at a British university with good compensation and appropriate working conditions. In our view, far from acting immorally, this person is doing a good deed. She is not only pursuing a worthy personal project; in addition, she is escaping bad institutions and making a decision that will enable her to benefit a larger number of people everywhere, including people in her native country. *This* is the typical scenario of an emigration of an educated person to a wealthier society.

Now consider a different (and less typical) scenario. A talented surgeon in a developing country affected by an epidemic works on alleviation and eradication of the disease. He is not at risk, and his compensation, while not particularly high, is adequate for him and his family. His team's contribution to eradication of the epidemic is pivotal, and he would be hard to replace in the short term. He then accepts a lucrative offer from a clinic in Beverly Hills to do cosmetic surgery. Let us concede, for the sake of argument, that this person is morally blameworthy. If so, in the absence of other circumstances to explain his decision, he may be properly subject to the criticism of his compatriots. As we said at the outset, *still* this does not authorize the state to enforce whatever moral rules the doctor may be thought to infringe. The state should not be in the business of enforcing *personal* morality, so it has nothing to say about the doctor's behavior. He is, at worst, morally at fault toward other persons, namely, his patients. But the principles of public justice that the state is entitled

Immigration Restrictions?" 433. A person's having a moral duty is neither a necessary nor a sufficient reason to justify state coercion against that person. The regulation that forces me to submit a form in triplicate is valid even if it does not enforce a moral duty. Conversely, my moral duties of loyalty to my friends, for example, should not be enforced by law.

to enforce do not include righting the doctor's personal wrong by making his exit harder or impossible.

These two examples show that whether the emigrant acts objectionably cannot be established in general terms. We need to look at all the circumstances. A person who leaves in the pursuit of a personal project that for some reason he cannot pursue at home can hardly be criticized. In contrast, someone who leaves just for greed may be criticized. But this means that the differences in personal histories matter, and for this reason, a wholesale criticism of those who leave is unwarranted. Any moral evaluation of the emigrant's behavior will draw on common morality and not on political obligations generated by the state's putative ownership of talents.

Moreover, as we saw in our first example earlier, it is far from clear that the emigrant who seeks greener pastures fails to help deserving persons. Although this is an empirical question, common sense tells us that the talented person will perform better under better conditions and thus will be more likely to maximize whatever benefits he provides to others. We would go further: even if the emigrant is leaving out of greed, his action may be valuable. If the work of a greedy immigrant is expected to benefit many people, especially the world's poor, then his decision to emigrate was a good decision in terms of its consequences, regardless of intent. Likewise, if the brain drain as an aggregative phenomenon benefits most people, especially the world's poor, then it is desirable regardless of private motivations.

THE QUESTION OF HARM

Two questions must be addressed. First, are those left behind really harmed? Second, even if those left behind are harmed in some sense, is it an *unjust* harm? Harm certainly means, at least, the setting back of someone's interest.[44] Whether emigration of talented persons harms those left behind is an empirical question, and judgments will vary in each case. However, the premise of harm in its general form is questionable. As indicated at the outset, the brain drain may be offset by a brain gain, brain circulation, and a brain bank. So considering *only* the home country, the premise that the brain drain is harmful is open to doubt.

Now let us concede, for the sake of argument, that talented citizens who leave harm (some of) those left behind. The question is whether the harm is unjust. The most serious forms of harm that the state must prevent are those with which the criminal law is concerned. But, as we will see in Chapter 6, it does not follow that the state's job is to redress as many harms as possible; in particular, the state should not be in the business of redressing competitive harm. If we apply this formula to emigration, there is no harm: when a doctor emigrates from Peru, she is not violating the rights of Peruvians, even assuming

---

[44] See our discussion of harm in the trade context in Chapter 6.

that she is setting back their interests. The person who leaves does not interfere with the personal projects of others, and therefore, the state has no business in interfering with his conduct.

Critics of the brain drain may concede that this argument is appropriate to reject exit visas but insist that it is not sufficient to reject other forms of regulation of the brain drain, such as taxation of foreign-earned income. Fiscal measures to curb the brain drain fall within permissible state policy, such as commercial and trade policy. In order for the measure to be justified, no strong notion of harm is needed. The government simply judges, in good faith, that something harmful is happening and decides to reduce the harm. Defenders of the Bhagwati tax (as it is called) focus on the presumed increase in welfare in the state that taxes. The argument for the tax proceeds in several steps. People in a developing country are not harmed if a few doctors leave. But if a sufficiently high number of doctors emigrate, then those left behind are harmed because there will not be enough doctors to provide health care in the country. The responsibility of the government is to address precisely these kinds of unintended consequences of otherwise permissible behavior. Although it would not be acceptable for the state to forcibly keep the doctor in the country because that would be too intrusive of liberty, it is surely permissible for the state to raise the cost of leaving by warning prospective emigrants that they will have to pay taxes to their native country.

This argument wrongly treats the exercise of a fundamental right as an *aggregative* phenomenon, thus overlooking the fact that rights are *distributive* in nature. The right to exit is pivotal to the pursuit of projects by all persons, talented or not, as we explained in Chapter 4. The state cannot say, consistently with acknowledging this right, that the emigration of 10 percent of doctors gives society just the right amount of freedom of movement it needs, so the government can subsequently impede the exercise of the right.[45] To do so would be to treat freedom of movement as an aggregative good, mirroring the aggregative harm allegedly caused by the brain drain. Only when emigration reaches a certain volume, it is thought, may the state intervene to stem it. But freedom of movement is not only an aggregative good but also a distributive good: *each* person holds a right to leave. As we indicated, individuals, not societies, are the right moral claimants. The aggregative approach wrongly assumes that persons are resources of the state and that the state is therefore free to regulate their behavior for reasons of public policy. Whatever the merits of this reasoning with regard to other social and economic issues, it is not applicable to behavior that constitutes an exercise of a fundamental right. Just as the government is not free to suppress a person's speech just because (it thinks) society has enough freedom of speech

[45] We borrow the example, *mutatis mutandi*, from Ronald Dworkin, *Taking Rights Seriously* (Cambridge, MA: Harvard University Press, 1978), 92.

already, so the government is not free to burden emigration just because (it thinks) too many talented persons have left already.[46]

RECIPROCITY

Critics of the brain drain may claim that emigrants owe a duty to those left behind because of benefits that the state has bestowed upon them. The argument has two versions. The specific-reciprocity argument claims that the talented citizen has received specific benefits from the state, such as subsidized education. The general-reciprocity argument claims that citizens owe associative, nonvoluntary obligations to their country. Under this view, citizens' talents are the inevitable outcome of social and political institutions, and for that reason, they owe something extra to their home state.

According to the specific-reciprocity argument, society has invested in the person's education, and therefore, the skilled citizen owes a corresponding duty to society to use her talents for society's benefit. She needs to give back part of what she received. The argument is contractual in nature: the skilled citizen has received a benefit from her fellow citizens who paid for her education; therefore, she has a moral duty to use her talents for their benefit.

This argument wrongly transposes principles of private contract into political relationships. Developing countries have few private schools and universities, so the typical student attends public schools and universities; usually, that is his only option. Because the government forces taxpayers to subsidize public education, the transaction is involuntary with regard to both parties. The student cannot choose where to attend school, and the taxpayers cannot choose to withhold payment either. These facts can hardly generate an obligation to give back to the country.[47] More generally, the argument that a person has a duty of reciprocity because he received an unsolicited benefit is questionable. To be sure, some political theorists do take this view (called the *principle of fairness*). They claim that persons owe obligations toward those who benefited them, even if the person never consented to the benefit.[48] This claim, however, is controversial. A number of writers have correctly observed that the fact that others have, without my consent, engaged in activities from which I benefited does *not* create an obligation on me, especially if I have not agreed, if I have no say on what others decide to do, and if I have no control

---

[46] We would go further. Imagine that *everyone* wants to leave a country. Can the government validly stop them or dissuade them from leaving by threatening them with future taxation? We think not. Rulers are, at best, mere agents of the people, and in a sense, their legitimacy is impugned if people do not want to stay and endure their governance.

[47] For an extended argument to that effect, see A. John Simmons, *Moral Principles and Political Obligations*, (Princeton, NJ: Princeton University Press, 1979).

[48] This argument is made in H. L. A. Hart, "Are There Any Natural Rights?" *Philosophical Review* 64 (1955), 185, and was adopted by Rawls, *A Theory of Justice*, 97.

over whether I receive the benefit or not.[49] And to think about such obligation as enforceable, perhaps in the name of preventing free riding, is even more objectionable. Even if an amended version of the argument could work by requiring *acceptance* of the benefits in order to generate the obligation,[50] the acceptance in most cases is vitiated by the beneficiary's lack of options. If a person in a developing country wants to study medicine and her only option is the local medical school, it matters little, for purposes of reciprocity, that she voluntarily attends school.

Moreover, if the taxpayers subsidize education, and if people are (presumably) paying their fair share to the public treasury, then the student, a taxpayer, has already paid for the education. The public treasury collects from citizens, and the government then spends that money on behalf of the whole citizenry on what it considers to be in the public good. The government is an agent; the "principal" includes everyone, including the student. Thus, unless the critics of brain drain take the position that public education is an objectionable forcible transfer of resources in favor of students, they cannot argue that the student owes back.

The general-reciprocity argument holds that we are who we are not because we possess pristine natural assets but because social and political institutions have shaped us into our present beings, and therefore, we owe a debt of gratitude to our society.[51] People could not have developed their talents without those institutions in place. This fact rebuts, they think, the primacy of personal projects and self-ownership: there is nothing that an adult person can exhibit as a purely natural asset. For example, a medical doctor benefited from the fact that his parents, also distinguished professionals, thrived under the political status and social recognition accorded to professionals; that social advantage accrued to their child. The doctor cannot, then, claim that his talents are natural. In the pursuit of his personal project, the doctor uses assets that are social in nature. Therefore, he owes something to the society that nurtured him.

At one level, this argument is tautological. We are all born into *some* social and political context. Does this mean that we always owe something extra to society (i.e., something in addition to our regular obligations) simply because

---

[49] See Jean Hampton, "Social Contract," *Cambridge Dictionary of Philosophy*, Robert Audi, ed. (Cambridge University Press, 1995), 746, and Nozick, *Anarchy, State, and Utopia*, 90–5.

[50] As suggested in A. John Simmons, "The Principle of Fair Play," in A. John Simmons, *Justifications and Legitimacy: Essays on Rights and Obligations* (Cambridge University Press, 2001), 1–26.

[51] This is one of Plato's arguments in the *Crito* dialogue. Authors who defend associative obligations, that is, duties a person owes to society for open or generic benefits (as opposed to specific benefits) she may have received, include John Horton, *Political Obligation* (Atlantic Highlands, NJ: Humanities, 1992), 146, 150, and Margaret Gilbert, "Group Membership and Political Obligation," *Monist* 76 (1993), 119–33. We are aware that the literature distinguishes between the associative-obligations argument and the gratitude argument, but for our purposes, they merge into the one claim that persons owe their societies a political obligation because of the generic benefits the state provides.

that society (with the police, the courts, and so on) was in place when we came into the world? The question is what normative consequences follow from the fact that we are born into a preexisting political setting. The answer to this question by those who think our talents are socially constituted is never clear. Presumably they would endorse strong taxation of talent-generated income because the person is simply using a social good. On this view, there are no personal projects: all projects that *seem* personal are really social in nature all the way through, and the fact that a person uses his natural assets does not affect the state's claim on his wealth. I own land, thanks to the political institutions in place, and I play the piano well, also thanks to the political institutions in place.

To the extent that this argument is not just an empty tautology, it must be rejected. Using the example of a medical doctor again, let us concede that what the doctor has now is in part the result of what her society is.[52] She could not be who she is but for those generic societal benefits. If so, either she received those generic benefits from her family, or from public institutions, or from private institutions. In the first and frequent case, the successful person has received most of the relevant benefits – those that arguably determine her present success – from her family. She had a good family that nurtured her and allowed her to be successful. If so, she owes her family, perhaps, but she does not owe something above and beyond her filial duties. In the second case, Nozick's argument, discussed earlier, applies: she does not incur obligation for benefits that were foisted on her by the state. If, however, she received those benefits from a private institution, either she paid for them or she did not. If she did, there is no residual obligation to society. Political institutions are set up in part to regulate and enforce contracts, including the provision of services such as private medical education. If I buy something from you, I owe you the price. I do not owe you the price *plus* something else to society. Someone may object at this point that I owe something *else* to society, namely, a tax to finance the cost of those institutions that facilitate exchange. But this is not the argument made here. The argument is that I owe the cost of the institutions, which are after all public goods, *plus* an extra obligation arising from the fact that the state nurtured me. As argued previously, this extra compensation is inappropriate because – assuming the relevant causal connection – the benefits were bestowed coercively. If, however, one has received private benefits for which one has not paid, then one owes that money to the benefit provider. Thus the doctor owes medical school loans. But again, the general-reciprocity argument claims that one owes that plus something else on account of the generic benefits in question. Simply put, there is no justification for such a duplication of debts. Interestingly, those who make the general-reciprocity argument are never too specific about the

---

[52] This is a big concession because it overlooks the role of genetic factors as determinants of natural talent.

generic benefits people received and for which they supposedly have to compensate others.[53]

A somewhat stronger version of the preceding argument will frame it not as revolving around dubious precepts of reciprocity but rather as unjust appropriation of property. Bennet has been the beneficiary, let us suppose, of prior investment in him by Country A that affords him the human capital that enables him to command a higher wage in Country B. By emigrating, he is therefore taking something that does not really belong to him, or not to him alone. It is, rather, the joint property of all the citizens of Country A. Unless Bennet first pays them back the investment they have made in him, he is not at liberty to deprive them of the return on that asset. Note that in this version the primary wrongdoer becomes Bennet himself, not the country that offers him entry.

We reject this version, too. It rests on the premise (one we already rejected) that one acquires partial ownership rights to persons by contributing to their future prospects whether or not they have solicited that contribution and, if they have, whether or not they have contracted with the provider to make repayment. Typically parents contribute time and other resources to the nurture of their children, but neither that nurture nor the original act of procreation bestows on them ownership rights in perpetuity. All the less plausible is it that states are entitled to claim ownership. Moreover, most of the human capital-building investment made in citizens occurs when they are too young to enter into a binding agreement to repay. Those made at a later stage, for example, a university education, may come attached to specific provisions of mandatory repayment, but this should not be taken to limit migration rights. Just the opposite: persons who exercise a liberty of mobility so as to enter a more remunerative job market are thereby rendered better able to repay an indebtedness previously incurred. When states improvidently insist on paying all or most of higher-education costs for citizens who attend university, they thereby affect a domestic transfer from the less-well-off to the more-well-off. This does not give them a later claim on the continuing presence of those on whom they have graciously bestowed their largesse – not even if the state possessed very little largesse to bestow.

In addition, the argument that prospective emigrants owe something to those left behind because the emigrants benefited from political institutions sounds strange when applied to the brain-drain phenomenon. We saw in Chapters 1 and 3 that good institutions are crucial for growth and prosperity. If so, under the view under discussion, the emigrants owe something to their society if it provided *reasonable* institutions. Yet people often leave because their native institutions are deficient. In many of those countries, people develop their talents *despite* the political institutions, not because of them, as the argument assumes. The argument we are considering must logically

[53] As Simmons observes. Simmons, "Associative Political Obligations," in *Justification and Legitimacy*, 88–90.

hold that the better the institutions left behind, the stronger the emigrants' duties because he would have received more valuable benefits. Thus a German doctor who emigrates to the United States is, in this view, doing something worse than the Ghanian doctor who emigrates to the United States because the German doctor, unlike the Ghanian doctor, is leaving good political institutions that nurtured him well. Notably, this claim clashes with the intuition that brain drain from poor countries is objectionable. Maybe this intuition is wrong, and supporters of the general-reciprocity argument should *praise* people who leave dysfunctional societies. If a country is poor as the result of bad institutions, then there is nothing wrong with leaving it; on the contrary, one would expect a reasonable person who cares about her future and her family to leave if she can. This conclusion is precisely the opposite corollary to the one that the argument was supposed to endorse. This dissonance occurs because the criticism of the brain drain trades on some vague notion of international justice that laments the loss of "human capital" that poor countries suffer for the benefit of rich countries.

We see, then, a sad truth about brain drain. All too often governments of developing countries do not discharge their justice-based duties (whatever they may be) with the taxes they collect.[54] Some of those regimes are outright oppressive, others are kleptocracies without being otherwise oppressive, and others are just disorganized, corrupt, and inefficient.[55] More often than not, governments in developing countries *mistreat* their talented citizens in various ways. Wage differential is certainly a major reason for the brain drain, but wage differential exists for a reason, and government failure should not be overlooked as a major cause. Poor political and social conditions diminish the returns that talented persons can expect, and those facts are not natural facts. This stagnation is often the result of vicious circles of economic and political depredation. If this is true, then the emigrants' present skills can hardly be credited to their political environment. In fact, they often perform a good deed by leaving not only because they are escaping mistreatment but also because they will be more likely to make valuable contributions with their talents in a society that does not exploit them. And emigrants will often make a better contribution to their native countries by developing their talents in a better place.

There is, then, a curious paradox here: critics of the brain drain purport to care about developing countries, but they overlook the fact that the governments of those countries are often the most oppressive, corrupt, and inept. The assumption that governments in developing countries are invariably

---

[54] For a full picture of the gravity of the issue, see the statistics compiled by Transparency International; available at: http://www.transparency.org/.

[55] A kleptocracy is a government that, while it does not politically oppress its citizens, *steals* from them. We discussed the concept in Chapter 1. For the case of Argentina, see Carlos S. Nino, *Un país al margen de la ley: estudio de la anomia como componente del subdesarrollo argentino* (Buenos Aires: Emecé, 1992).

acting in good faith, trying to get ahead, is unfortunately false. Many of those governments are among the worst violators of human rights and the most likely to pursue populist and demagogic policies with disastrous results. *That* is what causes the brain drain, not predatory practices from the rich countries. Developing countries need to improve their institutions and practices if they aspire to keep their talented citizens. Certainly any complaint about brain drain requires them to have clean hands in the first place.

A final problem with this argument, in any of its forms, is that it is hard to see why it applies only across national borders. No one objects if a doctor educated at Florida State University moves to California. Yet, under the reciprocity rationale, the doctor would have a duty to practice medicine in Florida because his education was subsidized by Floridians. Florida has its own political institutions that nurtured the doctor's talents. Someone could object that the doctor's move is acceptable because he does not harm the people of Florida. But there is often harm in the relevant sense. People leave economically depressed areas to move to other parts of the country, and although those left behind deplore it, no one claims that the local authorities should make emigration hard or impossible, as some claim for international migration of talent. Also, the argument's rationale is reciprocity, not harm. Under this rationale, the doctor owes Floridians a debt. Although relevant, harm beyond the harm of breach is not central to the argument.

NATIONALIST OR COSMOPOLITAN DUTIES?

Critics of the brain drain adopt a strangely nationalist position: talented citizens have a duty to stay so that they can benefit their own fellow citizens. This is a corollary of the flawed view that skilled citizens are the human capital of the state. But this position collapses under a cosmopolitan perspective. From this standpoint, the contribution by talented individuals should be measured by the value they add to the *world* (especially the poor) and not just to their compatriots. If this is the relevant consideration, then whether or not the emigrant's compatriots are the deserving beneficiaries of his output is an open question. From a global perspective, the AIDS research by a Syrian doctor working in the United States should benefit AIDS victims in Africa and not (just) the Syrians. The dubious nationalist position that talented persons owe to their own country parallels the dubious empirical assumption that the emigrant's work helps only the *host* country. The argument is that if some of the "human capital" migrates from Country A to Country B, then that represents Country B's gain, because Country B has increased its "human capital." In a sense, this is true, because the immigrant will pay taxes in his adoptive land. But this is not necessarily true of the benefits accrued from the immigrant's talents. Take, for example, a typical case of someone who studies physics in a developing country. He then earns a Fulbright Scholarship to pursue his PhD at a prestigious American university. After that, he decides to take an academic position in the United States, where he settles permanently. During his career, he will teach many students and publish a number of academic papers. This output will not benefit only the United States. Instead, he will contribute knowledge to the global public domain, knowledge that will improve scientific understanding and the technologies based on that understanding (this is the *brain-bank phenomenon*). If, because of inadequate working conditions, he could not possibly have produced this knowledge had he stayed in his home country, then leaving was the right thing to do – for himself and for others. He may even end up contributing more to his home country than if he had stayed there. Certainly, Amartya Sen's work on famines has done much more for India than anything he could have done had he stayed there instead of emigrating to the West to study economics with the top people in the field.[56]

THE HOST STATE

In light of the foregoing considerations, it is hard to see why rich countries that are hospitable to talented immigrants are acting wrongly. As we saw in Chapter 4, a cosmopolitan theory of justice recommends the liberalization of immigration generally, of skilled and unskilled workers alike. The host country provides opportunity to the nationals of a burdened country to pursue their personal projects by fully developing their potential; it is, then, doing a good deed. The possibility of emigration increases the chances that persons who would otherwise be trapped in their dysfunctional native land will realize their life plans. Any liberal should be sympathetic to this prospect. Further, as observed earlier, chances are that talented persons will help the largest number of people, including the world's poor, if they are allowed to work in optimal conditions. The host country thus provides a valuable global service by taking these talented immigrants and allowing them to develop their potential and bestow publicly available benefits. In some cases, the host country will even be saving the immigrants from oppression, corruption, and stagnation. Surely the fact that many Filipino nurses in Britain have been able to improve themselves and their families counts in any evaluation of the brain drain.[57] And finally, any claim that those nurses owe something to their compatriots collapses in light of our argument that people have a moral right to pursue their personal projects using the talents they own. The charge that rich countries prey on the poor countries' human capital is just nationalist rhetoric. Countries do not own persons, and the supposed "preying" is a free, voluntary transaction. To the extent

---

[56] For a telling account, see Amartya Sen, *Autobiography* (1998); available at: http://nobelprize .org/nobel_prizes/economics/laureates/1998/sen-autobio.html (accessed September 15, 2011).

[57] For an overview of this issue, see James Buchan, "New Opportunities: United Kingdom Recruitment of Filipino Nurses," in *The International Migration of Health Workers*, John Connell, ed. (New York: Routledge, 2008), 47.

that it produces a negative externality – a harm – it is not one that should be branded as unfair.

EVALUATION OF PROPOSALS

In light of these considerations, how should we evaluate the various proposals to regulate the brain drain? As an initial matter, all coercive measures should be rejected. As we saw, exit visas are inconsistent with liberty for obvious reasons. Other coercive proposals of control, such as requiring compulsory service before allowing skilled citizens to emigrate, are objectionable as well because they grossly intrude on individual liberty.[58] Bhagwati's milder proposal to tax the foreign-earned income of the emigrant also should be rejected for several reasons. First, because the state does not own the citizen's talents, it does not have the power to burden the emigrant's personal project by taxing her talent-generated foreign income. Second, whatever tax obligations the emigrant had in accordance with justice will from now on be discharged in her adoptive country, so the Bhagwati tax is unjust double taxation. And third, the rationale for the tax collapses together with the argument from reciprocity. If the fact that the government subsidized a person's education does not generate a duty of reciprocity, then collecting foreign-earned income cannot be justified.

However, noncoercive measures may be more acceptable. Rather than try to keep people against their will, it is much better for the state to address the causes of brain drain. The state can pursue better economic policies and create appropriate incentives for people to stay. It can secure the rule of law and enact market-friendly laws that, in turn, facilitate higher wages and good working conditions. A potentially more problematic practice is for a state to attach conditions to the provision of education, such as a commitment to stay or to return after state-subsidized foreign studies. These conditions are acceptable if genuinely voluntary. However, the conditions are unacceptable if the state is extorting the person, as is the case when the person has no option but to study at a public university. Similar considerations apply when a state pays for the person's education on the condition that he repay the tuition if he decides to leave. If these conditions are voluntary, they may be acceptable. If they are extortive because the person has no other place to study, they are questionable. Whether these conditions are defensible, then, will depend on context.

Finally, poor countries do not have a legitimate claim to compensation from rich countries. Poor countries do not own their nationals, and they cannot accuse rich countries of stealing their investment. Surely the fact that rich countries have better universities, better institutions, and better economies is not something for which those countries should apologize. As we saw in

---

[58] Brock recommends such measure. *Debating Brain Drain*, 101–4.

Chapters 1 and 3, the once-fashionable claim that successful countries built good institutions at the expense of poor countries is false in most cases. There are reasons why people seek opportunity elsewhere. Poor countries would do well in addressing those reasons instead of blaming others for the exodus of their disgruntled nationals. The brain drain should be praised, not criticized, because it is consistent with personal freedom and because in the long run it improves the lives of more people, including those who, under an appropriate theory of justice, we should care about.

6

Trade

The thesis we defend in this chapter was well put by a young John Maynard Keynes:

We must hold to Free Trade, in its widest interpretation, as an inflexible dogma, to which no exception is admitted, wherever the decision rests with us. We must hold to this even where we receive no reciprocity of treatment and even in those rare cases where by infringing it we could in fact obtain a direct economic advantage. We should hold to Free Trade as a principle of international morals, and not merely as a doctrine of economic advantage.[1]

This passage underscores two related claims: that trade is widely beneficial at the national and global levels and that tariff barriers unjustly hurt many while unjustly benefiting a few. The argument for trade, like the argument for open borders, is thus overdetermined. It is supported both by sound economics and by commonsense political morality, and it is a crucial staple in a humanitarian policy that seeks to alleviate poverty.

We have argued that justice requires us not to interfere with the pursuit of personal projects. We discussed in Chapter 5 governmental interference with mobility and association. Governments also frequently interfere with voluntary agreements. Justifying such interference is a large topic in political philosophy that we do not fully address here. This chapter addresses one form of governmental interference with contract: the enactment of protectionist laws. These laws assume various forms: tariffs, import licenses, export licenses, import quotas, subsidies, government procurement rules, sanitary rules, voluntary

[1] John Maynard Keynes, editorial in *Manchester Guardian Commercial Supplement*, January 4, 1923, in *The Collected Writings of John Maynard Keynes*, vol. 27 (Cambridge University Press, 2012), 451. Keynes later modified his views, but even then he did not reject his foundational opinions about trade: "Looking again to-day at the statements of these fundamental truths which I then gave, I do not find myself disputing them." John Maynard Keynes, "National Self-Sufficiency," *Yale Review* 22 (4) (June 1933), 755–69.

export restraints, local content requirements, national security requirements, and embargoes. All these trade barriers, while different in a number of respects, have this in common: they raise the cost (sometimes prohibitively) of importing goods and services.

We argue that, with very few exceptions, protectionist laws are indefensible on two grounds. First, they are indefensible on *principle* because they interfere with contracts for no plausible moral reason. Second, protectionist laws have objectionable *consequences*: they harm persons generally (they cause more harm than good), and they particularly tend to harm the poor. Following a robust consensus in the economic literature, we claim that liberalizing trade would contribute significantly to global and national growth and, mainly for this reason, will help in reducing poverty. An important corollary of our argument is that protectionist laws are indefensible not only under our own views on global justice but also under *any* plausible moral-political theory.

More specifically, protectionist laws are artificial, coercive obstacles placed by governments on voluntary transactions across borders. We saw in Chapter 2 that the world's poor have indeed been wronged, and we suggested in Chapter 3 that most of the harm inflicted on them is homegrown. Trade is a partial exception to this finding. The world's poor are doubly harmed by trade barriers. On the one end, protectionist barriers erected by governments of developing countries harm their own people. Seen from this perspective, interference with trade is one more instance of the market-unfriendly policies, discussed in Chapter 3, that have caused much of the stagnation in the developing world. Protectionism in developing countries goes hand in hand with unproductive public spending, corruption, and burdensome regulations – all features of economically and socially burdened societies. On the other end, though, protectionist laws in *rich* countries harm the world's poor as well by denying them access to rich markets. This *is* an injustice done by governments of wealthy countries to the distant poor. This particular injustice is a coercive interference with voluntary transactions – an unwarranted interference in the pursuit of personal projects.

We proceed as follows: first, we summarize the economics of trade presented by the mostly reliable *corpus* of research on international economics. The professional consensus is that free trade contributes to national and global economic growth and, mainly for this reason, helps the poor. We then examine the possible justifications for protectionist laws enacted by *rich* countries and find them wanting. We then examine the possible justifications for protectionist laws enacted by *developing* countries and conclude that those, too, are untenable. We discuss possible objections to our views.

THE ECONOMICS OF INTERNATIONAL TRADE

Economic models of international trade generally fall into two categories: the law of comparative advantages, which, in turn, has two versions, the Ricardian original version and the Hecksher-Olin version, and the endogenous-growth model.[2] The first model supports the view that liberalized trade is good for general economic growth and for the poor in particular. The second model is a version of the infant-industry argument, and while conceding that open trade is generally beneficial, it makes the case (we think unconvincingly) for sometimes supporting trade barriers in developing countries.

1. Comparative Advantage

The law of comparative advantages has long been one of the relatively few points of agreement among economists of all stripes.[3] According to David Ricardo, nations trade because technological differences lead each to specialize in the production of the good in which it has a comparative advantage.[4] In a model of two countries and two goods, Ricardo demonstrates that even if a country can produce one of the goods more cheaply than the other country, it still may import that good if doing so frees up its resources to produce a good in which its trading partner has an even greater cost disadvantage.[5] In all its

---

[2] This section draws on Jonathan Klick and Fernando R. Tesón, "Global Justice and Trade," in *Global Justice and International Economic Law: Opportunities and Prospects*, Chi Carmody, Frank Garcia, and John Linarelli, eds. (New York: Cambridge University Press, 2012), 217. The authors especially acknowledge Jon Klick's authorship of much of the original economic research in the section.

[3] For a useful summary, see Douglas A. Irwin, *Free Trade under Fire*, 3rd ed. (Princeton, NJ: Princeton University Press, 2009), 28–69.

[4] See David Ricardo, *On the Principles of Political Economy and Taxation*, 3rd ed. (1812) in *The Works and Correspondence of David Ricardo*, Piero Sraffa, ed. (Indianapolis, IN: Liberty Fund, 2004), 128–49.

[5] Assume two countries, Ruritania and Atlantis, and two goods, beef and computers. Ruritania has a comparative advantage in the production of beef relative to Atlantis if Ruritania's opportunity cost of producing beef (i.e., how many units of computers it can no longer produce if it produces an additional unit of beef for a given stock of resources) is lower than Atlantis' opportunity cost of producing beef. Or, more succinctly, Ruritania's marginal rate of transformation between beef and computers is lower than that of Atlantis. Ricardo offers an example in which England and Portugal both produce wine and cloth. If it takes 100 English workers one year to produce quantity X of cloth and 120 English workers one year to produce quantity Y of wine and it takes 90 Portuguese workers to produce X units of cloth and 80 Portuguese workers to produce Y units of wine in the same time period, Ricardo claims that Portugal will import its cloth from England and export wine to that country. To see this, if Portugal allocates its 90 cloth workers to wine making, in principle, it can ship units of wine to England. In turn, England now can allocate its wine workers to cloth production, sending units of cloth in return to Portugal. After this trade, employing the same total number of workers as before, Portugal has 20 percent more cloth than it previously produced (and the same amount of wine), and England has 12.5 percent more wine than it previously produced (and the same amount of cloth). While the exact split of the surplus generated by the trade will differ depending on the relative demands for wine and cloth in the two countries, in Ricardo's example, both countries have the potential to expand their consumption of both goods without using more resources. Joint consumption of both goods across the two countries is guaranteed to rise even though Portugal can produce both goods more cheaply

extensions, the theory's predictions are robust: trade increases welfare among the trading partners.[6]

Though the Ricardian model relies on differing technology to ground the concept of comparative advantage, the Heckscher-Ohlin model claims that the differences in the abundance of factors of production generate international trade. In the simplest form of the model, two factors are assumed (labor and capital) in the production of two different goods. One of the goods is capital intensive, and the other is labor intensive. This means that the marginal product of capital for good A exceeds the marginal product of capital for good B, whereas the marginal product of labor for good B exceeds the marginal product of labor for good A. Production functions are identical across countries, but one of the countries has a relative abundance of labor, while the other has a relative abundance of capital.[7]

Both comparative-advantage models (Ricardian or Hecksher-Olin) imply an aggregate gain from trade liberalization. Given the aggregate gains, if a country has well-functioning institutions, free trade will make every social group better off. Obviously, in the developing world, the assumption of well-functioning institutions is quite heroic. But, in general, because the poor are likely to be the owners of the abundant resource in developing countries (i.e., labor), liberalizing trade will increase the returns to the poor in those countries.

2. Endogenous Comparative Advantage

Supporters of the endogenous growth model do not dispute that free trade is likely to improve growth and welfare.[8] Instead, they worry that trade

than England can. That is, economic growth occurs even if Portugal has an absolute advantage in the production of both goods. Earlier, Adam Smith had argued the case for free trade when a nation has the opportunity to trade with a country exhibiting an absolute advantage in desired goods. In terms of modern microeconomic tools, by specializing in the good in which its comparative advantage lies, trade effectively allows both countries to shift their production possibility frontiers outward.

[6] According to a state-of-the-art treatise on international trade, "[T]he Ricardian model is as relevant today as it has always been." Robert Feenstra, *Advanced International Trade: Theory and Evidence* (Princeton, NJ: Princeton University Press, 2003), 1. The Ricardian model is extended to encompass a continuum of goods in R. Dornbusch, S. Fischer, and P. A. Samuelson, "Comparative Advantage, Trade, and Payments in a Ricardian Model with a Continuum of Goods," *American Economic Review* 67 (1977), 823.

[7] Feenstra, *Advanced International Trade*, 32. Before trade takes place (i.e., in a state of autarky), the domestic price of the capital-intensive good will be lower in the country with an abundance of capital. Because the Heckscher-Ohlin model assumes perfect competition, the price of the capital-intensive good will decrease because of its relatively large supply owing to the abundance of capital in the country. The same will be true of the domestic price of the labor-intensive good in the labor-abundant country. When trade opens, the capital-abundant country will be induced to export the capital-intensive good by the relatively high price of the good in the labor-abundant country, and vice versa.

[8] See Phillipe Aghion and Peter Howitt, *Endogenous Growth Theory* (Cambridge, MA: MIT Press, 1997), 392.

sometimes could displace growth-enhancing research and development. That is, if comparative advantage induces a country to specialize in a low-technology industry, technological spillovers from that industry will be less valuable than the spillovers that would have occurred had the country not specialized.[9] The endogenous comparative advantage is a version of the infant-industry rationale for protectionism. The idea is that in developing countries, protected industries will improve in productivity over time, eventually becoming competitive on the world market. If the long-term improvement in growth yielded by developing a comparative advantage in the previously protected industries is large enough, it could justify the short-run loss in efficiency generated by foregoing free trade.

Although these arguments are plausible at a broad theoretical level, implementing an infant-industry policy is a daunting task for any government. The policy requires governmental planners to be able to predict which industries will in fact generate large long-term gains. This predictive power is hampered by cognitive as well as political obstacles: not only are planners unlikely to manage the unintended consequences of protectionist laws, but they also will be especially vulnerable to rent-seeking special interests. Further, there is some question as to whether firms within the protected industries will have an incentive to improve their productivity. As the Friedmans put it, "[T]he so-called infants never grow up."[10] In addition, increased scale occasioned by *trade* can generate increased opportunities for research and development, as well as learning by doing, and these cumulative effects could be very large over time.[11] Lastly, protected industries may not be able to develop the scale necessary to maximize productivity.[12] Beyond these purely economic concerns, trading current costs (i.e., foregone current benefits of trade) for uncertain future benefits (i.e., the potential for achieving a higher long-run growth rate by developing a different comparative advantage) is quite problematic. Perhaps owing to these problems or perhaps because we do not really know the ways in which knowledge accumulation is affected by trade, the empirical evidence on the growth effects of infant-industry protection is mixed.[13]

[9] This view was first formalized by Paul Krugman, "The Narrow-Moving Band, the Dutch Disease, and the Competitive Consequences of Mrs. Thatcher: Notes on Trade in the Presence of Dynamic Scale Economies," *Journal of Development Economics* 27 (1987), 41.

[10] Milton and Rose Friedman, *Free to Choose: A Personal Statement* (San Diego: Harvest, 1990), 49.

[11] Luis Rivera-Batiz and Paul Romer, "Economic Integration and Endogenous Growth," *Quarterly Journal of Economics* 106 (1991), 531–56.

[12] See Mitsuhiro Kaneda, "Policy Designs in a Dynamic Model of Infant Industry Protection," *Journal of Development Economics* 72 (2003), 115, n. 4.

[13] See Dani Rodrik, "Trade and Industrial Policy Reform," in *Handbook of Development Economics*, Hollis Chenery and T. N. Srinivasan, eds. (Amsterdam: North Holland, 1995), 2925. For a modern defense of the infant-industry argument, see Bruce Greenwald and Joseph E. Stiglitz, "Helping Infant Economies Grow: Foundation of Trade Policies for Developing Countries," Columbia University working paper d, 2006; available at: http://www2.gsb .columbia.edu/faculty/jstiglitz/download/Helping_Infant_Economies_Grow.pdf (accessed February 2, 2007).

In general, the difficulty with the endogenous growth theory is that it relies heavily on very specific assumptions about the ways innovation occurs in the economy.[14] Accumulation of knowledge is in great part determined by the extent of trade among countries. Assuming that long-run growth and welfare are desirable, the wisdom of trade restrictions will depend on the relative importance of domestic vis-à-vis international innovations. If countries can learn a substantial amount from outside innovations, trade restrictions will hamper domestic productivity. If, however, the most important technological innovations presently occur in sectors outside a country's initial comparative advantage, trade theoretically might retard long-term growth. However, in today's globalized economy, it is quite likely that there will be more technological spillover across borders than that presupposed by the view under discussion.[15]

Under almost any plausible set of assumptions, short-term economic performance is harmed by trade restrictions. No one disagrees about this. The relevant policy decision then involves trading off short-term losses (due to foregone trade) against predicted future improvements (from having a "better" comparative advantage due to nurtured innovations) based on assumptions that are severely in dispute.

Under the Ricardian model, everyone who owns a factor of production (i.e., capital, land, or labor) benefits from open trade. Under the more complex (but not necessarily more accurate) Heckscher-Ohlin model, the owners of the more abundant factor, which for developing countries will be labor (owned primarily by the poor), will benefit from liberalized trade. Even under the endogenous growth model, trade liberalization will improve current economic conditions. At best, carefully targeted protectionist policies have the potential to improve conditions at some undetermined point in the future *if* some fairly restrictive assumptions hold and policy makers make the right decisions about which industries to protect. These conditions, needless to say, are hardly, if ever, met in practice.

When trade opens between nations, in all practical situations, joint gains occur and no country loses. In most situations, the gains of trade are split, so each of country gains. Therefore, not only does trade enhance aggregate wealth (i.e., the wealth of both nations added together), but in virtually every case it also enhances the national wealth of each nation. This improvement occurs because the resources in each country are used more efficiently. Long-run effects may be different in the endogenous growth model, but even under that model, restraints on trade generate short-term losses. Moreover, long-term gains from

[14] Dan Ben-David and Michael Loewy, "Knowledge Dissemination, Capital Accumulation, Trade, and Endogenous Growth," *Oxford Economic Papers* 52 (2000), 637.

[15] Moreover, the view that assigns more or less importance to technological innovations is obscure. What's wrong with Chile's efficiently producing fish, fruit, wine, and copper and exchanging those products for computers produced elsewhere?

the restraints are highly uncertain and depend on a high degree of foresight and predictive ability on the part of government actors. In particular, these models overlook the potential susceptibility of such actors to rent-seeking activities on the part of the industries seeking protection.[16]

The theoretical and empirical evidence shows that a country benefits even when it liberalizes trade *unilaterally*.[17] In this situation, all countries improve their steady state (i.e., their dynamic equilibrium path or the stable rate of economic growth). Moreover, the growth is most pronounced in the liberalizing country[18] – an insight that contradicts the folk belief adopted by much of the global-justice literature that the country that liberalizes unilaterally is the naive loser in the international trade game.

REJECTING MERCANTILISM

The finding that trade is a positive-sum game when nations are considered as units is of great importance because it contradicts the claim that the country that erects trade barriers helps itself and hurts other countries.[19] We routinely hear this claim from politicians and others not trained in economics, and it is based on a serious economic mistake: that exports are good and imports are bad. The view is known as *mercantilism*.[20] Mercantilism views trade as a zero-sum game where one country's gains come at the expense of other countries. It rests on the false assumption that a surplus in international trade must be a deficit for other countries. Mercantilists claim that exports, believed to benefit domestic producers, should be encouraged, whereas imports, believed to hurt domestic producers, should be discouraged. But national well-being is based on present and future increased consumption. Exports are valuable only indirectly: they provide the income to buy products to consume.[21]

---

[16] See Gene Grossman and Elhanan Helpman, "Protection for Sale," *American Economic Review* 84 (1994), 833.

[17] See the collection of essays in Jagdish Bhagwati, ed., *Going Alone: The Case for Relaxed Reciprocity in Freeing Trade* , (Cambridge, MA: MIT Press, 2002).

[18] See Ben-David and Loewy, "Knowledge Dissemination," 646.

[19] Thus we agree with Paul Krugman that "the essential things to teach students are still the insights of Hume and Ricardo. That is, we need to teach them that trade deficits are self-correcting and that the benefits of trade do not depend on a country having an absolute advantage over its rivals." Paul Krugman, "What Do Undergraduates Need to Know about Trade?" *American Economic Review* 86 (1993), 23–6.

[20] Mercantilism was refuted more than 200 years ago, notably by Adam Smith, *An Inquiry into the Nature and Causes of the Wealth of Nations*, vol. 1 (Oxford University Press, 1976), 429–98.

[21] See Thomas A. Pugel and Peter H. Lindert, *International Economics*, 11th ed. (New York: McGraw-Hill, 2000), 33. As these authors remind us, imports are part of a desirable expanding national consumption, not an evil to be suppressed. Equally problematic is the claim that imports reduce domestic employment. See Laura LaHayes, "Mercantilism," *Concise Encyclopedia of Economics*, Library of Economics and Liberty; available at: http://www.econlib.org (accessed February 8, 2010).

Mercantilism is so obviously wrong that we wonder why it continues to enjoy political and, in some circles, even academic success. We speculate that this is explained by the discursive pathologies of politics. First, Ricardian trade theory is *opaque and counterintuitive*. The public has trouble seeing that the country that protects hurts its own citizens and grasps instead much more easily zero-sum explanations of social outcomes.[22] Second, protectionists use the imagery of nationalism. We need to protect "us" against "them," our local industries against the invading products, our culture against immigrant invasion.[23] People use vivid imagery for political gain. To see the advantages of trade, people need to see that the country that protects *hurts its own people* because protection hurts consumers.[24] This is concealed by the notion of "protecting" *something that is ours*, in our country, against *something that comes from the outside*. Because that "something" is alien, external, politicians and rent-seekers can easily portray it as a threat. All one can say is a trivial truth: the government can protect *specific* producers and workers by protecting the industry from foreign competition. But trade barriers do not "protect" the employment rate in one's country because of their high opportunity costs (they artificially divest resources toward inefficient endeavors); nor do trade barriers "protect" the real value of wages. Conversely, trade barriers positively harm *all* consumers, which means everyone. When the rhetorical smoke clears, trade barriers benefit inefficient producers who prey on defenseless consumers.

One way to encapsulate the mercantilist mistake is this: mercantilists see protectionism as an *unsuccessful coordination game*: "Our country must protect because we know *they* will protect. If only they made a credible commitment to repeal their protectionist laws, we would do the same." However, protectionism is best characterized as a *successful rent-seeking game*: industries affected by foreign competition seek and obtain protection from their governments in exchange for political support and other benefits.[25] Two further facts explain the political success of protection notwithstanding the well-known fact that open trade benefits the great majority of the population. The groups that benefit from free trade, such as consumers, are *diffuse* and have high organizational costs. Further, while trade theory predicts that in the long run many of the

---

[22] This phenomenon is analyzed in Guido Pincione and Fernando Tesón, *Rational Choice and Democratic Deliberation: A Theory of Discourse Failure* (New York: Cambridge University Press, 2006).

[23] This rhetorical argument was criticized more than a hundred years ago by Henry George. See Henry George, *Protection of Free Trade: An Examination of the Tariff Question, with Special Regard to the Interests of Labor*, chap. 6 (1886); available at: http://www.econlib.org/library/YPDBooks/George/grgPFT6.html (accessed September 19, 2009).

[24] As Jagdish Bhagwati writes, "The fact that trade protection hurts the economy of the country that imposes it is one of the oldest but still most startling insights economics has to offer." Jagdish Bhagwati, "Protectionism," in *The Concise Encyclopedia of Economics*; available at: www.econlib.org/library/Enc/Protectionism.html.

[25] We thank Jon Klick for the insight.

workers and firms now hurt by foreign competition will be better off because free trade creates higher-paying jobs and higher returns to capital, workers and owners have trouble grasping these benefits.

THE EFFECTS OF FREE TRADE ON THE POOR

So far, the theoretical prediction is that freer trade causes global and national growth in *aggregate terms*. Yet nations must be disaggregated to find out who wins and who loses with open trade. Critics of free trade have long argued that the beneficial aggregate effect of trade is consistent with the bad effect of leaving the poor out because it is possible that the gains of trade fall on the rich or the middle class of both trading partners.[26] On this view, when we take *persons or families* as units, free trade may well lead to losses for the poor.

It is true that *if* free trade harmed the poor, governments in developing countries would be justified in erecting trade barriers. However, the factual premise of the argument is not supported by theory or evidence.[27] An analysis of the effect of trade on poverty centers on a simple two-step argument: trade enhances growth, and growth reduces poverty.[28] Even if openness to trade *at first blush* does not help the poor more than it helps others, why assume that the poor will end up worse than before? When a country grows, good things

[26] This is what critics of globalization mean by the cliché that "trade helps big business." Even philosophers of the stature of John Rawls echo such sentiments. Referring to the European Union, Rawls writes:

The large open market including all of Europe is aim of the large banks and the capitalist business class whose main goal is simply larger profit. The idea of economic growth, onwards and upwards, with no specific end in sight, fits this class perfectly. If they speak about distribution, it is [al]most always in terms of trickle down. The long-term result of this – which we already have in the United States – is a civil society awash in a meaningless consumerism of some kind.

John Rawls and Phillipe van Parijs, "Three Letters on *The Law of Peoples* and the European Union," *Revue de Philosophie Économique* 8 (2003), 9. Phillipe van Parijs calls this passage Rawls' "most explicitly 'anti-capitalist' text."

[27] The specialized research converges on this point. See L. Alan Winters, "Trade and Poverty: Is There a Connection?" 2000; available at: http://www.wto.org/English/news_e/presoo_e/pov3_e .pdf (accessed December 5, 2007); T. N. Srinivasan and Jessica S. Wallack, "Globalization, Growth, and the Poor," *De Economist* 152 (2004), 251; and David Dollar and Aart Kray, "Growth Is Good for the Poor," World Bank policy research working paper no. 2587, World Bank, Washington, DC, 2001.

[28] The evidence for this proposition is overwhelming. For a nontechnical account, see Jagdish Bhagwati, *In Defense of Globalization* (Oxford University Press, 2004), 51–67. For a more technical analysis, see Neil McCulloch, L. Alan Winters, and Xavier Cirera, *Trade Liberalization and Poverty: A Handbook* (Washington, DC: Centre for Economic Policy Research, 2001), and Jagdish Bhagwati and T. N. Srinivasan, "Trade and Poverty in the Poor Countries," *American Economic Review* 92 (2002), 180. As these authors show, the argument that free trade helps the poor is static (freer trade should help in the reduction of poverty in the poor countries that use their comparative advantages to export labor-intensive goods) and dynamic (trade promotes growth, and growth reduces poverty).

happen. More industries are created, more jobs are available, and so the opportunities for the poor expand. Further, when a country grows, so do societal resources that can be used to alleviate poverty. The assumption is that the more resources a country has, the more resources the government will have. And the more resources the government will have, the more effectively it will address the country's poverty. So whether a country's economic policies are laissez-faire or redistributive, the poor will benefit from access to global markets as producers and consumers. The main goal of development policy is to get poor countries to *develop*, even prior to computing distributional effects. Thus it is a bit strange for trade skeptics to reject a practice that concededly makes a poor country grow by saying, "No, not *that* kind of growth." At the very least, they should welcome free trade and then propose measures to correct the (perceived) undesirable distributional effects.

In general, empirical studies have found that "in most cases, trade reform increases the income of the poor as a group and that the transition costs are generally relatively small relative to the overall benefits."[29] However, a country may liberalize trade yet simultaneously pursue policies that are counterproductive for either growth or wealth distribution. This conflict of forces occurred in Argentina, where the liberalizing measures of the 1990s were accompanied by massive unproductive public spending and political corruption.[30] Under those circumstances, it is of course fallacious to attribute the cause of the country's collapse (and the corresponding increase in poverty) to trade liberalization.[31] It is therefore crucial to control for nontrade variables when assessing the effects of trade on the poor. Specialists recommend that governments accompany the country's adaptation to the law of comparative advantages, for example, by easing industrial adjustment or helping the country to diversify its exports, always in the light of its comparative advantages.[32]

Trade liberalization will produce winners and losers, and many of those losers will be poor. But our claim here is not that *each* poor person will improve as a result of trade liberalization; in fact, no policy can do that. The claim is that in virtually every instance, the poor *as a class* will improve. On the issue of cost of goods, trade liberalization will help the poor in the same way that it helps all consumers: by lowering the prices of imports and keeping the prices of substitutes for imported goods low, thus increasing people's real incomes. On the question of wages, the evidence seems to show a number of things. Labor markets need flexibility to adjust to comparative advantages.

[29] Geoffrey J. Bannister and Kamau Thugge, "International Trade and Poverty Alleviation," *Finance and Development* (December 2001), 50.

[30] See Jean-Cartier Bresson, "Economics of Corruption," *OECD Observer* (May 2000); available at: http://www.oecdobserver.org/news/fullstory.php/aid/239 (accessed January 12, 2007), and Joseph Contreras, "Argentina's Fiasco," *Newsweek*, December 21, 2001.

[31] The astute reader notes that we avoid the term "neoliberalism," preferred by critics of free trade and globalization. It is in truth a derogatory term devoid of any serious scientific meaning.

[32] See, e.g., Bhagwati, *In Defense of Globalization*, 55.

If firms are too constrained by labor laws from reducing their work forces, then the poor may suffer as a result. This is ironic, given that supporters of strict labor regulations claim to act *on behalf* of the poor.[33] Also, the gap between the wages of skilled and unskilled workers may increase, but this is hardly an objection to the claim that the poor as a class benefit from trade liberalization. The objection that liberalizing trade will reduce government revenues and thus its ability to fight poverty is also misplaced because it ignores the dynamic effects of trade liberalization. If trade liberalization produces growth, taxable incomes will grow as well, and government revenues will grow with them. And independently of whether the poor are able to export (i.e., independently of whether or not foreign markets are open to the goods they produce), the poor *benefit from having a wider variety of available imported goods to consume* either because the product was not available domestically or because trade lowers the price of the product, bringing it within the reach of the poor.

In sum, trade liberalization (1) increases *aggregate* wealth, that is, wealth measured aggregatively in both trade partners, (2) increases wealth in *each* of the trade partners, and (3) *at the very least*, within each trade partner, such growth is most often shared by the poor in various ways.

It is important to note the claims we do *not* make in support of free trade. Free trade does not necessarily reduce *inequality* among trade partners or among different groups or individuals within the trade partners. Further, free trade is not a panacea for economic success: as we saw in Chapter 3, countries with bad institutions are less likely to reap the benefits of trade. In particular, nations need to recognize well-defined property rights, freedom of contract, and the rule of law.

TRADE PROTECTION BY RICH COUNTRIES

Rich nations are, taken as a whole, less protectionist than developing nations.[34] However, they have enacted strong protectionist laws for targeted sectors – in particular, agriculture. The United States periodically reenacts the Farm Bill, which obligates the government to buy surplus from farmers in order to keep prices artificially high.[35] The European Union has long maintained the Common Agricultural Policy, a euphemism denoting, too, a vast system of state subsidies

---

[33] Thus, for example, critics of "sweatshops" claim that due in part to lax work conditions, "clothing companies benefit from free trade through BIG profits, and garment workers lose out." See http://www.sweatshopwatch.org/index.php?s=36 (accessed March 2, 2009).

[34] See the 2014 *World Index of Economic Freedom*, published by the Heritage Foundation and the *Wall Street Journal*; available at: www.heritage.org/index/. The study evaluates economic freedom generally, not just trade openness. However, trade openness is one of the components, and the ratings can be found in the section "Executive Highlights" of the report.

[35] This bill has been roundly criticized from right and left. See "A Disgraceful Farm Bill," *New York Times*, May 16, 2008. It was reenacted in 2014.

that keeps inefficient European farmers in business.[36] To these restrictions one must add a host of phony regulations, such as quality control, sanitary rules, government procurement rules, and even national security restrictions, the effect of which is often to virtually ban imported agricultural products. These restrictions certainly harm *consumers* in rich countries, who have to pay more for agricultural products. The law of comparative advantages predicts that in the absence of these restrictions, consumers would simply buy the cheaper (and usually better) agricultural products imported from developing nations while the resources now artificially channeled toward agricultural protection would be freed to produce goods and services where the rich nations are comparatively efficient.

These laws, of course, harm local consumers. But crucially, these laws harm *producers* in developing nations as well, who lose vast wealthy markets for their products. We have little to add to the extensive literature documenting this fact.[37] Farmers in developing countries experience catastrophic losses as a result of subsidies in the developed countries.[38] Unless these laws can be morally justified, they inflict an injustice on distant others by coercively interfering with their means of subsistence and growth.

Can these restrictions nonetheless be justified? Here we face an interesting problem for global justice. Domestically, these protectionist laws are redistributive: they transfer wealth from consumers to farmers. Supporters of these laws may invoke reasons of distributive justice. Let us assume, *gratia argumentandi*, that farmers in rich countries are, under appropriate principles of distributive justice, the rightful beneficiaries of societal subsidies. These laws still hurt *foreign* farmers and, in particular, farmers in developing nations. This means that even if the protectionist could successfully argue that the transfer is *domestically* justified, he cannot possibly maintain that the protectionist laws meet any test of global justice that focuses on alleviating world poverty because protectionist laws interfere with voluntary transactions between consenting sellers and buyers in such a way as to hurt the most vulnerable. By enacting these laws, rich countries *worsen* the situation of the world's poor.

This is a serious problem for mainstream theories of distributive justice, for they were originally designed to evaluate a basic *domestic* institutional structure, the goal of which was to benefit the *domestic* worst-off groups in society. Yet, when these theories add global reach, it turns out that the domestic redistributive policies they favor often hurt the distant poor, who almost always are

---

[36] For a useful description and summary of criticisms, see "Common Agricultural Policy"; available at: www.economicexpert.com/a/Common:Agricultural:Policy.htm (accessed March 11, 2010).

[37] See Thomas Pogge, *World Poverty and Human Rights* (Cambridge, UK: Polity, 2002), 17–19, and sources therein.

[38] See "EU Agriculture Policy Still Hurting Farmers in Developing Countries," *The Guardian*, October 11, 2011; available at: http://www.theguardian.com/global-development/poverty-matters/2011/oct/11/eu-agriculture-hurts-developing-countries (accessed December 15, 2014).

even worse off than the domestic poor. The startling conclusion is that enforcing redistributive programs in the name of *domestic* justice means violating *international* justice or, at least, international duties of humanity or charity toward persons elsewhere who are struggling for survival.

This essential incompatibility between domestic and international justice has led a number of influential philosophers to reject a justice-based global duty to redistribute wealth.[39] Under this view, justice mandates redistribution of resources only within state borders. Let us call this the "nationalist view." Now we claimed in Chapter 2 that as a matter justice we only owe distant others respect for their rights, nothing more. Someone may turn this tenet against us and say that under our own view, preferring compatriots is morally acceptable as long as we do not violate the rights of foreigners. Our farmers (farmers in rich countries) hurt by foreign competition are entitled to our solicitude and help; distant others are not. The Farm Bill is simply an instance of moral solicitude toward those who are closest to us and share a common project. As long as our government does not *directly* harm foreigners, the critic says, it is empowered to enact policies in accordance with its best understanding of domestic distributive justice. The government is not a global charity agency. It has been appointed by the citizens of the state to serve their needs and advance their interests as long as in so doing it does not violate the rights of foreigners. Raising the cost of imported goods is not a violation of a right that the foreign producer holds. True, foreign farmers suffer an indirect harm because their clientele has been reduced, but no one has a vested right in a clientele. If one is willing to export goods, one has to expect that foreign governments will sometimes intervene in markets in order to realize (domestic) social justice. On this view, given the fact that governments are the normal agents for realizing justice in their own societies, this is a risk that exporters in developing countries should assume. Thus, given the views we ourselves defended in Chapter 2, the nationalist concludes, we must concede that compatriots are entitled to our help and that therefore we cannot condemn protectionist laws just because they harm the distant poor.

This superficially attractive objection fails for several reasons. The main one is that trade barriers *actively interfere* with the rights of persons, namely, the rights of buyers (domestic consumers) and sellers (foreign producers). Thus it is incorrect, we think, to describe the situation as remote or indirect harm. It is a coercive interference with contract that directly harms the parties. Protectionist laws violate the rights of producers in developing nations – their right to freely

---

[39] In this sense, see John Rawls, *The Law of Peoples* (Cambridge University Press, 1999), 77, and Thomas Nagel, "The Problem of Global Justice," *Philosophy and Public Affairs* 33 (2005), 113, and our discussion in Chapter 3. There are important differences between these authors, but both favor a preference for compatriots in tax-based help (as opposed to voluntary charity). In the global-justice literature, this is known as the problem of the *scope of justice*. It is the most noticeable difference among writers who otherwise have similar views.

dispose of their property, a right that is central to their subsistence. Moreover, the inefficient local farmer does not have a right to foist her products on a public that no longer wants them. If consumers no longer demand the product (because they prefer the foreign product), it is hard to see what principle authorizes the farmer to enlist the government in force-feeding her products to consumers. Nor do farm workers retain a right to their jobs, given that their employer does not need them anymore. We cannot identify any principle that can justify state coercion to help people produce things that consumers no longer want.

The point can be put differently. What kinds of harm to its citizens can the state legitimately prevent? Certainly, the state should prevent unjust harms, such as those to which the criminal law reacts. But it is not the state's job to redress as many harms as possible. This would be absurd because most of what people do in their everyday lives affects and often harms others. For example, if Joe decides to marry Kirsten instead of Meredith, and Meredith loves Joe, Meredith will be harmed because her interests would be set back. If enough consumers decide to buy Apple computers because they judge them better, makers of PCs will be harmed. If two persons compete for the same job, the one who is not chosen will be harmed. Perhaps a necessary condition for legitimate state intervention is that the setting back of an interest be wrongful. That is, A harms B when (1) A sets back B's interest, and (2) A does this in a manner that violates B's rights.[40] Since in the preceding examples no rights are violated, the harms caused ought not be compensated.

If we apply this formula to international trade, the loss of a job as a result of foreign competition is not an unjust harm because it is a purely *competitive* harm. The worker was harmed because consumers are not interested in buying what he produces. Here we follow John Stuart Mill's lead:

In the first place, it must by no means be supposed, because damage, or probability of damage, to the interests of others, can alone justify the interference of society, that therefore it always does justify such interference. In many cases, an individual, in pursuing a legitimate object, necessarily and therefore legitimately causes pain or loss to others, or intercepts a good which they had a reasonable hope of obtaining.... Whoever succeeds in an overcrowded profession, or in a competitive examination; whoever is preferred to another in any contest for an object which both desire, reaps benefit from the loss of others, from their wasted exertion and their disappointment. But it is, by common admission, better for the general interest of mankind, that persons should pursue their objects undeterred by this sort of consequences. In other words, society admits no right, either legal or moral, in the disappointed competitors, to immunity from this kind of suffering; and feels called on to interfere, only when means of success have been employed which it is contrary to the general interest to permit – namely, fraud or treachery, and force.[41]

[40] Joel Feinberg, *Harm to Others* (Oxford University Press), 1987, 65.
[41] John Stuart Mill, *On Liberty* [1859], chap. 5, sec. 3, in John Stuart Mill, *On Liberty and Other Essays*, John Gray, ed. (Oxford University Press, 2008), 104–5.

Competitive harms do not violate rights. A free society should allow them because competition benefits society as a whole. Mill's rationale should be extended to our present globalized economy. The competitive harm rationale underlies the World Trade Organization (WTO) Treaty: market agents who lose in competition are not entitled to redress (the exceptions to this in the WTO Treaty, such as the permission to protect agriculture, are, of course, objectionable). A global system of free trade benefits everyone in the long run and should be preserved, and this can only be done by disallowing redress for competitive harm.[42]

The protectionist could reply that workers have acquired certain expectations that the government must try to preserve. It is not the worker's fault, he may argue that his industry is now inefficient. He got this job, started a family, bought a home; in short, he made life plans that are now frustrated by events that he cannot control. For this reason, the worker harmed by foreign competition is a proper beneficiary of societal help. In this view, trade barriers are justified not so much to enrich the local employer (although it does that) but to preserve jobs. And it is appropriate for consumers to pay for this: society (the consuming public) subsidizes fellow citizens (the workers of the affected industries) who are suffering hardship. It is no different from other forms of wealth redistribution.

Responding to this argument brings us to the final argument against protectionism. Even if we assume, contrary to what we have suggested, that the government is generally empowered to interfere with trade, protectionist measures are indefensible because they fail to achieve their goal: they do not and cannot effect just redistribution of wealth.[43] When a government protects an industry, it *aborts the creation of jobs in other industries*. This occurs because as the economy is unable to adjust to the efficiencies of production, resources are artificially directed to the less efficient endeavors. The government assists workers in those inefficient industries by erecting trade barriers. But what should we say about the person who is now unemployed *because new industries* that would have employed her have been aborted by the strangling effect of protectionist laws? Seen in this light, producers and workers who benefit from protection are *not* deserving of transfers of wealth in their favor because protection is harming *other* persons in that society. Because those persons

---

[42] A useful discussion of competitive harm can be found in Richard A. Epstein, "The Harm Principle – And How It Grew," *University of Toronto Law Review* 45 (1995), 369. Mill's consequentialist may be recast in nonconsequentialist terms. For example, Arthur Ripstein, "Beyond the Harm Principle," *Philosophy and Public Affairs* 34(3) (2006), 215, provides a Kantian justification for disallowing compensation for competitive harm.

[43] Mill makes exactly the same point: "Restrictions on trade, or on production for purposes of trade, are indeed restraints; and all restraint, *qua* restraint, is an evil: but the restraints in question affect only that part of conduct which society is competent to restrain, and are wrong solely because they do not really produce the results which it is desired to produce by them." Mill, *On Liberty and Other Essays*, sec. V, "Applications."

are the unemployed, they are worse off than the protected workers. Just as the firms obtaining protection get rich at the expense of foreign firms, so the workers in protected industries keep their jobs at the expense of the poor *in their own countries*. Because the protectionist harm is the opportunity cost of inefficient laws, it can only be gauged by asserting counterfactuals and is, for this reason, opaque. The public cannot easily see it.

And finally, even if the nationalist is right that the state can legitimately aid workers hurt by trade, erecting trade barriers is a bad remedy. Domestic transfer policies such as industrial retraining are more efficient and fair ways to help those workers.

Thus, even assuming the nationalist premises of the argument, protectionist laws in developed countries are objectionable because (1) they violate the rights of foreign producers by interfering with their voluntary transactions, (2) they do not benefit persons or groups that, on any plausible theory of domestic justice, are entitled to a transfer of wealth in their favor, and (3) they hurt the domestic poor (by aborting the establishment of efficient industries) and domestic consumers (by raising prices). When we add the fact that protectionist policies, far from being the outcome of a quest for justice, are ordinarily the reaction to political rent-seeking and other forms of predatory behavior, the argument based on domestic justice vanishes. Well-organized protected industries hire powerful lobbyists who essentially "buy" the protectionist legislation from politicians interested in incumbency.[44] If protectionist barriers in rich countries are objectionable even without considering their effects on foreigners, they become particularly offensive when they harm the distant poor.

TRADE PROTECTION BY DEVELOPING COUNTRIES

Some people who criticize protectionism by rich countries are nonetheless reluctant to condemn protectionism by developing countries. This is a mistake. The arguments against protectionist laws apply equally to developing nations. Powerful local monopolies enlist the government in protecting them against foreign competition, thus hampering economic growth and perpetuating economic stagnation. The debate, once again, suffers from a fatal rhetorical glitch caused by a failure to understand the economics of trade. Critics of rich-country protectionism correctly see that it hurts producers in developing nations, thus hampering the growth of those nations. But they do not believe that poor-country protectionist laws will hurt producers in rich countries much, and even if they do hurt those producers, it will not matter much from the standpoint of global justice because the pressing moral concern is to alleviate the plight of the world's poor. So the implied reasoning is that protectionism

[44] The politics of protectionism is well summarized in John O. McGinnis and Mark L. Movsesian, "The World Trade Constitution," *Harvard Law Review* 114 (2000), 521–31. See also Grossman and Helpman, "Protection for Sale."

in developing countries is, at worst, morally neutral because it does not harm foreign persons in a way that is an issue for global justice: producers in rich countries have vast markets at their disposal, in particular, their own wealthy domestic markets. In fact, some have gone further and insisted that protectionism by developing countries *benefits* those countries. This approach enjoyed considerable vogue during the 1960s and 1970s mainly as a result of a promotion by the Economic Commission for Latin America and the Caribbean (ECLAC) (the Spanish acronym is CEPAL), an agency of the United Nations. It recommended a nationalist economic policy based on import substitution and massive public spending as prescriptions for growth and development. This policy ("Cepalism") was implemented in Latin America and Africa with disastrous results.[45] Vastly discredited today, this theory is still sporadically invoked by populist demagogues to justify their nationalist policies.[46]

The view that protectionism by poor countries is benign ignores the central premise of international economics, which bears repetition: the country that protects *hurts itself*. Protectionism is self-destructive. In developing countries, the problem is not that these laws hurt producers in rich countries but rather that they prey on *domestic* consumers by forcing them to forego the economic choices generated by international trade, and they abort the creation of new industries by redirecting resources toward inefficient activities. As we indicated earlier, this harm is opaque. Tragically, the unemployed person in suburban Buenos Aires cannot *see* that a main reason for his predicament is that inefficient producers and their powerful unionized workers have successfully lobbied the Argentine government to get protection against foreign competition. In this way, the labor unions have improved their situation vis-à-vis our unemployed person because the latter now will not be employed by an industry that was *aborted* by the perverse incentives created by protectionist laws. Because understanding this requires not only knowing the complex and counterintuitive law of comparative advantages but also positing a *counterfactual* that is itself hard to grasp, the victim of this depredation does not see himself as such and, sadly, continues to support the populist demagogues in the hope that he, too, will benefit from some subsidy or other.

A final point: it is no mere coincidence that, with some exceptions, the wealthier countries have *fewer* trade barriers than the developing countries. If protectionist barriers were so good for developing nations, we should see some evidence of this in the numbers. Not so. As we discussed in Chapter 3, nations who succeeded in defeating poverty did so mostly by establishing

---

[45] For Latin America, see Hernando de Soto, *The Invisible Revolution in the Third World* (New York: Harper Collins, 1989); for Africa, see George B. Ayittey, *Africa Betrayed* (New York: St. Martin's Press, 1992).

[46] For the example of Hugo Chávez in Venezuela, see Álvaro Vargas Llosa, "The Rise of Hugo Chávez," *The Independent Institute*, September 19, 2007; available at: www.independent.org/newsroom/article.asp?id=2028.

market-friendly institutions and fixing their noneconomic institutions, such as the judiciary. Trade openness is a component of economic openness, and as we saw, the correlation between market-friendly institutions and economic prosperity is undeniable.

TRADE AND COERCION: THE PROBLEM OF STOLEN GOODS

International trade takes place mostly between private agents. A private producer in Country A attempts to sell her product to private consumers in Country B, but the government of Country B interferes by placing trade barriers, thus raising the cost for consumers. Our argument is that governments have no justification to interfere with these voluntary transactions. But sometimes this voluntariness has been vitiated. Trade presupposes legitimate ownership over the traded goods, but suppose that the goods are stolen. This may occur in two ways. In the first scenario, rich people in developed nations presently hold resources that they obtained in the past from people in developing countries through theft, force, or deception. Trading with the poor the very resources that the owner stole from them is deeply wrong. This is the *imperialist thesis*: resources were stolen, it is argued, by rich nations or their citizens from their rightful owners in poor nations. In the second scenario, a despot stole resources from his own subjects and then illegitimately sold them to foreigners (usually in rich nations) mostly to advance his own interests and consolidate his power. This is the *dictator-thief thesis*. It may be argued that in these two cases, before opening trade, we must implement corrective measures: we must return the stolen goods to their rightful owners. Only then we could start talking about free trade. We consider both theses separately.

We have two replies to the imperialist thesis. The first is simply that its factual premises are, for the most part, wrong. As we discussed in Chapter 3, the reasons why some nations are rich and others are poor have little to do with theft. Rather, they have to do with different equilibria between productive and predatory forces in society, as reflected in the quality of institutions and, in particular, on the success or failure of market-friendly practices. But there are surely some instances (some colonial cases comes to mind) where perhaps some of the resources currently held by persons in rich countries are ill gotten. We distinguish between two vantage points from which to address the problem: ideal theory and nonideal theory.[47] Ideally, the best international system would be one where free trade would be accompanied by compensation for wrongdoing. Compensation, however, would be hampered in most cases because determining what part of the current wealth held by individuals should

---

[47] The distinction between ideal and nonideal theory was introduced in John Rawls, *A Theory of Justice*, 7–8. Allen Buchanan applied it to international relations in Allen Buchanan, *Justice, Legitimacy, and Self-Determination: Moral Foundations of International Law* (Oxford University Press, 2004), 54–5.

be returned to their rightful owners is a daunting task. Surely not all wealth, not even its greatest part, is stolen. Still, if we could determine who rightfully owns what, corrective transfers would be justified.[48] Freedom to trade would be accompanied by corrective justice.

From the standpoint of nonideal theory, however, a worthy goal is to *reduce poverty here and now*. That is, international institutions should help to reduce poverty. If corrective measures are unfeasible either because the theft took place too far back in time, because we cannot possibly know the percentage of wealth that was stolen, because the amount of coercion needed to restore the status quo ante is morally prohibitive, or simply because international politics pose insurmountable practical obstacles or for some other reason, then that should not be a reason to refuse to liberalize trade, here and now, as a way to alleviate world poverty.

The dictator-thief thesis is harder to answer.[49] A defense of free trade rests on the moral worth and beneficial effects of voluntary transactions. Yet, as Leif Wenar points out, dictators in the poorest countries often appropriate the resources from the people and then sell them to foreigners, most of the time for their own enrichment.[50] In these cases, the international transaction was *coerced* when the tyrant appropriated the resources at gunpoint. This case evinces an egregious failure of *domestic* institutions, aggravated by a defective rule of international law – the so-called principle of effectiveness. Under international law, whoever politically controls a country has a right to sell its resources. This rule is obviously unjust not only from the standpoint of basic human rights but also from the standpoint of market rules themselves. The result is objectionable in principle because it countenances the sale of stolen goods and in terms of its consequences because it aggravates poverty (because the tyrant does not use the resources to benefit the people but rather to increase his own power and wealth). Because the gains from trade are achieved at the expense of the victims of theft and oppression, these persons arguably have a fairness complaint against the trading partner, that is, the buyer of the stolen goods.[51] An evaluation of free trade from the standpoint of justice therefore must recommend, as Wenar does, abolishing the rule in question and substituting a rule of respect for the principle that resources belong to the people and not to their rulers.[52] We think, therefore, that the point is essentially correct

---

[48] See Robert Nozick, *Anarchy, State, and Utopia* (New York: Basic Books, 1974), 150–3.

[49] The argument is made by Mathias Risse, "Justice in Trade I," *Politics, Philosophy, and Economics* 6 (2007), 356, and Leif Wenar, "Property Rights and the Resource Curse," *Philosophy & Public Affairs* 36 (2008), 2.

[50] See the horrific examples offered by Wenar, "Property Rights and the Resource Curse."

[51] Risse, "Justice in Trade," 362.

[52] This same point was made by Thomas Pogge, "Recognized and Violated by International Law: The Human Rights of the Global Poor," *Leiden Journal of International Law* 18 (2005), 717, and Peter Singer, *One World: The Ethics of Globalization* (New Haven, CT: Yale University Press, 2004), 96–105.

and that the international trade system should be reformed to require that goods traded from one country belong to their rightful owner – either the private owner or a democratic government that has acquired those goods under acceptable democratic procedures that respect individual rights, including private-property rights.[53]

However, it is unclear that the government in the country where the prospective buyers reside will address this injustice by erecting protectionist barriers. The dictator-thief problem dramatically underscores the fact that most injustices are homegrown, as we have claimed. While opening international trade alone will not remedy these injustices, closing trade will not do the job either. Here, as elsewhere, protectionism is an ill-suited remedy to cure the problem. Something different is required: establishing a system for restoring the stolen goods to their owners while maintaining free trade. The dictator-thief objection accurately identifies a problem in international trade: the system legitimizes objectionable rulers. *This* problem, however, cannot simply be solved by protectionist laws.

THE PAUPER LABOR ARGUMENT

Less persuasive is the view that domestic workers in rich countries are entitled to protection if the imported goods arrive to our shores not through oppression or theft but as a result of lower labor standards in the countries of origin – the *pauper labor argument*. Mathias Risse has given a qualified defense of this argument. For him, if labor laws in rich countries are established for moral reasons, then, for the sake of consistency, workers harmed by imports deserve compensation from the government.[54] The idea is that the moral reasons that underlie labor standards are universal, so while the government cannot enforce those standards in the country of origin, it should acknowledge the universality of those standards by compensating domestic workers harmed by imports.

It is doubtful, however, that many stringent labor standards are always or often enacted for moral reasons. The overwhelming evidence is that

---

[53] We think that Wenar is too generous with the international law provisions that assign ownership collectively to the people (see, e.g., Article 1, *International Covenant on Civil and Political Rights*). He says that those rules are compatible with either private or public ownership of the resources. According to Wenar, for the government to be legitimately entitled to sell the resources, the process of public acquisition must meet democratic strictures. Wenar, "Property Rights and the Resource Curse," 20–1. However, it is unlikely that many signatories of that provision intended that. More likely than not, dictators of the world believe that placing the collective ownership on "the people" entitles them, the dictators, to dispose of the resources. In other words, many signatories of those treaties assumed the very archaic rule that Wenar (and us) decry. But this does not detract from Wenar's point, because he makes a moral argument for reform of the system, not a legal point about the proper interpretation of those treaties. One last point: for a variety of reasons, including public-choice concerns, we are less sanguine than Wenar about the legitimacy of *democratic* governments' expropriating private owners. See our discussion of kleptocracies in Chapter 1.

[54] Risse, "Justice in Trade I," 366–9.

governments enact them for a host of political reasons, including protectionist reasons.[55] However, perhaps labor standards are *supported* by moral reasons, even if the government had other reasons for enacting the standards. This
will largely depend on the labor standard in question. Take wages: it is highly
unlikely that high wages in rich countries are supported by moral reasons.
These salaries are the result of self-interested bargaining by workers, either
individually or through unions, at a time when world labor markets were
highly segmented. With the rise of globalization, it became obvious that labor
in developing countries was more competitive. Understandably, labor unions in
rich countries speak of sweatshops and slave labor, thus implying that workers
in developing countries are in the same moral category as the oppressed, that
they are coerced into working for miserly salaries, almost at gunpoint. This
rhetoric conceals the fact that unionized workers in rich countries have been
outcompeted. Assuming voluntary relationships, including a right to terminate
the contract, one does not have a right to an ongoing high wage if the employer
finds someone who can perform the same work at a lower wage.[56] In fact, our
intuition is exactly the opposite to Risse's: domestic workers in rich countries
are acting *immorally* when they demand protection against cheaper imports
because in so doing they are knowingly enlisting the state in the aggravation
of world poverty.

   Quite apart from this, the evidence does not support the view that opening trade with developing countries has been the main cause for the depres-
sion of wages in rich countries. Rather, trade with poor countries may well
have *improved* wages in the sense that it has moderated the decline that might
have occurred as a result of nontrade factors such as labor-saving technological change.[57]

   Suppose, though, that some labor standards, such as occupational safety
rules, are morally required in the sense that workers have a *right* to those standards.[58] Even then, it is not clear that this right is *inalienable*. Imagine that the
government of a developing country offers workers in a particularly successful

---

[55] See Risse's example of the 1930 U.S Tariff Act, ibid., 367. Horacio Spector has identified
   labor standards precisely along these dimensions and has concluded that many of them do
   not reflect moral principles but rather rent-seeking and desire to avoid competition. Horacio
   Spector, "Philosophical Foundations of Labor Law," *Florida State University Law Review* 33
   (2006), 1119.
[56] Of course, parties must abide by their contracts, so employers could be contractually committed
   to paying higher wages even if cheaper labor is available elsewhere. For an excellent discussion
   of the sweatshop issue, see Matt Zwolinski, "Sweatshops, Choice, and Exploitation," *Business
   Ethics Quarterly* 17 (2007), 689–727.
[57] Bhagwati, *In Defense of Globalization*, 124.
[58] We are unsure even about the claim that safety standards are morally required. Why not think of
   different levels of safety as labor benefits offered by businesses so that workers can freely choose
   between accident risk and economic welfare? But we do not pursue the matter. We concede that
   some labor standards might be morally based. For an inquiry into which labor standards may
   be morally justified and which may not, see Spector, "Philosophical Foundations."

industry a choice. The government offers to enforce the standards, but workers have to understand that this would make their product more expensive and less competitive overseas. Because the market for this particular product is largely foreign, the workers' own welfare will be adversely affected. Alternatively, the government offers to relax the standards and keep the industry internationally competitive. If the workers accept this offer, they *consent* to lower standards (i.e., to give up their right to the higher standards) in exchange for their overall economic welfare. They trade the risk of a workplace injury or illness for their enhanced prosperity. We cannot see why this would be objectionable unless one thinks, implausibly, that individuals are morally forbidden from making tradeoffs of this kind. The case of accepting a higher occupational risk in exchange for a better economic prospect seems far removed from the standard cases of inalienability, such as consenting to being tortured or even selling an organ. It seems to us that in this case workers in rich countries have no claim to protection.[59]

A NOTE ON THE WORLD TRADE ORGANIZATION

Given the advantages of free trade, we agree with those who have defended the role of the WTO in enforcing the most-favored-nation clause, that is, the trade nondiscrimination rule that, in turn, has resulted in a dramatic lowering of tariffs and other trade barriers in the last fifty years or so, with corresponding global economic growth.[60] However, whereas the current WTO regime is preferable to a generalized protectionist regime, it has a number of imperfections from the standpoint of justice and efficiency. First, current arrangements allow governments, rich and poor, to overprotect, thus hampering the chances that the poor will participate in the world economy. One problem with the WTO Treaty, therefore, is that it *does not liberalize trade enough.*[61] In particular, the WTO rules that allow protection of agriculture by rich countries are highly objectionable, as Thomas Pogge and others have pointed out. The WTO should enforce the most-favored-nation clause without exceptions if it is to be consistent with global justice. Second, although generally structured to gradually

---

[59] Here again, the evidence does not support the much-feared "race to the bottom," that is, the view that allowing imports from countries with low standards will cause governments to relax theirs, thus creating a desperate race to lower production costs. Rather, the evidence shows exactly the opposite, a race to the *top.* As incomes rise in poor countries, their growing middle class expects and demands improvements in workplace conditions. See Bhagwati, *In Defense of Globalization,* 127–34.

[60] See McGinnis and Movsesian, *The World Trade Organization,* 529–47.

[61] For an earlier appraisal of the protectionist features of the WTO (then the GATT), see Jagdish Bhagwati, *Protectionism,* in *The Concise Encyclopedia of Economics* (1988); available at: http://www.economlib.org (accessed January 2, 2010). Our criticism of the WTO, therefore, is diametrically opposed to the criticism by the antiglobalization forces: the latter blame the WTO for being too biased toward free trade; we, however, believe that it does too little to advance free-trade principles.

lower trade barriers, the WTO regime is partly predicated on outdated mercantilist notions: governments seek to secure foreign-market access for exporters, thus treating access to *their* markets as a bargaining "chip." Because imports benefit consumers, the notion that granting access to one's markets is a *concession* to other countries is false. A government that lowers tariffs helps its own citizens. This is yet again a fact concealed by the nationalist rhetoric of protectionism. So the organization is suboptimal from the standpoint of global justice, and it is certainly inferior to more liberal alternatives, such as unrestricted trade.[62]

Still, however bad the present system may be, protectionism is worse. Current critics of the WTO, while rightly criticizing protectionism in rich countries, wrongly claim that developing nations can sometimes help their economies by enacting protectionist measures. The institutional solution that could bring the world closer to the ideal of unrestricted trade is a WTO-like organization whose sole purpose is to ensure that nations liberalize trade. However, excessive international regulation *restrictive* of trade, even if meant to address a genuine market failure, often may be counterproductive with regard to the poor.

[62] See Amartya Sen, "How to Judge Globalism," *American Prospect* (Winter 2002), 2: "Global interchange is good; but the present set of global rules needlessly hurts the poor."

7

States

In October 2011, the Libyans, with aid from the North Atlantic Treaty Organization (NATO), overthrew and killed Muammar Qaddafi, their ruler for more than forty years.[1] Between 1969 and 2011, the world treated the Libyan government in all important respects as the genuine representative of the Libyan people. Under Qaddafi's rule, Libya enjoyed the fundamental powers that international law grants to every state: diplomatic immunities, treaty-making capacity, the right of self-defense, and most important, plenary jurisdiction, that is, the right to enact and enforce laws in its territory. Libya participated normally in regional and global organizations, often in positions of leadership.[2] Qaddafi's envoys were received as proper ambassadors in the United Nations and in foreign capitals. Qaddafi's Libya was, in short, a member in good standing of the international community. This regal treatment continued even after it became obvious that the Libyan regime was responsible for the bombing in 1988 of Pan American Flight 103 that killed more than 200 innocent people. Two staunch antiterrorist Western leaders, George W. Bush and Tony Blair, rejoiced at Qaddafi's renunciation of weapons of mass destruction and welcomed an apparently redeemed Qaddafi to the family of nations.[3] And in 2009, U.S. Senator John McCain (not known for his softness toward dictators) praised Qaddafi for his peace-making efforts in Africa and recommended expanding U.S. relations with Libya.[4]

---

[1] *BBC News*, "Libya's Col. Muammar Gaddafi Killed, Say NTC Officials"; available at: www.bbc .co.uk/news/world-africa-15389550 (accessed 17 May, 2013).

[2] In May 2010, Libya was *elected* to the Human Rights Council, a post from which it was suspended when the rebellion grew (as if before the rebellion the human rights record of the Libyan government would have been exemplary.) See *ABC News*, "Libya, Thailand Elected to Human Rights Council," May 14, 2010; available at: http://www.abc.net.au/news/2010-05-14/libya-thailand-elected-to-human-rights-council/435128 (accessed May 24, 2013).

[3] *BBC News*, "Libya to Give up WMD," December 20, 2003; available at: http://news.bbc.co.uk/2/hi/3335965.stm.

[4] Reuters, "McCain Says Congress Backs Expanding Libya Ties," Friday, August 14, 2009; available at: http://www.reuters.com/article/2009/08/14/idUSLE528109 (accessed May 27, 2013).

However, as soon as the rebels grew stronger and popular support for Qaddafi subsided, observers changed their tune: they started using the words "tyrant" and "dictator" to refer to Qaddafi. These words, of course, were as accurate in 2011 as they had been during the forty-two years of Qaddafi's rule. We do not think that it is an exaggeration to say that the Qaddafi regime was a criminal outfit that ruled by sheer force and intimidation. Yet, for more than four decades, outsiders treated this regime with deference and respect. They might not have liked Qaddafi, but they accepted him as the legitimate representative of Libya. What accounts for this phenomenon? Was there anything that justified this presumption of legitimacy of a state that, on any reasonable philosophical account, was (to use St. Augustine's words) no more than a den of thieves?[5] Was there anything about Qaddafi that gave him the right to be obeyed by the Libyans and the right to be treated with respect by foreign dignitaries? And can we say that even if the Libyans did not have an obligation to endure Qaddafi's tyrannical rule, *foreigners* had nonetheless the obligation to respect him as the lawful Libyan authority, to treat him as if he were legitimate? If so, why?[6]

This chapter addresses the moral standing of states and, correspondingly, the principles that govern permissible interference, short of war, with them (war is subject to different principles, which we address in Chapter 8). Things have changed significantly in the last fifty years or so, but nation-states are still central in international relations. A discussion of the state, therefore, belongs in a book about global justice.

We said that we must respect the moral rights of all persons, including foreigners. This is essentially an obligation of noninterference with *personal* projects and does not depend on whether those persons have political obligations toward their states. The obligation to respect persons does not always translate into an obligation to respect *states*; in fact, as we shall see, sometimes the opposite is true. However, the principle of noninterference with persons entails a duty to respect good institutions in other societies. Good institutions allow persons to pursue their personal projects – they respect their moral rights. Our prescription for a liberal foreign policy is, then, that persons, privately or through their governments, may pursue their legitimate interests in the international arena in a manner consistent with the rights of everyone. Everyone should respect *good* institutions in other states. But we do not have an obligation to be deferential to *bad* institutions; on the contrary, everyone should, within the boundaries of prudence, help persons suffocated by bad governance. These duties to distant others do not depend on there being *any* legitimate state. We go further: we suspect that the only legitimate state is a voluntary state. Since

---

[5] Phillip Schaff ed., *Confessions and Letters of St. Augustine, with a Sketch of His Life* [395 A.D.] (Whitefish, MT: Kessinger, 2004), 254.

[6] We pick Libya, but the same questions can be asked about East Germany, Iraq, Liberia, and many other states.

there are no actual voluntary states, no actual state is legitimate. But again, this does not mean that we should be agnostic toward actual institutions; on the contrary, we should encourage good institutions and discourage bad ones.

STATES DEFINED

What is a state? A good place to start is the legal definition. International law defines a sovereign state as a population ruled by an independent government in a territory. A government is independent when it is not subordinate to a superior authority (other than the authority of international law, if any.)[7] A state is typically a stable independent political community.[8] International law grants powers to the state, that is, to each stable independent community.[9] These powers define the mutual relations between these communities. But a full concept of a state is more complex. We can say (following David Copp) that a state consists of the *animated institutions of government*.[10] A state is made of persons, institutions, and territory; it consists of populated institutions, as it were.[11] Institutions may endure over time and be animated by different persons at different times, or institutions may change. The state has different incarnations at different times: sometimes the institutions of government remain the same but the persons who occupy them rotate, as in liberal democracies. Other times the institutions change but the persons are the same, as when a king enacts liberal reforms and turns an autocratic monarchy into a constitutional monarchy. And sometimes both the institutions and the persons change, as when revolutionaries replace the previous government and the previous constitution. This is a nonmoral definition of the state; nothing normative follows from the definition. A state thus defined may or may not be morally justified.

THE CONCEPT OF LEGITIMACY

There is considerable confusion in the literature on state legitimacy.[12] Most writers consider legitimacy a *binary* concept. It does not admit of degrees.

---

[7] Article I of the 1933 Montevideo Convention (widely considered to reflect customary international law) provides: "The state as a person of international law should possess the following qualifications: (a) a permanent population; (b) a defined territory; (c) government; and (d) capacity to enter relations with other states." Montevideo Convention on the Rights and Duties of States, entered into force December 26, 1934.

[8] See Ian Brownlie, *Principles of Public International Law*, 7th ed. (Oxford University Press, 2008), 71.

[9] International law speaks about rights and duties of the state, but we prefer the term "powers" because we are skeptical about the "domestic analogy": only persons can have rights.

[10] David Copp, "The Idea of a Legitimate State," *Philosophy & Public Affairs* 28 (1999), 6–7.

[11] We briefly discuss territory in a separate section; in what follows, we assume that the society that underlies the state has some kind of title to the territory it occupies.

[12] For a helpful survey, see Thomas Christiano, "Authority," in *Stanford Encyclopedia of Philosophy*; available at: http://plato.stanford.edu/entries/authority/ (accessed January 31, 2014).

A state is legitimate if it meets the applicable moral threshold, even if it commits discrete injustices, and it is not legitimate if it does not meet that threshold, even if at times it does justified things. Writers disagree wildly about what makes a state legitimate. Here are some examples: legitimate states are those that exercise coercion

- Consistently with the rights of persons
- In pursuit of the common good, however defined
- In accordance with a given constitution
- Consistently with the conception of the good historically upheld by the people
- Authorized by a democratically adopted law after public deliberation
- That serves essential societal needs
- Accompanied by a public justification, that is, one that the coerced person can accept
- To provide public goods
- That is de facto effective, that is, obeyed and applied, in a territory

And so on. Of course, these standards can be combined, yielding complex standards of legitimacy.

More recently, authors have suggested that state legitimacy has two aspects: political *authority* and political *obligation*. Political authority is the *right to rule*, that is, the right that the state has to make laws and enforce them against members of society. Political obligation is the obligation (subject to certain exceptions) to *obey governmental commands*, even in circumstances that one would not be obligated to obey those commands if issued by a private person.[13] Writers who define state legitimacy as the state's right to rule do not hold that subjects must obey *any* command by the state: they typically propose substantive constraints on the kinds of commands that the state may legitimately enact. They typically adopt one of two views:

1. A state that satisfies a legitimacy threshold (say, general respect for basic human rights) has the right to enact even unjust commands, and the subjects have the correlative obligation to obey in spite of the injustice because the state is legitimate.
2. A state that satisfies a legitimacy threshold has the right to enact even unjust commands, but the subjects do *not* have the correlative obligation to obey.

We do not have to take sides on this issue because we do not believe that the state has a right to rule, and we do not, therefore, agree that subjects have an obligation to obey the commands of the state *qua commands of the state*. Others have discussed this question at length, and we defer to their

---

[13] We follow here Micahel Huemer, *The Problem of Political Authority* (London: Palgrave Macmillan 2013), 5.

analysis.[14] The main point (on which we expand later) is that the concept of "obligation to obey the law" is ambiguous. Suppose that the state prohibits murder. We indeed have an obligation to refrain from murdering, but the reason is not that the state has said so. All the work is done by the moral prohibition against murder. The same analysis applies to less dramatic rules – the rules of traffic, for example. The state decrees that we should drive on the right side of the road. We have an obligation to drive on the right, but not because the state said so, but because we owe an obligation to our fellow drivers to drive safely, and the coordination point chosen by the state (the right as opposed to the left) is as good a coordination point as any. We take advantage of the fact that the state has identified one coordination point among many. If all the drivers decided to drive on the left instead, there would be no residual obligation to drive on the right just because the state said so.

On the traditional view, when the state has a right to rule (because it exercises coercion in accordance with the applicable standard, whatever it is), outsiders have an obligation to *respect* that domestic governance. Whatever makes a state domestically legitimate creates a duty on others to respect that state.[15] That is, whatever makes a state worth respecting by other states has to do with how that state relates to the persons that inhabit the state. The reason is that by respecting the state, foreigners respect the subjects of the state, with regard to whom the state rules legitimately. Using a metaphor, one can say that outsiders must accept the state because the subjects themselves accept the state. For foreigners to respect a legitimate state is a way to honor, indirectly, the duty not to interfere with personal projects. The intuitive idea is, then, that the international standing of the state derives from its standing vis-à-vis its subjects. If the regime has no standing with its subjects, it has no standing with outsiders, in the sense that outsiders have no reason to treat the regime as a lawful agent of its people – no reason to treat the regime as a member in good standing of the international community.

Suppose (contrary to what we have intimated) that there is a standard of legitimacy, such as general respect for human rights. That a state is legitimate is a *sufficient* condition to create the duty on others to respect that state. It is not a *necessary* condition. Subjects may have an all-things-considered duty to obey the laws of the state, even an illegitimate one. Often it will be wrong to upset existing institutions. It does not follow from the fact that a state does not have the right to rule that subjects are free to disobey the laws.[16] These considerations apply equally to foreigners. They, too, will often have reasons to respect (in the sense of refraining to upset, modify, or attack; see later) illegitimate

[14] See, in addition to Huemer, A. John Simmons, *Moral Principles and Political Obligation* (Princeton, NJ: Princeton University Press, 1981).

[15] See Bas van der Vossen, "The Asymmetry of Legitimacy," *Law and Philosophy* 31 (2012), 565–92.

[16] See A. John Simmons, *Justification and Legitimacy: Essays on Rights and Obligations* (Cambridge University Press, 2001).

states. It is possible, as we said, that *no* state is legitimate, that is, that no actual state has the right to rule. Yet this cannot mean open season for foreigners to upset the institutions of other states. There are many reasons why this will be the wrong thing to do in a great majority of cases.

In this book we set aside the concept of state legitimacy as traditionally understood. Because, as we said, it is likely that *no* state is morally legitimate, we organize our proposals, following previous chapters, around the idea of *good and bad institutions*. Put succinctly, a state cannot be legitimate *in totum*. Rather, states perform permissible and impermissble *acts of coercion*. Only *acts* of coercion can be legitimate in the sense that they are morally justified. The United States respects free speech but unjustly incarcerates many people. The United States does not get a pass for the unjust incarceration merely by invoking the status of legitimate state, for those acts of coercion are precisely the ones that were supposed to define legitimacy in the first place. Yet there are better and worse states – in fact, some states (e.g., liberal democracies) are *much* better than others. But this does not mean that they are legitimate in a philosophical sense. It only means that they have better institutions, those that (relatively) allow persons to flourish in freedom. And it is for this reason that foreigners must respect them, all things considered.

DE FACTO AND DE JURE LEGITIMACY

Before examining the various standards of state legitimacy proposed in the literature, we must remove an ambiguity. When people say that a state is legitimate, they may mean two different things. They may mean that the government has the *right to rule* over its subjects in the sense explained earlier. But people may refer to a second sense of legitimacy, namely, that a state is legitimate when the government *actually controls the resources of the state*, and for this reason, it is the only agent who in fact is in a position to speak for the state, as it were.

This second concept of legitimacy, *de facto legitimacy*, is outward looking and pragmatic. Suppose that State A is interested in a treaty with State B. We may say that such and such individual is the "legitimate" government of State B when he is the public official to whom State A's officials should address themselves if they want to negotiate a treaty. Here the concern is pragmatic, operational. State A's officials do not look at whether State B's government is morally or constitutionally legitimate: State A just wants to make sure that it is dealing with someone who in fact can be trusted to implement the treaty. State A is interested in results. The government of State B is the de facto ruler of the state. This means that it *controls the resources of the state* and so can act effectively (it can arm or disarm, sign a ceasefire, repeal a treaty, vote for State A's position in the United Nations, and so on). Thus, for example, imagine that Eastland wishes to prevent Westland from attacking Southland, Eastland's ally. In this case Eastland will try to exact a commitment by Westland through a treaty, a nonaggression pact. Eastland does not care whether Westland is morally legitimate or illegitimate, liberal or illiberal, tyrannical or democratic: all Eastland cares about is that Westland refrain from attacking Southland. The domestic relationship between that government and its subjects is irrelevant. All that matters is whether this de facto regime can deliver the goods. If we use the word "legitimacy" to mean de facto control in this sense, then, of course, every de facto government is legitimate.

The point is this: it is perfectly consistent to say that a state is illegitimate in the first sense while treating it as legitimate (as the de facto agent of the state) in the second sense. To resume our example: Eastland, a democracy, is anxious to get Westland, a dictatorship, not to attack Southland. Eastland then enters into a nonaggression pact with Westland. Eastland reasonably believes that the Westland government will abide by the treaty, perhaps because Eastland has warned Westland of the dire consequences of breach. Now Eastland's government believes that Westland is an outlaw regime, a criminal outfit headed by thugs. Still, it treats those thugs as the agents for Westland because *only they can perform their treaty obligations*. This shows that legitimacy-as-de-facto-agency has nothing to do with moral justification. It is a strategic concept, governed as such by the rules of strategic interaction. Eastland treats the Westland government as an agent because it is rational for it to do so given the structure of payoffs.

What is the relationship between both concepts? As we just observed, one can consistently say that a state is morally illegitimate but should still be treated as the de facto agent for the subject because the government controls the state's resources. In this trivial sense, the moral quality of governance does not affect agency. But this concept of legitimacy is uninteresting: it is akin to treating the power of a hostage taker as legitimate. The hostage taker controls the hostages, and this is why we have to negotiate with him. If our purpose is to free a kidnapped child, it will not help to negotiate with the de jure agent (say, his parent) because she lacks the power to free her child. Legitimacy-as-de-facto-agency will always be present in international relations, of course: any state that has control is a de facto agent just for that reason. But we will not call this "legitimacy." All states that have control are de facto agents for their subjects, but only states that meet a (as yet unspecified) substantive standard of governance are legitimate.

Again on the mainstream view, if a state has the right to rule, if it is legitimate in the normative sense, some important consequences follow. We can treat this state as a full member of the international community. We deal with its government much in the way we deal with a peer: we will tend to cooperate with that state not just in strategic terms but also in recognition of the fact that it is not simply wielding de facto power but *justified* power. A state is legitimate if it has the right to rule, and if it has the right to rule, it is a de jure agent for its people. International relations rest on the assumption that governments *represent* their subjects. It makes sense for a government to treat another government as an agent of its subjects if there is, in fact, an agency relationship. Agency is established by contract; it is a fiduciary relationship between people and government. That contract was either executed or it was not; someone is the agent of the principal or he is not. A government who is not an *actual* agent – has not in some sense been appointed by the principal – is a usurper that purports to represent persons when it does not.

As we anticipated, the main difficulty with the normative account of legitimacy is that no actual state is really legitimate, for no state really exercises delegated power. Rather, the justice or injustice of governance is measured via a continuum. Persons have moral rights that they need to pursue their personal projects. Good institutions enable persons to pursue their projects; bad institutions interfere with those projects. The institutions of government and the actions by officials and others often violate the moral rights of citizens to different degrees. They unjustly intrude with liberty or property. Virtually all governments do this. The United States allows great freedom of speech but permits the incarceration of many morally innocent persons. Singapore restricts political freedom but enables citizens to trade and produce. Argentina does not persecute dissenters but steals from its people. For this reason, we reject the sharp distinction between liberal and illiberal states that dominates the literature.[17] A state will be better or worse depending on its degree of respect for the moral rights of its subjects. Now, of course, some states protect freedom better than others. On their balance sheet, they can show a significant surplus in the freedom column. We can call these states, for convenience only, *liberal states*. They are the ones that possess *relatively* unobtrusive institutions not only in the formal sense but also in the way that they are applied by public officials. These institutions deserve respect, and it is highly desirable that more actual states become liberal in this sense of acquiring good institutions.[18] But bad institutions and practices, even in these relatively benign states, do not deserve respect and are vulnerable to criticism and acts of diplomacy calculated to counter them. In other words, a state is not shielded by its good institutions from (otherwise permissible) actions aimed at undermining its bad institutions. China's improved record on economic freedom does not shield its government from international criticism of its political censorship. Greece's relatively good record on civil liberties does not excuse its predatory economic behavior.

In summary, the bivalent concept of legitimacy is not particularly helpful for two reasons. First, as we suggested, it may turn out that *no* current state is really legitimate. Indeed, our inclination is to say that only voluntary states are legitimate, and none of those exist. Second, the bivalent concept of legitimacy

---

[17] This includes the abandonment of the black-or-white distinction between liberal and illiberal states by one of your authors. See Fernando R. Tesón, *A Philosophy of International Law* (Boulder, CO: Westview), chaps. 1 and 2.

[18] In the rest of this chapter, we mean "liberal state" in this sense: a state that in relative terms allows its subjects to pursue their personal projects with a (relative) minimum of unjust intrusions.

is not granular enough to account for the moral diversity of political practices. Rather, the proper targets of evaluative judgments are the *acts of state coercion*. States exercise coercion in their territory. When these acts of coercion cohere with the moral rights of its subjects, they are morally permissible. When they infringe on the moral rights of its subjects, they are morally impermissible. It follows that a theory of global justice cannot rest on a moral switch between legitimate and illegitimate states. There are no states as such worthy of respect: only their acts can be evaluated. Once this is understood, we can talk about states that deserve *more* respect than others because they interfere *less* with the pursuit of personal projects than others.

At any rate, a state's moral standing derives from the way the state relates to its subjects. The more a government respects them, the more respect, in turn, it deserves from outsiders. If a regime's violation of the moral rights of its subjects is substantial, it will have little standing with outsiders, in the sense that outsiders will have little reason to treat the regime as a de jure agent of its people. Whatever reasons outsiders may have to tolerate bad regimes, it is *not* a belief that those regimes are "equal participants in good standing of the Society of Peoples."[19] There is no magical threshold of rights violations at which states become equal to one another.

GOVERNMENTAL ILLEGITIMACY AND NATIONAL SELF-DETERMINATION

A state may be considered illegitimate in two ways. In a first sense, a state may be considered illegitimate because its rulers (the persons who populate the institutions of government) lack the moral authority to enact and enforce laws for their own subjects. An example would be an unjust regime that, for this reason, is not entitled to the allegiance of its subjects. This is the question of *governmental illegitimacy*. We said that the state consists of the animated institutions of government. This definition allows us to speak generically of the state as legitimate or illegitimate, with the understanding that we are referring to the state's right to rule at a given time. To ask whether a state is legitimate is to ask whether the persons who populate the institutions of government have the moral authority to enact and enforce binding laws in a territory. A state may be legitimate at one time and illegitimate at another time. If a military junta takes over the government of Argentina at gunpoint, then Argentina would be an illegitimate state at that time, even if the state of Argentina could regain legitimacy in the future and even if, of course, Argentines retain their moral rights. By state legitimacy here, we mean *only* the right to rule. Governmental illegitimacy is not limited to undemocratic usurpation of power. A government may be democratically elected yet rule under an unjust constitution or enforce unjust laws. Here we speak indistinctly of state illegitimacy and governmental

---

[19] These are John Rawls's words. John Rawls, *The Law of Peoples* (Cambridge, MA: Harvard University Press, 1999), 59. See discussion later in this chapter.

illegitimacy to refer to any situation where, for whatever reason, the state does not have the right to rule vis-à-vis its own subjects. To return to the Libyan example: when we say that under Qaddafi Libya was an illegitimate state, we mean that the Libyan government, that is, the persons who occupied the institutions of government, did not have a moral right to rule.

In a second sense, a state may be considered illegitimate because it has *usurped* jurisdiction over a *territory*. The government, let us assume, is substantively just (it respects the rights of its citizens), but it has "stolen" someone else's territory. This state may be said to be illegitimate not because the government or the institutions are unjust or abusive but rather because the territory over which that government exerts its authority does not *belong* to the society in question but to some other society. Many of those who question the legitimacy of the state of Israel make precisely this kind of argument: Israel is illegitimate not because it rules unjustly but because it rules over a land that does not belong to the Israelis but to the Palestinians (whoever the Israelis or the Palestinians are). A state that respects the moral rights of its citizens may still exercise its powers over a territory that (in some sense to be specified) the society does not own. This is the different question of *national self-determination*. It is the only significant situation where the legitimacy of a *state* is different from the legitimacy of the government. The issues that national self-determination raises are many and complex, but except for a brief reference to territory later, we do not address them here.[20]

THE MORAL STANDING OF STATES

What makes a state legitimate? We anticipated our answer: no state is really, that is, philosophically, legitimate. There are better and worse states. All states violate the moral rights of their subjects, but some do so less than others. We examine three answers found in the literature before restating the one we favor. The *Westphalian* view treats any state that exercises de facto power as legitimate. The *Rawlsian* view treats any state that meets a minimal standard of decency as legitimate. For the *Kantian* view, only liberal states are legitimate. Finally, under the *Lockean* view, which we favor, we have moral obligations only toward persons. This entails the obligation to respect good institutions, even if no state turns out to be legitimate in a strong philosophical sense.

1. The Westphalian View

The Westphalian view claims that any state that meets the legal definition of a state (a population ruled by a government in a territory) is legitimate. Outsiders must treat the de facto power exercised by governments over their territories as de jure power, thus merging the two concepts of legitimacy discussed earlier.

[20] See Fernando R. Tesón, "The Mystery of Territory," *Social Philosophy and Policy* (in press).

Internally, the government must be able to maintain minimal order. Externally, it must be able to relate to other sovereign states within the standard rules that govern diplomacy: it must be able to make treaties, send ambassadors, and so forth. Above all, it must be willing and able to abide by international law. These conditions are harder to satisfy than one would think, but still the threshold is quite low. The state does not have to meet any moral standard to be legitimate; for example, it does not have to respect human rights, nor does it have to be democratic – let alone liberal. To be sure, under this conception, a government has to ensure minimal internal order, so at the very least it has to protect individuals against one another and against foreign aggression. But the government can otherwise be oppressive on any modern account of human rights and democratic legitimacy.

For a long time, this was the view held by international lawyers, and it continues to be the default legal rule today. It is known as the *rule of effectivité* (effectiveness). Whatever else international law requires a state to do, what makes an entity a legitimate state for legal purposes is the ability of its government to exercise political control over the population in a territory plus the willingness and ability to comply with international law. Thus modern international law requires states to respect basic human rights, but for international purposes, even states that fail to do so are still considered legitimate in the sense that they represent their citizens in the international arena. To return to our Libya example: Qaddafi was considered to be the legitimate government of Libya for forty-two years *precisely* because he secured these minimal state functions. However, once Qaddafi lost his grip over his subjects, he lost his legitimacy. Under the Westphalian view, the rest of the world acted properly in withdrawing their recognition of legitimacy at the point when Qaddafi ceased to provide those minimal functions. Nations withdrew their recognition from Qaddafi not because he was a tyrant but because he lost de facto power. Conversely, nations subsequently recognized the Transitional Council not because it turned out to be a model of democratic rule but because it wielded de facto power in Libya.[21] On this view, then, international legitimacy has little to do with moral tests. This is true even if international law today requires states to respect human rights. International law draws a distinction between the legal standing of states and their compliance or otherwise with the rules of international law. International human rights law has not repealed the rule of *effectivité*. The view that in order to be legitimate, all a state has to do is to maintain minimal law and order is alive and well.

While authors in this camp agree on this minimal standard, their differences are important. Some claim that any sovereign state is legitimate. Others argue that legitimate states must provide certain minimal functions. Yet others

---

[21] Libya has descended again into chaos. See "Little to Celebrate," *The Economist*, February 22, 2014; available at: http://www.economist.com/news/middle-east-and-africa/21596974-power-struggles-are-intensifying-little-celebrate (accessed November 3, 2014).

defend a standard of de facto power grounded on self-determination, understood as the value of the community. Let us examine them in turn.

The Realist View

One view, associated with Thomas Hobbes, regards international relations as anarchical. Nations compete globally for resources in an arena where none of them is bound by superior authority. In this arena, national interest, not morality, reigns supreme.[22] The view, Realism, has many versions, some of which are committed to various forms of moral skepticism or relativism. The most plausible Realist account sees international law as a modest global *modus vivendi*. The idea is that to survive, the liberal state must coexist with societies of all kinds, most of which are not liberal. Many of those societies are perhaps objectionable, but international law ensures a modicum of international peace that allows the liberal state to endure in a world replete with dangers. This explains why international law must include the rule of *effectivité*. Only by protecting the sovereignty of all societies can international law protect the sovereignty of the liberal state. Conceived in this way, international law's role is modest: it lays down a few rules designed to channel the use of coercion and to demarcate spheres of jurisdiction. These basic rules of the game do not aspire to reflect any robust morality, liberal or otherwise. Their purpose is solely to enable all sovereign entities to coexist and, by consequence, to enable liberal states to protect freedom within. Notice that this view is not relativist or skeptical. It treats international relations as an arena where morality is out of place, as a veritable state of nature, but it is compatible with a belief in the moral superiority of liberal institutions. The Realist approach simply sees international relations as morally unregulated. The most rules can expect to achieve is a precarious peace, which, in turn, is a condition for the ability of the liberal state to preserve its own institutions.

There are three reasons to be attracted to this view. First, if one assumes, with Hobbes, that any political organization is preferable to the state of nature, then one could say that all states are legitimate because they have succeeded in ending the chaos and perpetual insecurity that characterizes anarchy. Second, the structure of international relations creates serious problems for spontaneous international cooperation. Those who ignore the corrosive logic of the Prisoner's Dilemma in a semianarchical world do so at their peril.[23] And finally, Realism is unpretentious: unlike other defenses of the Westphalian view we will soon consider, it does not attempt to suggest that deference to de facto political power reflects any kind of morality. Simply put, the state's spheres of power must be respected as a condition for survival.

---

[22] This position is well described in Hedley Bull, *The Anarchical Society: A Study of Order in World Politics*, 2nd ed. (New York: Columbia University Press, 1980), 65–70.

[23] See Tesón, *A Philosophy of International Law*, chap. 3.

The Realist view is certainly possible, although we do not find it particularly interesting. We would like to go further and say that there are important differences *among* these states, even if we accept the premise that in all these cases the state of nature would have been worse (a nonobvious premise: think about North Korea.) Because we believe, *contra* Hobbes, that persons have rights that are not just conventional but natural (prepolitical), we moor global justice to assessments of the degree to which persons can pursue their personal projects. The Realist position cannot do this job. It is vulnerable to arguments analogous to those that Lockeans have used against Hobbes: even if sovereign nations are in a state of nature, ethical considerations apply there as well.[24] Contrary to Hobbes, moral principles are prepolitical; they do not depend on the kind of common life that characterizes an organized political society. Morality is universal, and it is difficult to sustain the view that any de facto power must be treated as legitimate or the view that any action by any state that pursues its national interest is immune from judgments of right and wrong. Moreover, a sophisticated account of morality makes room for the legitimate national interest. To say that governments should pursue their national interest *is* to take an ethical position, a position, moreover, that is compatible with ethical behavior. One can easily accommodate the fiduciary duties of governments – their duty to advance the interests of their citizens – within a global theory of justice.

Realism blocks cosmopolitan moral considerations in foreign policy. Such a move would be more defensible if it were true that diplomacy could not possibly have an effect on the lives of persons. But this premise is false. Diplomacy can and should contribute to the welfare of individuals, more precisely to the removal of barriers to the pursuit of personal projects. If so, a theory of global justice should have something to say about state power. Realism lacks resources to make distinctions based on how states treat their subjects; indeed, it has no resources to criticize *any* state behavior. From a cosmopolitan standpoint, Realism is hard to defend: if all persons have moral rights, then it matters whether those who rule over them respect those rights. Finally, the premise of the argument is dubious: it is just not true that for a state to treat *all* other states as legitimate is a condition for its survival. Such a view may have been plausible in the nineteenth century, but, at least today, judgments of legitimacy, right or wrong, do not seem to undermine the chances of survival of those governments that make them. More generally, one should be wary of a theory that lifts moral restraints from state action, thus in practice condoning the many crimes that states have committed historically in the name of security and national interest. In the end, the Realist view confuses the two meanings of legitimacy discussed earlier. We can *choose* to say that legitimacy *means* "wielding effective power, " but that, as indicated, is trivial, uninteresting. The

---

[24] For cogent responses to Realism, see Charles Beitz, *Political Theory and International Relations*, 2nd ed. (Princeton, NJ: Princeton University Press, 1999), chap. 1, and Marshall Cohen, "Moral Skepticism and International Relations," *Philosophy & Public Affairs* 13 (1984), 299–346.

interesting problem is what governmental acts, if any, contribute to the realization of individual projects.

The Minimal-Functions View

David Copp has put forth another version of the Westphalian view. He joins A. J. Simmons and Michael Huemer in rejecting robust justifications of the state, such as contractarian views, but he likewise rejects their anarchical conclusion – the view that no state is legitimate. He proposes instead a minimalist conception: states are legitimate just in case they are able to satisfy basic societal needs, such as "the ability to enact and enforce the law, where compliance promotes the state's ability to meet its needs."[25] The argument does not distinguish any one state from another. Any state, even an unjust one, is legitimate in this sense, and it will only cease to be legitimate when it is no longer able to meet the basic needs of the society over which it rules. There is a "threshold of efficiency" below which a state is no longer legitimate. But, of course, since most states meet this threshold, most states are legitimate, and all existing states are *presumptively* legitimate. Outsiders may not deny the state its right to rule, no matter how unjust that rule may be, as long as the state is meeting basic societal needs. The argument equates internal and external legitimacy: outsiders must respect the state's right to rule because the subjects themselves must respect the state's right to rule (although, for Copp, subjects do not have to obey unjust laws).

Copp rejects contractarian justifications of the state because no actual state can possibly meet contractarian tests, whether expressed in terms of actual or hypothetical consent. Because the anarchical alternative (no state is legitimate) is untenable, Copp thinks that the test for legitimacy must be sought elsewhere. Crucial to the argument is a distinction between justice and legitimacy. Copp thinks that his conception is superior to more robust alternatives because it explains why citizens of unjust states must obey "morally innocent" laws, such as the laws that prohibit murder, the laws of traffic, and so on. If the injustice of the state destroyed its right to rule, then subjects would be free to disobey morally innocent laws. This is implausible, Copp thinks: citizens have an obligation to obey these laws regardless of the injustice of the regime. If so, the view that only just states are legitimate is mistaken. This argument relies on a distinction between the right to rule, which the state has, and the duty of obedience, which the subjects may or may not have. Citizens do not have an obligation to obey unjust laws, but they have an obligation to obey morally innocent laws, even when enacted by an unjust regime. This latter obligation can only be explained, Copp thinks, by assuming that the state (even an unjust one) has the right to rule over its territory.

The problem with this line of argument is that our obligations to obey innocent laws are due to our fellow citizens, not to the state. I must obey these laws

[25] Copp, "The Idea of a Legitimate State," 40.

for coordination or reciprocity reasons, not out of recognition that the current regime has any right to rule. The regime happens to promulgate laws that I accept for independent reasons. This explains why we have to obey traffic laws even under an unjust regime. Copp trades on the already noted ambiguity of the concept of legal duty. The sentences "the government enacted this law, and I have a duty to obey it" and "the government enacted this law, and *for that reason* I must obey it" say different things. In the first one, my obligation is not generated by the legal enactment; in the second, it is. Copp wrongly infers that the unjust state has a right to rule from the fact that the state has enacted a law that we must obey *for independent reasons*. No one denies that unjust regimes often perform useful functions, such as providing courts for adjudicating controversies among citizens and so on. Copp is correct in observing that citizens cannot refuse to abide by a court ruling or disobey traffic laws merely because the current regime is unjust. But these obligations are a subspecies of moral obligations. They are owed to the fellow human beings with whom I have to interact daily. They are not owed to the state.

To see why this is so, consider someone who committed a crime, say, armed robbery, in Libya circa 1988, and was arrested by Libyan police shortly thereafter and brought to justice. Copp thinks that if we deny the Libyan state the right to rule, we cannot explain the legitimacy of this arrest because if the Libyan state is illegitimate, so would be the Libyan police and the punishment visited on the criminal. Yet, Copp thinks, we know that the arrest and punishment are justified; therefore, the Libyan government, distasteful as it is, has a right to rule. The problem with this argument is this: the arrest is justified not because the Libyan government is legitimate but because, by committing the crime, the robber forfeited his immunity against coercion. It follows that *anyone* can exercise the natural right of punishment, understood as an enforcement right against a right violation. The Libyan police exercised the enforcement rights held by the victim of the robbery. Since the only relevant change in the moral landscape is that the robber lost his own right not to be coerced, it follows that the Libyan police may act against him, just as may any other person who wishes to exercise those enforcement rights. We do not need to postulate the legitimacy of the Libyan state to consider the arrest as morally justified.

Copp finds support for his argument in the fact that virtually all current states originally emerged through skulduggery – fraud, aggression, theft, and deceit. It is a historical fact that states that we now consider just (say, Britain) were originally unjust: maybe they usurped the authority of a preexisting state, maybe they obtained their present territory by aggression, or maybe the original governmental authority was tyrannical and only subsequently matured into a liberal democracy. Given this history, no state can possibly meet a robust test of legitimacy – certainly not a pedigree test. But, Copp thinks, the conclusion that no actual state is legitimate is implausible; for example, we treat the United Kingdom as a legitimate state notwithstanding the fact that it arose out of centuries of unjust rule. How can this be? Because, Copp says, the English monarchy *was* a legitimate state, say, in the thirteenth century. If the King of England had a right to rule, then the test of legitimacy cannot be justice but something else: the government's ability to meet society's basic needs.

The answer to this argument is that the English King did *not* have a right to rule in the thirteenth century. To be sure, the King provided useful functions, and the subjects at the time had natural duties toward their fellow citizens, as we explained earlier. Obeying the King (e.g., by abiding by his rulings in deciding controversies) was an indirect way for subjects to discharge their moral duties toward one another. But they did not have a political obligation toward the King himself. Thus, for example, the taxes collected by the King to pursue wars in search of glory or conquest failed to generate any obligations for the subjects. Morally, they amounted to theft, and the subjects were justified in evading them. Then as today, all the work is done by external moral principles. Talking about the authority of the state is a shorthand for referring to the complex ways in which moral principles govern social life.

Finally, it is a mistake to dismiss, as Copp does, the possibility that *no* state may have the right to rule. As we observed earlier, it is possible that the obligations we have toward fellow citizens have a source other than the authority of the state. The arguments by A. John Simmons and Michael Huemer in support of philosophical anarchy seem, to us at least, quite compelling.[26] Copp assumes that philosophical anarchy (the view that no state is legitimate) is false; thick accounts of legitimacy fail; therefore, legitimacy must be grounded in a thinner account: de facto political power. However, if the premise falls, so does the argument.

The Communitarian View

Michael Walzer offers yet another version of the Westphalian thesis.[27] Like Copp, Walzer thinks that states are presumptively legitimate, but his normative foundations are different. Walzer distinguishes between internal and external legitimacy. According to Walzer, a state is *externally* legitimate when it represents the political life of its people. Walzer expresses this idea in various ways. He writes that a state is legitimate when there is a fit between government and people.[28] By this, he means that the government reflects in some sense the political forces, the history, and the values of the population over which that government rules. For Walzer, citizens are bound to one another in a kind of Burkean contract; they are not, however, bound to obey their government. Citizens are free to reject their government; strictly speaking, they have no political obligation to the regime. Apparently, then, for Walzer, no state is

---

[26] See Simmons, *Moral Principles and Political Obligation*, and Huemer, *The Problem of Political Authority*.

[27] See Michael Walzer, "The Moral Standing of States: A Response to Four Critics," *Philosophy and Public Affairs*, 9 (1980), 209–29.

[28] Ibid., 222.

internally legitimate, or if it is, the standard is significantly more demanding than the external standard. However, the right of subjects to reject their government does not extend to foreigners. Foreigners may not deny the reality of the "union of people and government."[29] States, even unjust states, enjoy external legitimacy, even if they are domestically illegitimate. A state is the arena where the political process unfolds, where people fight for liberty. It is this arena that foreigners have a duty to respect. Walzer, then, adopts an *asymmetrical* concept of legitimacy: the reasons for *citizens* to disobey their government do not affect the obligation by *foreigners* to respect that government. Notice that Walzer does not simply say that foreigners must treat governments as agents for the strategic reasons we discussed earlier. He does not say that the fact that the government is in control creates an obligation of noninterference by foreigners. That obligation arises instead from the *cultural fit* between government and people.

Walzer says, of course, that states are protected against military intervention, but he extends the prohibition to actions that do not involve the use of military force. Walzer expressly says that his theory of external legitimacy is not limited to military intervention: *diplomatic* interference would still be disrespectful because, in his view, the indigenous political process has independent normative value. An attempt to interfere with a morally valuable social relationship is presumptively wrong, even if the intervener uses diplomacy instead of force. We should respect those political processes that are not meant to include us as participants. We read Walzer's argument, then, as prohibiting or at least discouraging the use of diplomacy (and not just force) to interfere with political processes, even if the aim is to end rights violations.

To show that diplomatic (and not just military) pressure to effect political changes in a state is impermissible, Walzer uses a hypothetical example. Imagine an illiberal state where the political practices are unjust but consistent with that society's culture and traditions (he calls it Algeria.) Suppose, he says, that we (liberals) had a wondrous drug that, when introduced into Algeria's water supply, would magically turn Algerians into Swedish social democrats (apparently Sweden is Walzer's political Nirvana). Such an action, Walzer contends, would be impermissible. Algerians, as a society, have a collective right to their own political process. Foreigners are banned from this arena and especially precluded from altering the arena artificially, even by these nonmilitary means.[30]

The hypothetical is inapposite. Using the drug is impermissible not because it would interfere with the political process but because it would turn *persons* into different persons without their consent. It would alter their individual identity by medical means. Using the drug is prohibited for the same reason that lobotomies are prohibited, even if they improve the patient's character.

[29] Ibid., 220.
[30] Walzer, "Moral Standing of States," 233–4.

Administering the drug without the patient's consent is a violation of individual, not communal, autonomy.[31] In a way, Walzer's premises lead him to construct this inapposite example, for once he assumes that the object of moral concern is the political process, then he automatically assumes that any external pressure must be aimed at changing that process. Yet once we change the focus to persons, the hypothetical loses its force. Diplomatic pressure aims at changing politics but not because the intervener wants to replace one process with another one he likes better but because he wants to protect persons.

To illustrate our objection, we propose a different experiment. Let us call it the "green-button hypothetical." A state is violating the rights of its subjects. I own a fabulous machine activated by a green button. By pressing the button, I can instantly discontinue all rights violations. The green button will not alter anyone's personality nor have other undesirable consequences. Unlike Walzer's drug, it will not turn persons into different persons, nor alter their psyches or beliefs. It will simply block rights violations. Pressing the green button, we suggest, is morally justified. In fact, we cannot imagine reasons why anyone should not press the button. Diplomatic pressure may be costlier than pressing the button, of course, but the hypothetical shows that contrary to Walzer, there is no independent normative value in a rights-violating social or political practice: the costs of diplomatic pressure should be measured in terms of individual welfare. The costlier the means to end the offensive practice, the less permissible it will be (which is why pressing the green button seems right), but not because the practice in question embodies anything inherently valuable. Diplomatic pressure, unlike war, will be less costly than allowing the rights violations; for this reason, it will be permissible just that often.

Walzer's communitarian version of the Westphalian view must be rejected. There is no reason to make an exception to the standard duty that we all have to help victims of injustice, provided that we can do so at an acceptable cost to everyone. Although diplomatic efforts are not costless, they do avoid the terrible costs of war, so it is hard to understand why they would be impermissible. Walzer reasons to the contrary do not persuade. For example, he claims that foreigners do not have enough knowledge of the society in question and that citizens are expected to resist foreign interference. Again, Walzer has war in mind, but, of course, it is perfectly possible that citizens may resist diplomatic interference as well: in fact, this happens often. We assume that Walzer would follow the same kind of reasoning: if our domestic political process is valuable, then foreigners have no business interfering with it. However, these empirical guesses are dubious. As to the first claim, it defies belief to suppose that foreigners do not know enough about events in other societies, especially when those events consist of denials of rights. The second claim is questionable as well on empirical and normative grounds. Empirically, it is just not true that citizens who suffer injustice will not welcome diplomatic efforts by other governments

---

[31] Charles R. Beitz, "Nonintervention and Communal Integrity", 9 *Philosophy and Public Affairs* (1980), 389–90.

to end that injustice. Normatively, citizens are not entitled to oppose diplomatic efforts by foreigners on behalf of the victims of injustice. If the government denies my rights, you have no standing to block efforts to restore them. Walzer here adopts the collectivist approach: if a clear majority of the population opposes foreign interference, then it would be wrong to interfere.[32] But this is unacceptable. Oppression by a majority is not better than oppression by a minority. In fact, we would think that in the case of tyranny of the majority, it would be more urgent to interfere because often the minority is powerless.

Another way of putting this objection is to ask what obligations are generated by the supposed Burkean social contract that Walzer posits. Walzer thinks that citizens are bound to one another. Now imagine that the state denies many persons their moral rights. A neighboring state is planning to put diplomatic pressure on the local government to end the injustice. According to Walzer, the neighbor cannot permissibly do this because a majority of citizens will oppose such interference. Walzer concedes that the victims have a right to resist the injustice. If this is true, then those who domestically resist foreign attempts to end the injustice are in the wrong; they are collaborators of the unjust regime. What kind of social contract is this? I do not have a social contract with persons who aid and abet the violation of my moral rights; it is more accurate to say that their collaboration with injustice is a *breach* of contract. If so, outsiders do not have an obligation to respect the political process that, far from reflecting communal values, is a cover for rights violations.

To conclude, the Westphalian view reflects a conception of state sovereignty that privileges political power at the expense of morality and justice. Whether based on a crudely Hobbesian view of the primacy of order or on a romantic communitarian idealization of political bonds, it cannot resist an analysis moored to individual rights and individual welfare. Maybe no state is legitimate in a philosophical sense, but surely a justified foreign policy can and must draw distinctions based on how state institutions treat persons.

2. The Rawlsian View

A second group of writers endorses a stronger notion of state legitimacy but denies that only states that satisfy a particular set of political-philosophical principles (e.g., liberal principles) are internationally legitimate. For these authors, the standard of international legitimacy is more modest than the standard of internal legitimacy, but it is nonetheless a substantive standard and not a mere de facto standard of political control. Only states that meet *thin* moral conditions, such as respecting *very* basic human rights, are legitimate. John

---

[32] Richard W. Miller follows a similar approach in the context of Afghanistan. See Richard W. Miller, "The Ethics of America's Afghan War," *Ethics & International Affairs* 25 (2011), 103–42, and the reply by Fernando R. Tesón, "Enabling Monsters: A Reply to Professor Miller," *Ethics & International Affairs* 25 (2011), 165–82.

Rawls and his followers have defended this view.[33] In this view, the standard is moral decency. To be legitimate, a state must respect minimal human rights; those who do not are outlaw states. But many states that respect these minimal human rights fall short (even significantly short) of the demanding standards of political liberalism. These states can still be members in good standing of the international community. For these authors, it would be a mistake to treat only liberal states as legitimate; such a standard is too demanding to serve as the basis for international law. Global justice must be tolerant and accept a diversity of conceptions of the good. We call this the *Rawlsian view*.[34]

Rawls attempts to formulate the principles of a justified foreign policy of a liberal democracy. He sees global justice as an outward extension of liberalism: the question is how should liberal governments treat other regimes, especially regimes that are not liberal. One of the issues that citizens in a liberal democracy must resolve is how to treat outsiders. Rawls's proposal rests on distinctions among various kinds of foreign societies ("peoples").

The "Law of Peoples" extends to international relations a central idea in Rawls' later work: reasonable pluralism.[35] The project is *not* to formulate a theory that reflects the best principles of political morality, but rather the best set of principles consistent with the hard fact of reasonable pluralism. Many societies disagree about the right conception of the good. Philosophical liberalism is but one of such conceptions, and for this reason it cannot sustain a global theory of justice. Many societies around the globe sincerely endorse illiberal conceptions of the good, and liberal foreign policy, as well as the principles of international law, must acknowledge this fact. Rawls' theory is, then, relativist in the important sense that even if moral truths are discoverable, they are not invokable against others who sincerely endorse incompatible views. For Rawls, reasonable pluralism is a hard fact with normative consequences. Given that persons in different societies have different political conceptions, it follows that societies *must* respect one another (provided that they meet certain minimal conditions). It is not just that liberal societies must accommodate illiberal ones for obvious reasons of peaceful coexistence. Liberal leaders must *respect, tolerate*, and *cooperate with* those societies. These illiberal regimes, Rawls thinks, must be treated as free and equal members of the international community. These illiberal conceptions are still decent enough to warrant respect. Liberal

---

[33] See Rawls, *The Law of Peoples*; Charles Beitz, "Rawls's Law of Peoples," *Ethics* 110 (2000), 669–96; David A. Reidy, "Rawls on International Justice: A Defense," *Political Theory* 32 (2004), 291–319. Beitz doubts that Rawls got this right but also thinks that the standard should be *sui generis*.

[34] The discussion that follows focuses on Rawls' version. In previous chapters we sympathized with Rawls' views on global redistribution. In this chapter we part company with him on the question of state legitimacy. For an early criticism of Rawls' view along similar lines, see Tesón, *Philosophy of International Law*, chap. 4. Here we expand on what was then said.

[35] As formulated in John Rawls, *Political Liberalism* (New York: Columbia University Press, 1999).

and decent illiberal societies share a common public reason anchored in their adherence to minimal moral values and mutual tolerance. Of course, some illiberal regimes do not even qualify for a variety of reasons: they are outlaw regimes, and they should not be respected (except for prudential reasons).[36]

The first problem with this view is methodological. Since *Political Liberalism*, Rawls has insisted that the task of philosophy is to find principles that can accommodate decent but incompatible worldviews so that persons who disagree about fundamentals can still lead cooperative, productive lives. The view is attractive because it allows persons who disagree about fundamentals to endorse a social and political order, that is, common institutions. The state, then, would be neutral toward the inconsistent fundamental conceptions of the good that persons have. In extending this idea globally, Rawls' vision is one in which the international community and international law would be neutral toward the inconsistent conceptions of the good that various societies endorse.

But the whole enterprise depends on Rawls' conception of the role of political philosophy – usually labeled "public-reason liberalism." If this conception fails, the whole proposal crumbles, especially for international relations. Public-reason liberalism is questionable because either persons are perfectly (or highly) morally and epistemically rational, in which case they will agree, and there is no need to accommodate anything, or they are less morally or epistemically rational, in which case their views should not prevail.[37] Some views approximate the truth more than others. The task of a theory of global justice is to argue for the *best* conception of politics, one that accords with the better empirical and ethical theories, even if the chances of implementing that conception in the real world turn out to be slim. The fact that many people have illiberal beliefs adds nothing to the plausibility of those beliefs. Whatever plausibility illiberal views may have will result from the reasons marshaled in their support, not from the fact that many people hold them. Public-reason liberals are forced to resort to an idealization of the rational person to get the substantive results they want.[38]

The liberal conception we defend in this book rejects attempts at locating political morality in overlapping consensus or other forms of majority validation. Rawls' proposal, in contrast, comes close to an argument *ad populum*: many societies have illiberal values; therefore, liberals (within some limits) must respect them. This might be a colorable program for politicians trying to get along in the corridors of the United Nations, but it is not acceptable for a

[36] Rawls, *The Law of Peoples*, 90.

[37] See Richard Arneson, "Toleration and Fundamentalism: Comments on Gaus"; available at: www .cato-unbounjd.org/2011/10/12/richard-arneson/toleration-and-fundamentalism-comments-on-gaus/ (accessed December 1, 2013). Arneson puts it well: "Why should people prone to error and false belief be allowed in the set of theoretical determiners of right and wrong, of what are the legitimate principles that fix what we owe to one another?"

[38] See David Enoch, "Against Public Reason", available at: https://www.academia.edu/5794576/ Against_Public_Reason (accessed June 20, 2014).

theory of global justice. If there *are* moral truths, if persons have rights, then liberals have no *moral* reasons to respect the rights-violating acts of political regimes. Of course, there are many reasons to act peacefully toward these regimes. But these reasons have nothing to do with a belief that when these regimes mistreat their subjects, they are worthy of respect.

Even if we accept Rawls' approach, though, there are deeper problems with his concept of liberal toleration. When Rawls writes about decent illiberal regimes, he assumes that they sincerely implement an illiberal but decent societal conception of the good. Just as a liberal state must accommodate incompatible *individual* conceptions of the good, so principles of global justice must accommodate incompatible *societal* conceptions of the good. But there is no such thing as a societal conception of the good. The analogy does not work. Consider Rawls' view of *domestic* reasonable pluralism, that is, within the liberal state. Citizens have differing conceptions of the good. They are incompatible, however, so liberal institutions should accommodate them as long as they are reasonable. Now let us try to extend this idea internationally. Surely, on Rawls' own account, it is still a hard fact of social life that *persons* have different, incompatible conceptions of the good *within each society*. This is true of citizens in illiberal states as well. So what does an illiberal state do? Its rulers coercively impose *one* conception of the good among the many that their subjects have. The regime is illiberal precisely because it imposes this conception. Rawls' liberal toleration, then, amounts to this: in the name of liberal toleration, the liberal state must treat with respect and deference regimes that, domestically, do *not* accommodate differing *individual* conceptions of the good but, on the contrary, suppress all but one of them.

The consequences of this failure of the analogy are fatal for Rawls' thesis because the spurious extension of reasonable pluralism to the international arena poses an *internal* irresolvable tension within the theory: liberal toleration of illiberal regimes means acceptance that governments are under no duty to tolerate diversity *within* – that is to say, they have no duty to accommodate their citizens' incompatible (but reasonable) conceptions of the good. This anomaly arises because of Rawls' failure to see that *only persons* have conceptions of the good, and plausibly, the state should attempt to accommodate them, just as Rawls says. But a society does not have a conception of the good: if reasonable pluralism holds, then persons in a society will differ in their conceptions of the good. Even if sometimes we speak of a societal *ethos*, in Rawls' own view, many people will dissent from that *ethos*. Certainly political *regimes* should not have conceptions of the good; indeed, their *job* is not to have them but rather to arbitrate among the diverging conceptions held by citizens. So the whole project of "tolerating" illiberal regimes fails not only for pretty obvious commonsense reasons (these regimes are quite distasteful) but also for conceptual reasons.

There is yet another problem with the idea of reasonable pluralism, pointed out by Eric Mack. Liberal institutions should indeed strive to accommodate the different *ends* that people have. But liberals do not have to accommodate the various *means* that people want to use to achieve those ends, especially the various coercive means that governments around the world use to impose religious, ethical, or political ends.[39] In our view, people should be free to pursue their own ends of individual excellence as long as those ends do not consist of interfering with the personal projects of others, nor *imposing* their ends on others. Trying to accommodate paternalistic or authoritarian coercion is, for a liberal, unconditional surrender.

Close examination of Rawls' more concrete proposals only increases these worries. He believes that liberal societies must tolerate illiberal societies (meeting certain minimal conditions) not just in the weaker sense of refraining from military and political sanctions but in the stronger sense of "recognizing these illiberal societies as equal participating members in good standing in the Society of Peoples."[40] To qualify as decent, an illiberal society must respect "basic human rights," be peaceful and nonaggressive, and provide for a "decent hierarchical structure" within which its citizens can participate in decision making, albeit in a nondemocratic way. If an illiberal society meets these criteria, liberal societies must treat it as legitimate and cooperate with it. Rawls expressly bans liberal regimes from applying military, economic, and/or political measures to get such a regime to improve.

But this notion of liberal tolerance leads to strange results. Whereas Rawls writes that liberal governments should not adopt diplomatic and military sanctions against these regimes, his view logically precludes liberal *criticism* of illiberal societies as well (Rawls himself does not say this) because the liberal representatives do not have, within the "Law of Peoples," the intellectual resources to criticize illiberal practices. In Rawls' own view, liberals have already *accepted* that these illiberal regimes comply with the conditions required of all states to be members in good standing of the international community. If at an international conference a liberal representative criticizes the illiberal state for not allowing free speech, the illiberal representative, armed with Rawls' book, can retort that, on liberal principles of toleration, the liberal must keep quiet.

What *is* a decent illiberal regime anyway? As we saw, to be decent, a regime must meet three conditions: it has to be peaceful, it has to respect what Rawls calls "basic human rights," and it has to provide for a "decent hierarchical consultation." The first condition that decent regimes must pursue their aims peacefully, by diplomacy and trade, and not militarily,[41] seems harmless enough. Indeed, barring the extreme circumstances that justify war, any aggressive behavior by any government, liberal or not, is inadmissible. Close inspection,

39 See Eric Mack, "Peter Pan Strikes Back," *Cato Unbound*, October 14, 2011; available at: http://www.cato-unbound.org/2011/10/14/eric-mack/peter-pan-strikes-back/ (accessed January 25, 2014).
40 Rawls, *The Law of Peoples*, 59.
41 Ibid., 64.

however, reveals that the requirement does not assuage concerns about these regimes' illiberal practices. Let us take a real-life example. A coalition of states, the Islamic Conference, has recently sponsored, with some success, the criminalization of blasphemy.[42] Most, but not all, of the coalition's members can be characterized as decent illiberal regimes in Rawls' terminology; at any rate, these states dominate the coalition. The move to criminalize blasphemy is certainly peaceful because these states act through normal diplomatic channels. Moreover, the leaders of these countries sincerely believe that their conception of the good requires criminalizing blasphemy; indeed, their laws do exactly that.[43] According to Rawls, therefore, the attitude of liberal states should be one of respect, deference, and cooperation. The most they could do is politely refuse to adopt such a norm in their domestic legal orders. Otherwise, they must tolerate the blasphemy movement and continue cooperating with the regimes that sponsor the measure.

Yet any liberal government worth its salt must vigorously oppose such diplomatic moves. It matters little that proponents of this measure act peacefully and that they act out of a sincerely held conception of the good. By promoting the criminalization of blasphemy, those governments incite repressive behavior and denial of important moral rights. Liberal governments must confront diplomacy that promotes rights violations with the conviction that such policy is not just a diverse conception of the good deserving of toleration and respect but a morally objectionable policy, one that tries to rationalize repression at home and promote it outwardly.

But at least promoting a rights-violating policy is just that, promotion. Domestically, these regimes actually *violate* the moral rights of persons, often extensively. According to Rawls, liberal outsiders must respect those rights-violating policies. His conception of basic human rights is remarkably stingy even compared with the modest achievements of international law. Rawls requires that the right to life and personal security should be guaranteed. Then he mentions liberty: for Rawls, ensuring liberty means freedom from slavery and "a sufficient measure of freedom of conscience to ensure freedom of religion and thought." Notable here is what Rawls does *not* require: that these regimes respect freedom of speech, including the freedom to dissent, the right

---

[42] On March 27, 2009, The UN Human Rights Council adopted a resolution sponsored by the Islamic Conference recommending the criminalization of "defamation of religions." See http://ap.ohchr.org/documents/E/HRC/resolutions/A_HRC_RES_7_19.pdf. Fortunately, this document has no legal force. Western observers have widely criticized the move. See Paula Schriefer, "The Wrong Way to Combat 'Islamophobia,'" *New York Times*, November 9, 2010; available at: www.nytimes.com/2010/11/10/opinion/10iht-edschriefer.html.

[43] For example, the Pakistani criminal code, Section 295-C, reads

Use of Derogatory Remarks in Respect of the Holy Prophet Whoever by words, either spoken or written, or by visible representation, or by any imputation, innuendo, or insinuation, directly or indirectly defiles the sacred name of the Holy Prophet Muhammed (peace be upon him) shall be punished with death, or imprisonment for life and shall also be liable to fine.

to remove a government by vote or similar procedures, and principles of non-discrimination. These "decent" societies must have a hierarchical structure in which the authorities fairly hear everyone, but once a measure is enacted, the police can put the critics in jail.

Similar worries arise with regard to property rights. In line with most egalitarian liberals, Rawls requires only the respect of "personal property." A regime that confiscates all means of production and all resources is therefore beyond criticism, even if those measures can seriously frustrate the subjects' pursuit of their personal projects. We extensively documented in Chapters 1 and 3 the centrality of property rights and freedom of contract in the makeup of good institutions. Anyone concerned with global poverty should worry about these applications of "liberal toleration." Toleration of theft comes close to complicity. Rawls' hierarchical regimes violate many important moral rights that persons have and thus impermissibly interfere with their projects. For these reasons, they should not be elevated to members in good standing of the international community.

It might be thought that Rawls' vision is an improvement over the Westphalian view, under which *any* state that secures minimal order is a member in good standing of the international community. At least the Rawlsian conception *seems* to require a threshold of legitimacy in terms of the rights of subjects. However, Rawls' view is more dangerous than some of the versions of the Westphalian view because it purports to reflect the best political principles as applied to international relations. The "Law of Peoples" is supposed to reflect the best international political morality. In contrast, the Realists recommend using prudence and not morality when confronting illiberal regimes; unlike Rawls, Realists do not endorse those regimes.

Rawls thinks that some of these concerns may be assuaged by requiring that to be a decent illiberal regime, the leaders must *sincerely* believe in the conception of the good they advance. In this way, he excludes from the "club of decent regimes" opportunistic illiberal rulers whose assertion of (supposedly) decent values is merely pretextual. We have serious doubts about the value of sincerity, however. Violating someone's rights is not made better by the perpetrator's belief that he is sincerely implementing a true maxim that authorizes him to act in that way. The virtue of sincerity is entirely parasitic on the value of the maxim in question. Because the illiberal maxim is false (it recommends rights violations), the value of the enforcer's sincerity is zero. On the contrary, a principled evildoer is *worse* that an opportunistic evildoer because he cannot be easily persuaded or bought. Acting on an evil maxim is worse that acting on no maxim.[44]

---

[44] On this, see Fernando R. Tesón, "Targeted Killing in War and Peace: A Philosophical Analysis" in *Targeted Killings: Law and Morality in an Asymmetrical World*, Claire Finkelstein, Jens Ohlin, and Andrew Altman, eds. (Oxford University Press, 2012), 403

In fact, Rawls' view is far removed from any vision that can be called liberal. If the "decent hierarchical society" harbors liberal dissenters, their only remedy, according to Rawls, is to emigrate.[45] The dissenter, in the Rawlsian vision, is a misfit in her own culture, and her only hope is to persuade enough of her fellow citizens to change the political system. She cannot (in Rawls' world) expect even moral sympathy from liberal governments because the regime that suppresses her speech is abiding by Rawls' "Law of Peoples." Liberal regimes just should stay out of it. This is an ultraconservative position that not even the modest international human rights movement is willing to endorse. If a liberal government believes that suppressing speech is wrong, it should say so, and it should be free to exert diplomatic pressure to get the illiberal state to enact political reforms because under the liberal view only individuals matter. Governments have no independent moral standing.

The Rawlsian may protest as follows: objecting to specific policies by illiberal regimes (e.g., the criminalization of blasphemy) is compatible with treating these regimes as members in good standing of the international community. After all, he may say, liberal regimes also make moral mistakes, and we still treat them as legitimate. Similarly, we may (calmly and politely) object to specific laws without denying these regimes their place as members in good standing of the international community. The question of the moral standing of a regime is distinct from the question of what human rights principles regimes must observe. Just as a person who committed a crime does not lose his status as a member of the community, so a regime that violates rights (below a certain threshold of iniquity) does not lose its status as a member of the international community.

This move illustrates the problem with Rawls' proposal. Rawls' "reasonable pluralism" directs us (liberals) to *respect* the practice of throwing people in jail for criticizing the official religion because the practice is part of a sincerely held conception of the good. On Rawls' account, the liberal state *cannot* criticize, oppose, or block the move by the Islamic Conference because it is part of such a conception. But an illiberal society is called that, illiberal, precisely because the regime sustains and endorses illiberal laws, practices, and policies. In respect to those policies (e.g., the criminalization of blasphemy) that violate the subjects' moral rights, the illiberal state has no moral power to coerce. Every imprisonment of a blasphemous citizen is an impermissible act of coercion. When those acts of coercion multiply, the regime's moral claim to rule shrinks in proportion to the denial of its subjects' rights. This claim is weakened rather than strengthened by the sincerity of the rights-violator's beliefs. Put differently, there is no threshold of legitimacy or "good standing" beyond which a state's violation of the moral rights of its subjects is entitled to approval by anyone, including outsiders. And we do not claim an exemption for liberal regimes. The practice of the United States of incarcerating millions

[45] Rawls, *Law of* Peoples, 74.

of persons for morally innocent behavior (e.g., personal drug use) is immoral, and its immorality is not cured by the fact that the U.S. Constitution and its laws are better than those of most other nations.

In Chapter 2 we expressed sympathy with Rawls' view about international distributive justice, especially with his assertion that "[t]he great social evils in poorer societies are likely to be oppressive government and corrupt elites."[46] Here, however, we disagree with his view of international *political* justice. An illiberal society, even a decent one, is a society that violates many moral rights of its citizens. Liberals should not accept those violations, and the more serious the violations are, the lesser should be the liberal disposition to treat such regimes as "free and equal" members of the global community. Liberals should be free to criticize and (*contra* Rawls) sometimes adopt stronger diplomatic measures to protect the moral rights denied by those regimes. There is nothing decent in the denial of speech, confiscatory expropriation, the enforcement of discrimination among groups, or the denial of the right to hire and fire your government.

If our natural-rights premise (or something like it) is accepted, then liberals are not obligated to treat regimes that violate the moral rights of their subjects as members in good standing of the international community because their illiberal practices are morally impermissible. Nor do liberal states have any principled obligation to cooperate with rights-violating regimes. We all have obligations to *persons* grounded in common morality, not on the supposed decency of illiberal practices, regardless of whether the practices are sincerely endorsed by the regime and its collaborators. More generally, political morality is not about finding what we agree on so that we can all get along. All persons have rights, and in international relations as elsewhere, we have an obligation not to interfere with the exercise of those rights and to insist that those in power respect the rights of everyone.

The foregoing analysis shows, again, that the dividing line between legitimate and illegitimate regimes is too coarse to guide foreign policy: liberal regimes should accept the exercise of coercion by foreign regimes that are consistent with the moral rights of the subjects and oppose that coercion when it violates those rights. The less liberal a regime is, the more reasons liberals will have to refuse to accept the regime because a larger quantum of state coercion will be morally tainted. So it is not a question of legitimacy or illegitimacy. There is no magical threshold at which a regime becomes legitimate or descends into illegitimacy. It will be a matter of degree, but one thing is sure: liberals must not cooperate with rights violations, and regimes that engage in significant rights violations should not be considered members in good standing of the international society. The dividing line should not be between liberal and illiberal regimes but between rights-respecting regimes and rights-violating regimes. This can allow the flexibility of shaping the foreign policy of a rights-respecting

[46] Ibid., 77.

state based on individual freedom, not on formal notions such as democratic rule or empty enunciations of bills of rights.

A final word to clarify an ambiguity. In this chapter we ask when a regime deserves *respect*. The concept of respect, however, is ambiguous. In the foregoing discussion, we rejected the view that a regime's sincere belief in the conception of the good in the name of which it infringes the moral rights of its subjects earns that regime the respect of outsiders. In the Rawlsian view, the illiberal (but "decent") regime deserves respects *because* it is acting out of a sincerely held worldview. This is a *strong* notion of respect: we respect someone who acts out of a sincere moral belief. As a consequence, we are not allowed to adopt any measures (military, political, or economic) against such a regime; those regimes act within their "rights" when they behave illiberally.[47] We have rejected this idea: no rights violation, sincere or insincere, deserves respect.

But there is another, weaker sense of respect, suggested by the Westphalian view discussed earlier, that even these illiberal regimes should receive. Because these regimes are de facto rulers, and because (by definition of "decent") they allow a modicum of individual freedom, outsiders should not try to destabilize them and certainly should tolerate them in everyday diplomatic intercourse. But this is very far from Rawls' prescription of treating them as *full* members in good standing of the international community. Outsiders do not have to accept the rights violations that characterize such regimes and are certainly permitted to use hard diplomacy, including, *contra* Rawls, political and economic measures, to discourage those practices. Common prudence (which is also part of common morality) counsels tolerance of their actual sovereignty. But this is a different notion of respect from the one the Rawlsian view commends. The *reasons* to leave these regimes undisturbed are different for each view. For Rawls, the rights-violating practices of these regimes are themselves worthy of respect because they reflect a sincerely held worldview. For us, those rights-violating practices are *not* worthy of respect: we would be justified in pressing the magical green button to end those violations and are justified in pressuring those regimes to desist. However, we have, most of the time, *other* reasons to allow these regimes to rule in their territories.[48]

3. The Kantian View

A third view is that only liberal states are internationally legitimate.[49] A liberal state is defined, approximately, as a relatively well-functioning constitutional

---

[47] See ibid., 59.
[48] We do not say that Rawls has moral reasons to respect illiberal regimes while we have only *prudential* reasons to do so because the reasons that we have are also part of common morality. They involve the usual reasons for actions – principles and consequences.
[49] This is the view defended in the past by one of the authors of this book. See Tesón, *A Philosophy of International Law*, chap. 1. Allen Buchanan offers a well-argued variation of this approach in Allen Buchanan, *Justice, Legitimacy, and Self-Determination: Moral Foundations of International Law* (New York: Oxford University Press, 2003), 247–60.

democracy such as the United States, Germany, or Japan. In this conception, there is only one sense of legitimacy, and it operates internally and externally. Only liberal principles can justify political power, so states that fail to satisfy liberal principles wield illegitimate power over their citizens. They are illegitimate. Only states that meet the *thick* moral demands of constitutional liberalism, such as, perhaps, current liberal constitutionalism, are legitimate. Global justice requires this arrangement, so only liberal states enjoy the full rights of sovereignty. Justice also requires that all other societies strive toward liberalism. The regulative idea of international relations is a free federation of independent liberal democracies. Here again, the Kantian view does not recommend coercive action against illiberal states in most cases, but the reason for this restraint is not that illiberal states are, in some sense, legitimate.

The Kantian view is supported by two arguments, one normative, the other one empirical.[50] The normative argument is simply that liberalism is the correct view. An argument of this sort may rely on hypothetical or actual consent. Kant favored hypothetical consent: legitimate states are states that would be chosen by rational agents, and these agents would rationally choose to live in a liberal state. In "Perpetual Peace," Kant suggested that only an alliance of liberal states (he calls them "republican") can secure global peace.[51] Kant is sketchy about the conditions for legitimacy, but his thoughts on this can be pieced together from other texts, such as the "Doctrine of Right." There Kant specifies the conditions for lawful state coercion. Persons in the state of nature have an *obligation* to enter into the social contract, the civil condition. Coercion in the civil condition is justified when it complies with the universal principle of right, according to which an action is right only if "on its maxim the freedom of choice of each can coexist with everyone's freedom in accordance with a universal law."[52] A justified world order is the one in which all nations comply with this precept. This political arrangement is, for Kant, *rationally* required in the sense that it is the one that would be chosen by ethical agents willing to turn the lawlessness of international anarchy into a legally protected web of political relationships.

Alternatively, the Kantian view (that only liberal states are internationally legitimate) can rely on actual consent (although this was not Kant's view). Legitimate states are states that are voluntary, that is, formed by the free choices of individuals. Because (it is supposed) only liberal states meet these conditions, only liberal states can be considered legitimate. Here the idea of agency, discussed earlier, plays an important role. Starting from the premise that governments wield de jure power only if individuals have delegated that power to

---

[50] See Tesón, *A Philosophy of International Law*, chap. 1, for an expanded treatment of both arguments.

[51] See Immanuel Kant, "Perpetual Peace: A Philosophical Sketch," in *Kant: Political Writings*, Hans Reiss, ed., 2nd ed. (Cambridge University Press 1991), 99–105.

[52] Immanuel Kant, *The Metaphysics of Morals* [1795], Mary Gregor, ed. (Cambridge University Press, 1992), 56–7.

them, this argument concludes that governments have international standing if they can meet a double test: they can show that their power to rule has been duly delegated by the citizens, and they can show that they *exercise* this power consistently with the scope of the delegation, that is, that they respect individual moral rights minus the amount of coercion authorized by the delegation.

Kant's empirical argument is that justice requires an alliance of liberal states because they do not wage war against one another – the *democratic peace thesis*. Because liberal states are inherently peaceful, the global system should encourage all states to ultimately become liberal. Why the democratic peace endures is a bit of a mystery.[53] Anticipating political scientists by more than two centuries, Kant argued that liberal democracies have an in-built system of incentives that incline those societies toward peace. The soundness of this theory continues to be debated, but one thing is clear: the democratic peace is a *fact* for which an explanation is needed, so the burden of proof is on those who think that a stable peace can be secured in a world of liberal and illiberal regimes alike.

The Kantian view is tempting because it tells an attractive story about how prepolitical rights may end up justifying political power. If actual states were really the result of rational agents' having delegated some of their unlimited freedom to government, then we would have a true liberal theory of the state. Unfortunately, as several authors have shown, consent cannot justify political obligation in existing states.[54] No present state, not even the most admirable, draws its authority from a free delegation of powers from its citizens. States are not voluntary associations; they are in the coercion business. Even if a voluntary state is not logically impossible, surely no existing state exercises delegated power.

Appeal to *hypothetical* consent has seemed more promising to many: legitimate states are states that would be consented to by rational persons. However, the difficulties with this position are well known and have been put forth by many critics. Three general points are worth noting here. First, hypothetical consent cannot bind us to the state; only *actual* undertakings can.[55] Second, no state today can meet the hypothetical consent test, for actual constitutions have many features that reasonable persons may reject.[56] And third, if rational persons are those who would choose the right principles, then those principles, and not consent, are doing all the work. We can *call* a state legitimate if, and only if, it satisfies appropriate principles of justice. But then all the work is done by those principles, not by contractarian devices.

---

[53] See the discussion in Chapter 1.

[54] See Simmons, *Moral Principles and Political Obligation*, chaps. 3 and 4; Beitz, *Moral Principles and Political Theory*, 78–83; Huemer, *Political Obligation*.

[55] The point was made early by Ronald Dworkin, *Taking Rights Seriously* (Cambridge, MA: Harvard University Press, 1978), 150–2; see also Copp, "The Idea of a Legitimate State," 12.

[56] An example would be monarchy in the United Kingdom. See Copp, "The Idea of a Legitimate State," 31.

Moreover, drawing a bright line between liberal sheep and illiberal goats is too coarse a method for two reasons. First, having formal democratic institutions and general respect for traditional liberal rights is not *sufficient* to secure the respect for personal projects. Take the example mentioned in Chapter 1 of *kleptocracies*, that is, regimes that are democratically elected and respect traditional liberal rights but systematically *steal* from their citizens. These regimes are morally objectionable because they actively interfere with personal projects through denial of property rights and freedom of contract. Economic liberties should be listed among the moral rights that persons have because they are important vehicles for the pursuit of personal projects.[57] Second, although respect for traditional liberal rights is morally required for obvious reasons, majority rule is not strictly *necessary* to secure many moral rights of individuals, as a number of case studies show (including the case of Singapore discussed in Chapter 3). What matters is the aptitude of a given *institutional package* to facilitate the personal projects of its citizens. The most truculent rights violations (e.g., summary executions, arbitrary arrests, torture, censorship, and so forth) would disqualify any regime for straightforward moral reasons. But disrespect for the rule of law, failure to secure property rights, confiscatory taxation, erection of protectionist barriers, and heavy interference with freedom of contract are likewise bad institutions when seen through the prism of personal freedom.

The upshot is that not even citizens of the better states have political obligations. If so, outsiders cannot invoke the state's right to rule in a territory as the basis for international legitimacy because there is no right to rule. There are no legitimate states. The Kantian view requires strong philosophical assumptions, and for this reason, attractive as it is, it should be rejected.

Our discussion would not be complete without a brief comment on the authority of democracy. We have spoken about liberal democracies, and as we indicated, we accept that, for practical reasons, many decisions are properly adopted by democratic vote (although we do not think that democratic vote generates per se obligations to obey[58]). However, we deny the very broad authority that many writers assign to majority rule. We endorse the classical view that democratic decisions should be constrained by individual rights. To us, the rights-protected sphere is considerably larger than is usually accepted. It includes not only a robust version of the traditional liberal civil rights but also, for the reasons developed in previous chapters, the rights to private property and freedom of contract. These rights are central to the pursuit of personal projects and, consequently, to the alleviation of global poverty. To give but one example: say that citizens have saved privately for their retirement, but the legislature democratically votes to confiscate those private funds for a variety

---

[57] For a recent argument in this sense, see John Tomasi, *Free Market Fairness* (Princeton, NJ: Princeton University Press, 2012).

[58] See Huemer, *The Problem of Political Authority*, 59–80.

of stated reasons that range from alleviation of public debt to the presumed intention of paying retirement to everyone (and not only to those who contributed).[59] To us, such a law cannot be described as anything other than theft. Mainstream egalitarians, in contrast, lack the resources to criticize such acts of governmental depredation. The reason is their favored combination of an ample scope for democratic rule with the denial of moral property rights.[60] Such a position, we insist, prevents the realization of the global-justice goals that these writers profess. Allowing regimes unlimited power to appropriate private resources as long as they do so democratically is inconsistent with the respect for rights and with the goal of lifting persons out of poverty.[61]

When all is said and done, the value of majority rule is that it is preferable to dictatorship, and with this, of course, we agree. But there is a big gap from this dictum to the view that virtually *all* the important decisions should be made by vote. The Churchillian dilemma of democracy or dictatorship is false. There are other alternatives, for example, a society that strongly protects the rights of its citizens, including property rights, and in which, consequently, majority vote operates on a much narrower scope than the one we see today.

4. The Lockean View

If perhaps *no* state is really legitimate, our duties toward distant persons rest on reasons unrelated to the political obligations that those persons may have. Only persons have moral rights, and we owe duties to *them*, not to states or governments. To our knowledge, no one has argued this position in the global-justice literature, but there is a rich tradition in political philosophy that can be transposed to the problem of international legitimacy addressed here. For the *Lockean view*, the yardstick of a morally justified foreign policy is the respect of the *moral rights* that all persons have. This view does not require holding *any* state legitimate: a democratic government may fail to respect moral rights as much as an autocratic government. It will be a matter of degree.

---

[59] This expropriation has occurred in several countries such as Russia, Poland, and Argentina. For Russia, see Allison Schrageer, "Unlike Russia, the U.S. Government Won't Take Your Pension Outright," *Bloomberg Business Week*, August 18, 2014; for Poland, see "Poland Piggish Pols—They're Not Alone," *Forbes*, October 7, 2013; for Argentina, see See Alexei Barrionuevo, "Argentina Nationalizes $300 Billion in Private Pensions," *New York Times*, October 21, 2008; available at: http://www.nytimes.com/2008/10/22/business/worldbusiness/22argentina.html?_r=0 (accessed November 5, 2014). See Chapter 1 for a more extended discussion.

[60] Samuel Freeman, for example, defines high liberalism as the view that denies "that the economic liberties and property rights are nearly coequal with the basic personal liberties" and according to which property rights are simply things to be "relativized or adjusted to meet the requirements of antecedent principles of justice." Samuel Freeman, "Capitalism in the Classical and High-Liberal Traditions," *Social Philosophy and Policy* 28(2) (2011): 19–55.

[61] As we discussed in Chapter 6, our disagreement with Leif Wenar, "Property Rights and the Resource Curse," *Philosophy and Public Affairs* 36 (2008), is that he fails to acknowledge kleptocracies: to him, a government that appropriates resources democratically is blameless.

That persons have moral rights does not mean that they owe *allegiance* to this or that institution. In this sense, a justified foreign policy does not have to make distinctions among regimes to provide guidance for action.

To see why, assume that the applicable standard for legitimacy is the respect of people's Lockean rights. Only states that exercise coercion consistently within Lockean rights are legitimate. The standard encompasses the moral rights of persons as specified by a Lockean conception. This includes self-ownership with its corollaries about the rights to life and personal integrity, speech, conscience, and so forth plus property rights over legitimately acquired external assets with the usual incidents such as freedom of contract. If *this* is the standard of legitimacy, it is plain that no state is legitimate, for even the most benign states routinely disregard Lockean rights.[62] Thus, to accommodate this possibility, that no state is philosophically legitimate, we suggest that outsiders have the obligation to respect *good institutions*, defined as those that *relatively* allow persons freedom to pursue their projects. Outsiders will have this duty even if the states that have good institutions are not legitimate.

There are two distinct advantages to this approach. First, it eliminates the problem caused by the binary nature of legitimacy. If the duty to respect states is anchored to the quality of institutions, then deference to states will be a matter of degree. It may be that no state is legitimate, but states surely vary in how much they allow people to pursue their personal projects. Second, this approach dovetails nicely with the institutionalist literature summarized in Chapters 1 and 3. That literature does not inquire into state legitimacy. Rather, it inquires, usefully, into the correlations between institutions and prosperity. A theory of global justice, therefore, is well advised to avoid the conceptual rigidity of state legitimacy and anchor the duty of noninterference to the more workable concepts of the social sciences.

We thus bypass the debate on whether or not internal or external legitimacy is symmetrical. Both internal legitimacy and external legitimacy are symmetrical in the sense that if a state meets the standard of legitimacy (whatever it is), it has a right to rule, and citizens and outsiders alike must respect it. But citizens and outsiders alike may have duties to respect existing state institutions even if the state is not legitimate (we have speculated that no actual state is legitimate). These reasons may differ for one or the other group, and they are measured through a continuum of institutional quality.

If the institutions under which persons live are good (i.e., they are institutions that enable the exercise of their moral rights), then outsiders must respect them. But this is not because the citizens owe any allegiance to those institutions but rather because those institutions – those states – reasonably respect their moral rights. Good institutions allow persons to lead productive lives in the pursuit of their personal projects; bad institutions fail to do so. There is nothing about states per se or about sovereignty per se that requires

---

[62] We expand on this point later.

moral respect, although there are, of course, many reasons to exercise restraint in our relations with foreign rulers. While the rationales of the Kantian and Lockean positions are somewhat different, they yield in practice an analogous result: foreigners must respect institutions that protect moral rights and allow persons the freedom to pursue their personal projects. Of the current states, well-functioning liberal democracies come closer to this ideal. We prefer the Lockean position because we accept, with Locke, that all persons have prepolitical moral rights. Individuals have moral obligations, but it does not follow that they have political obligations. If citizens of a state do not owe any allegiance to the state, *a fortiori*, outsiders will have no reason to consider that state legitimate. However, there are good and bad states, good and bad institutions. Some states allow persons to live good, productive lives; others do not.

Therefore, we propose a different way to look at the issue. A justified foreign policy is one that is maximally compatible with the pursuit of personal projects by all persons. Many states interfere substantially with those personal projects; others interfere less. When the interference with individual moral rights is great, we say that those institutions – those regimes – are bad, deficient. When the interference with individual moral rights is tolerable, we say that those are good institutions. Outsiders should not interfere with good laws and institutions but *may* interfere with bad laws and institutions, with unjust states. Because in today's world liberal states are, as rule, more respectful of the moral rights of their subjects, our view converges for the most part with the view that only liberal states are legitimate and thus is consistent with favoring "clubs" of liberal democracies and the like (these clubs are desirable for other reasons as well). Were we forced to use the word "legitimacy," we would *call* legitimate states that, comparatively, respect the moral rights of their subjects.

A NOTE ON TERRITORY

Current states wield political power in their territories inwardly by enacting and enforcing laws against all residents and outwardly by controlling access of persons and goods into their territory – most often, as we saw, impermissibly. Until recently, though, the question of territory has remained elusive, a bit of a mystery.[63] What gives a state a *title* to territory? And why does a state (say,

---

[63] The first in recent times to identify the importance of territory was Lea Brilmayer, "Secession and Self-Determination: A Territorial Interpretation," *Yale Journal of International Law* 16 (1991), 177–202. Since then, there has been a flurry of literature on the issue. See Cara Nine, *Global Justice and Territory* (Oxford University Press, 2012); Avery Kolers, *Land, Conflict, and Justice: A Political Theory of Territory* (New York: Cambridge University Press, 2009); Margaret Moore, *A Political Theory of Territory* (Oxford University Press, 2015); Anna Stilz, "Nations, States, and Territory," *Ethics* 121 (2011), 572–601; Anna Stilz, "Why Do States Have Territorial Rights?" *International Theory* 1 (2009), 185–213; David Miller, "Territorial Rights: Concept and Justification," *Political Studies* 60 (2012), 252–68; A. John Simmons, "On the Territorial Rights of States," *Philosophical Issues: Social, Political, and Legal Philosophy*

the United Kingdom) have authority to legislate for that particular territory, the British Isles, and not for another? Theories of territory have fallen into two categories: individualist and collectivist. Individualist theories of territory have been defended by writers of Lockean persuasion.[64] Collectivist approaches to territory, in turn, can be subdivided into nationalist, statist, and group views.[65] While our sympathies lie with views that respect methodologic and normative individualism, in this book we do not address the issue, except to say the following: whoever it is thought to have ultimate title over land, states have an obligation to exercise their regulatory powers in a manner consistent with the principle of noninterference that we defend here. Thus state-enforced systems of property that prevent persons, in particular, the poor, from participating fully in the market as producers and consumers are unjust. By the same token, justice condemns the appropriation by rulers of their subjects' wealth, including land and other resources. Any theory of territory therefore must cohere with the imperative, binding on individuals, states, international institutions, and groups of all stripes, to respect the pursuit of personal projects that lies at the core of the theory of justice we defend in this book. This excludes other pursuits, such as the search for a group destiny or identity, or aggrandizement of power, or similar goals, as the proper ends of government.

DIPLOMACY

A large part of the debate about state legitimacy has centered on humanitarian intervention, that is, on whether outsiders may intervene *militarily* in unjust states to end the injustice.[66] This emphasis (important as it is) muddles the question of state legitimacy because, as everyone knows, war is presumptively wrong for a host of reasons, most of which are unrelated to the illegitimacy of the regime.[67] It is important, therefore, not to confuse the question of state legitimacy (is this entity a member in good standing of the international community?) with the different question of forcible intervention (does the fact that this state is unjust or

---

11 (2001), 300–26; Hillel Steiner, "Territorial Justice," in *National Rights, International Obligations*, Simon Caney, David George, and Peter Jones, eds. (Boulder, CO: Westview, 1996), 139–47; and Bas van der Vossen, "Locke on Territorial Rights," *Political Studies* (2014), available at: http://onlinelibrary.wiley.com/doi/10.1111/1467-9248.12106/pdf.

[64] See the works by A. John Simmons and Hillel Steiner just cited; Tesón, "The Mystery of Territory," (in press).

[65] David Miller offers the strongest defense of the nationalist position in "Territorial Rights." The statist view is developed by Anna Stilz, "Nation, States, and Territory." The group view has been advanced by Nine, *Global Justice*. See Tesón, "The Mystery of Territorial Sovereignty," for a full analysis and critique.

[66] For a full treatment of humanitarian intervention, see Fernando R. Tesón, *Humanitarian Intervention: An Inquiry into Law and Morality*, 3rd ed. (Ardsley, NY: Transnational, 2005), and Chapter 8 of this book.

[67] We use the term "legitimacy" for convenience, bearing in mind our observations earlier that there is a legitimacy continuum. A legitimate state is a state that is *relatively* unobstrusive.

tyrannical authorize the use of force against it?)[68] In most (but not all) cases where the answer to the first question is negative, the answer to the second question also will be negative. Few situations authorize war.[69] For this reason, in this chapter we bracketed the question of use of force[70] and addressed the different question of how should liberal states, that is, citizens and the liberal governments that represent them, treat rulers and subjects in other states. Should illiberal states be considered members in good standing of the international community? If the answer is no, what are the consequences for the foreign policy of a liberal democracy? What tools can citizens in liberal states, through their governments, use (short of war) to promote reforms in illiberal states? In other words, when can liberal states *interfere* (short of war) in other countries?

A useful classification of diplomatic acts is between *soft* and *hard* diplomacy. Soft diplomacy uses noncoercive means, and for this reason, it does not entail *interference* (we avoid the word "intervention" because it suggests military force). Most regular diplomatic interaction is of this kind and is therefore entirely permissible. Diplomacy is usually guided by what governments perceive to be the national interest, that is, the interest of their citizenry.[71] We should not lament this fact because governments should be the agents of those who have appointed them. In a typical liberal state, the government acts as the foreign relations agent of its subjects. It has been appointed by them to pursue their interests in the international arena. Just as citizens in civil society engage in peaceful self-interested transactions for mutual gain, so governments engage in peaceful self-interested political and economic transactions for mutual gain. These relations are normally at arm's length, vary considerably depending on the issue, and are in general desirable. Many interactions, such as trade, are positive-sum games. Others are more complicated, such as, for example, a government's asking another to prevent violation of the latter's territory of intellectual property rights held by citizens of the former.

The traditional view is that given the self-interested nature of diplomacy, the quality of the governments with which the liberal state interacts is irrelevant. The liberal government has a fiduciary duty to advance the interests of its citizens relative to everyone else, friend or foe. But this is misleading: issues of governmental quality crop up at every turn in these interactions. Suppose that the liberal state wishes to settle the boundaries with its southern neighbor, which at the moment is ruled by an authoritarian regime. The two states make a treaty to that effect. The neighbor's regime arguably has no moral authority

---

[68] Walzer at times seems to mesh both questions. See Walzer, *Moral Standing of States*, 224. Rawls writes that liberal states may not adopt "military, economic, or political sanctions" against illiberal regimes. Rawls, *The Law of Peoples*, 59.

[69] We discuss war, including humanitarian intervention, in Chapter 8.

[70] As Beitz does in the same context. See Beitz, *Political Theory*, 72.

[71] This is how it should be ideally, but in the actual world, things are different because politicians often use diplomacy to further *their own* interests. The agency costs of having a state are high indeed.

to bind its subjects. That regime is not a valid consenting agent. Indeed, if the people later get rid of the dictator and establish a democratic government, they may well question the boundaries agreed to by the defunct regime. Or consider trade. If a liberal state trades with an illiberal state, there may be an issue of legitimate ownership of the traded goods, as discussed in Chapter 6. The dictator may have stolen the resources from her people. In this case, not only are the trade interactions morally problematic, but also the liberal state, again, may suffer a backlash when the people of the state in question get rid of the dictator.

In contrast, *hard* acts of diplomacy *interfere* with the behavior of other governments. A diplomatic act is an act of interference when it satisfies two conditions. First, the act involves a significant amount of *pressure* or *coercion* (short of war). Second, the state tries to coerce another government to do what it rather would not do or to abstain from doing something it would rather do.[72] Thus an offer to engage in trade, a proposal to form an organization for mutual benefit, or a simple diplomatic demarche to ask another government to vote a certain way in the United Nations is not an act of interference, even if, should it persuade, it may have important consequences for the citizens in both states. The requested regime can decline the offer. Similarly, a peremptory request *lacking* political pressure is not an act of interference because it does not coerce the other state to do something it would rather not do. The government of Argentina's angry requests to the United Kingdom to return the Falkland Islands is not an act of interference because the amount of political pressure is insufficient. Notice that the definition here is nonmoral, descriptive: an act of interference may or may not be morally justified. When the United States imposes economic sanctions on Syria in response to the latter's human rights violations, the United States *is* interfering with Syria in the sense defined, but depending on the consequences, it may be a *justified* interference.

We propose to redefine the concept of *permissible* international interference. We start with a very rough characterization of the role of government *within* the state. A government has a general duty, domestically, to allow and enable persons to pursue their personal projects. This is a general duty of *noninterference* with those projects; however, it may sometimes entail a duty to *interfere* with those who would unjustly interfere with the projects of others. Here we follow Kant's definition of justified coercion. To him, coercion is justified when it is a hindrance to a hindrance to freedom.[73] Determining which particular laws and institutions satisfy this test well exceeds the limits of this chapter, but the idea is that the state's interference with the personal projects of some is justified only when, in turn, those projects consist of or imply unjust interference with the personal projects of others. Thus the government is justified

---

[72] The standard here is loosely suggested by the *Case of Military and Paramilitary Activities in and against Nicaragua*, International Court of Justice, 1986 ICJ Reports, 14, 107–8.

[73] Kant, *Metaphysics of Morals*, 57.

in interfering with a thief's personal project because that project consists of hindering the personal projects of others.

How does this idea translate into international relations? We can say that a government has a fiduciary *duty* and a moral *permission* to advance the interests of its citizens in the global arena, provided that in doing so it does not unjustly interfere with the personal projects of foreigners. This is a duty of noninterference with *persons*, not with states. States are not persons and therefore cannot have personal projects. As noted earlier, we are skeptical of assertions of permanent national interest, manifest destiny, or collective goals. The government's chief job is to facilitate the pursuit of personal projects by the citizens who inhabit the state. Sometimes, in order to enable persons in *other* states to pursue their personal projects, states will permissibly interfere with *states* that unjustly interfere with the freedom of their own citizens. Just as the state can permissibly interfere with *domestic* freedom deniers, so too can a state permissibly interfere with *foreign* freedom deniers. There is a difference, however: whereas the state normally has a *duty* to interfere with *domestic* freedom deniers, it normally has only a *permission* to interfere with foreign freedom deniers. The reason is that the state owes a fiduciary duty to its citizens. The state has an obligation to protect its own citizens against one another but only a *permission* to protect strangers (meaning persons to whom the state does *not* owe a fiduciary duty) from one another, including their own governments.

We suggest that a state may permissibly advance the interests of its citizens in the global arena subject to the duty not to violate the moral rights of foreigners. We define a violation of moral rights as an unjust interference with a personal project. Interferences are unjust whenever they are aimed at persons *other* than freedom deniers. *Soft* diplomacy, then, is entirely permitted because, by definition, it does not interfere with anyone. A state may permissibly interfere with another state, that is, use *hard* diplomacy (defined as acts to coerce another government into doing something it would rather not to), whenever the act interferes with that government's unjust interference with the personal projects of individuals (its own citizens or others). Hard diplomacy takes several forms:

1. A state may adopt nonforcible sanctions against another state, for example, embargoes, economic sanctions, freezing of funds, boycotts. It would be a mistake to think that because these measures are nonforcible, they are therefore noncoercive: on the contrary, they can be quite coercive in the sense that they may create an irresistible incentive for the target state to do things it would not otherwise want to do.

2. A state may adopt a number of less robust measures to criticize or condemn other states. It may bring a lawsuit in an international court for human rights violations or express publicly its disapproval of another state's trade political practices at international forums and in bilateral

communications; in short, a state may lobby internationally to get another state to change its ways. Someone may retort that these actions are irrelevant to a theory of global justice because they are normal diplomatic actions and therefore entirely permitted. This, however, is a mistake. First, this kind of treatment can be mildly coercive: states have reputational interests and a desire to be treated as honorable. When another state denies them this treatment, it refuses to accept them as honorable members of the community. Second, we want to know whether a government that complains about the political practices of another state is *justified* in doing so. This will be so only if the complaint is based on a reasonable theory of global justice. It will not do for the complaining state to invoke *its* own conception of political morality because in that case the criticized government may reject the principle on which the complaint is made. (Notice, in passing, that many of these actions would not be justified under John Rawls' "Law of Peoples" if the coerced regime is "decent.")

3. Finally, in the pursuit of its own national interest, a state may adopt measures that are not necessarily directed at a second state but that nonetheless affect the second state substantially. The common agricultural policy of the European Union is an example of this. These measures with *incidental* effects on persons in other societies require specific analysis.[74] The main issue here is to what extent can governments adopt self-interested policies that have negative externalities on citizens of other states. While traditionally these actions have not been seen as interventions, they must be accounted for in a theory of global justice.

The distinction between force and diplomacy is crucial, for even if it is true that in most cases force ought not be used against states that violate the rights of their subjects, the reasons for this restraint are often unrelated to the institutional quality of that state. Conversely, when a liberal government considers another state burdened with bad governance, its attitude toward that state may be quite different than if it considered it a peer: for example, a state may engage in diplomatic efforts to get an offender state to change its ways – for example, to get it to respect the moral rights of its citizens – or it may cast negative votes in international organizations, or it may adopt a variety of unfriendly measures against that state. Crucially, the state would not be entitled to adopt such measures if the target state were a "member in good standing" of the society of nations. In fact, the idea of "member in good standing" is dysfunctional here. No one is in good standing. We only have acts of coercion by governments. There is no "membership" that allows a state to acquire immunity for rights violations.

---

[74] We argued in Chapter 6 that these particular protectionist measures are unjust.

One can legitimately ask what the stakes are here. International intercourse is replete with cheap talk. Diplomats say many things about other regimes, and they know that others know that they are just posturing and that the words carry little effect. Thus, one can ask, as long as the words do not become deeds, why should one care about diplomacy? There are two reasons to distinguish between permissible and impermissible diplomacy, one philosophical and the other practical. A number of writers have emphasized the importance of tolerance in international relations. As we saw, John Rawls contends that illiberal regimes should be immune from *diplomatic* measures as long as they comply with certain features that make those regimes "decent." Chief among those features is the regime's sincere endorsement of a conception of the good. If one accepts this view, then one *does not have the resources to oppose illiberal practices* because those practices are covered by something like Rawls's global public reason. Our proposal instead focuses on the degree of violation of moral rights. If a regime violates the moral rights of its subjects, then the fact that it does so in the name of a particular conception of the good does not make the regime invulnerable to outside criticism or pressure (short of war) to change its ways. There is no reason for philosophers to treat these regimes as legitimate, nor is there an obligation by outsiders to cooperate with these rights-violating regimes, and there is certainly a prohibition to *enable* them in their ongoing rights-violating practices.

This takes us to a second reason to underscore the importance of diplomacy: sometimes diplomatic pressure can enhance freedom. Diplomatic actions by outside powers may well facilitate not only the end of the actual repression but also the demise of an objectionable regime. Thus, while there is indeed a lot of useless cheap talk in the media and the corridors of international power, sometimes leaders can, with the various political and economic tools at their disposal, improve people's lives.[75]

NONINTERFERENCE WITH PERSONS AND NONINTERFERENCE WITH STATES

Once we exclude war, why exactly is *diplomatic* intervention into the affairs of other states undesirable? One argument relies on the *domestic analogy*. States, like persons, pursue their own ends, their own conceptions of the good.[76] When outsiders interfere, they attempt to substitute their own ends for the ends of the target state. Just as it is wrong for me to substitute my ends for yours, so it is wrong for one state to impose its ends on another. It is in this spirit that some complain that the West attempts to impose political and economic liberalism on unwilling states. This action is wrong, it is thought, for the same reasons that interfering with persons is wrong.

---

[75] Diplomacy is seldom publicized; secret diplomacy has a long and not always honorable tradition.
[76] See the discussion earlier on Rawls' *The Law of Peoples*.

Now surely there are instances where the analogy works. If there are elections in State A and the Green Party defeats the White Party, it is wrong for State B to put pressure on State A to change the election results (assuming that the Green Party is morally reasonable). State A had a "right" that its election results be respected. State B can regret the defeat of the White Party, but it should refrain from diplomatic pressure to get the results overturned. We can generalize by saying that it is wrong to interfere diplomatically in another state to get that other state to do something that it does not want to do *and* that state had a "right" to abstain from doing that thing.

However, in many other situations, the domestic analogy fails. Suppose that the *government* of State A violates the moral rights of its citizens. If the *government* of State B adopts diplomatic measures to get the government of State A to cease and desist, it is misleading to say that State B is interfering in State A. Rather, this may well be (depending on other factors) justified action in defense of others: the government of State B interferes with the attempt by the government of State A to violate the rights of its citizens. States must be disaggregated. Traditional analysis has treated states as sovereign black boxes in which people and government are lumped together. This has allowed analysts to speak of outside interference in states as if they were attempts to coerce this amorphous entity, the state, into doing something it does not want to do. And of course, no one likes coercion. But, in fact, there are cases of justified interference: coercion is acceptable when (paraphrasing Kant) it is an *interference with an interference with freedom*. As we saw earlier, societies do not have ends, and it is a mistake to identify the ends of a particular government with the ends of the persons over which that government rules. When Rawls says that states pursue different conceptions of the good, he cannot be describing a collective entity that includes the government and the people of a given state. It would be more accurate to say that sometimes the ruling elites pursue ends and that those ends may or may not consist of frustrating the ends of the ruled.

States are artificial constructs created by men and women to serve their needs and allow them to pursue their life plans. A foreign policy that ignores the differences among states is deficient because it fails to consider facts that should be relevant for action. A liberal state that tolerates rights violations by another state might well be cooperating with those violations. Liberal governments should, as a moral matter, take a stand against oppression, even if they can do so only symbolically.[77] Another way of putting this is to say that citizens have a right to expect that their government will show concern for those whose life plans are frustrated by rulers who wield power over them. How should this concern be expressed is another matter, but certainly bad regimes should not be treated with deference and respect.

---

[77] But not if the symbolic action is counterproductive. The embargo on Cuba is an example of such self-defeating political behavior. See generally Guido Pincione and Fernando R. Tesón, "Self-Defeating Symbolism in Politics," *Journal of Philosophy* 98 (2001), 636–52.

The upshot of all this is that the principle of noninterference, which we defended in Chapter 2, is a principle of noninterference with *persons*. This principle does *not* automatically translate into a principle of noninterference with *states*. In fact, the opposite often will be true: an interference with *governments* will be an attempt to restore the moral rights of persons, that is, to secure the noninterference by their government with their personal projects. Yet it may well be that the all-things-considered correct response to a bad state is to do nothing. The judgment that a state or government violates significantly the rights of its subjects does not entail the permissibility of just any action with regard to that state. In particular, some acts of interference with objectionable states may be prohibited because those acts, in turn, impermissibly interfere with the projects of individuals.

NATION-STATES, SPONTANEOUS ORDER, OR WORLD GOVERNMENT?

We conclude this chapter with a brief reflection about the optimal political organization of the world. We presently have a world divided into states. An abundant literature addresses the extent to which a world state, or world government, would be preferable to the current status quo.[78] In this book we have argued for expansion of free trade and liberalization of immigration. Should these goals materialize, the world as we see it today would be greatly changed. We would be much closer to a global liberal order in which states would perform subsidiary functions – that is, subsidiary to the workings and outcomes of the market.

A thorough exploration of the possible scenarios is impossible within the confines of this book. We content ourselves, therefore, with a few general observations.

It is quite clear from what we have said so far that while states perform important functions, they are nonetheless a major obstacle to the pursuit of personal projects. The interferences with the lives of millions in the form of political oppression, senseless wars, useless regulations, and trade and immigrations barriers are so far removed from the idea of the common good that only an incurable idealist can today place faith in the nation-state as the sole instrument available for the realization of justice and improvement of the human condition. As we said, our proposals would lead, if implemented, to a considerable softening, even perhaps the disappearance, of national borders.

But the idea of globalizing freedom is compatible with a variety of institutional arrangements. We describe two of them and leave open which of those arrangements (or others that our readers may conjure) should be preferred

---

[78] See Catherine Lu, "World Government," *Stanford Encyclopedia of Philosophy*; available at: http://plato.stanford.edu/entries/world-government/ (accessed November 7, 2014).

on the merits and whether or not and to what degree any of them would be feasible.

THE UNIVERSAL PEACEFUL ORDER

F. A. Hayek suggested in 1968 that

[F]rom the first establishment of [trade] which served reciprocal but not common purposes, a process has been going on for millennia which, by making rules of conduct independent of the particular purposes of those concerned, made it possible to extend these rules to ever wider circles of undetermined persons and eventually might make possible a universal peaceful order of the world.[79]

Hayek's vision has a predictive and an evaluative component. The predictive component is that increased globalization will eventually lead to a global liberal society. Such a society will be held together by the shared benefits of millions of voluntary transactions driven by local purposes. There will be no central authority to impose a national project or a common goal. Government will have only the role of enforcing the rules of just conduct. These are the classical rules of criminal law and the enforcement of property and contract needed to protect the wealth-creating game called *market*.[80] This universal order, for Hayek, can *only* result from the enlargement of markets and not from government's deliberate actions. Hayek's vision conjures up a borderless global liberal order governed by institutions charged with the limited but essential function of enforcing the rules of the game. Why this order will be peaceful is unclear in this argument. Presumably, the structure of incentives generated by full globalization will incline people to trade and not to plunder.

VOLUNTARY COMMUNITIES

In the second model, there is no global state. People form voluntary associations according to their preferences. People can permissibly associate with others who share their same taste, religion, or language as long as they do not coerce anyone and do not impose burdens on third parties. Suppose that someone is a devout Catholic. He may wish to be *surrounded* by a Catholic community – to live in an environment where, he thinks, he can best flourish. This is his life project. This project may not be our readers' cup of tea, but there is nothing inherently wrong with it as long as no one is coerced.

The world we imagine, then, will be populated not, as now, by nation-states with inherent coercive power governed by constitutions that (in the best

---

[79] F. A. Hayek, *Studies in Philosophy, Politics, and Economics* (University of Chicago Press, 1967), 168.

[80] F. A. Hayek, *Law, Legislation, and Liberty Chicago* (University of Chicago Press, 1973), 2, 123–32.

scenario) secure basic rights and leave other decisions to majority rule. The world we imagine is populated by voluntary communities.[81] These are characterized by a number of features. Persons join voluntarily to form the societies they like. Some may form a Christian society, others may form a laissez-faire society, others might prefer a welfare state, and yet others can pool their resources in a socialist state. Individuals come to these communities with their resources, themselves and their property. These societies are entirely voluntary. No one can be coerced to join any society, and no one can be coerced by majority vote to behavior he cannot be deemed to have agreed on in advance. By the same token, the voluntary society provides ample right to exit. The society's borders are constituted by the private-property boundaries of its members and whatever land they have voluntary transferred to the state. Persons are deemed to have natural rights to life, liberty, and property that they can partially waive when they join a particular society. We also may imagine common-law courts that resolve problems within and among the different voluntary communities. In this utopia, persons are truly allowed to pursue their personal projects, even when those projects include communal preferences. The fact that no one may coercively enroll anyone else in her project allows for the preservation of freedom throughout.

There are many gaps in both visions, of course, and only systematic research and argument could fill them. But we think that the main recommendation in this book (leave people alone!) implies a substantial transformation of the political organization of the world. Contrary to the global-justice mainstream literature, we do not think that the weakening of states should lead to stronger international institutions or a global coercive government that sets ends for everyone. On the contrary, persons should choose their own destinies by interacting freely with others. The universal peaceful order based on trade and the constellation of voluntary communities, incomplete and utopian as they are, reflect this idea.

---

[81] This view, which we can only sketch here, is developed in a bit more detail in Guido Pincione and Fernando R. Tesón, *Rational Choice and Democratic Deliberation: A Theory of Discourse Failure* (New York: Cambridge University Press, 2006), chap. 9. It is inspired by Robert Nozick, *Anarchy, State, and Utopia* (New York: Basic Books, 1974), 297–334.

8

War

War is the most terrifying and destructive form of violence. A war of aggression inflicts a great injustice on others; it is a major crime. But not all wars are criminal. Most people believe that a state that is unjustly attacked has the right to defend itself. If these were the only truths about the morality of war, the right to wage war (*jus ad bellum*) would have a binary structure. A war is either unjustified aggression or justified self-defense; there would be no moral space between the two. This is the traditional view about *jus ad bellum*, supported, with variations, by most governments and scholars.

In this chapter we argue that the traditional view is too coarse, not granular enough, and that once the rationale for a just war is properly analyzed, it turns out that it is possible to think about wars that are not in defense to aggression but that nonetheless can be just. The issue is extremely thorny because the justice of a particular war will depend not only on the cause but also on its consequences. Even a war fought for a just cause may turn out to be unjust for other reasons – for example, because it brings about the death of many innocent bystanders. This is true even if one accepts the binary traditional view. In lawfully resisting an attack, a state nonetheless may inflict an unacceptable amount of harm. But before addressing these issues, we must see why war has such a special place in international relations.

Each sovereign state establishes the monopoly of force within that state. States have police, courts, and armies, and individual violence is narrowly confined. Sometimes these arrangements fail, and states plunge into anarchy, and often the monopoly of force plunges into oppression. But the ideal role of the state is to protect citizens against one another and to tame violence through the prism of the rule of law, accepted procedures, and constitutional guarantees. The modern state, when it works well, outlaws interpersonal violence by monopolizing force. It prohibits both opportunistic plundering and private retribution while providing means of redress to those wronged by the aggressive behavior of others.

The international society, however, is not a state. Its central feature is precisely that it does not establish a monopoly of force on any sovereign. At its inception, the United Nations Charter was meant to create a system of collective security, but its weaknesses are well known.[1] Suffice it to say that international law does not provide a satisfactory remedy for wronged nations, groups, or individuals. To be sure, international society has made great strides in developing *norms* to curb war. International law has codified in detail the laws that govern combat (*jus in bello*.)[2] This is an area of international law that makes a difference in actual conflicts because the degrees of compliance and enforcement are reasonably high. The *jus ad bellum*, however, is a different story. The United Nations Charter reads *as if* it prohibits most interstate violence and *as if* it empowers the Security Council to respond to aggression on behalf of the international community. Because of this discursive consensus, if today a state invades another for no good reason, observers are more ready to condemn the invasion than they would have been only seventy years ago. Yet the mechanisms available to actually restrain war are woefully weak. They are certainly much weaker than the corresponding mechanisms within a functioning state. Before the United Nations Security Council authorizes the use of force against an aggressor *and* a member is willing and able to act on that authorization, many improbable things have to happen. For one thing, the five permanent members of the Security Council have the right to veto. This means that the Security Council will not authorize force against permanent members or their allies. But more important, although domestic law *obligates* the government to act in response to private violence, international law merely *authorizes* governments to respond to aggression. Assuming, against the facts, that the Security Council acts expeditiously in every case of aggression or genocide and authorizes the use of force to address it, still governments are not *bound* to react. To begin with, only a powerful state (as we write, usually, but not always, the United States) can act. Unless weaker states can forge a sufficiently powerful alliance (another implausible scenario), they will free ride on the powerful state. But the powerful state will not act unless its government believes that its national interest is at stake (this, again, is a rosy scenario: politicians will go to war if *their* own interests are thereby advanced, especially their electoral interests). States in a position to respond to aggression can simply decline the invitation. Now imagine if someone invades your home and threatens your family. You call 911, and the voice on the other end says, "What's in it for me?"

---

[1] For a traditional, sympathetic discussion of the UN system on the use of force, see Thomas M. Franck, *Recourse to Force* (Oxford University Press, 2003). For a more critical view, see Fernando R. Tesón, *Humanitarian Intervention: An Inquiry into Law and Morality*, 3rd ed. (Ardsley, NY: Transnational, 2005).

[2] In the Geneva Conventions.

You'd be rightly appalled because the police have an institutional obligation to protect you against aggressors.

Because of this, when threatened, states continue to rely on self-help, and war, of course, is the extreme form of self-help. If State A plans to invade State B, State B cannot call the police for the good reason that (most of the time) there are no police. And if an attacked state wants redress for the destruction caused by the aggressor, it cannot sue the aggressor for the good reason that (most of the time) there are no international courts of compulsory jurisdiction. If you refuse to pay me the thousand dollars you owe me and I punch you in the nose to "enforce" my rights, my action is morally reprehensible because I have legal avenues to seek redress (sue you in court and so on). But if a neighboring nation refuses to honor a treaty, most of the time the aggrieved party cannot seek judicial redress. The wronged state is on its own. To be sure, international law prohibits wars to enforce run-of-the-mill treaties, but certainly wronged states can and do resort to various forms of self-help in the form of retaliatory countermeasures short of war. The point here is that self-help is omnipresent, and as a result, given the sobering fact that states and others will continue to commit aggression and other serious wrongs, war is here to stay, regrettably, for the foreseeable future.

In this chapter we examine the morality of war. The topic has an old and rich tradition in political philosophy. Despite the recurrent suspicion that war somehow escapes evaluation (*inter armas silent leges*), philosophers have attempted to tame war, as it were. We examine some of the views that have been advanced in the literature and defend two views. First, war can only be justified in defense of persons and, where applicable, just institutions. This is the only just cause for war. We hasten to add that even if a government has a just cause, it may still be wrong for it to wage war. Just cause is a necessary but not a sufficient condition to justify any war. Second, the threshold for permissible collateral damage in a just war depends on the moral urgency of the cause.

JUST CAUSE FOR WAR: THE DEFENSE OF PERSONS

With the exception of pacifists, people agree that states are justified to fight in response to aggression. By the same token, a sizable number of writers believe that almost any *other* kind of war is problematic. This view is supported by a conventional reading of the United Nations Charter and, with sizable dissent, by the international law establishment.[3] The gist of the view is that there is something unique about aggression that authorizes the victim to fight in self-defense. It is unreasonable to ask a state that is wrongfully attacked not to react, given that, as we saw, that state cannot seek protection from a higher authority. Moreover, it would be irrational to prohibit self-defense anyway because victims of aggression will continue to react regardless of what

---

[3] Typical of this view is Simon Chesterman, *Just War or Just Peace?* (Oxford University Press, 2001).

philosophers say. So wars in self-defense are (reluctantly, perhaps) morally justified. Supporters of this mainstream view observe that since 1945, the default
rule in international law has been the prohibition of war.[4] This means, to
them, that the only justified wars are defensive wars. Other wars are offensive
because they are not a response to attack and are, for that reason, unjustified.
In particular, the mainstream view contends that humanitarian intervention (a
war to save persons in other states) is impermissible.

In order to evaluate the mainstream view, we must go deeper and explore
the concept of just cause. It is said that wars in self-defense are justified. But
defense of whom and what? A natural response is defense of the state, the state
that is attacked. But surely the state matters, morally, because it is inhabited
by persons. Its institutions matter because they serve persons. And land matters because it belongs to persons (privately or held in trust by the state). As
Michael Walzer argued in his classic treatise, the crime of war is that those who
initiate it force *persons* to abandon their regular lives and projects and fight
for their survival.[5]

We submit, therefore, that war has *only one general justification: the defense
of persons*. This is the important truth behind the mainstream position: all
justified violence is defensive violence. But the proper entity that deserves
our defense is the individual – and only derivatively the state. If this is correct, then there are no reasons to confine a justified war to a war of *national*
self-defense. A justified war also may be a war in defense of persons in *other*
states. The traditional dichotomy between national self-defense as a defensive
war (and justified for that reason) and humanitarian intervention as an offensive war (and unjustified for that reason) is problematic. The same reasons
that justify self-defense can justify other nonaggressive wars and, in particular, *humanitarian intervention*, that is, military action aimed at stopping or
preventing large losses of human life. Although there are important differences
between self-defense and humanitarian intervention, it is misleading to contrast *defensive* with *offensive* wars and consider national self-defense as an
instance of the former and humanitarian intervention as an instance of the latter. Humanitarian intervention is *also* a defensive war: it is, like self-defense, a
war in defense of persons who have been wrongfully attacked.

We can see this more clearly by applying a well-known matrix used in criminal law. Persons are entitled not only to defend themselves against unjust
attacks but also to defend others who are victim of unjust attacks. If Attacker
unjustly attacks Victim, Victim is entitled to use defensive force. In this case,
though, Third Party is also morally permitted to defend Victim by force. We
can say that Attacker's attack on Victim is unjust whenever Victim has a right

---

[4] Among philosophers, this view has been defended (with qualifications) by Michael Walzer,
who calls it "the legalist paradigm." See Walzer, *Just and Unjust Wars: A Moral Argument with
Historical Illustrations*, 4th ed. (New York, Basic Books, 2006).
[5] Walzer calls it the "tyranny of war," *Just and Unjust Wars*, 31.

not to be attacked. Therefore, if Attacker attacks Victim and Victim has a right not to be attacked, Attacker forfeits his own right not to be attacked. To be justified, an attack by Third Party against Attacker must presuppose that Attacker has lost his moral shield, as it were. Humanitarian intervention, then, is Third Party's attack against Attacker, who is unjustly attacking Victim. Third Party assists Victim in her defense against Attacker's unjust aggression. We will see later that this matrix must be applied with caution to the case of international aggression, but the central idea remains valid: if a state is entitled to defend its own citizens against aggression, it is also entitled to defend third parties, foreigners, against aggression.

But we should refine the analysis further. Because states are not persons, the application of the criminal-law matrix to war recognizes at least four distinct cases:

1. **National Self-Defense.** National self-defense is Victim's justified use of force against an unjust Attacker. But, unlike the individual case, Victim's force aims to protect herself *and others, her compatriots*. We can say that in war, my use of force to repel an aggressor is a use of force partly in defense of self (because Attacker is forcing me to defend my life, rights, and possessions) and partly in defense of others (because I participate in the coordinated effort to repel Attacker).

2. **Collective Self-Defense.** Collective self-defense is the use of force by Third Party, usually a government, in defense of an ally, Victim, who has been attacked by another *state*, Attacker.[6] Here Third Party defends the citizens (and perhaps the government) of the Victim, all of whom are unjustly attacked by Attacker. This is also a Third Party defense of persons (Victim's citizens, unjustly attacked by Attacker's army).

3. **Humanitarian Intervention.** Humanitarian intervention is the use of force by Third Party, usually a government, in defense of persons, Victim, who have been attacked by *their own government*, Attacker. This war, as the other two, is also a Third Party defense of persons, Victim, unjustly attacked, this time not by another state but by their own rulers.

4. **Humanitarian Crisis Relief.** Humanitarian crisis relief is the use of force by Third Party to save Victim, not from Attacker, but from a natural disaster such as a tsunami or an earthquake. In this case, the local government is unable or unwilling to help *and* also unwilling to allow Third Party to provide relief. Therefore, Third Party must overcome the government's resistance by force in order to save Victim. Perhaps we could say that the government becomes Attacker by omission.[7]

---

[6] We use the legal language in Article 51 of the UN Charter, where "collective self-defense" is a term of art that means the use of force by a state in aid of another state that has been attacked.

[7] We consign this variation here, but we do not explore it further. What we say about humanitarian intervention applies, *mutatis mutandi*, to humanitarian crisis relief.

Because the case for collective self-defense stands or falls with national self-defense and the case for humanitarian crisis relief stands or falls with humanitarian intervention, we address the two master cases: national self-defense and humanitarian intervention.

SELF-DEFENSE

Self-defense in international relations is the military action by a state against an unjustified military attack. The notion is deceptively simple: national self-defense is the response to aggression, and aggression is an unjustified attack. There are a number of difficult issues lurking under the surface, however. Why exactly is national self-defense justified? What is the extent of the franchise? Can a state that has been unjustly attacked pursue the war *after* having successfully repelled the aggressor? Are anticipatory and preemptive wars justified? Are wars in aid of *other* states justified?

As Michael Walzer has written, international self-defense relies on the *domestic analogy.*[8] Sovereign states are analogized to persons. Just as individuals live in civil society, so states live in international society. This allows us to transpose the categories of criminal law (i.e., trespass, aggression, and self-defense) into international relations. Because international institutions, as we saw, are weak and imperfect, the analogy cannot be carried too far. For example, whereas in domestic law self-defense is limited to repelling someone's attack, in international law the victim of aggression can pursue and to an extent punish the aggressor. But the analogy is good enough, Walzer thinks, to characterize war as a criminal act and to legitimize defensive-punitive wars.

The domestic analogy is appealing, but it must be amended. Self-defense is morally justified not because it is a defense of *states* as such but because it is a defense of the *individuals* who populate the states. The defense of persons includes the defense of their basic rights, including their property, and their valuable social processes and customs. To the extent that states reflect these valuable structures and protect the lives and freedoms of their citizens, they are morally protected against external encroachment. These structures are shielded by sovereignty. To this extent, *but to this extent only,* Walzer is right that states are worth defending. But we disagree with Walzer's view that even unjust states are protected by sovereignty. Walzer thinks that even objectionable domestic political processes should be shielded from intervention because those processes embody "communal integrity," the life in common. For us, only morally defensible political processes are shielded from foreign intervention. When, in addition to having valuable social structures, a society has good institutions, they will be protected as well.[9]

---

[8] See the discussion in Walzer, *Just and Unjust Wars,* 58–63.
[9] We have more to say about this later.

To be sure, in most cases we will agree with Walzer on the morality of particular defensive wars. Whereas he will see a defensive war as a justified defense of the state as the *locus* of the life in common, we see it as a justified defense of persons, their rights, their valuable social structures, and, if applicable, their institutions.

But is even national self-defense justified? We can distinguish *normal* self-defense from *extended* self-defense. Both are military actions in response to an unjustified attack. But "normal self-defense" is confined to the military actions that are necessary to repel the aggressor. By "extended self-defense," we understand military action originally launched to respond to aggression but pursued beyond the action that was strictly necessary to repel the aggressor. Virtually everyone agrees that normal self-defense is morally justified. David Rodin, however, has argued that national self-defense as currently understood in international law is unjustified precisely because it authorizes extended self-defense. He claims that because soldiers fighting defensive wars typically do things that are not morally justified under a plausible philosophical account of self-defense, such as the strict self-defense rationale found in the criminal law, the standard account of self-defense is morally objectionable.[10] For example, under the current law of war, soldiers fighting defensive wars can kill enemy soldiers who are sleeping or marching. Also, under the current *jus ad bellum*, states can adopt proportionate military actions well beyond those needed to repel the aggressor. Yet the rationale for permitting someone to use force in self-defense is that the aggressor is threatening him. Because international law allows killing enemy soldiers who are not threatening us, national self-defense as conventionally understood, Rodin thinks, is morally untenable. Killing non-threatening persons is unjustified; therefore, national self-defense (other than strict physical response to aggression) is unjustified. The same objection applies to other extensions of self-defense, such as punitive wars or wars pursued to disarm the aggressor or replace the regime.[11]

There are two answers to Rodin's objection. The first is that national self-defense can be reduced to a collection of individual rights to self-defense. National self-defense lies in a continuum between self-defense and defense of others.[12] If we suppose that an individual can legitimately use force in self-defense, then we can expand that case into the increased number of persons who coordinate their defensive efforts against a common threat. These persons are justified in killing sleeping or marching enemy soldiers because those soldiers have already attacked and are preparing to attack again. They *are* threatening their victims. The threat is part of a complex action developing at different periods of time starting with the initial acts of aggression. This

[10] See David Rodin, *War and Self-Defense* (Oxford University Press, 2003).

[11] Notice that we are not addressing here the killing of *civilians*. The originality of Rodin's argument is that it questions the morality of killing enemy *soldiers*.

[12] Here we follow Jeff McMahan, "War as Self-Defense," *Ethics & International Affairs* (2004), 75.

conception explains why it is morally *prohibited* to kill enemy soldiers who are retreating. Unlike those who are sleeping in order to restore their strength to continue their aggression, retreating soldiers presumably pose no future threat.

The second reply is that international law of war does not necessarily track the morality of war. Rodin reasons that national self-defense, as regulated by international law, allows states who have been attacked to respond by killing enemy soldiers who are not threats – for example, soldiers who are sleeping or eating. Therefore, he claims, the right of self-defense is untenable. But this does not follow. The only thing that follows, if Rodin is right, is that international law should be reformed. If Rodin is right that morality only allows soldiers to kill enemy soldiers who threaten them, then the Geneva Conventions, which allow killing nonthreatening soldiers, should be reformed by prohibiting such killing. The right of self-defense, then, would be circumscribed and reformed in accordance with morality but would not disappear.

1. National Self-Defense by a Good State

In Chapter 7 we suggested that while it is likely that no actual state is legitimate (because even the best states perpetrate illegitimate acts of coercion), some states are better than others. Those are the states that have relatively better institutions, defined as those that allow persons to pursue their life projects. Foreigners must respect persons (by not attacking them) and their good institutions (by not upsetting them). If this is sound, then it follows that citizens have an obligation to defend not just each other's life and property but also *the good institutions they have created*. Let us call this the "liberal view." The liberal view indeed relies on more than individual self-defense. Citizens defend not merely one another but also the just institutions they have created together and under which they live. The government is their instrument. The justification of self-defense thus combines principles from political and moral philosophy. Soldiers fighting a defensive war defend, first, the citizens' lives and property threatened by the aggressor (this is the reductive account of national self-defense explained earlier); second, they defend their good institutions; and third, they defend the state's territory, understood as the *locus* for the exercise of their rights and the functioning of institutions.

Rodin has a couple of objections to this account. The first is that the liberal view wrongly views self-defense through the same moral lense as humanitarian intervention. As we saw, both are wars to defend persons. If self-defense is action by a government to defend citizens, then humanitarian intervention is simply an extension of self-defense thus defined. The difference would simply be that in humanitarian intervention, the government comes to the rescue of citizens other than its own. Yet, the objection goes, it is wrong to consider humanitarian intervention and self-defense as having the same underlying rationale because "common sense tells us that humanitarian intervention is a very different creature from self-defense." They are even "antagonistic" and "in deep tension" with each other.[13] This is so because when a government invades another country, say, to stop ongoing domestic atrocities, "one of the moral considerations weighed against this action is the defensive rights of the subject of the intervention." In Rodin's words:

[I]f there is a right to humanitarian intervention, this is because the moral basis of the right of national self-defense can in certain circumstances be justly overridden, not because the right of humanitarian intervention is, in some sense, an application of those moral considerations.[14]

We certainly plead guilty to Rodin's charge: a war in self-defense *is* a humanitarian war. Rodin's reply begs the question: to him, "everyone knows" that self-defense and humanitarian interventions are different creatures; therefore, self-defense cannot be based on defending persons. Rodin finds the two rationales separate because if an army invades a neighboring country to prevent mass murder (say) of the population by its local dictator, and the dictator resists the invasion, then (he thinks) there is a clash between the alleged right of the invading army to stop the murder and the defensive rights of the dictator. But this reply fails: simply put, *tyrants do not have defensive rights aimed at them because they, the tyrants, are unjust attackers.* They have attacked the population and thus become morally vulnerable to attack themselves. If humanitarian intervention is justified, the defensive rights of the *government* that is the target of humanitarian intervention disappear. There is no tension between self-defense and humanitarian intervention. Despotic rulers have no defensive rights against justified humanitarian action. They, and their loyalists, must depose arms and go home (or face justice for their crimes). So our response to this objection is to reject the claim that the rationales for the two kinds of war are different. Self-defense and humanitarian intervention share the same rationale – defense of persons.

National self-defense, then, is morally overdetermined. When liberals write about the duty of governments to defend citizens against aggression (and the assault to their rights that it entails), they presuppose that the government's action is not simple defensive rescue of persons but protection of good institutions as well. This gives self-defense additional grounding when compared with humanitarian intervention. A government has an obligation to defend its citizens – this is what it has been validly authorized to do. Self-defense is more than the implementation of a general obligation to rescue random persons in danger. The government is fiduciarily obligated to defend the citizens of the state. It is a protection agency. In contrast, many people speak of the right, not the duty, of humanitarian intervention because in this case the intervention is justified only on general humanitarian grounds, not on a fiduciary relationship.

---

[13] Rodin, *War*, 130–1.
[14] Ibid., 131.

The second objection Rodin makes to the liberal view is the objection from bloodless invasion. When an aggressor occupies a remote or uninhabited territory, the standard view of self-defense authorizes deadly force to expel the invader. Yet, because this exercise of self-defense is not an action in defense of persons (the territory is uninhabited), the liberal view fails. Just as property owners whose lives are not threatened may not use deadly force against squatters, so defending armies may not use deadly force against unlawful occupiers who threaten no lives.[15]

We have two replies. First, territory is a space *delegated* in some form to the state by its citizens. The concept of territory in international law is complex, but the least that can be said is that states exercise jurisdiction over territory based on some form of *title* loosely analogous to property in land in domestic law.[16] The government who holds this territory in trust has a right to expel trespassers. Doing so is a form of defending persons. Second, the analogy with the property owner fails. The reason the property owner may not use force against the trespasser is that she can call the police and get the intruder evicted. If he resists, he will be dragged out by force, and if he uses deadly violence, he may even be killed. In contrast, international society is semianarchical. In the international example, the defending government requests the invader to leave the unlawfully occupied territory, and the invader refuses. The defending government then must evict the trespasser by force because no one else will do it for him. Despite the deceiving terminology inherited from criminal law, in international law and ethics, self-defense is a term of art. It encompasses not only the right to repel an aggression but also, as Locke argued, the rights to enforce and punish as long as the force used is proportionate. This extension of self-defense, one comprising other forms of self-help against an aggressor, becomes necessary because of the absence of international enforcement and judicial institutions.[17]

2. National Self-Defense by a Bad State

Good states can permissibly defend themselves, but what about bad states, understood as those that have bad institutions and where the government has usurped power and performs many unjust acts of coercion against its subjects? The government ostensibly lacks the power to use force against anybody. Moreover, there are no good institutions worth defending. Yet it stands to reason that citizens ruled by tyrants have defensive rights. True, they have

---

[15] Ibid., 132.

[16] For discussions of territory, see Cara Nine, *Global Justice and Territory* (Oxford University Press, 2013), and Fernando R. Tesón, "The Mystery of Territory" *Social Philosophy and Policy* (in press).

[17] UN Security Council action under Chapter VII of the UN Charter is a partial exception to this. However, under Article 51 (self-defense broadly understood), states may unilaterally evict invaders.

not *delegated* authority to their government, including the authority to defend them against foreign attacks. The government is a de facto ruler, a usurper. Yet citizens have a right to defend their lives and property just as citizens in good states do. Because the tyrant in fact controls the resources of the state, its armies and weapons, only he is in a position to defend the state against aggression. Therefore, while he has not been duly empowered to defend the citizens, he still has a duty to do so. This obligation derives from the *role* the tyrant occupies. The citizens say: "You are illegitimate, we do not recognize your authority, but given that you have grabbed control of our resources and thus have de facto political power, the least you can do is defend us against attacks." The citizens have a right to defend themselves, the dictator is the only one who can do it, and he must do it because he has deprived citizens of the means to do so themselves.[18] So the standard view is essentially correct: all states, even bad ones, hold the right of self-defense against *unjustified* attacks. Citizens of liberal states, then, are entitled to defend themselves against aggression under the reductive rationale mentioned earlier, and the dictator is morally entitled – indeed, obligated – to coordinate the defensive efforts despite his spurious pedigree.

Now the criminal-law analysis was originally devised to explain self-defense of individuals against other individuals. Application of the basic matrix to interstate wars, where armies and governments are involved, must be done with care. To begin with, the factors that make a government morally protected against military attack by another government are not exactly the same factors that make an individual morally protected against attacks. Individuals have a natural right to life and physical integrity; this is why an attack against them (even by their own government) is impermissible. The government, *qua* government, does not have any natural rights. Its status is entirely conventional. Moreover, military action produces costly externalities that affect third parties in a way that individual attacks against persons often do not. Even in justified defensive wars, the just army will bring about the deaths of innocent persons. In the criminal-law matrix, the costs of acting are internalized. The third party that rescues the victims does so at his own risk. In contrast, the invading army imposes risks on nonculpable parties.

HUMANITARIAN INTERVENTION

A war of national self-defense is a war to defend compatriots. However, as we saw earlier, sometimes persons other than compatriots are in serious danger. Imagine that the government of a neighboring state, dominated by members of an ethnic group, is killing large numbers of members of the rival group. Assume (to simplify for now) that the powerful neighbor's costs of

---

[18] Someone who has unlawfully abducted a person still has the moral duty to protect the person from harm, even if he is not the person's lawful "protector."

intervening are minimal. Can that neighbor invade to stop the killings? This is the problem of the permissibility of humanitarian intervention. This problem has many facets that have been discussed extensively elsewhere.[19] Often the discussions concern issues of institutional design and other important practical matters of implementation. Here we sidestep those practical questions. We are interested in devising general moral principles to evaluate humanitarian intervention, that is, whether or not, and in what circumstances, humanitarian intervention can be justified. To do so, we address humanitarian intervention from two points of view: that of the *target* of the intervention and that of the *intervener*.[20]

We said earlier that humanitarian intervention is justified as a defense of persons attacked by their own government. When can we say that a government attacks its own subjects? Provisionally, we define such an attack as the perpetration of grave acts of impermissible coercion. The idea is this: governments are in the coercion business. In order to provide the services it is supposed to provide, a government has to tax people, imprison criminals, and the like. The acts of coercion that a government can perform, then, can be classified into two categories: morally permissible acts of coercion and morally impermissible acts of coercion. Citizens (let us assume) do not have a right to defend themselves against permissible acts of coercion, and *a fortiori*, outsiders do not have any right to assist them. If an outsider uses violence against the government in such a case, it violates the moral shield of that government, a shield that protects it from attempts to interfere with the permissible acts of coercion that it performs.

So a humanitarian intervention, to be justified, must target impermissible acts of coercion. But, of course, not every impermissible act of coercion generates an entitlement to use military force against the government that performs it. It is doubtful that even the individual victim has a right to resist by force just any act of impermissible coercion. (We do not address here what circumstances justify such resistance, the individual right to resist authority.) But it is certain, we believe, that relatively minor impermissible acts of coercion do not generate a right of outsiders to defend the victim by force. But why? Because military action is extremely costly, so it must be confined to actions necessary to defend victims of major impermissible acts of coercion. The threshold cannot be decided mechanically. We need a theory of just war that includes the crucial requirement of proportionality.

---

[19] See Tesón, *Humanitarian Intervention.*

[20] There is a third point of view: that of the international society at large. They are discussed at length in Tesón, *Humanitarian Intervention.* A brief comment is in order, however. Writers point to the danger of abuse of the doctrine of humanitarian intervention. But this danger is also attendant to the right of self-defense and could perhaps be curbed by appropriate institutions and procedures. The point is that the danger of abusing a right does not negate that right.

INTERVENTION AND STATE LEGITIMACY

Some writers have proposed a different reason why outsiders may not use force to assist the victims of (most) impermissible governmental acts of coercion. They have suggested that the government has a *right to rule* that must be respected, even if some or many of the acts that the government performs in the exercise of its right to rule are morally impermissible. This is the large question of state legitimacy. One of your authors has suggested in the past that the concept of legitimacy plays a crucial role in judging intervention.[21] In this view, humanitarian wars are impermissible against *legitimate* regimes precisely *because* those regimes are legitimate. Legitimate states have a moral shield against others, a right not to be attacked. However, for a humanitarian war to be permissible, the targeted regime must be *illegitimate*, and other conditions must obtain as well. In this view, illegitimacy is a necessary (though not a sufficient) condition of the permissibility of humanitarian intervention. In a sense, this is correct: that an intervention is permissible against a regime entails, analytically, that that regime has lost its moral shield that it no longer enjoys a right not to be interfered with, just as Attacker forfeits his right not to be attacked when he attacks Victim in the matrix discussed earlier. However, the facts that cause the collapse of that moral shield are impermissible acts of coercion against its own citizens, not the property of being illegitimate. It is true that only intervention against illegitimate regimes is (sometimes) permissible, but not *because* it is illegitimate, as the statement wrongly suggests. Permissible intervention does not aim at restoring political legitimacy but rather at ending or preventing impermissible violence against persons.

As indicated earlier, all states perform acts of coercion, acts of violence, against their citizens in their territories. Some of those acts are morally justified, and some are not. We may say, perhaps, that coercive acts of the state that are consistent with the moral rights of subjects are justified, and coercive acts of the state that are inconsistent with those rights are unjustified. A humanitarian intervention is, in principle, justified only to end or prevent the most seriously wrong acts of coercion perpetrated by governments. This is so not because states have a right to perform mildly wrong acts of coercion but because war to redress those mild wrongs will often be disproportionate. For this reason, whether or not governments have a "right to do wrong" is irrelevant for purposes of justifying humanitarian intervention. Intervention is impermissible against any act that is not seriously wrong *if*, as is almost always the case, the military intervention will impose significant costs. For the same reason, that a state is internally illegitimate (on whatever standard of legitimacy one chooses) is insufficient reason to intervene because the prospective intervener must comply with the strictures of the proportionality principle as well.

---

[21] Tesón, *Humanitarian Intervention*, esp. chaps. 3 and 4. See also Andrew Altman and Christopher Heath Wellman, *A Liberal Theory of International Justice* (Oxford University Press, 2011), 78.

Let us consider first states that are illegitimate, judged under some standard of substantive justice. These states perform unjustified acts of coercion. But here again, it will often be the case that a military intervention would be very costly, that is, disproportionate or counterproductive. When the military invasion is likely to cost significantly in terms of blood and treasure, it will be permitted *only* to end or prevent serious assaults on persons – seriously wrongful acts of state coercion – *because* only in such cases will the intervention be proportionate, and only then will the costs of war be justified. Consider the case of a government that has rendered itself guilty of less extreme rights violations. A military junta, say, has taken power by undemocratic means and has suspended constitutional guarantees – perhaps to prevent revolutionary activity. Let us assume that this undemocratic seizure of power violates the moral rights of the subjects and (to avoid complications) that this junta has little support in the population. Now suppose that the democratic forces can secure the help of a powerful neighbor, and suppose further that the mere border crossing by the foreign army will predictably cause the junta to surrender without a fight. It seems to us that this military intervention is morally justified because the military invasion will *not* impose unacceptable costs (the junta will surrender without resistance), *and* the violations of rights are relatively serious (although not egregious). The intervention, in other words, is proportionate. So the general proposition that only severe tyranny justifies humanitarian intervention will be true in most cases, but it is not strictly correct. The proposition has a hidden premise: that in less serious cases the intervention will impose unacceptable costs, as wars are prone to do. But if the military intervention, as in the example, is not costly, then the threshold of justification, in terms of the gravity of the cause, is lower. Thus the answer to the question "Is it justified to intervene by force to restore democracy?" is that it depends. If the intervention will kill many innocents, destroy vast amounts of property, or likely make things worse, the answer is no. If, on the contrary, the intervention will not have those dire consequences (e.g., if the intervener achieves the humanitarian objective by merely *threatening* force), then the answer may be yes. We hasten to add that the epistemic barriers faced by prospective interveners in calculating the likely costs of the war are so severe that perhaps the legal rule should confine the permissibility of intervention to really egregious cases.

Now consider legitimate states (judged as such under some standard of justice).[22] We said that intervention against legitimate states is prohibited, but not *because* those regimes are legitimate and therefore outsiders must respect what they do. Suppose that a state is considered legitimate, again, on some standard of substantive justice, such as general compliance with human rights.

[22] In accordance with our discussion in Chapter 7, we use "state legitimacy" loosely here, meaning "good enough." Good enough states are those that relatively allow persons the freedom to pursue personal projects.

Such a state *also* perpetrates unjustified acts of coercion – usually on a minor scale and usually less serious. *These* illegitimate acts of coercion, these violations of the moral rights of persons (say, incarceration of morally innocent people, as in the United States, or systematic governmental acts of theft, as in Argentina) are *not* deserving of protection. If someone could press the wondrous "green button" (discussed in Chapter 7) and stop the rights violations without any collateral cost, then that "intervention" would be morally permissible. But because *military* intervention is extremely costly, it will never be allowed against the impermissible acts of coercion of otherwise (presumed) legitimate states. For one thing, these states have reasonable avenues of redress against rights violations. More than that, these states have valuable institutions that, on the whole, allow persons to pursue their personal projects, and for this reason, violence against them, even if animated by a just cause such as ending illegitimate acts of coercion, is banned. Again, though, the reason for not intervening is not that those morally impermissible acts of coercion are somehow legitimate (whatever this statement may mean).

We can see, then, that the concept of state legitimacy does not do any work in the justification of humanitarian intervention. Contrary to some suggestions,[23] states do not have any *rights-based* shield against foreign intervention directed at ending their wrongful acts of coercion. States do not have a *general* right to rule, that is, a right to rule *beyond* what the rights of the subjects (one could say, the social contract) allow. All the work is done by the requirement of proportionality in war. War is justified *only* to end serious and systematic rights violations, that is, to protect persons against *attacks* by their own governments, because otherwise war in most cases would be disproportionate. If the rights violations are less severe, the principle of proportionality indicates less severe remedies. Because war is *the most severe* remedy in terms of blood and treasure, it must be reserved to redress the most urgent situations. To see this, imagine an even less severe situation. Imagine a state that harasses political dissidents; for example, it closes newspapers that are critical of government, and it persecutes dissidents with phony charges of tax evasion and the like. Outsiders (say, liberal democracies) are perfectly authorized to put diplomatic pressure, even coercive pressure such as economic sanctions, on this regime to stop these rights violations but are not authorized to invade – unless, as already indicated, the invasion itself will be costless (very unlikely in such a scenario). The reason for the prohibition to invade is *not* (as conventional wisdom would have it) that sovereignty shields nonegregious governmental misdeeds. The reason is that a military intervention would be patently disproportionate.

---

[23] Bas Van der Vossen, "The Asymmetry of Legitimacy," *Law and Philosophy* 31 (2012), 567–76; David Copp, "The Idea of a Legitimate State," *Philosophy and Public Affairs* 28(1) (1999), 26–9; John Rawls, *The Law of Peoples* (Cambridge, MA: Harvard University Press, 1999).

THE TARGET OF INTERVENTION: THE MORAL VALUE OF SOVEREIGNTY

We are not generally sympathetic, then, to the objection that humanitarian intervention violates the sovereignty of the target state. However, the objection must be examined more closely. Perhaps the idea is that there is something valuable in confining political processes to the citizens of the state and that the principle of sovereignty protects precisely this collective autonomy. Foreigners who use force to alter these processes are disrespecting the citizens of the target state.

To evaluate this objection, we need to distinguish *states* from *governments*. International law establishes the principle of state sovereignty. But states are artificial constructs created to protect and respect persons. The principle of sovereignty, therefore, is entirely derivative from the interests and rights of individuals. The objection that foreign intervention violates state sovereignty has some force *only* in cases where the well-intentioned intervener will radically change the valuable social structures built by persons in that state. When they have cemented their social relations through cumulative processes over time, the resulting institutions are prima facie worthy of respect by foreigners, provided that the institutions are morally justified. One can think of sovereignty as protecting nonoppressive social structures from foreign interference. To this extent, and to this extent only, the sovereignty argument against intervention is plausible. Foreigners do not have the right to change nonoppressive political structures.[24]

By the same token, cumulative historical processes do *not* deserve respect if they are oppressive. We are thinking here not of oppressive *regimes* but of social institutions and practices that originated from the bottom up, as it were, yet are unacceptable from the standpoint of justice. For example, the historical subjugation of women in many cultures is not acceptable from the standpoint of justice, so the objection that a foreign intervention will alter *that* practice is unavailable to those who oppose the intervention. It does not follow, of course, that military intervention is justified *just* to reverse those oppressive social practices. But the critic of intervention cannot point to those oppressive practices as valuable elements of the social fabric that (he thinks) the intervention will upset. Sovereignty does not protect those.

Citizens *hire* the government to do a certain job: the government is, in Nozick's terms, a protection agency. Now, when the government attacks its own citizens, it becomes itself morally vulnerable to attack. Such a government cannot be said to be an international agent for the citizens it is victimizing. The principle of sovereignty is no longer available to that government to fend off intervention aimed at rescuing the victims. The rhetoric of sovereignty has

---

[24] One of the sins of colonialism was precisely to alter many nonoppressive local customs and institutions.

muddled much discussion of this topic. Sovereignty is supposed to protect the "black box" of the state. Within that black box, people and government are lumped together in an undifferentiated amorphous object called "the state." But the phenomenon of tyranny *severs* government from people. If we disaggregate the state, we have three parties: the tyrant (joined by his henchmen and collaborators), his victims, and the bystanders. An intervention that removes the tyrant affords a remedy to the injured party. The bystanders have an obligation, perhaps, to do something, to aid the victims, as opposed to remaining on the sidelines. If they do remain on the sidelines in a war or revolution, they are partially protected by the doctrine of double effect (DDE) discussed later. Tyrannical regimes forfeit the protection afforded them by international law. They do not have defensive rights against force aimed at them – against humanitarian intervention. Tyranny causes the collapse of sovereignty.

Critics of humanitarian intervention think that national borders are morally significant barriers against intervention. But it is hard to see why this should be so. Consider the following two hypothetical examples[25]:

Genocide in Rodelia. Rodelia is a federal state. One of its provincial governments has unleashed its troops against an ethnic group within that province. Casualties mount rapidly. The Rodelian federal government sends federal troops to the province to stop the genocide. The provincial army resists, however, and a civil war follows. After several months of fighting with significant military and civilian casualties, the Rodelian federal troops subdue the rebels and save the victims.

Revolution in Andinia. A military junta in Andinia has overthrown the democratic government. It has indefinitely suspended constitutional liberties and unleashed a military campaign against dissenters. This includes widespread torture and summary executions. Democratic forces regroup and take to the streets to fight the junta. After several months of fierce fighting, with significant military and civilian casualties, the revolutionaries succeed in deposing the regime and restoring the liberal constitution.

Most people would endorse (perhaps reluctantly) the *internal* use of force in these two cases. Yet, in the Rodelia case, many will object if *foreign* armies invade to stop the atrocities in the Rodelian province (imagine that the Rodelian federal government is unable to act). And in the Andinia case, they will likewise object to *foreign* troops aiding the liberal revolutionaries against the junta. In both cases, noninterventionists will oppose foreign involvement even if everything else remains the same, that is, even if the number of casualties and other destruction caused by the violence remain constant. In fact, noninterventionists would likely oppose intervention even if it would cause more good than harm (reduce casualties and so forth). Yet there is no moral difference between the internal political violence in these imaginary cases and the

---

[25] Adapted from Tesón, *Humanitarian Intervention*.

foreign interventions having identical purpose and effect. Noninterventionists think that national borders operate a change in the *description* of the acts of humanitarian rescue (Rodelia) and justified revolution (Andinia): the actions are no longer humanitarian rescue or revolution but war. The rationale for this difference is entirely mysterious.

If opposition to humanitarian intervention is not grounded on state sovereignty but on other factors such as the impermissibility of killing innocents, then the noninterventionist cannot adequately explain her endorsement of the use of *internal* force to stop genocide or liberal revolutions to depose tyrants because in these instances innocents also die. There is no relevant difference between the national army rescuing victims of genocide and a foreign army doing the same thing. And it is inconsistent to praise justified revolutions but oppose foreign aid to them, even when that aid is the revolutionaries' only hope of getting rid of the tyrants.

What humanitarian crises justify foreign interventions? The issue is that of just cause. Scholars who accept the legitimacy of humanitarian intervention agree that the threshold should be quite high. For example, the well-known report on the "Responsibility to Protect" suggests that only a massive loss of human lives justifies foreign intervention.[26] Our own suggestion is that a justifiable intervention must be aimed at ending severe tyranny or anarchy. The standard does not necessarily require that genocide or a similar massive crime should be afoot.[27] To see why, consider the Andinia hypothetical earlier. No genocide is occurring there, yet the democratic revolutionaries need help from the powerful neighbor to succeed. Again, if unaided revolution is justified, aided revolution is also justified, provided that the other factors remain constant. If those factors do not remain constant, for example, if the intervention predictably will greatly increase civilian casualties, then the intervention may be unjustified. But the intervention cannot be condemned if the revolution is not condemned. It follows that sometimes the goal of ending humanitarian crises *other* than genocide or massive murder may constitute just causes for intervention.

THE LIBERTARIAN OBJECTION

Libertarians think that only defensive war is justified. This belief about war is an extension of their beliefs about individual violence. Just as persons cannot permissibly attack other persons, so nations cannot permissibly attack other nations. The late Harry Browne's statement is representative:

Most libertarians believe you shouldn't initiate force against someone who has never used force against you. Force is to be used only in self-defense – not used just because

---

[26] See International Commission on Intervention and State Sovereignty, 32–4; available at: http://www.iciss.ca/pdf/Commission-Report.pdf.

[27] See the discussion in Tesón, *Humanitarian Intervention*, 157–60.

you don't happen to like someone, or because someone doesn't like you, or because
he might become dangerous in the future, or because some third party has attacked
you and you want to prove you're not a wimp. The same principles must apply to our
nation – that it shouldn't use force against a nation that hasn't attacked us.[28]

This view, assimilating states to persons for the purpose of evaluating
aggression, has a venerable lineage. Kant, for example, treated states as "free
persons" and held that "a foreign power's interference in a civil war would
violate the rights of an independent people struggling with its own ills."[29] For
Kant, the state is a moral person considered as living alongside other moral
persons – other states – in a condition of natural freedom.[30] This view was
followed by Hegel in altered form and informs a large part of the modern
international-relations literature as well as international law.[31]

We reject this view of the state. However useful it may be for other purposes
to emphasize civic bonds within states, wars kill persons and destroy property.
Under a normative-individualist premise, states are no more than artificial constructs to serve human needs. They have no independent moral standing. A war
is an act of violence against individuals and not (primarily) against an abstract
construct such as the state. We can speak derivatively of an attack against a
state, of course. With this expression, we describe an army's attack against
another state's citizens, plus its impermissible border crossing, plus, perhaps,
its attempt to destroy the institutions of the state. But all these things are, in
a sense, possessions of individuals. They, the individuals, are the real victims
of the attack. And, despite nationalist rhetoric (let the nation rise against the
aggressors!), an act of national self-defense is an act in defense of self and others against an aggressor.

Let us start by accepting the impermissibility of aggressive interpersonal
violence. This rule has a corollary: the permissibility of defensive violence. If
someone initiates aggression against me, I am entitled to defend myself. Now,
as we saw earlier, defensive violence includes not only defense of self but also
defense of others. Suppose that I am passing by and see a villain (Attacker)
assault a defenseless person (Victim). Surely I have the right to defend Victim
by using force against Attacker. Victim's defensive rights are transferable to me.
(I assume that other requirements for permissible violence are met: Victim is
innocent, Attacker is culpable, Victim has consented to my defending her, and
my response is proportionate.)

---

[28] Harry Brown, "Libertarians and War"; available at: http://harrybrowne.org/articles/
LibertariansAndWar.htm.

[29] Immanuel Kant, *To Perpetual Peace: A Philosophical Sketch* [1792] in Immanuel Kant, *Perpetual
Peace and Other Essays*, trans. by Ted Humphrey. (Indianapolis, IN: Hackett, 1983), 109.

[30] Immanuel Kant, *The Metaphysics of Morals* [1797], Mary Gregor, ed. (Cambridge University
Press, 1992), 114, para. 53.

[31] The view of the state as a moral person has been dubbed the "Hegelian myth" by Fernando
R. Tesón, *Humanitarian Intervention*, chap. 3.

Let us now transpose this reasoning to war. Most libertarians say that defensive war is justified. How so? Because a defensive war is the use of violence by persons who have been unjustly attacked by a foreign army. Under the libertarian principle of nonaggression, if the evil enemy invades, we may permissibly defend ourselves and our fellow citizens (also victims of the attack) against the attackers. This means that my violence against the attackers is an action *both* in self-defense and in defense of others. And the government's job is to coordinate our defensive actions. Many views of the state (including libertarian views) list this defensive role as a raison d'être of the state.

If this analysis is correct, then it turns out that a defensive (and therefore justified) war is a war in defense of persons, self and others, as we explained earlier. It is not a defense of the state or the government per se. We can generalize by saying that, for the libertarian, the only justified violence is violence in defense of persons (self and others) who are victims of unjust attacks. Wars waged to achieve territorial aggrandizement, national glory or dominance, or similar nondefensive reasons are never justified.

Now take Rwanda, April–June 1994. One ethnic group, the Hutus, attacked a rival ethnic group, the Tutsis, and in 100 days killed about 800,000 of them.[32] Now suppose that the United States could have stopped this genocide at a low cost to everyone. Standard libertarian doctrine says that this would have been an offensive war, an initiation of violence against Rwanda. Because neither Rwanda nor the Hutus would have attacked the United States, the United States would not have had any business intervening in Rwanda. It would have been an unjustified war.

But this cannot be right if we accept (as libertarians do) the legitimacy of defense of others. The action of the United States in this hypothetical situation is an instance of defending Victim against Attacker. As we saw earlier, the distinction between defensive and offensive wars is misleading because it treats the state as a "person" who can be Attacker or Victim. But states are not persons. When we disaggregate the state, what we have is a group of human beings unjustly attacking another group of human beings. A defense of the victim here is not an offensive war: it is a defensive war, a war in defense of unjustly attacked persons. As such, it should not be banned by the libertarian principle that condemns the offensive use of violence.

Of course, problems remain. First, empirical and epistemic considerations may lead us to oppose any war, even defensive ones.[33] Let us accept this *arguendo*. Still, if those epistemic barriers could be overcome, then interventions to protect persons from genocide could *in principle* be justified under the libertarian principle of nonaggression and its corollary, the permissibility of defending

---

[32] For a gripping account, see Samantha Power, *A Problem from Hell: America and the Age of Genocide* (New York: Harper, 2007).

[33] See Bryan Caplan, "Pacifism Defended," in *Library of Economics and Liberty*; available at: http://econlog.econlib.org/archives/2011/04/pacifism_defend.html.

others. In other words, this is a different argument against war. It does not support the view that humanitarian interventions are impermissible because they are offensive wars.

Second, unlike what happens in many individual cases, in most wars innocent bystanders die. It could then be argued that war, but not individual defense of others where there is no collateral harm, is banned precisely because it inflicts collateral harm. This is a serious problem that we address later. All we say here is that this objection proves too much, for in the defensive war that the libertarian does allow (a reaction against the invader), there is collateral harm as well. States that defend themselves also kill innocent women and children when they repel the aggressor. Thus, if the reason to oppose the war in defense of the Tutsis attacked in Rwanda is that it kills innocent bystanders, then the libertarian has to oppose the defensive force by the Tutsis themselves.

Finally, it may be argued that our government has a limited mandate: to protect ourselves and our territory and nothing more. This fiduciary duty prohibits the government from using our resources to defend others, even in Rwanda-like cases. Defending Tutsis is just not part of our government's job description. This position is consistent with allowing private persons to rescue victims of genocide and with contractual arrangements to defend others. Imagine that a government proclaims that from now on it will abide by the principle of nonaggression. The government announces that it will not initiate any military action for any reason other than defending actual victims of unjustified attacks. The government inserts a clause to this effect in all enlistment contracts. This would authorize enlisted soldiers to refuse to participate in any war that was not a defense of persons against unjustified attacks. Such an arrangement, we believe, would be consistent with sending forces to Rwanda to stop the genocide.

The libertarian opposition to foreign wars, then, cannot be based on the distinction between defensive and offensive wars. If, as the libertarians and we believe, only the defense of persons, self or others, can possibly justify war, then some foreign wars are justified as well.

THE INTERVENER

Thus cases of severe oppression overrule the principle of sovereignty that protects the state. But it still may be wrong to intervene for a number of reasons; for example, the moral costs of intervening may be unacceptably high. Here we examine a different family of reasons: those relating not to the target state but to the state that contemplates intervention. We avoid the important institutional question of whether intervention should be conducted by an international organization, an alliance of states (say, liberal states), or individual states. We focus instead on the question of whether a liberal government may validly use the state's resources (troops and taxes) to liberate victims of severe tyranny in other societies. This is the problem of the internal legitimacy of humanitarian intervention.[34]

A government, we saw earlier, has a fiduciary duty toward its subjects. This includes the obligation to respect human rights at home. But because morality is universal and all persons have rights, a good government also has an obligation to respect human rights abroad. A government may not collude with another government in the latter's oppression of its citizens. Thus a principle of justice in foreign policy is the *obligation not to cooperate with tyranny*.[35] We think that this purely negative obligation can be reinforced by adding a softer obligation to promote human rights globally, provided, of course, that this can be done at reasonable cost. Now these principles for a liberal foreign policy yield the following consequence for the topic at hand: if promoting human rights globally includes sometimes saving foreigners from severe tyranny, then the government can *tax* citizens for that purpose. If the government in a liberal state can tax citizens to contribute, say, to the establishment of a human rights court, then it can tax citizens to support an army to free foreigners from tyranny. In both cases, the government is using the citizen's *economic* resources (taxes) to improve the lives of others. In neither case is the government literally *forcing* people to defend others. So both cases are morally indistinguishable from the standpoint of the taxpayer. It may well be that *neither* taxation is justified, of course. The point here is that taxing to finance a human rights court and taxing to finance a humanitarian intervention entail the same demands on taxpayers. The degree of intrusion into the citizens' freedom is the same. Humanitarian intervention is not a more egregious case of government demands on citizens' resources.

The more pressing question is whether the government can validly send people to fight for the freedoms of foreigners. Recall that the humanitarian crises we have in mind are of such gravity that the target state is not protected by the principle of sovereignty: it is morally vulnerable to intervention. Assuming that an intervention is otherwise justified, who can the liberal government ask or force to fight? There are four theoretical possibilities: spontaneous private brigades, a forcibly conscripted army, a voluntary army, and mercenaries.

Volunteers may form private brigades to invade the country and end the tyranny there. This possibility raises a host of questions about the legitimacy of private wars. However, in theory, a private brigade is a satisfactory solution to *this* problem (i.e., whether the government can legitimately use the citizens' resources to liberate foreigners) because the government does not force anyone to do anything: the privateers voluntarily undertake the intervention.[36]

---

[34] We adopt Allen Buchanan's terminology. Allen Buchanan, "The Internal Legitimacy of Humanitarian Intervention," *Journal of Political Philosophy* 7 (1999), 71–87.

[35] See Loren Lomasky, "Liberalism Beyond Borders," *Social Philosophy and Policy* 24 (2007), 206–33.

[36] Apparently, bikers are joining in the fight against ISIS. "German Motorcycle Club Members Join Dutch Bikers in Fight against ISIS," *The Independent*, Tuesday, December 9, 2014; available

The government does not even tax anybody. As a matter of principle, if geno-cide is occurring and outsiders have a moral obligation to rescue the victims if they can do so at a reasonable cost to themselves, it seems arbitrary to require that their rescue mission should be approved or endorsed by their government. It is true that international law places liability on the state of the privateers, but perhaps this is yet another state-centered feature of international law that requires revision. Nonetheless, for all their advantages, relying on privateers is likely to be inefficient for obvious reasons. The coordinating function of the government plays a decisive role in military issues, at least as long as the world is populated by the current kinds of nation-states. Still, it is unclear why a the-ory of just war must include the requirement (first introduced by Aquinas) that war can only be conducted by "the Prince."

Conscription is morally objectionable for many reasons, but especially so for humanitarian intervention. To see why, let us start with conscription for self-defense. The government forcibly enlists persons and orders them to fight, thus putting them at risk of death. Even here, conscription may well be a seri-ous violation of freedom. Suppose that the country is invaded by an evil and ruthless enemy. Our democracy and everything that citizens value will collapse unless they can succeed in their defensive war. If defensive force is merely *per-mitted*, not obligatory, the victim of an attack is free to decide whether he will fight for his life, property, or freedom. He may choose not to fight and submit instead to the aggressor. Others (the government especially) cannot coerce him into combat. This libertarian argument, then, contends that the only legitimate collective force occurs when citizens rise spontaneously against an aggressor. Those who choose not to fight are within their rights and should be left alone.

In this view, no conscription is ever justified, even in these extreme cases. But let us assume, for the sake of argument, that conscription is permissible in the extreme defensive circumstances just described.[37] Even if conscription can be justified for national self-defense, it cannot be justified for humanitar-ian interventions. To see why, let us consider how conscription for national self-defense may be justified. The argument relies on the fact that national defense is a *public good*. If people are allowed to choose individually whether they should contribute to national defense against the kinds of serious threats we imagine, they will be tempted to free ride on the defense efforts of others. National defense is vulnerable to market failure: everyone wants to repel the aggressor, but each one hopes that others will risk their lives to do so. Because everyone reasons similarly, the public good (defense) is underproduced, and

at: http://www.independent.co.uk/news/world/europe/german-motorcycle-club-members-join-dutch-bikers-in-fight-against-isis-9804525.html.

[37] Arthur Ripstein writes: "[I]n extreme circumstances when ordinary arrangements break down, extraordinary demands may be placed on individuals who are selected for no better reason than their availability." Arthur Ripstein, "Three Duties to Rescue: Moral, Civil, and Criminal," *Law and Philosophy* 19 (2000), 777–8, n. 25.

the state succumbs to the aggressor. One can, of course, recast this argument in normative terms: we have sometimes, in extreme circumstances, a *moral* duty to defend our fellow citizens and the social contract.[38] This argument, then, reluctantly accepts that the government may use the military draft to defend the state against attack.

However, this argument does not support the legitimacy of conscription for humanitarian interventions.[39] The public-goods argument that served as a justification for military conscription for self-defense does not work very well in the case of a war to defend distant others. The argument depends on the assumption that the good in question is demanded by a sufficient number of people. Because the demand for national defense is likely to be strong, conscription is arguably needed to eliminate free riders. Those who object to national self-defense, where they face their *own* destruction, are hardly credible: they are likely to be free riders. But, while humanitarian intervention also may be a public good in the sense that it allows for opportunistic moves ex post (people who would agree ex ante to intervene will refuse to fight once the veil of ignorance is lifted), the demand for humanitarian intervention by the intervener's public surely will be much weaker than the demand for national defense. There will be genuine objectors who are not, by definition, opportunistic agents. Therefore, a liberal argument must balance respect for these genuine dissenters against the moral urgency to liberate victims of foreign tyranny. The duty to promote global human rights is relative: it must cohere with other moral-political considerations, such as the need to respect nonopportunistic exercises of individual autonomy.[40]

If this analysis is correct, the two alternatives left are voluntary armies and mercenaries. Voluntary soldiers have contractually consented to fight in wars, the justice of which is decided case by case by their employer, the liberal government. Voluntary soldiers have agreed ex ante to fight in cases where the legitimate government believes that there is a sufficiently grave reason to fight.

---

[38] Sidgwick offers a utilitarian rationale: "Still I conceive that where compulsory military service is rightly introduced, the decisive reason in its favour is the economic reason, that the army required is too large to be raised by voluntary enlistment except at a rate of payment which would involve a greater burden in the way of taxation than the burden of military service." Henry Sidgwick, *The Elements of Politics* (London: Macmillan, 1908), 173.

[39] The view in the text departs from the previous view expressed in Fernando R. Tesón, "The Liberal Case for Humanitarian Intervention," in *Humanitarian Intervention: Ethical, Legal, and Political Dilemmas*, J. L. Holzgrefe and Robert O. Keohane, eds. (Cambridge University Press, 2003), 123–8. There it was argued that the government must *first* resort to a voluntary army to dispatch a humanitarian intervention, and only if that turned out to be insufficient could it resort to conscription. For the reasons in the text, we now think that conscription is not available for humanitarian intervention regardless of whether or not it is available for self-defense.

[40] John Rawls disagrees. He writes that "conscription is permissible only if it is demanded for the defense of liberty itself, including here not only the liberties of the citizens of the society in question, but also those of persons in other societies as well." John Rawls, *A Theory of Justice* (Cambridge, MA: Harvard University Press, 1971), 380.

This includes humanitarian interventions. The advantages of a voluntary army are well known. For one thing, the market is likely to select the better fighters. Also, a voluntary army mitigates the problem of conscientious objection because the voluntarily enlisted soldier has contractually authorized the government to decide on the justice of particular wars.[41] Someone may object that the enlistment contract contains an implicit clause under which the person inducted into the armed forces only consented to fight in self-defense or a clause under which the enlistee has retained the right to decide on the justice of particular wars. We doubt that such contracts can reasonably be construed in this way; more important, the whole point of a voluntary army would be defeated if the enlistee could pick and choose among the wars he will be asked to fight.

A possible solution to the problems of conscription and enlistment is to allow the liberal government to hire national or foreign mercenaries. Mercenaries are private entrepreneurs who offer military services for a price. As long as they have existed (since antiquity), they have been the target of scorn and contempt by governments, scholars, and the general public.[42] However, an unprejudiced look at the issue reveals that most of the reasons for this hostility are questionable.[43] It is argued, first, that because killing for money is morally wrong, it is impermissible for the liberal state to hire people who do that. But surely enlisted soldiers kill for money, too: it is their profession. Moreover, it is not altogether clear what is the mix of self-interested and altruistic motives in both mercenaries and enlisted soldiers. Arguably, enlisted soldiers risk their lives not only for love of country but also for solidarity with comrades. If this fact is true, then it seems equally true of mercenaries, who presumably take pride in what they do and feel solidarity with their comrades as well. The point here is that monetary compensation is one element in a richer range of motives, many of which are self-interested. Enlisted soldiers receive salary, benefits, prestige, and social esteem. All these motives are self-interested, yet a romantic tradition has emphasized the honor and glory of fighting for one's country. Because this altruistic motive seems to be lacking in mercenaries, they are supposed to be bad people. But once we disaggregate motivation in both cases and we see the patriotic prejudice for what it is, the two cases do not seem that different.

---

[41] It does not totally eliminate the conscientious objector: a soldier who has agreed contractually to fight may still in good faith believe that the cause is unjust, and that belief may conceivably override his contractual obligations. Any law allowing conscientious objection must detect the bona fide objectors and distinguish them clearly from opportunistic free riders.

[42] The law of war reaffirms this contempt: Article 47 of the Additional Protocol to the 1977 Geneva Conventions denies mercenaries the right to claim prisoner-of-war status. Of course, the word "mercenary" is already loaded because it denotes especially greedy people who will only work for a price.

[43] The objections that we discuss in the text are formulated by James Pattison, "Deeper Objections to the Privatisation of Military Force," *Journal of Political Philosophy* (2009), 1.

Another reason offered against mercenaries is that using them will weaken the communal bonds in society. But communal bonds are not very useful if the country *loses* the war. Imagine that the country is fighting a just war against a powerful enemy. At one point the voluntary army becomes insufficient. Should, then, the government conscript soldiers or hire mercenaries? The answer is not clear at all. Conscription is objectionable for liberty reasons, so hiring mercenaries solves the problem. Moreover, mercenaries are professional soldiers who will presumably increase the chances of victory, so they are preferable for efficiency reasons as well. As we saw earlier, the hostility toward mercenaries is the result of the patriotic prejudice that it is honorable to fight and die for your homeland, and that this noble motive should not be tainted by the profit motive. As we said, though, enlisted soldiers are also fighting for a host of motives, many of which are self-interested, and there is no reason to think that they are nobler persons just because they become a part of the state's bureaucracy as opposed to being mere contractors.[44]

To sum up, sometimes taxing people for war is justified, and this includes, sometimes, humanitarian interventions. We have doubts about whether conscription is ever legitimate, but if it is, it only covers national self-defense because self-defense is a public good that is vulnerable to being underproduced, with disastrous consequences for the state itself. In contrast, the state can only ask voluntary soldiers, that is, those voluntarily enlisted or mercenaries, to participate in military operations aimed at liberating distant victims of tyranny or anarchy.

Humanitarian interventions, like all wars, are still subject to the criticism that they cause the deaths of innocent persons. We turn to this all-important question next.

THE PERMISSIBILITY OF KILLING IN WAR

Under what circumstances is killing in war permitted? We need to address two questions. The first is the question of who has, in principle, the right to kill. The second is the question of collateral deaths – the deaths of innocent persons in an otherwise justified war.

According to the traditional view, combatants on both sides of a war are morally equal on the battlefield. Anyone who is a lawful combatant has a right to kill enemy combatants, provided that the means are also lawful. Henry Sidgwick, for example, argued that in order to evaluate the morality of killing in war, we must "abstract from all consideration of the justice of the war."[45]

---

[44] Guido Pincione and Fernando R. Tesón have identified the tendency to romanticize certain professions over others as a form of *discourse failure*. See Guido Pincione and Fernando R. Tesón, *Rational Choice and Democratic Deliberation: A Theory of Discourse Failure* (New York: Cambridge University Press, 2006), 50–3.

[45] Henry Sidgwick, *The Elements of Politics*, (London: Macmillan, 1908), 267.

Sidgwick's view influenced Michael Walzer, who also analyzed the morality of killing in war apart from the question of the justice of the cause.[46] Walzer amended Sidgwick's purely utilitarian test on this point by noting that the restrictions on *how* to fight could not be subject entirely to that test.[47] But Walzer adopted Sidgwick's "moral equality" approach: in principle, a soldier on *any* side of a war has a right to kill enemy soldiers, provided that he abides by the restrictions of *jus in bello*. International law reaffirms the moral equality of combatants. The Geneva Conventions, which establish important constraints on the means of warfare, sever the justice of the cause from the legality of killing. As long as soldiers are engaged in a legally defined armed conflict, they have the right to kill enemy troops, even if they fight for the wrong side. The neutrality of nongovernmental organizations that provide war relief, such as the Red Cross, also reflects this view. The Red Cross is not supposed to take sides in a conflict but only assist the sick and wounded and remind belligerents of their obligations under the Geneva Conventions.[48]

We join Jeff McMahan in his rejection of this traditional view.[49] If State A unjustifiedly attacks State B, only the soldiers of State B have the moral right to kill enemy soldiers in combat. The moral right to kill in war is confined to soldiers fighting a just war. As McMahan points out, "[t]hose who fight solely to defend themselves and other innocent people from wrongful attack, and who threaten no one but the wrongful aggressors, do not make themselves morally liable to defensive attack."[50] So every killing by a soldier on the wrong side of a war is an objectively wrong killing. By not referring back to the justice of the cause, the international law of war perpetuates the old belief that we can never tell who is on the just side of a war and that all we can do is alleviate war's destructive effects. For example, under current law, it is unlawful to use poisonous weapons; this holds for both sides in a war, the aggressor and the victim. *This* moral symmetry is, of course, correct: restrictions on permissible ways of fighting apply to everyone. The Allied bombings of Dresden were morally wrong notwithstanding the fact that the Allies were fighting a just war against Germany. But the deaths caused by the German soldiers in World War II were unjust *even* when those soldiers complied with the restrictions. If a war is unjust, every killing in pursuance of that war is unjust.[51]

What is the moral responsibility of an unjust combatant?[52] Once we have established that the deaths he causes are objectively unjust, the issue is whether

---

[46] See Walzer, *Just and Unjust Wars*, 128.

[47] Ibid., 129–33.

[48] See International Committee of the Red Cross, "Neutrality of the red Cross"; available at: https://www.icrc.org/eng/resources/documents/misc/57jncv.htm.

[49] See Jeff McMahan, *Killing in War* (Oxford University Press, 2009), 1–103.

[50] Ibid., 14.

[51] McMahan makes the interesting point that unjust combatants can never meet a plausible proportionality test. Ibid., 15–32.

[52] By "unjust combatants," we mean here combatants fighting for an unjust cause.

he can nonetheless be morally *excused*. As is well known, the *laws* of war do not condemn unjust combatants who fight in accordance with the relevant rules; they are not legally liable, and there are good reasons to maintain this legal position.[53] The question is one of moral blameworthiness. We agree with McMahan that one cannot give a unified answer to this question. Some of those who fight an unjust war are very culpable (soldiers in high places, perhaps), some are partly culpable, and some could be morally excused.[54] At any rate, we think that the standard foot soldier on the wrong side should be morally excused for the injustice of the killings in most cases. One difficulty with assigning moral responsibility is that in many cases the justice of the war is not apparent.[55] Take the 2003 Iraq war: many soldiers may have believed in good faith that the war was justified either as an effort to find weapons of mass destruction or as an effort to overthrow a brutal tyrant or both.[56] We are not revisiting that debate here. We simply point out that the principles of *jus ad bellum* are considerably more *indeterminate* than the principles of *jus in bello*. Whereas the latter is not free of ambiguity, the former is plagued with major uncertainties. The main problem, already noted, is that many people regard the *jus ad bellum* as essentially binary: any war that turns out not to justified, for whatever reason, is deemed aggression.[57] This crude distinction does not do justice to the complex morality of war. A war may be wrong for many reasons. The warrior may have an objectively unjust cause, he may wage the war in violation of the *jus in bello*, he may have a just cause but cause disproportionate harm, he may have a just cause but his acts may not be conducive to the realization of the just cause, he may have an objectively just cause but harbor a wicked design such as domination, and so on. In which of these situations is the soldier supposed to *know* the immorality so that we can withhold the excuse from him? If philosophers cannot agree on the justice of the Iraq or Kosovo wars, how can we expect the soldier to have moral certainty?[58]

---

[53] See the reasons for legal immunity in McMahan, ibid, 105–10.

[54] Ibid., 128.

[55] Francisco de Vitoria got it right: if the injustice of the cause is patent, the soldier should not fight, but if there is "provable ignorance of either fact or law," the unjust combatant may be morally excused ("free of sin"). *Vitoria: Political Writings*, Anthony Pagden and Jeremy Lawrance, eds. (Cambridge University Press, 1991), 307, 313.

[56] For humanitarian arguments defending the war in Iraq, see Fernando R. Tesón, "Ending Tyranny in Iraq," *Ethics and International Affairs* 19 (2005), 1, and the essays collected in *A Matter of Principle: Humanitarian Arguments for War In Iraq*, Thomas Cushman, ed. (Berkeley, CA: University of California Press, 2005).

[57] This difficulty explains why it has been so hard to define aggression for the purposes of individual criminal responsibility. For a discussion of some of the philosophical issues, see Larry May, *Aggression and Crimes against Peace* (Cambridge University Press, 2008).

[58] We thus disagree with McMahan on this point. He thinks that the same reasons that excuse the combatant who fights for a just cause apply to the soldier who commits war crimes (duress and uncertainty). We do not excuse the latter; therefore, we should not excuse the former either. Ibid., 128. But this is doubtful. The *content* of the law (and morality) of the *jus in bello* is highly

This indeterminacy of the *jus ad bellum* explains why superior orders sometimes may excuse a subordinate's fighting in (what may turn out to be) an
unjust war, whereas superior orders may not excuse violations of the *jus in
bello*. Still, soldiers who participated in a war that later turns out to be clearly
unjust should answer to the fact that they were the instruments of the wrongful war. After the war is over, others should make clear to those veterans that
they did an injustice to their victims. Thus, for example, war education should
not endorse the moral-equality approach and should not treat the veterans of
unjust wars as heroes. Rather, it should emphasize that the destruction caused
by the aggressor was unjust. This implies that those who carried it out under
the mistaken belief that they were simply defending the homeland should not
be glorified or vindicated. They should not be scorned either – after all, they are
morally excused. But it certainly would be appropriate for them to apologize
for having participated (unwittingly) in the unjust war.[59]

COLLATERAL HARM: THE DOCTRINE OF DOUBLE EFFECT

A vexing problem in the philosophy of war is that virtually any justified war
effort will cause the deaths of innocent civilians caught in the crossfire.[60]
Pacifists have sometimes relied on the moral impermissibility of killing the
innocent as a reason to claim that *all* wars are immoral.[61] The idea is that
because the just warrior cannot confine his destructive actions to morally permitted targets, then all war is impermissible. The problem does not arise as
acutely in unjust wars because, as we saw earlier, *every* killing by an unjust
combatant is wrong. Of course, an unjust combatant who also violates the
laws of war commits aggravated murder. But does the just warrior who brings
about the deaths of innocent persons commit *simple* murder? If he could confine his military actions to purely military targets, then the just war would be
surgical, as it were: no innocent people would die. Alas, this is not possible.
Since noncombatants have not waived their right to life, those killings seem

---

detailed and specific (though not totally free from ambiguity). This increases the probability that
the soldier will be subjectively certain (that he will *know*) that a contemplated act is criminal.
In contrast, the content of the *jus ad bellum* is indeterminate and highly contested – witness the
debates about humanitarian intervention in general and as applied to particular cases such as
Iraq and Kosovo. Given this epistemological problem, it is unfair in many cases to hold the soldier morally culpable for fighting an unjust war. But we agree with McMahan that one cannot
draw bright lines: some *will* be culpable.

[59] We think that this atonement is the only practical consequence of rejecting moral equality. We
do not take McMahan to argue that the moral accountability of the soldier who fights in good
faith for an unjust cause should go further than this. Certainly, he does not argue that all soldiers
who fought an unjust wars should be legally prosecuted.

[60] In what follows, we use interchangeably the terms "civilians," "noncombatants," "innocent persons," and the like to refer to victims of war other than those who have taken arms. We assume
that these persons are innocent in the relevant sense. We ignore the problem of culpable civilians.

[61] In this sense, Robert Holmes, *On War and Morality* (Princeton, NJ: Princeton University Press, 1989).

unjustified. So the moral warrior faces a dilemma: if he wants victory over the evil enemy, he must regrettably cause the deaths of innocent persons; if he decides to refrain from anything that will result in the deaths of innocent persons, he will lose the war and surrender to the evil enemy. One who upholds an absolute prohibition of killing the innocent must, it seems, reject the permissibility of all wars. She must be pacifist.

One may be tempted to resolve this question by reflective equilibrium. If collateral deaths are absolutely prohibited, then we should indeed be pacifists. But pacifism clashes with our intuitions that some wars (such as World War II) were rightly fought. We *know* that some wars and revolutions are morally justified. Therefore, the absolute prohibition on killing innocents and its corollary, pacifism, must be rejected. This, however, is too easy: maybe the pacifist is right, and the wars that we thought justified were objectionable. Perhaps we should revise our intuitions and become pacifists.

Just war scholars have replied to this objection by invoking the "doctrine of the double effect."[62] The DDE distinguishes between *intended* killings and *merely foreseen* killings. It is morally wrong to deliberately target innocent persons. The commander who decides, in pursuit of a just cause,[63] to aim the guns at a school in order to kill children and in this way demoralize the enemy is guilty of murder because he *wills* the deaths of the children. This immorality is not cured by the justice of the cause. But the commander who aims the guns at enemy soldiers while merely *foreseeing* that this action may kill innocent children is on a different moral footing. The deaths of the children are not essential to his destruction of the enemy; he would spare the children if he could. Some authors say that in the first case the commander treats the children as *means* to his end of winning, whereas in the second case the commander does not treat the children as means. This intent-based distinction between the two cases is essential to the DDE.

The formulation of the doctrine varies considerably in the literature. As a first approximation, we can state the doctrine thus:

An act with two effects, one good, one evil, may be performed

1. If the act is right (or not wrong),
2. If the good effect is intended, though the evil effect may be foreseen,
3. If the good effect does not come through the evil effect, and
4. If the good achieved by the good effect is significant enough to permit the evil of the evil effect to come to pass.[64]

---

[62] A previous, tentative discussion of the DDE in connection with humanitarian intervention can be found in Tesón, "The Liberal Case for Humanitarian Intervention," 93. The discussion in the text attempts to improve on that earlier attempt.

[63] Unless stated otherwise, the discussion that follows assumes that the warrior has a just cause in the sense defined earlier: he fights to defend persons or just institutions against unjustified assaults.

[64] R. G. Frey, "The Doctrine of Double Effect," in *A Companion to Applied Ethics*, R. G. Frey and Christopher Heath Wellman, eds. (Oxford, UK: Blackwell, 2003), 464. Joseph Boyle, Jr.,

Now let us adapt this formulation to the problem at hand, that is, the collateral deaths of noncombatants in a just war:

An act of war aimed at a good result (i.e., defeating an enemy who sufficiently harms or threatens persons) that results in the deaths of noncombatants is permissible if, and only if

1. The act itself is permitted by the laws of wars; for example, the weapons used are permissible (thus, no poisonous or biological weapons);
2. The agent aims at a good result (i.e., a result conducive to the defeat of the enemy defined earlier), although he also foresees the deaths of noncombatants;
3. The good effect (i.e., the defeat of the enemy or acts conducive to it) does not come through the deaths of noncombatants; and
4. The good result (the defeat of the enemy or an act conducive to it) is significant enough to permit the death of noncombatants to come to pass.

Condition 1 stipulates that the means used by the warrior have to be themselves acceptable. For example, if the commander uses poisonous or other prohibited weapons, the act will be unjustified even if he complies with the other conditions. Most of the literature has focused on condition 2: the warrior should not intend the deaths of noncombatants, even though he foresees those deaths. To it we now turn.

THE DISTINCTION BETWEEN INTENTION AND FORESIGHT

According to DDE scholars, the collateral deaths of innocents are not *intrinsic* to the just warrior's action, and this means that in some important sense the agent does not intend those deaths. But the language of intention is misleading because the evil effect is certainly *imputable* to the agent. He willingly and knowingly brings about the deaths of those innocent persons.[65] In what sense, then, can we plausibly say that he did not *intend* their deaths? The commander was informed that if he fired his guns, innocent civilians would die. He went ahead and fired. On a plausible meaning of "intending," he intended those deaths: he knew that if he fired, he would kill those persons. In view of this difficulty, proponents of the doctrine have conceded that in these cases the agent

formulates the doctrine somewhat more succinctly: "It is morally permissible to undertake an action when one knows that the undertaking will bring about at least one state of affairs such that, if this state of affairs were intrinsic to the action undertaken, the action would be rendered morally impermissible, if and only if (i) the state of affairs is not intrinsic to the action taken – that is, it is not intended – and (ii) there is a serious reason for undertaking the action." Joseph Boyle, Jr., "Toward Understanding the Principle of Double Effect," in *The Doctrine of Double Effect: Philosophers Debate a Controversial Moral Principle*, P. A. Woodward, ed. (Notre Dame, IN: Notre Dame University Press, 2001): 12. Critics of the DDE include Jonathan Bennet, "Morality and Consequences," in *The Morality of War*, Larry May, Eric Rovie, and Steve Viner, eds. (Upple Saddle River, NJ: Pearson-Prentice-Hall, 2006), 187, and Horacio Spector, *Autonomy and Rights* (Oxford, UK: Clarendon Press, 1992), 109–13.

[65] See Boyle, "Toward Understanding the Principle of Double Effect," 9.

intends the evil and have distinguished between *direct* intention and *oblique* intention. The commander intends all the predictable causal consequences of his behavior. But he *directly* intends the killing of the enemy soldier, whereas he *obliquely* intends the death of the noncombatants. An agent aims at achieving *X* (a good consequence) but knows that by achieving *X*, he also brings about *Y* (a bad consequence). We ask the agent the following question: "Would you have proceeded in achieving *X* if you had been told that *Y* would not happen?" If the answer is yes, then the agent intended *Y* obliquely. The evil effect is irrelevant to the agent's goal, which is to prevail in a just war.

Yet this is just a terminological move. The question is not conceptual (what counts as intent?) but normative: why exactly are collateral deaths in a just war morally permissible? The most promising candidate is this: action aimed intentionally at an evil is *guided* by that evil.[66] Direct harmful agency is, therefore, more *disrespectful* than collateral harm, and therein lies the moral difference between both actions (or between both effects of the same action).[67] The commander who does not aim at noncombatants does not really wish to cause the deaths of innocent persons; he would spare them if he could. The bad effect is nothing to his intent; his action is not guided by evil. The commander who aims at noncombatants wishes their deaths; he does not want to spare them. Their deaths are essential to his intent; his action is guided by evil. The distinction, then, is plausible and establishes the moral difference between direct and oblique harmful agency.

But it does not follow from the fact that there is a *moral difference* between direct harmful agency and oblique harmful agency that the latter is *morally permissible*. As Warren Quinn observed, the DDE raises the bar for the moral permissibility of killing; it does not lower it.[68] The doctrine does not justify collateral deaths in war but merely says that collateral deaths are less bad than direct deaths. The pacifist may concede that a commander who directly kills civilians in order to demoralize the enemy is morally abject while insisting that the commander who merely causes collateral deaths of civilians is still acting immorally – less immorally than the other one, to be sure, but still immorally. He agrees with the DDE's moral differentiation of the two cases but maintains that even the more benign case is objectionable. For the pacifist, all wars are unjust, although, of course, there are gradations of injustice. The most reprehensible warrior is the unjust warrior who violates the DDE. Less blameworthy but still bad (perhaps) is the unjust warrior who abides by the DDE. The second place (perhaps) goes to the just warrior who violates the DDE (we are unsure about how to rank the last two categories). And the least blameworthy is the just warrior who abides by the DDE. But even this one, the least blameworthy of all, is acting unjustly because he performs an act of war

[66] Thomas Nagel, "Agent-Relative Morality," in P.A.Woodward ed,. *The Doctrine of Double Effect: Philosophers Debate a Controversial Moral Principle* (University of Notre Dame Press, 2001), 46.

[67] See Warren Quinn, *Morality and Action* (Cambridge University Press, 1994), 192–3.

[68] Ibid., 188.

that will predictably kill innocents, and this is *still* morally impermissible. We can see now why merely invoking the distinction in condition 2 of the DDE, that is, the distinction between direct harm and oblique harm, does not answer the pacifist's objection. To respond to the pacifist, we must focus on condition 4: the requirement that the good effect (the vindication of the just cause) be "significant enough" to allow for the moral cost represented by the deaths of noncombatants.

THE ROLE OF THE JUST CAUSE IN THE DOCTRINE OF DOUBLE EFFECT

The fourth condition is widely held to embody a requirement of proportionality. What counts as proportionate action, however, is noticeably obscure. The modern literature on the DDE generally has rejected a purely utilitarian test, but the solutions proposed do not seem to improve much over a crude calculation of costs and benefits, perhaps in terms of human lives.

The DDE may play one of two related yet distinct roles. It may be used to distinguish between fighting morally and fighting immorally *without reference to the justice of the cause*, or it may be used to justify collateral killings (and conversely condemn direct killings) in otherwise just wars. As we saw earlier, Michael Walzer adopts the first strategy. He writes that an act of war satisfies the DDE when

1. The act is good in itself or at least morally indifferent, which means ... that it is a legitimate act of war.
2. The direct effect is morally acceptable – the destruction of military supplies, for example, or the killing of enemy soldiers.
3. The intention of the actor is good, that is, he aims only at the acceptable effect; the evil effect is not one of his ends, nor is it a means to his ends.
4. The good effect is sufficiently good to compensate for allowing the evil effect; it must be justified under Sidgwick's proportionality rule.[69]

Walzer's condition 2 stipulates that the good effect must be morally acceptable. By "morally acceptable effect," Walzer, following Sidgwick, means here the effect that the soldier thinks is conducive to victory of *his* side. Similarly, under condition 4, a "good effect" means exactly the same: a good effect given the war objectives of the combatants, independently of the justice of the cause. As we saw earlier, Walzer and Sidgwick want to isolate the morality of fighting from the justice of the cause. They want to be able to distinguish between legitimate and illegitimate fighters on *both* sides of the war. This is understandable: a soldier who violates the war restrictions commits a crime even if he fights for a good cause. The Sidgwick-Walzer approach tries to capture this important difference. Moreover, Walzer adds an important requirement: the

---

[69] Walzer, *Just and Unjust Wars*, 153. For Sidgwick's proportionality rule, see later.

soldier who foresees the deaths of civilians must take steps to prevent those deaths, even at some cost to himself. In addition to having the right intent, the soldier, "aware of the evil involved ... seeks to minimize it, accepting costs to himself."[70] The sole requirement that the deaths of civilians not be directly intended is too permissive. Because the foreseen victims of an act of war are innocent and it is in principle wrong to kill innocent persons, the soldier has a moral duty to transfer some risk to himself.

Useful as it is, this approach disables the DDE from justifying *just* wars. Thus, if we are to justify war at all, we must not only distinguish between good and bad soldiers but also respond to the pacifist who thinks that *even* the collateral deaths brought about by the just warrior are immoral. The pacifist claims that no act of war can ever be justified, not even those performed by just warriors, *because* they predictably will bring about the deaths of innocent persons. As we saw in the preceding section, the deaths inflicted by the soldier on the wrong side are always unjustified, even if he abides by the restrictions imposed by the DDE.[71] If the soldier on the wrong side abides by the Sidgwick-Walzer strictures, he will avoid court martial, so Sidgwick and Walzer are correct that there is a moral difference between the soldier on the wrong side who fights decently and his comrade who fights indecently. But because both good and bad soldiers fight an unjust war, their killings are ultimately unjust.

The DDE's more interesting role is in responding to the pacifist's claim, that is, in justifying oblique deaths of noncombatants in a just war. In our judgment, this can only be done if condition 4 is understood not only as a quantitative proportionality test (a calculation of costs and benefits) but also as a *qualitative* evaluation of *how just* the just cause is.

We start with Sidgwick's proportionality rule and amend it by stages to respond to the worries we have identified. The general idea of proportionality is that the good effect of the war (or of a particular act of war) must outweigh the bad effect under a suitable proportionality rule. According to Sidgwick, the aim of the moral combatant must be to disable his enemy and force him into submission "but not do him (1) any mischief which does not tend materially to that end, nor (2) any mischief of which the conduciveness to the end is slight in comparison to the amount of mischief."[72] Because Sidgwick thinks that the morality of killing in war is independent of the justice of the

---

[70] Walzer, *Just and Unjust Wars*, 155.

[71] As Cavanaugh writes, "[F]or one's conduct in war to be just, both the war and the individual act must be just." T. A. Cavanaugh, *Double Effect Reasoning: Doing Good and Avoiding Evil* (Oxford University Press, 2006), 181. A reading of Walzer's book makes it clear that he, too, thinks that a justified war must have a good cause. Like all just war theorists before him, he thinks that a completely just war includes just cause *and* just fighting. However, his use of the DDE in the chapter on the justice of fighting obscures the fact that the doctrine plays a crucial role in responding to the critic who says that even just fighting (in the DDE sense) by a just warrior (in the sense of having a just cause) may be immorally impermissible.

[72] Sidgwick, *Elements*, 268

cause, this definition will be useful to our purposes only if suitably amended to include *jus ad bellum* considerations and, in particular, address the problem of collateral deaths.

So we amend Sidgwick's rule as follows: an act of war undertaken for a just cause which collaterally brings about the deaths of innocents will *not* be permissible if either (1) the act is not materially conducive to the realization of the just cause; or (2) the conduciveness to the just cause is slight in comparison to the number of collateral deaths.

This amendment introduces the concept of just cause as the morally justified war objective. But the amended version still does not capture the qualitative dimension of the concept of just cause. To be justified, a person who performs an act of war must have a grave reason to do so. The term "significant enough" in condition 4 of the DDE embodies the degree of moral urgency that animates the just warrior. The war must be *sufficiently* justified to compensate for the bad effect. This requirement is not quantitative but substantive. The more *compelling* the reason to fight is, the lower will be the threshold for justifying collateral deaths. We suggest, then, a further addition: an act of war undertaken for a just cause which collaterally brings about the deaths of innocents will *not* be permissible if (1) the act is not materially conducive to the realization of the just cause; or (2) the conduciveness to the just cause is slight in comparison to the degree of collateral harm; or (3) the cause is not *grave* enough to outweigh the collateral harm.

These three components of proportionality must be distinguished because the justification of war includes all of them. The act of war must be conducive to the realization of the good; the harm done (the bad effect) should be kept to a minimum and, at any rate, must be quantitatively proportionate to the good effect, and the reason to fight must itself be normatively compelling. Compliance with these three cumulative conditions justifies war in general (i.e., *starting* a war) and any particular act of war.

We can now formulate an updated version of the doctrine. An act of war is justified if, and only if, it meets the following six conditions:

1. The warrior uses permissible means of fighting, that is, permissible weapons.
2. The warrior does not directly *intend* the deaths of civilians. If he foresees the deaths of civilians, he must try to minimize them, even at some cost to himself. He must transfer some risk to himself.
3. The warrior has a *just cause* (a) to start the war and (b) to perform that particular act of war. Only the defense of persons and free institutions counts as a just cause.
4. The act of war is materially conducive to the realization of the just cause. This rule condemns cases where the intensity of the act of war is *unnecessary* to the realization of the just cause. The rule applies *both* to the war as a whole and to particular acts of war.

5. The degree to which the act of war is materially conducive to the realization of the just cause is great enough to compensate for the collateral deaths of civilians.
6. The just cause mentioned in condition 3 must be *compelling enough* to compensate for the collateral harm. This condition recognizes that there are degrees of moral urgency, so not all just causes will justify collateral harm. The more compelling the cause, the lower will be the threshold for collateral harm.

A couple of comments are in order. We have omitted the requirement that the good effect should not come through the bad effect because it is contained in the requirement of intent in condition 2: a warrior who uses the innocent as means to achieve the good effect is not complying with the requirement that the bad effect should be intended only obliquely. We also have subdivided the proportionality requirement into three distinct requirements in accordance with the foregoing discussion. In particular, to the usual proportionality requirements discussed in the literature, we have added condition 6: the permissibility of war turns on whether the collateral harms that will inevitably occur are justified by the *moral urgency* of the cause. If the collateral harm is too great compared with how important it is to realize the good effect, the action will fail the test. Notice that unlike the test established by condition 5, the test in condition 6 is qualitative, not quantitative. It takes into account *how* just the cause is. If leaders of a free society wage a war against a powerful evil enemy bent on the destruction of everything decent, then the threshold for collateral harm is lower. If the cause is still just but less morally urgent (see, later, the example of a military intervention to help a neighboring country restore its democratic institutions after an unconstitutional coup), then the threshold for justifying collateral deaths will be higher.

The justice of the cause informs all moral questions in war. Under condition 5, the collateral killings, say, of 50,000 civilians, to gain a small military advantage is unjustified because it is *materially* disproportionate. Under condition 6, however, even a smaller number of collateral deaths may be unjustified if the cause of the war, while just, is not sufficiently compelling. The action will be *morally* disproportionate. There are degrees of moral urgency, and correspondingly, there should be degrees of moral permissibility of bad things done in our way to the realization of a moral goal. The upshot is that to justify an otherwise impermissible bad effect, it is not enough for the agent not to directly intend that bad effect. *Why* he causes the bad effect and *how* that effect measures (materially and morally) against the good one are decisive factors as well.

Here we must heed Sidgwick's warning that particular judgments about proportionality are extremely hard. In particular, the conditions laid down by the DDE are imprecise. The kinds of questions that a moral warrior asks himself are very hard to answer: Is the just cause *compelling* enough to justify the destruction this war will cause? How much will the war (or a particular act of war) contribute *causally* to the achievement of the good result? This is not surprising: few things are more difficult and momentous for any leader who cares about human life and liberal values than the decision to go to war. If there is anything certain about war, it is that there is no mechanical procedure readily available to identify the right thing to do. Having said that, we hope that we have identified the *kinds* of factors that responsible leaders and commanders should weigh in making these tough decisions.

Consider the following typology of *just* warriors that illustrate the several requirements of the DDE:

The Terrorist Warrior. A commander knows that a despicable tyrant who has led his country to a war of aggression against its neighbors is hiding somewhere in a city that the commander's forces now occupy. He reasonably predicts that the capture of this person will seriously demoralize the enemy and lead to victory. There are people in the town who know where the tyrant is hiding. In order to force people to come forward, the commander announces that he will start executing random civilians, including women and children, one per day, until someone turns the tyrant in. This action is prohibited notwithstanding the importance of the good effect (apprehending the tyrant and winning the war). The prohibition is not overruled by the justice of the cause. This commander violates condition 2.

The Bumbling Warrior. This commander aims only at permissible military targets in his pursuit of the just cause, say, defeat of the aggressor or tyrant. However, because of failures in intelligence, he has chosen to attack an empty depot lacking in military importance, and in so doing, he collaterally causes the deaths of noncombatants. This agent violates condition 4 because the act he initiates that obliquely brings about the bad effect is not materially conducive to realization of the just cause. Many people think that this is the reason why the 2003 invasion of Iraq was unjustified. If one thinks that the just cause there was to disable Saddam Hussein from using weapons of mass destruction against his neighbors, then the invasion was not conducive to realization of the just cause because, apparently, there were no weapons of mass destruction.[73]

The Out-of-Control Warrior. This commander leads his country's forces in repelling a minor invasion by his neighbor. He, too, aims only at military targets yet brings about collateral deaths of noncombatants. He knows that all he needs to do is to drive back the enemy forces, perhaps defeat them soundly to teach them a lesson. He is reasonably sure that the neighbor's little military adventure is unlikely to recur. However, he decides to go ahead and take the country's capital. In the course of this action, many noncombatants die. The action was unjustified because the oblique harm

---

[73] We say "apparently" because no one has explained to our satisfaction why *everyone* (U.S. intelligence, foreign intelligence, the United Nations) thought the WMDs were there. Even Saddam Hussein behaved as if he had WMDs. But we do not pursue the issue.

caused was too great in comparison with what the commander needed to do to realize the just cause (here the expulsion of the aggressor and the prevention of future attacks). To be sure, the commander achieved the good effect: the neighbor will not attack again. However, that goal could have been achieved with less destructive means. This agent violated condition 5: the degree to which the act of war was conducive to the good effect was not marginally great enough to compensate for the collateral harm. He used unnecessary violence.

The Overzealous Warrior. In a neighboring democratic country, a military junta has taken power by a coup d'état and suspended all constitutional guarantees. No massive killings are occurring. The democratic leaders, who have fled the country, ask a powerful neighbor to intervene to restore democratic order. The neighbor's army invades the country and, after a protracted war where it aims only at military targets (but knows it is causing collateral deaths), restores the ousted democratic leaders. However, when the smoke clears, it turns out that the civilian casualties have reached the tens of thousands. Arguably, this carnage cannot be justified by the urgency to restore democracy in the country. The cause is just and quite compelling but not compelling enough to compensate for the intense oblique harm. We must concede, however, that this is a hard case. Perhaps the citizens of the country have a duty to bear the costs of returning to democracy. But even here proportionality applies, unless one can assume that those who died did so willingly, as it were, as a sacrifice for victory.

The Humanitarian Liberator. Compare the preceding case of the overzealous warrior with the case of the commander who invades a neighboring country where the government and its allies are about to perpetrate genocide against an ethnic group. As in the previous examples, the commander fights justly and aims only at military targets. After a few weeks, the war is successful and stops the genocide. However, as in the preceding example, the war caused the collateral deaths of tens of thousands of noncombatants. Arguably, those deaths are justified in light of the moral urgency to stop the genocide. This commander has satisfied all six conditions of the DDE.

At this juncture, someone may object that conditions 5 and 6 are not really different. Both are based on a calculation of costs and benefits in terms of casualties. The distinction between the two cases arises because the cost in human lives of having an undemocratic government are smaller than the cost in human lives of genocide. For this objector, the cost-benefit calculation in terms of lives lost accounts for the moral difference between the two cases. We do not need some qualitative judgment about the moral urgency of the respective reasons to fight. We think, however, that the cogency of the evil in the latter case creates a greater moral urgency *even* if it turns out that, after all is said and done, the number of victims of the unconstitutional regime in the overzealous warrior case turned out to be greater than the eventual victims of genocide in this other case. The degree of *evil* is higher in the latter case, and that, we think, makes the military intervention more compelling. The notion of moral cost should include *both* qualitative and quantitative elements. To take another example, think about a state where the members of the dominant ethnic group have enslaved their ethnic rivals. There are no massive deaths here, and the enslavement may very well continue indefinitely in an atmosphere of civic "peace." Suppose that the slaves ask the neighboring state to help them. The neighbor then invades and frees the enslaved millions. In so doing, the invading army brings about collateral deaths of some number of civilians. These deaths cannot be justified by comparing their number with the number of deaths avoided because, by construction, the victims were enslaved, not killed. Plausibly, ending slavery is a sufficiently urgent moral cause that justified the intervention in this case notwithstanding the collateral harm.

To sum up: to be justified, a war must comply with the strictures of the DDE. The requirements are demanding, but if an act of war satisfies them, regrettable as the necessity to fight may be, it will escape the criticism of the pacifist.

POLITICAL ASSASSINATION AND TARGETED KILLINGS

In war, soldiers fighting for a just cause are allowed to kill enemy combatants. But if this is justified, what about killing the *leader* of the enemy, the real villain, if this will reduce the miseries of war?[74] If assassinating Hitler would have ended World War II, perhaps the Allies should have attempted it instead of embarking on a war that predictably had terrible moral costs. And assuming, controversially, the justice of the cause, perhaps the U.S.-led coalition in Iraq should have prevented the deaths of thousands of innocent persons in 2003 by killing Saddam Hussein, assuming that this action would have achieved the desired result.

"Assassination" is the extrajudicial intentional killing of an identified person for a political purpose. There are two main kinds of assassination. "Targeted killing" is state-sanctioned assassination; "tyrannicide" is assassination not sanctioned by the state (in the rest of this section, the term "assassination" refers only to targeted killing). Now killing is prima facie a deeply immoral act. The prohibition, however, has some exceptions. As we saw earlier, killing in war is permitted. Here we examine whether the liberal state can ever assassinate persons in the course of a justified war – whether it is a defensive war or a justified humanitarian intervention.

What can justify assassinations? To even begin to justify such a repugnant act, at least four conditions must be satisfied. First, the liberal state must be

---

[74] For a full treatment, see Fernando R. Tesón, "Targeted Killing in War and Peace: A Philosophical Analysis" in *Targeted Killings: Law and Morality in an Asymmetrical World*, Claire Finkelstein, Jens Ohlin, and Andrew Altman, eds. (Oxford University Press, 2012), 403

on the right side of a war. This can be a traditional symmetrical war, that is, a war against another state, or an asymmetrical war, such as the war against terrorists. It can be a defensive war – a response to aggression – or a non-defensive war, such as a humanitarian intervention. Second, large numbers of innocent persons must face a deadly threat. This condition is crucial because it makes assassination justifiable only to save innocent persons. Third, the targeted person must be *culpable* of posing that threat, a true villain. The assassin is not allowed to kill someone affiliated with the villain if that person is not sufficiently culpable (but the assassin may target a sufficiently culpable henchman if the other conditions are satisfied). And fourth, alternatives to assassination, such as capture, must be unavailable, maybe because they are likely to result in the deaths of those innocent persons. Here again, the justification emphasizes that assassination is an extreme measure to avoid deaths of two groups of innocent persons: those the enemy itself is threatening and those the liberal state foresees will collaterally die as the price of victory. Saving the innocent, then, alone may justify assassination.[75] This argument does not condone assassination just to achieve victory or restore freedom or just in case the expected benefits outweigh the expected costs.

We saw that just war theory normally condones two kinds of killing. Soldiers may permissibly kill enemy soldiers; in addition (and disturbingly), soldiers may permissibly bring about the deaths of noncombatants, many of them innocent, as long as the soldiers do not directly aim at those victims, that is, as long as the deaths are a proportionate side effect of the destruction of a legitimate military target. But if sometimes incidentally causing the killing of *innocents* is justified, it seems *a fortiori* that killing a *culpable* person to avoid those other deaths not only should be justified but also preferable.

A possible way to justify assassination is this: given the permissibility of killing enemy combatants, assassinations can be defended by treating the political leader of the enemy (the one who plans or directs aggressive war, say) as a combatant, perhaps as the enemy's commander-in-chief. In this case, the argument goes, he can permissibly be killed.[76] Because here assassination is morally equivalent to killing in combat, this argument condones assassination for similar reasons, that is, just to prevail in a just war. This rationale does not require that the failure to kill the leader cause the deaths of large numbers of innocent persons because the leader is treated just like any enemy soldier. But, if part of the rationale to allow killing of enemy soldiers is that they are threatening us, maybe assassination cannot be justified in this way. If the target of assassination is unarmed and removed from the battlefield, assassination may be morally problematic, especially if the liberal state has some options, such as arresting him (see later).

---

[75] Andrew Altman and Christopher Wellman, *A Liberal Theory of International Justice* (Oxford University Press, 2009), 116–21.

[76] Stephen Kershnar, "The Moral Argument for a Policy of Assassination," *Reason Papers* 27 (2004), 43–66.

Asymmetrical war against terrorists poses further problems (assuming the war to be just) because the enemies have chosen not to identify themselves as such, thus preventing the laws of war to operate.[77] Under the conventional rules, whereas the conventional enemy can be either killed in combat or captured, the terrorist can only be captured. He claims combatant license to kill others but civilian immunity when the army is looking for him. This does not seem satisfactory. Writers who justify assassinating terrorists think this permission solves the problem by becoming the functional equivalent of killing in combat. Notice here again that this argument is more permissive than the first because it does not require that the assassination be the indispensable means of avoiding the deaths of large numbers of innocent persons. Killing terrorists raises a host of other problems, however. Typically, terrorists lead normal lives while they are "off duty": they do not camp with other terrorists, nor are they deployed in military or similar formations. They live civilian lives. As a result, most attempts to target them will wreak havoc on civilian populations, especially if assassinations are extended (as they would be in symmetrical war) to persons who harbor or aid the terrorists.

All arguments for assassination must account for the justice of the cause. Of course, the war has to be just to allow those killings. But *how* just? Fighting for democracy is a just fight, but less compelling than fighting to resist genocide or aggression. The test for the permissibility of assassination, then, must factor the degree of moral urgency of the aim in the name of which the killing is contemplated. The less urgent the cause is, the less likely assassination will be justified. Thus the justice of the cause plays an analogous role here, as it did in our previous discussion of collateral killings: the stronger the urgency to realize the cause, the more likely assassination (under the conditions just specified) *and* collateral killings can be justified.

Such is the case for the moral permissibility of assassination. The argument, however, is far from conclusive. What are the arguments against assassination? Possibly four. The first is epistemic: the assassin cannot possibly *know* that the assassination will bring about the desired result. Thus, for example, assassinating Saddam Hussein as a way to avoid the 2003 invasion might or might not have prevented the deaths of large numbers of innocents (in fact, violent insurgency continued *after* Saddam's execution). The objection is stronger in the case of the assassination of a terrorist who is not a notorious leader (although, as we saw, this act may be defended as a kind of killing in combat). As noted earlier, targeting terrorists poses difficult epistemic problems, not the least of which is identifying them as such.

The second objection rests on considerations of political virtue. A liberal government is not supposed to assassinate people. It is supposed to conduct

---

[77] Seumas Miller, *Terrorism and Counter-Terrorism* (Oxford, UK: Blackwell, 2009), 139–45; Michael Gross, *Moral Dilemmas of Modern War* (Cambridge University Press, 2010), 104–9.

itself in accordance with the civic virtues for which it stands. We can think of an analogous objection to tyrannicide. The would-be assassin who seeks restoration of democracy and human rights may be deterred by virtue considerations: the liberal, humane society that he seeks to restore is, perhaps, incompatible with assassination.

The third objection denies that assassination is ever necessary to achieve the desired result. If the assassins can reach their victim, they can presumably apprehend him. Now either the victim surrenders or he resists arrest. If he surrenders, then it is morally impermissible to kill him; his captors should bring him to justice. If, however, the victim resists arrest, then the assassins can permissibly kill him under the rules applicable to resistance to justified arrests. This view condemns killing a person, no matter how culpable, without giving him a chance to surrender. Yet sometimes surrender is not possible. Suppose that all the right conditions apply (killing the person will prevent innocent deaths and the victim is morally culpable), but the target is unreachable. The only way to kill him is shooting from afar or using drones or similar devices. In this case, the objection we are considering is inapplicable. Yet the objection would have succeeded in severely limiting the instances of permissible assassination. Assassination is never permitted when the victim can be captured.

The fourth objection is that assassination is incompatible with the transparency and trust that will make a lasting peace possible in the aftermath of war.[78] The idea is that the way armies fight decisively shapes the behavior of victor and vanquished after the war. If the victor, who had right on his side, succeeded by assassinating enemy leaders (as opposed to fighting in accordance with the rules), presumably the vanquished will have no compunction in conducting a guerrilla war that also includes assassinations and other terrorist tactics. We doubt that this objection has much weight, though. The guerrilla fighters, loyal to the defeated regime, by definition supported a tyrant or an aggressor (the unjust side in the war). If so, they are not likely to have ethical constraints anyway. Refraining from assassination as a way to give an example of virtue is unlikely to work too well on such people.

Assassination is puzzling because even in the confined circumstances in which it might be morally permitted our consequentialist intuitions collide with our deontological intuitions. *Someone* has to do the deed, and it is plausible to think that in an important sense the act is wrong regardless of consequences. Moreover, the conditions for the moral permissibility of assassination are so strict that it will rarely be justified. For this reason, some have argued that liberal democracies should enact a blanket *legal* prohibition against assassination – perhaps to be waived by the (liberal) government only in the extreme circumstances described earlier.

[78] See Kant, *Perpetual Peace*, 110.

A NOTE ON *JUS POST BELLUM*

What is the right policy for the just victorious side in a war? Recent experiences in Afghanistan, Iraq, and elsewhere have rekindled this difficult question. If a war is successful in countering aggression or stopping genocide, should the victorious army leave immediately? Or is military occupation permissible? Does it depend on the circumstances? Which? As we write these lines, an army called ISIS is terrorizing entire populations in Iraq and Syria. Suppose that the only way to end this nightmare is for the United States and its allies to defeat ISIS and then to occupy those countries for a long time, build democratic institutions, strengthen local forces, and shore up the economy so as to prevent forever the resurgence of that terrible threat. What would be the objection? Perhaps, as John Stuart Mill argued, that free institutions are valuable only if the native populations can build them themselves.[79] Only then will they learn their value and muster the courage to defend them. We can extend Mill's dictum to *jus post bellum* and say that the only valuable test of a people's having become fit for good institutions is that they or a sufficient portion of them are willing to brave labor and danger to build them. If foreigners do it for them, they spoil them, as it were. But what is wrong with spoiling the vanquished by helping them get back on their feet? This is what the Allies did with Germany and Japan, with good results. So Mill's dictum seems a tad dogmatic: "[O]nly the natives can build their institutions because their future is at stake" is a tautology or else a non sequitur. Sometimes we need help to achieve good outcomes, even if they are *our* good outcomes.

We cannot here offer a full theory of *jus post bellum*,[80] but we think that the general approach of the victor should be forward and not backward looking. Some authors have suggested that a main task of the occupier is to purge "dangerous, corrupt, or culpable remnants of the previous system."[81] We agree that sometimes bringing the major war criminals to justice is proper and necessary, but we think that for the most part *jus post bellum* should focus on the future and not the past. The main task of the victorious power is to help build strong and lasting free institutions. At this stage of this book, it should be clear that free institutions include at least three things: the establishment of solid order to prevent a fall into anarchy; the establishment of political and civil freedoms, especially by creating an independent judiciary; and the establishment of robust markets to enable prosperity. Eradication of the bad economic policies of the past is as important as eradication of the vestiges of tyranny. How much the task will take cannot be decided in a vacuum, and all factors should be considered in making such decisions. And yes, there will be times when the

---

[79] John Stuart Mill, "A Few Words on Non-Intervention" [1859]; available at: http://www.libertarian.co.uk/lapubs/forep/forep008.pdf.

[80] See generally *Jus Post Bellum: Mapping the Normative Foundations*, Carsten Stahn, Jennifer S. Easterday, and Jens Iverson, eds. (Oxford University Press, 2014).

[81] Yvonne Chiu, "Liberal Lustration," *Journal of Political Philosophy* 19 (2011), 440.

situation will be hopeless. In such cases, there is little to do but withdraw and test Mill's dictum. If the occupiers could not do the trick, perhaps the natives, unaided, ultimately will. Or perhaps that society is destined to sink further into misery.

INTERNATIONAL LAW AND THE MORALITY OF WAR

This book is concerned with global *justice*, not law, and this chapter addresses the *morality* of war, not its legality. Still, someone can object to our argument for the morality of certain nonaggressive wars, such as humanitarian interventions, as follows: states have a content-independent obligation to obey international law, even if the law is morally incomplete or defective. This is so because international law fulfills an important coordination role in the relations among nations. Since international law bans the use of force except in self-defense, governments who intervene by force are committing a wrong, even if they have a valid moral reason to intervene – say, preventing genocide. International law, as a convention, plays an independent role in the evaluation of state action. Therefore, the fact of violation counts against humanitarian intervention even if the latter achieves a morally desirable outcome.

This argument is unconvincing. First, it rests on a dubious premise. The argument proceeds with great assurance about what international law stipulates, as if it were undisputedly clear that humanitarian intervention is unlawful. Yet the view that positive international law prohibits humanitarian intervention is itself controversial.[82] It springs from a specific interpretation of treaties and state practice that already presupposes the importance of preserving the status quo. State practice is at the very least ambivalent on the question of humanitarian intervention, so any interpretation of that practice (for or against) has to rely on values. There is no such thing as a "state practice" staring at the interpreter and yielding a legal rule, especially in this area. Diplomatic history has to be interpreted. If this is correct, the positivist rejection of humanitarian intervention is far from objective or undisputed. It is informed by a set of values that privileges the preservation of governments and political regimes over the protection of human rights. Legal analysis is not conceptually autonomous in contested areas such as this one, so the morality of war has an important role to play in *determination* of the law.

Second, international law does not map out the morality of the *jus ad bellum*. Unlike the positive laws of *jus in bello*, the legal materials pertaining to *jus ad bellum* are highly indeterminate. Essentially, the critic we are considering has, as we noted, a binary view of the law of use of force. To him, wars fall into two kinds: justified wars (self-defense and Security Council–authorized actions) and acts of aggression (everything else). He overlooks the range of justifications (or lack thereof) for war that a proper philosophical analysis may yield. This view

---

[82] This question has been discussed *in extenso* in Tesón, *Humanitarian Intervention*.

of the law is crude and simplistic, so it cannot provide a principled basis for the argument we are considering. There is no reason to accept that this binary view should inform the grave decisions about life and death that governments must make when facing the prospects of war. In other words, not only is the critics' understanding of international law dubious as a matter of positive interpretation, but it is also philosophically unsophisticated. This fact weakens the *pro tanto* obligation to obey international law that animates the objection.

There is a final answer to this objection. As we saw earlier, whether humanitarian intervention is legally prohibited is controversial. But let us assume, *gratia argumentandi*, that international law does prohibit humanitarian interventions. The intervener, let's suppose, would be violating international law. But humanitarian interventions are meant to put an end to *other* egregious violations of international law: genocide, crimes against humanity, and so on. Thus it is not a question of violating or not violating the law. It is a question of which illegal situation we prefer. Do we prefer the illegality of intervention that ends (and because it ends) the illegality of genocide? Or do we prefer the illegality of genocide undisturbed? Whatever legal position we take, we will end up tolerating a violation of *some* fundamental rule of international law. Either the government intervenes and puts an end to the massacres, in which case it violates the prohibition of war, or it abstains from intervening, in which case it (and the lawyers who support it) will tolerate the major crime of genocide. The maxim "other things being equal, states must obey international law" can hardly mean "other things being equal, states must obey international law even if doing so enables an ongoing and considerably more egregious violation of international law." Of course, the morality of intervention is governed, as we saw, by the cumulative requirements of just cause and proportionality. Tolerating tyranny may be the right thing to do if intervening would be disproportionate, where proportionality is understood in the nonutilitarian way discussed earlier.

The obligation to abide by international law, then, does not help the noninterventionist. His position depends on a dogmatic judgment that an international war is always worse than tyranny or anarchy. But this, of course, cannot be determined a priori for all cases. At least sometimes the cost of military action to stop genocide or other massive assault on persons is sufficiently low to warrant its permissibility.[83]

---

[83] The modern example is the Rwanda genocide of 1994. As former President Clinton recently admitted, the United States could have saved 300,000 lives had it intervened at the start of the genocide. See Kiran Moodley, "Bill Clinton: We Could Have Saved 300,00 Lives in Rwanda," CNBC, March 13, 2013; available at: http://www.cnbc.com/id/100546207 (accessed January 7, 2014).

9

Beyond Justice at a Distance

The persistent theme of this book is that the first precept of justice toward distant others (not to mention those who are close at hand) is to *leave them alone*. Much of the misery of the world's downtrodden is attributable to violation of this precept. The lion's share of baleful interference is produced domestically, but wealthy countries are not without their own share of blame for creating avoidable distress. It is not acceptable to block trade activities that cross borders or peaceful mobility by persons who wish to work, study, or reside in a country other than the one whose citizenship they hold. Nor is assistance tendered to foreign despots in service of oppressing their own nationals consistent with respect for rights. We have also insisted that these wrongs to foreign nationals simultaneously violate the rights of nationals. A Michigan employer who is prevented from hiring a willing Mexican national is interfered with in his projects just as much as if he were not allowed to contract with someone from Massachusetts. Trade protectionism harms would-be consumers of goods produced abroad. And so on. These restraints are so drearily familiar that they are not apt to impinge on our consciences with the vivacity of a mugging, yet our policies toward distant others – and toward our own conationals – constitute literally millions of muggings annually.

However, although noninterference is the first precept of justice, there are others. One is compensation for prior violations. For example, a wedding party rained on by errant drone missiles deserves recompense for harms done. This sort of case is clear-cut. More arguable are claims to compensation for historical wrongs such as American slavery or African colonialism. Our view is that these are doubtful for at least two reasons. First and most important, many of those who were the direct victims of these practices have long since passed from the scene, so it is beyond the capacity of any earthly justice to make them whole. Second, the assessment of historical counterfactuals is pervasively conjectural and thus is not capable of strongly supporting claims for compensation.

Let us assume that, say, French occupation of Algeria constituted wrongs to the inhabitants of that territory; do contemporary Algerians stand as victims of that episode or perhaps as beneficiaries? These questions are grist for the mill of historians but are not likely to persuade taxpayers of erstwhile colonial powers that they are obliged to pay the alleged debts incurred by their grandparents.

A second additional requirement of justice can be to provide easy rescue of those in distress. A ship that encounters a foundering craft is not at liberty to proceed blithely on its course instead of pausing to lend assistance. To the extent, however, that the danger is chronic rather than acute or that an attempt to rescue would be significantly perilous to the benefactor, the existence of a duty of justice becomes less plausible. This does not mean that there is no moral case to be made for positive assistance, but it will occupy some terrain other than justice, for example, compassion or generosity. In this final chapter we wish to venture onto that terrain. Even if, strictly speaking, the rich countries of the West (and, increasingly, the East) are not *obligated* to extend positive provision to the distressed abroad, is it not unseemly narrow to justify turning one's back on such legalistic grounds? After all, like justice, compassion, too, is a virtue, and its scope extends beyond national borders. Philosophers may have reason to scrutinize moral foundations, but is not what properly matters most to ordinary citizens that they do the right thing? The question to be taken up here is whether that right thing incorporates the provision of aid.

VARIETIES OF AID

Although we normally think of *foreign aid* as a transaction between governments, transfers also can be made from governments to private parties, private parties to private parties, and even private parties to governments. These total four distinct species of aid to be appraised. In fact, the possibilities are more extensive than this because among the actors in the aid arena are organizations that are theoretically nongovernmental (NGOs) but which often are involved at arm's length (or considerably closer) to state agencies. [Additionally, either under the auspices of the United Nations or through other international protocols, intergovernmental organizations (IGOs) also serve as aid providers.] A case for provision of aid is incomplete; it is necessary also to consider who the providers should be and who the recipients. Most development aid is currently extended by governmental or quasi-governmental agencies; it totaled a bit over $135 billion for the year 2011.[1] Under one accounting, worldwide private philanthropy amounts to less than half this amount, but if remittances

---

[1] See   http://data.worldbank.org/indicator/DT.ODA.ALLD.CD/countries/1W?display=default. This figure is somewhat arbitrary in that it incorporates judgments about how to include loans extended at below-market rates and complicated issues of distinguishing development from other purposes that grantors may have.

are included, the figure dwarfs official aid.[2] As might be expected, a vast literature appraising the effectiveness of aid has been generated, and as might also be expected, these appraisals differ markedly. A number of studies find a positive or conditionally positive correlation between aid and economic growth, whereas others offer a bleaker assessment of zero efficacy or worse.[3] It is neither our ambition nor our capability to offer a meta-analysis of these studies here. Instead, we take as a given that this remains much-disputed territory. In the presence of such empirical murkiness, we argue that there is a strong presumption in most circumstances for preferring private aid to state-sponsored aid.

Why give aid at all? The indicated answer is *to do some good.* Yet this raises the further question: *good for whom?* Even aid packages ostensibly directed toward relieving the distress of the world's least-well-off may feature other rationales no less important. This is especially true with regard to aid packages extended by governments. From Thucydides to the present, theorists of international relations have taken pains to emphasize that states act to advance their own self-interest, offering up copious amounts of lip service to humane ideals but only dribs and drabs of genuine sacrifice for the well-being of other polities with which they interact. One need not be a card-carrying political realist, though, to surmise that even when states do act altruistically, this is not the full extent of their motivations. Advancement of their material interests is unlikely to be far from the surface. This is most obvious in the case of military aid meant to buttress allies against potential foes, but whether via guns or butter, realpolitik must be served. This goes a long way toward explaining why so-called development aid since World War II generated so distressingly little development. Especially in the context of the cold war, humanitarian assistance for completely disinterested purposes was virtually impossible. No matter how stunted and dysfunctional a country might be, better to enroll it in one's own camp than to see it fall under the influence of the other side. And if the choice is between aid that serves the well-being of the distressed and aid that cements allegiance, only an exceptionally optimistic observer would predict that the former predominates. Now, some two decades on from the demise of that bipolar world, it remains the case that diplomatic imperatives cannot but affect the nature of transactions among nations.

That governments have agendas does not imply that private parties are immune from self-regarding motives. However, these are likely to be comparatively benign. A philanthropy that is devoted, say, to combating African river blindness will prosper only if it competes successfully in the market

---

[2] See the Hudson Institute, 2012 *Index of Global Philanthropy and Remittances*, 15; available at: http://www.hudson.org/content/researchattachments/attachment/1015/2012indexofglobalphilanthropyandremittancs.pdf (accessed December 28, 2014).

[3] For an overview of the literature, see Christopher Coyne, *Doing Bad by Doing Good* (Stanford, CA: Stanford University Press, 2013), 51–4. Particularly useful insight concerning causes of aid successes and failure is provided in William Easterly, *The White Man's Burden* (New York: Penguin, 2006).

for charitable benefactors who are especially concerned about global health outcomes. Honoring conspicuous donors at a black tie dinner may be a useful tactic, but probably some demonstrable inroads against the disease also will be required to keep them coming back. That is, there is a strong complementarity between the interests of benefactors and those of beneficiaries. Complementarity does not ensure that effective means to desired ends will be taken, but it does suggest that there will be a strong impetus to focus on those ends and to seek to distinguish between those means that actually advance them and those that may look good on paper but that, when put to the test, disappoint. When a governmental aid program stumbles with regard to advancing its ostensible humanitarian ends, however, it may nonetheless be nicely advancing its own internal bureaucratic imperatives. Indeed, failure may be the greatest success of all insofar as it supports the case for an expanded budget.

The case of Egypt is instructive. For more than thirty years, that country has been among the major recipients of American aid, with the total extended in excess of $30 billion. Not all that amount was for development; a significant fraction was earmarked for "peace and security," a loosely defined category that ranges from operations against drug smugglers to supporting the military forces of friendly countries. In 2011, the amount budgeted for peace and security was $1.3 billion out of a total $1.5 billion aid appropriation.[4] Despite the extended history of aid, Egypt's record of development has been distinctly mediocre. Its success with regard to peace is more debatable. On the one hand, the great desideratum of no further warring against Israel after 1979 was achieved. Moreover, the hold of the Soviet Union over Egyptian policy that was so strong under the Nasser regime was progressively relaxed in favor of the United States. On the other hand, political stasis under the 1981–2011 presidency of Hosni Mubarak frustrated aspirations of the Egyptian people and stoked animosities that erupted during Arab Spring. How, then, should this overall aid experience be evaluated? Despite official U.S. pronouncements suggesting otherwise,[5] we believe it fair to conclude that development assistance played second fiddle to other considerations and did little for the well-being of ordinary Egyptians.

In response, it could be argued that generalizations from the case of Egypt are illegitimate, that Egypt is a special case precisely because of its location as a linchpin in one of the world's great hotspots. Diplomacy necessarily trumps all other matters. We concede the point but observe that diplomatic considerations, whether overwhelmingly powerful or latent, are ubiquitous. To a greater or lesser extent, they influence all else. Governments are simply unable

[4] Brian Wingfield, "Making Sense of U. S. Foreign Aid to Egypt and Elsewhere," *Forbes*, January 29, 2011; available at: http://www.forbes.com/sites/brianwingfield/2011/01/29/making-sense-of-u-s-foreign-aid-to-egypt-and-elsewhere.

[5] See http://egypt.usaid.gov/en/aboutus/Pages/usaid_egypt_history.aspx.

to make development abroad their first priority; they have too much else to worry about.

The practice of country-to-country development aid rests on something of a paradox. Either a country's population is economically advancing or it is not. If it is on a growth track, then aid is not necessary. If it is stagnant, the likely cause is deficient local institutions featuring counterproductive policies and predatory politicians. In this case, aid is hardly likely to be productive. Indeed, to the extent that it augments the resources available to those who have already given evidence of their incompetence or venality, their position is reinforced. Theoretically, disbursements could be used as a lever to elicit good behavior, but this requires the donor nation not only to know which structural readjustments are called for but also to have the gumption to insist on their imposition subject to withdrawal of support. If along with its humanitarian inclinations an aim of the donor is to remain on diplomatically good terms with the recipient country, authoritative quid pro quos are not likely. Rather, each side will agree that much has been learned and that they will do better in the future. There will then be time for photo opportunities and press releases.

Because the natural interlocutor of a government is another government, states are essentially trammeled in their pursuit of humanitarian activities. Almost always they are precluded from bypassing official channels to engage directly with their would-be clients. To do otherwise is an affront to sovereignty. Many of the countries that are recipients of aid have long memories of suffering impositions by colonial powers; they are not apt to welcome reruns of that experience. Therefore, although donors have their own ideas concerning which interventions are appropriate, to a greater or lesser extent they must step lightly and take in-country instructions from the host government – the party that has been supervising the ongoing futility that the aid is meant to counter. If that government is seriously motivated to advance the welfare of its population, then it might be willing to own up to its prior incompetence and shift course, but such humility on the part of presidents-for-life is unusual. More likely is that old habits and relationships will persist unchanged. It is in the interests of the receiving government that the flow of aid resources continues unabated, but it will also be in the interest of the functionaries of the aid agency that they be permitted to carry on business as usual. This is not meant as a cynical critique of those who staff aid bureaucracies. We are comfortable in supposing that the vast majority are genuinely motivated by humanitarian concerns. They realize, though, that they operate within constraints, the most significant of which is that without the cooperation of host governments, they cannot continue their operations. That current efforts are largely fruitless is a matter for regret, but perhaps they will improve in the future – either under current leadership or perhaps that of the next set of generals who assume power.

As noted earlier, the question of how (un)successful official development aid has been has generated an enormous literature. That on balance results have been negative may perhaps be an overly pessimistic assessment, but it hardly constitutes a ringing endorsement of some $3 trillion in spending that it may after all have done some good. About the best that is said about the activity is that over the years its practitioners have learned something about what works and what does not; this time, as the saying goes, will be different.[6] Perhaps, although a decades-long history of the fruits of aid being oversold prompts caution. Countering disappointment induced by aid failure are the records of many countries launched into a trajectory of growth despite little or no official aid.[7] It is simply not the case that hundreds of millions of people are consigned to lives of destitution unless the rich nations of the world fork over massive sums to lift them out of distress. Rather, receipt of aid money is consistent with unabated misery, and the absence of aid is consistent with economic advance.

If aid transfers were necessary and sufficient to ratchet distressed populations out of misery, then there would be a strong case for the existence of a duty of rescue. Because such transfers are neither necessary nor sufficient, however, there can be no such duty. Rather, the relevant moral obligation is that which obtains between governments and their citizens. Individuals may permissibly be taxed to support necessary and proper functions of government such as defense, provision of public goods, and maintenance of a basic safety net; they are not an open-ended piggy bank for whatever flights of fancy may have captured the affections of ruling elites. If transfers are not mandatory as a matter of justice, if they are of dubious efficacy in improving the lot of hard-pressed populations, then they are strictly impermissible. States may not permissibly extract resources from their own citizens to send abroad on wild goose chases.

American citizens seem to be cognizant of the morally dubious status of foreign aid. Routinely, when polled, they declare it their least preferred governmental program.[8] Critics respond that this result bespeaks ignorance and insensitivity, but we reject that verdict. As the next section argues, moral sensitivity to the world's most distressed can and does take other forms than state provision, with American private citizens near the front of the pack. And although it is unarguably the case that few nonspecialists are apt to be conversant with the intricacies of federal aid policy, citizens' sense that it is not among

---

[6] For example, Jeffrey Sachs, *The End of Poverty* (New York: Penguin Books, 2005).

[7] See Easterly, *White Man's Burden*, 346–7, for a table listing the ten best and ten worst per capita growth rates, 1980–2002. The median aid/GDP ratio for the former is 0.23 percent; for the latter it is 10.98 percent. This should not be read as an indicator that aid causes low growth; more plausible is that low growth (and regress) prompts donors to provide greater quantities of aid. Without investigating complex questions of causality, one plain moral is that with regard to development, aid is neither indispensable nor a panacea.

[8] Foreign aid is identified by more citizens than any other federal program in a recent Pew Research poll as the one they would prefer to see cut. See https://www.devex.com/en/news/poll-foreign-aid-cut-tops-america-s-priority/80388. They also tend to overestimate by a factor of 10 the percentage of the budget devoted to foreign aid. This may explain why it is so unpopular. Alternatively, its perceived flaws may make it loom larger in citizens' eyes. For documentation of citizen ignorance, see http://www.worldpublicopinion.org/pipa/articles/brunitedstatescanadara/670.php.

the more notably successful governmental undertakings is well grounded. We do not expect all the readers of these pages to share our views concerning the proper boundaries for limited government, but under any reasonable estimation of bang for the buck, aid expenditures are unjustifiable.

Some will take these reflections to be a council of despair. Because the aid industry has been in an extended slump, are we to give up on raising the lot of the world's most distressed people? Our answer is no. To reject a program is not the same as rejecting the ends that the program aims to serve. Rather, it is to say that different means are required. With a few exceptions to be identified later, humanitarian aid is a business in which governments do not belong. There are, though, nonstate alternatives to which we now turn.

PRIVATIZING AID

In Chapters 4 through 6 we have argued that liberties to travel and to transact do not abruptly come to an end at national borders. Neither does basic compassion. People who are hungry, whether they live next door or across the world, need food, and if they are unable to secure it through their own activities, then they stand in need of the assistance of others. Charities operating internationally can, at the margin, make a difference. The private aid arena is a disparate lot including the Red Cross, Oxfam, Doctors Without Borders, the Gates Foundation, and dozens of less well-known religious and philanthropic organizations whose stated purpose is to relieve distress around the world. To advance that end, they draw on the resources of millions of donors. Their efforts are admirable, although it is important not to overestimate the good they are likely to do. Generosity from abroad is not an antidote to wretched domestic institutions, but in some cases it can effect improvements at the margin. For those whose situation is intolerable, this matters.

At least six reasons count in favor of private philanthropy as the preferred alternative to state-operated aid. First and foremost, it is *voluntary*. No moral credit accrues to someone from whom resources are coercively extracted to serve some purpose that may or may not be her own. Choice, though, gives effect to one's identity as a morally responsible agent. Through one's decision to direct one's time, energy, or money to a particular cause, one makes a statement about what is personally valued. In the best case, one's activity is efficacious toward advancing that valued goal, but in any event, one has *intended* the desired outcome and *expressed support* for it. This is the sense in which choice is morally eloquent. There is, then, some irony in the position of those who declare that tendering foreign aid is a moral imperative but then play down the importance of individually motivated acts of assistance as against the workings of impersonal policy. Individual human beings can be generous or callous, but states cannot. If acting well matters, then there is prima facie reason to support practices in which decision making is delegated to the level of personal choice rather than filtered through the workings of a ponderous bureaucracy. This is, of course, a defeasible conclusion; some determinations – defense policy, regulation of the money supply, what to serve at state dinners for visiting worthies – cannot reasonably be left to choice by private individuals. But concerning those choices for which one size does not fit all and reasonable individuals differ, it is dubious policy to impose from above and all the more so when that top-down decision making displays an extended history of unsatisfactory outcomes. A skeptic may inquire why if devolution of decision making is appropriate for foreign philanthropic efforts that it should not be repatriated domestically so as to replace various of the functions of the welfare state. We acknowledge the logic of this criticism.

A second and related point is that private philanthropy gives effect to distinct *ideals*. Those who donate may have in mind not simply a goal of improving overall well-being but specific conceptions of how that well-being is best understood. Consider well-known financier George Soros, who, in his capacity as philanthropist, has given away billions of dollars to causes he finds personally meaningful. These include major benefactions to newly decommunized Eastern Europe, including most especially endowment of the Central European University in Budapest. His many philanthropic and political activities in the United States as well as Europe cohere as expressions of a Popperian commitment to the ideal of an open society.[9] Soros' political and economic views are highly controversial. This would be a liability in an official state operation but is entirely appropriate for private parties endeavoring to change the world for the better as they so judge. Few of us are in a position to operate on the level of a Soros, but even those of modest means enjoy a liberty to direct their contributions toward what they find meaningful.

Previously, we glanced at Egypt's history as an aid recipient. Like Egypt, Israel has persistently been at or near the top of the listing of beneficiaries of U.S. aid, and as with Egypt, that money has been directed primarily toward security needs. Unlike Egypt, however, Israel also has been on the receiving end of a great deal of private aid. For many decades, even before there was such a state as Israel, dollars from the Jewish diaspora streamed into that nation's forerunner. The funds supported economic development but also cultural enhancement, planting trees, a wide range of humanitarian initiatives, and yes, defense. The donors were of one mind with regard to the need to create and sustain a Jewish homeland, but beyond that, they were divided along lines of religious observance, political philosophy, willingness to pursue territorial compromise with Arab populations, and much more. It is not extreme to say that absent the support generated from this broth of dynamic ideals, there would not exist a state of Israel today. And if it did exist, it would not be as economically dynamic. At its founding, Israel confronted severe economic obstacles. One was the need to allocate much of its budget to settling impecunious immigrants and defending its borders against threats from uniformly

---

[9] Soros' statement of principles can be found at http://www.georgesoros.com.

hostile neighbors. Another was the socialist ideology of its founding gener-ation. The drag that these created on growth would have been considerably worse but for external transfers. Aid from the United States and reparations from West Germany supplied much-needed capital, but private donations were crucial for Israel to come into its own. Many of the diaspora Jewish donors had amassed fortunes through distinctively capitalistic means, and their willingness to put their financial acumen where their hearts were led Israel in an ascent from middle-income status to membership as of 2010 in the elite Organisation for Economic Co-operation and Development (OECD) club of the world's most economically successful nations.[10]

A third factor recommending decentralized private philanthropy is its *edu-cational* superiority to monolithic collectivization. When our governments adopt hundreds of policies about which we know little, there is no incentive to concern ourselves with their ramifications. It is literally and figuratively not our business. When, however, we are the ones to whom appeals for support are addressed, then it is indeed very much our business whether to respond with aye or nay. Even to block one's ears so as not to hear pleas for assistance is a gen-uine choice that can be grist for the mill of reflection. The knowledge that one *could* have done otherwise may prompt consideration of whether one *should* have done otherwise. Or it may not. We do not claim that expanded choice is a magic elixir for promoting reflective consciousness; the human capacity to remain dully disengaged should never be underestimated. But if individuals are precluded from playing an active role in significant undertakings other than casting the odd ballot every two or four years, then their moral consciousness will to that extent be stunted. It is not only distant others who bear the costs, so too does the capacity of individuals to engage in responsible citizenship.

Against this it can be argued that the point of aid is to relieve the distress of the world's poor, not to serve as a civics lesson for those comfortably off. It is, of course, true that the point of aid is aiding, but it does not follow that other complementary goals should be excluded from consideration. *What is done* matters, but *how it is done* matters, too. If there were strong reason to believe that state enterprises are uniquely capable of alleviating global distress, then the case for retaining official aid bureaucracies would be powerful. If anything, however, evidence points to the contrary. States have enjoyed limited success meeting their stated humanitarian goals, and neither have they done well by engaging their own citizens in morally meaningful activity at a global level. Therefore, it is appropriate on several grounds to question the hegemony of the status quo.

A fourth reason to prefer private philanthropy is the fruitfulness of *diversity*. Just as competitive markets provide incentives to learn how to do things better,

---

[10] A useful overview of Israel's economic development is provided by Nadav Halevi, "A Brief Economic History of Modern Israel," Economic History Association; available at: http://eh.net/encyclopedia/a-brief-economic-history-of-modern-israel/.

a variety of independent aid organizations each aiming to do at least as well as their collaborators/competitors in bringing resources to bear on problems encourages discovery. Organizations that cannot demonstrate achievement are liable to lose the support of donors, whereas those that can point to concrete results will attract greater support. If there are numerous "products" on the humanitarian relief market, we can hope that those that function most effectively will grasp a greater share of that market.

It is a bit too glib to affirm that what works to achieve efficiencies for vendors of cell phones, steak dinners, and shoes will similarly make aid more efficient because there is a fundamental discontinuity between the two. In the former case, those who purchase the item are the ones who receive its benefits, whereas those who fund aid services are not their ultimate beneficiaries. (Compare the inefficiencies, amusing or otherwise, that accompany the practice of buying Christmas presents for others.) It is possible, then, that the motives of providers are not perfectly aligned with the interests of the recipients. That duly acknowledged, it nonetheless seems clear that a world of many competing private agencies will more closely approximate the dynamics of economic markets than will state agencies that compete for funding not against other and potentially more adroit aid providers but rather against other departments of the government that covet whatever appropriations are up for grabs.

Fifth, private aid organizations are less subject to *conflicting organizational imperatives* than are state agencies. Diplomatic concerns of necessity figure centrally for governments but have little or no purchase on private organizations. Many pages would be required to list the names and crimes of all the tyrants and kleptocrats who have been lavishly supported by the United States, allegedly to spur development in their countries but where the bottom-line imperative was alliance building. This is a deplorable record but is in an odd way defensible. The primary rationale of states is to serve the interests of their own citizens, and if these should conflict with the interests of foreign nationals, then it is proper to give priority to the former. This is not to endorse the various adventures and imbroglios that America's strategists conjured over previous decades, but this is a matter of our political leaders' competence, not their proper calling. Aid simply as aid will do better if detached from other governmental functions and allowed to follow its own internal dictates. We do not believe that this is possible as long as governments call the tune. It is not the sincerity or integrity of, say, United States Agency for International Development (USAID) functionaries that is doubted but rather their ability to swim against more powerful governmental currents. In virtue of being inherently less conflicted, private philanthropy is in a position to do better.

Sixth, private agencies enjoy greater freedom to *deal directly with intended beneficiaries*. Because a charity or NGO is not as great a potential threat to the sovereignty of the host nation as are the agents of powerful foreign governments, there is a decent chance that they may be left alone to perform the activities that, from the point of view of the ruling elite, are essentially innocuous.

Indeed, to the extent that private aid providers succeed in delivering various welfare services, they moderate the onus on the government to do so. If they are perceived as catalyzing political opposition, they will be unwelcome, but this holds at least as strongly true for official governmental delegations.

An upside of privatizing aid, then, is that it affords more cover than do state-to-state interactions. A downside is that private parties may be more vulnerable to interference by those with their hands out soliciting bribes. This is an occupational hazard for those attempting to operate in dysfunctional political environments against which guile, toughness, and some useful connections are only a partial defense. If corruption and obscurantism are entrenched enough, there simply may be nothing useful that can be accomplished at reasonable cost. In this case, the best available alternative may be to shut down operations and move elsewhere. This is unfortunate, but at least is not likely to spawn a diplomatic incident of the sort that can be occasioned by a government-versus-government contretemps.

WHAT, THEN, IS LEFT FOR GOVERNMENTS TO DO?

In the realm of aid, private organizations should do most of the heavy lifting, but states can serve as important adjuncts. Specifically, they should take on the roles that only they can fill. One of these is to run interference for their own nationals who are engaged in global aid activity. Precisely because only governments can engage on equal terms with other governments, they are in a position quietly yet firmly to suggest to host nations that they moderate their predations against those who endeavor to assist. This is the liberal ideal of state neutrality extended beyond borders. States properly enable the project pursuit of their citizens by protecting them against wrongful intrusions. Bakers, brewers, and university professors merit such support, but they will not usually face challenges of the magnitude experienced by aid workers in challenged countries. Therefore, carrying out this proper state function may demand more overt measures than are usually required to protect individuals in their undertakings.

The second area in which states are indispensable is after the occurrence of catastrophic acts of destruction. Private philanthropies may be up to the challenge of confronting chronic conditions of underdevelopment, but their resources are overwhelmed by massive disaster. On Sunday, December 26, 2004, one of the most massive earthquakes ever recorded caused a devastating tsunami that killed over 200,000 people in more than a dozen countries around the Indian Ocean while injuring and displacing many others. The challenge of relief was too much for domestic governments, even those blessed by reasonably effective institutions. People around the world generously opened their pocketbooks, and both private philanthropies and quasi-governmental agencies distinguished themselves for dedication and zeal. Only states, however, were in a position to contribute technical support such as humanitarian satellite imagery and transportation by U.S. navy ships – not to mention billions of dollars in financial appropriations. Although ordinary aid relief is properly consigned to private philanthropies, when horrific disaster strikes, states properly can be called on to serve as the ultimate backstop, We include in this category not only natural disasters but also the product of human evil. We do not believe that governments tend to do this very well, but there is no other alternative.[11]

On anyone's list of the most successful aid ventures that have ever been undertaken, the postwar Marshall Plan certainly must rank very high. In retrospect, it can be seen that all the stars were aligned for success, but it is worth observing in particular that this intervention was much more like the response in the wake of an acute disruption than chronic underperformance.[12] The European nations that had suffered catastrophic losses of materiel and personnel were lying prostrate, and American aid crucially helped to lift them off the floor. We are, then, not opposed in principle or practice to state aid initiatives, but we insist as a matter of some urgency that governments come to understand better where their entry is called for and where it is likely to be valueless or worse.

Other than the two functions of riding shotgun for individual project pursuers and responding to acute crises, the proper place of states with regard to humanitarian aid is on the sidelines. Please note the qualifier "humanitarian." There should be no illusions that in the realm of state-to-state relations, humanitarian concerns are a prime mover. The practice of statecraft now and always incorporates a distinction between allies – sometimes misleadingly termed "friends" – and enemies. Accumulating the former and diminishing the number and heft of the latter constitute one of the rules governing how the game is played, and an important tactic is transferring assets to those who might thereby be influenced. Without doubt, this can be done poorly – the classic instance is U.S. support for Saddam Hussein during Iraq's war with Iran – but it is excessively utopian to urge abandonment of aid for the sake of diplomatic or military ends. There would, however, be a great gain in clarity

---

[11] Western liberal democracies did a splendid job of condemning after the fact the Rwanda genocidal massacre in 1994 of close to a million Tutsis. Unfortunately, neither any of these countries nor any instrument of the United Nations intervened to stanch the rivers of blood while rescue remained possible. Natural disasters are less politically problematic, but here too the record of governments is decidedly spotty, even when confronting domestic emergencies. Hurricane Katrina's devastating winds could not have been meliorated by any earthly power, but the aftermath was thoroughly mishandled by the world's richest and most powerful state. Christopher Coyne offers in *Doing Bad by Doing Good* a provocative and important post mortem of Katrina bungling with which we largely agree, although we believe that Coyne does not give enough credit to the power of human incompetence to take a bad situation and make it so very much worse.

[12] It was suggested to us in private conversation that what Europe needs now is another Marshall Plan. The proposal was, we think, only semiserious, but it nicely underscores the theoretically fundamental difference between acute distress and chronic dysfunctionality.

if it were called what it is rather than camouflaged under the rubric of "development." To be sure, diplomacy is the quintessence of the art of obfuscation, but a democracy ought to be able to derive some benefit from communicating straightforwardly with its own citizens and with the world.

IS PRIVATE PHILANTHROPY ENOUGH?

In a word, no. We are under no illusions that where governments have failed in the task of remaking the world, private charities will succeed. The very best that can be realistically expected is that intervention will ameliorate episodes of immediate distress but will rarely alter the trajectory of burdened social and economic life. This is far from negligible. If millions of lives are saved through improved sanitation and enhanced availability of medical care, this is a humanitarian triumph of the first order. We are enthusiastic, if sometimes critical, fans of Oxfam, Doctors Without Borders, and the Gates Foundation; the world is much better for their existence, especially the underdeveloped precincts of the world. However, even though they relieve much distress, their contribution to long-term development is minimal. This is not because they operate inefficiently but because, as we have insisted over and over, poverty is mostly homemade. Faltering institutions and venial rulers are an almost unfailing recipe for poor performance. (This is true in wealthy countries as well, but they enjoy the inestimable luxury of starting from a much superior position.) All the goodwill in the world – and a thick slab of money, too – will not loosen the grip of corrupt elites; all too often they exacerbate it. In *Republic*, Plato opined that in order to master troubles, either kings must become philosophers or philosophers kings. Fortunately, the past two centuries have demonstrated that the job attributes necessary for growth-sustaining rule are less demanding. Nonetheless, Plato's basic point is correct: an internally disordered regime is uncongenial to the good life. External charity is welcome but secondary.

Other forms of external provision are more important than philanthropy. *Remittances* are many times greater in toto than all aid transfers, official or private. When economic times are good, foreign remittances expand; when economies falter, as after the 2007 recession, they contract. According to the World Bank, remittances amounted to some $372 billion in 2011.[13] Not only is this a larger sum than the aid industry commands, dollar-for-dollar remittances probably are more effective because providers are motivated by love coupled with intimate knowledge of the needs of those to whom the money is directed. In the absence of remittances, millions more people will go to bed hungry at night, lack treatment for disease, and die prematurely. Insofar as wealthy countries adopt measures to exclude impoverished migrants, though, they cut into the flow of life-sustaining transfers. In Chapter 4 we argued that

[13] http://web.worldbank.org/WBSITE/EXTERNAL/TOPICS/0,,contentMDK:21924020~pagePK:5105988~piPK:360975~theSitePK:214971,00.html.

blocking personal mobility directly violates the liberty rights of those who are precluded from entry; here we observe that indirect harms are also considerable. Many people who argue in favor of a Rawlsian-type global difference principle simultaneously support the prerogative of local governments to keep out nonthreatening foreign nationals. We find this juxtaposition to be incoherent. Valuing the good of the world's least-well-off should entail endorsing realistically attainable practices that predictably enhance their welfare. (Massive financial transfers in pursuit of global egalitarianism are not realistic.) Insofar as they tend to reinforce cultures of dependency, remittances are not ideal, but they are acceptable as a second-best solution to the problem of providing for hard-pressed inhabitants of stagnant societies.

The most desirable form of international transfer is *direct foreign investment*. Accumulating capital is the key to economic takeoff, but impoverished states lack sufficient domestic resources to provide a base for speedy development. During the nineteenth century, the United States and Argentina were major recipients of European investment that generated industrial goods and infrastructure. Over that span, they transformed themselves from backwaters to the top tier of the world's economies. In the century that followed, one of those countries managed to remain in that neighborhood. Why did one of them eventually fall back into the pack, and why do poor countries today fail to achieve prosperity by attracting productive investment? The crucial problem they confront is that investors have numerous options for where they will put their money in play, so to be near the head of the financial queue requires some sort of advantage. Most often this will be tolerably effective government that vindicates property rights and the rule of law. To be sure, regardless of the rectitude of rulers, finance will find its way to countries where pools of oil are oozing out of the ground, but this so-called resource curse generates wealth for a small fraction yet does little for the vast preponderance of the population. General betterment is built on the back of perspicuous investment, and capital follows good institutions that turn abstract possibilities into concrete opportunities.

Those who wish to promote development abroad would do well, then, to construct industrial enterprises in decently governed polities. If Warren Buffett is looking at these pages, then there is at least one reader of this book who is in a position to act on this advice. For the rest of us, different thoughts are more pertinent. It is to these we turn in the next and final section.

CONCLUSION

What, then, shall we do? The most stringent principle is the Hippocratic dictum *to do no harm*. It is strictly impermissible to violate the rights of foreign nationals (or the rights of compatriots). For those of us who are not regular globetrotters or elected officials, this is mostly of theoretical interest; actual opportunities to trespass are infrequent. Of greater relevance is the derivative principle not to support the doing of harm. All advanced Western nations, not least the United States, encroach rightful liberties to trade and to associate across borders. To the extent that as citizens we support such illiberal policies, we morally compromise ourselves. A critic might respond that no one individual or small group of individuals is in a position to move governmental policies, especially xenophobic incursions that enjoy wide popularity. We take the point but reject the assumption that only consequentially potent activities come in for moral appraisal. It is not only what one *achieves* but also that which one *supports* that morally matters.[14] There is no likelihood that the Nazi Party is going to make a comeback, but one who speaks fondly of the trains that ran on time (to the extermination camps) when the Fuhrer was in charge is reprehensible. Protectionism is not on that order of evil. Many people honestly believe it to be justified on nationalistic or pragmatic grounds. They should know better, and once they do know, they should give effect to that knowledge in words and deeds.

It is wrong either to violate rights or to support the violation of rights; does it follow that one is morally obliged to combat policies that do so? Not if among the liberties worth cherishing is a liberty to stay away from the practice of politics. We have expressed reservations concerning the scope of duties of positive assistance, and this extends to alleged duties to campaign against repressive governmental policies. Nonetheless, we encourage those of a genuinely liberal disposition to support the extension of liberty – including liberty at a distance. One way of doing so is to speak out against both those who claim that social justice requires massive global redistribution and those who oppose liberty to trade and to migrate across borders for innocent purposes. Another is to protest aid and comfort extended by one's own government to tyrants who abuse their own populations.

Most of this chapter has dealt with the provision of humanitarian aid. Although we are moderately hopeful that at least some of this will do some good, we hold out few hopes for major structural improvement. There is, perhaps, need for less conventional thinking about how to plant seeds of reform. The next time you are urged to make a donation to Oxfam or UNICEF, think instead about whether an even more promising investment in human flourishing would be to take the money you would have otherwise donated to one of those groups and instead use it to purchase copies of Friedrich Hayek and Milton Friedman works to be discretely inserted into countries short on economic and political freedom. This may strike you as unserious, but there is some evidence that just this kind of libertarian proselytizing paid dividends in Eastern Europe after the implosion of the Soviet Union.[15] Although not likely,

[14] An expressive ethics with special reference to voting is discussed in Geoffrey Brennan and Loren Lomasky, *Democracy and Decision: The Pure Theory of Electoral Preference* (Cambridge University Press, 1997).

[15] Former president of the Czech Republic Václav Klaus often speaks of his debt to Hayek. See on his website http://www.klaus.cz/clanky/3345.

it is possible that rumblings of opposition to tyrants in Africa and the Middle East will take a liberal turn, and any opportunities for encouraging such movement should be encouraged.

Another useful, if not inspiring, task is to be a voice of moderation and benign skepticism when enthusiasm soars in the wake of the next grand international declaration. These have periodically been issued by the "Great and the Good" in a line that extends from Bretton Woods to the announcement of "Millennium Goals" at the 2005 Gleneagles G-8 meeting. Popping optimistic balloons is not a recommended path to popularity, but it is a necessary corrective to the underlying assumption that prospects for the world's have-nots mostly depend on outside benefactions. Much of the literature of global justice maintains that the persistence of poverty around the world is attributable to a shameful dearth of goodwill and money from the rich countries of the West. Sometimes this is presented as a failing of charity[16]; other times as a breach of justice.[17] These injustices can be ongoing, as with World Trade Organization (WTO) trade agreements unfairly weighted in favor of the rich. They may be historical relics, as is the legacy of imperialism. None of these claims is bogus. Charity, at least when intelligently directed, can ease at least some of the rough edges of stunted lives. Nor do we believe that trade practices as they have emerged in the postwar period from a sequence of General Agreement on Tariffs and Trade (GATT) and WTO rounds are admirable. Agricultural barriers in particular inflict harms on producers in the developing world (and on consumers in rich countries as well). Contemporary trade rules are not exemplary, but they are incomparably better than in the bad old days of the Smoot-Hawley tariff and its progeny. Imperialism is perhaps too easy a catchall scapegoat for the ills of former colonies, but we thoroughly agree that almost all imperialists systematically violated rights, and some, including Belgium and the Soviet Union, were thoroughly horrific.[18] Let all these points be conceded; nonetheless, it should be hammered home again and again that no normative theory of global poverty is adequate if it does not emphasize the primary role of domestic factors. To suppose that significant advance will finally be achieved if only benefactors agree to raise the quality of their game is to whistle past the graveyard – literally so for millions whose lives have been cut short by the oppression of their own rulers.

We would dearly love to be able to produce an edifying book of the quick-fix genre: *How to Lift Up the World's Downtrodden*. It saddens us that we cannot. There is nothing that we can advise the readers of this book to do that will accelerate development by so much as a speck – unless, to our surprise, a copy

---

[16] Peter Singer epitomizes this strand.

[17] This is the central theme of Thomas Pogge's works.

[18] A gripping account of inhumanity in the Congo is Adam Hochschild, *King Leopold's Ghost: A Story of Greed, Terror, and Heroism in Colonial Africa* (Boston: Houghton Mifflin, 1999). Accounts of Soviet infamies are legion.

has been picked up by Kim Jong-un, Robert Mugabe, or Christina Fernandez. OECD member states can do better in this regard than philosophers, but not if they remain wedded to the failed policies of the past. Official aid gets depressingly little bang for the buck. Enormous economic gains are achievable if international borders are softened to allow more goods and, especially, people to pass through, but currently the political likelihood of change in this direction is discouragingly low. As we write, the Doha round of trade liberalization talks barely survives on life support, and in many Western countries, parties compete at elections over which will be strictest on limiting immigration.

An economic forecaster of a previous era declared, "The poor you will always have with you." Perhaps he knew something that the mandarins of the contemporary aid industry do not. Nonetheless, there is nothing to do but to persist in trying to understand why many have achieved wealth in recent decades, why too many others have not, and how the gap between them can be bridged.

Index